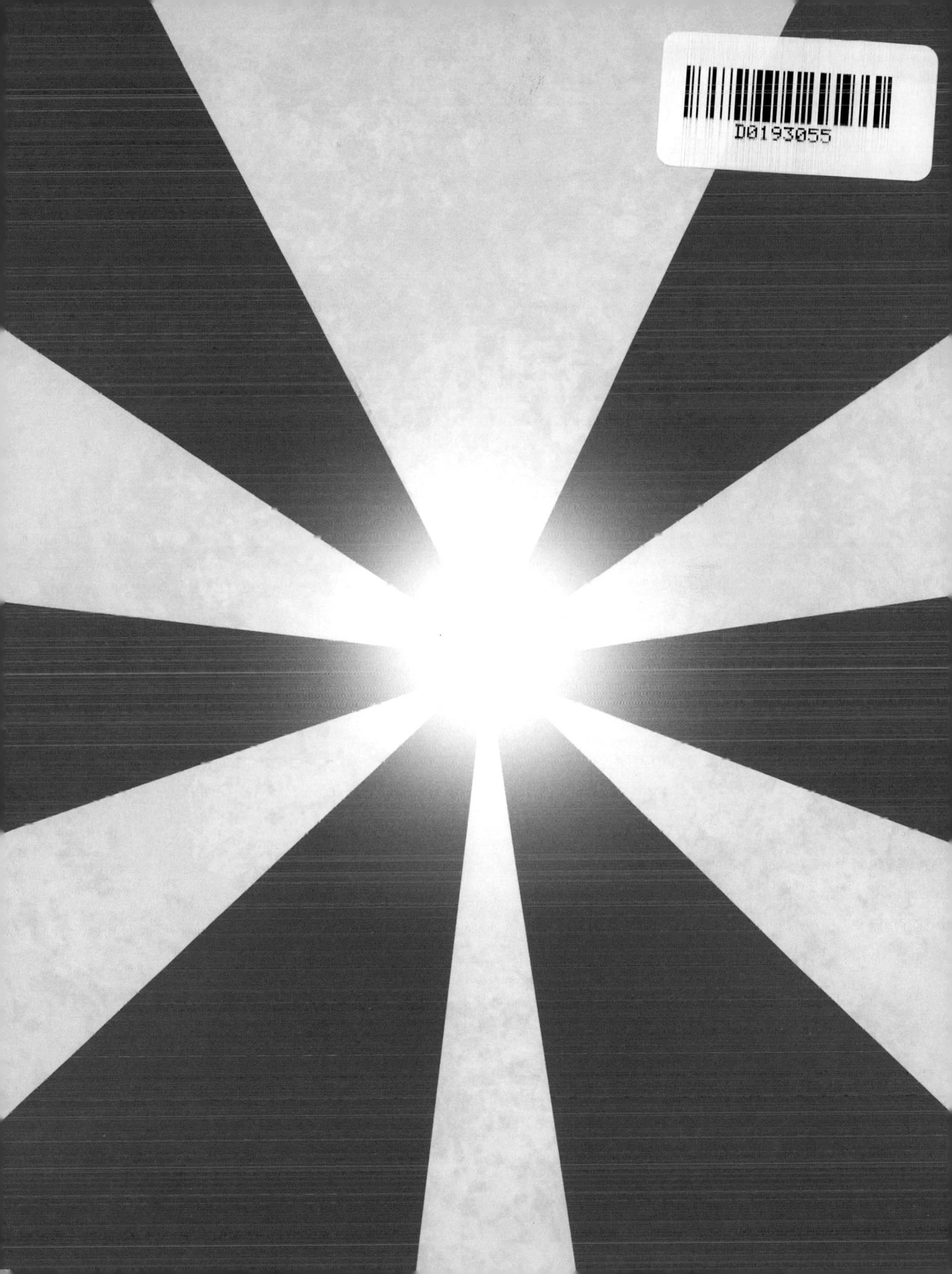

KUNG FU HERO AND THE FORBIDDEN CITY

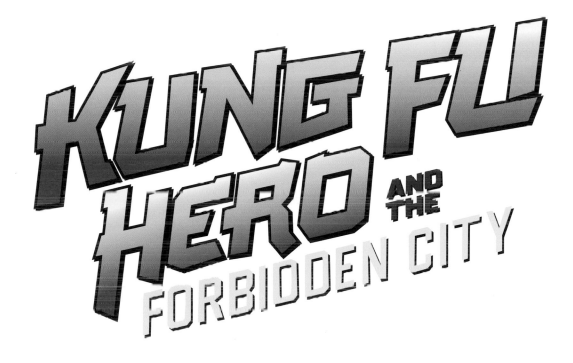

KUNG FU HERO AND THE FORBIDDEN CITY

A COMEDY SHORTS GAMER GRAPHIC NOVEL

DEJI OLATUNJI

TRAPEZE

FIRST PUBLISHED IN GREAT BRITAIN IN 2017 BY TRAPEZE
AN IMPRINT OF THE ORION PUBLISHING GROUP LTD
CARMELITE HOUSE, 50 VICTORIA EMBANKMENT
LONDON EC4Y ODZ

AN HACHETTE UK COMPANY

1 3 5 7 9 10 8 6 4 2

A CIP CATALOGUE RECORD FOR THIS BOOK IS AVAILABLE FROM THE BRITISH LIBRARY.

ISBN 978 1 4091 7428 8
ISBN (EBOOK) 978 1 4091 7429 5

PRINTED IN GERMANY

MIX
Paper from responsible sources
FSC® C104740

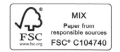

WWW.ORIONBOOKS.CO.UK

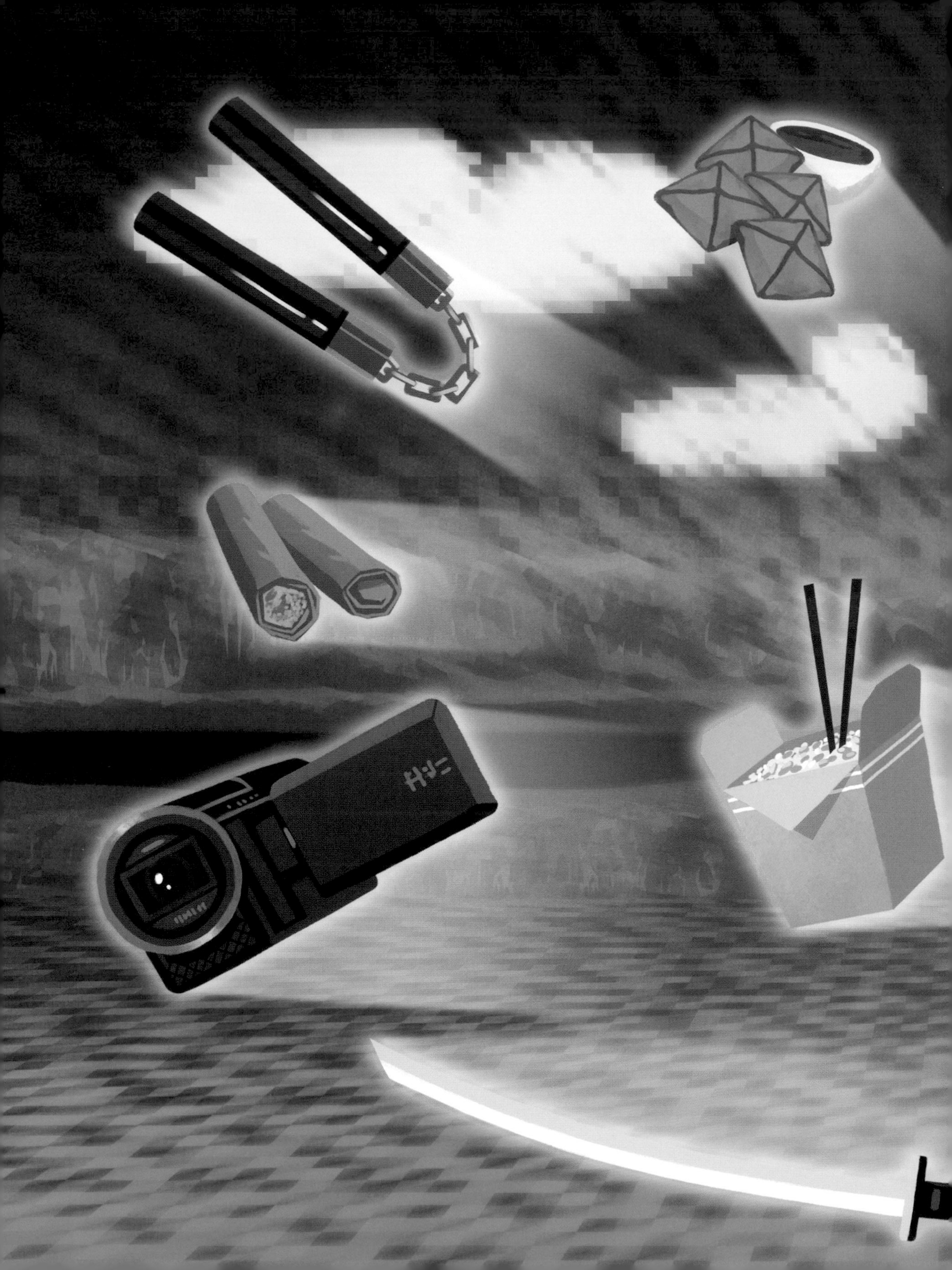

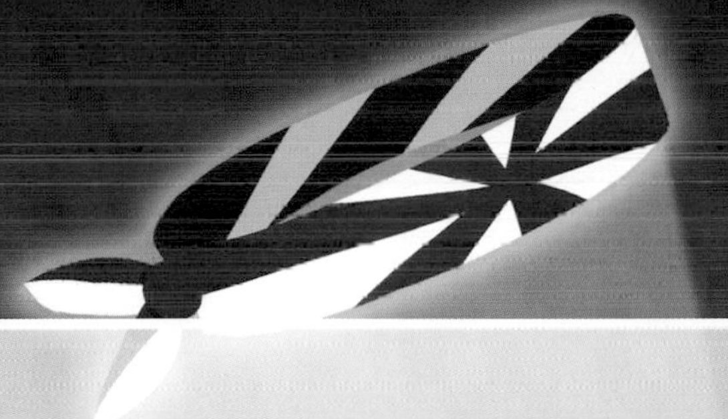

HEY GUYS! IT'S *COMEDYSHORTSGAMER* HERE AND MAN ARE WE ALL ABOUT TO HAVE SOME SERIOUS FUN!

NO DOUBT MANY OF YOU HAVE BEEN FOLLOWING MY VIDEOS ON YOUTUBE FOR THE LAST FEW YEARS AND YOU'LL KNOW THAT I LOVE PRANK VIDEOS, KUNG FU AND CHINESE FOOD. AND YOU'LL ALSO KNOW THAT ME AND MY BRO DON'T ALWAYS GET ALONG...

ANYWAY, I LOVE MAKING VIDEOS, AND MAKING YOU GUYS LAUGH, BUT SOMETIMES IT'S HARD TO FILM SOME OF THE CRAZY IDEAS THAT GO ON IN MY HEAD. AND IF I TRIED THE COST WOULD PROBABLY BE MORE THAN A MARVEL COMIC BOOK MOVIE!

THANKFULLY, WRITING A BOOK WAS AN AMAZING OPPORTUNITY TO FINALLY SPLATTER MY BRAIN ONTO THE PAGE. AND MAN HAVE I LOVED IT! A LOT OF THESE IDEAS I'VE HAD SINCE I WAS A KID, WHILE OTHERS CAME TO ME AMID LATE NIGHT TEKKEN SESSIONS, OR WHEN MY BROTHER WAS GETTING ON MY NERVES.

I AM SO EXCITED TO FINALLY BE ABLE TO SHARE THIS STORY WITH YOU AND WANT TO THANK YOU ALL ONCE AGAIN FOR YOUR AMAZING SUPPORT ALONG THE WAY. IT'S THANKS TO YOU GUYS THAT I GET INCREDIBLE OPPORTUNITIES LIKE THIS AND I HOPE THE STORY BRINGS A SMILE TO YOUR FACE.

SO, SIT BACK, AND PREPARE TO BE HURLED INTO THE WEIRD AND WONDERFUL WORLD OF MY BRAIN. IT'S NOT PRETTY IN THERE...

LET'S DO THIS!

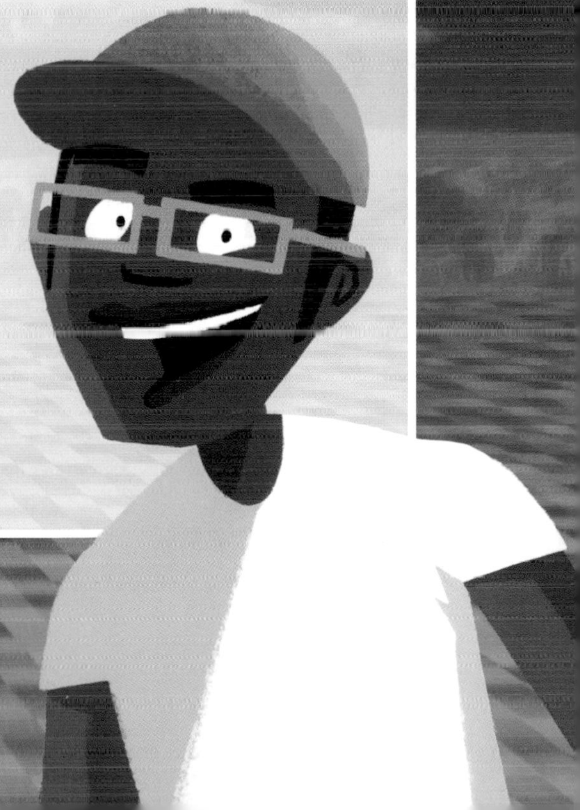

STREET PUNKS

HARD AS NAILS NINJAS WHO ROAM THE STREETS DOING CHEN CAGE'S BIDDING, ALWAYS HOT ON THE HEELS OF DEJI. THESE GUYS HAVE MAD MARTIAL ARTS SKILLS AND ARE ARMED TO THE MAX WITH NUNCHAKUS, SAMURAI SWORDS AND ASSORTED WEAPONRY. BAD ASS HAIRCUTS ALSO INCLUDED.

CHEN CAGE

THE TRIAD CRIME BOSS OF BEIJING. FEARED BY EVERYONE IN THE CITY, CHEN CAGE IS AN EVIL MASTERMIND WHO WILL STOP AT NOTHING TO GAIN MORE POWER. HE'S SLICK, RICH, COLD-BLOODED AND SHOWS NO MERCY TO THOSE WHO DON'T FOLLOW ORDERS.

MEI-LING IS DEJI'S SMOKIN' HOT LOVE INTEREST. SHE'S SASSY, CONFIDENT AND CAN TAKE DOWN HOT SAUCE LIKE NO ONE ELSE. SHE IS THE VOICE OF REASON WHEN DEJI'S CRAZY IMAGINATION IS ABOUT TO CAUSE A SICK ACCIDENT.

SHI IS A TALKING CHINESE LION DOG STATUE BROUGHT TO LIFE. HE IS SMALL BUT HE PACKS A HUGE PERSONALITY -- MAINLY BEING UNIMPRESSED WITH DEJI'S ANTICS. HE SMOKES, DRINKS AND IS VERY INAPPROPRIATE. HE WOULD MUCH RATHER BE DRINKING A BEER AND WATCHING WOMEN'S VOLLEYBALL THAN ENGAGED IN SUCH A HIGH STAKES ADVENTURE.

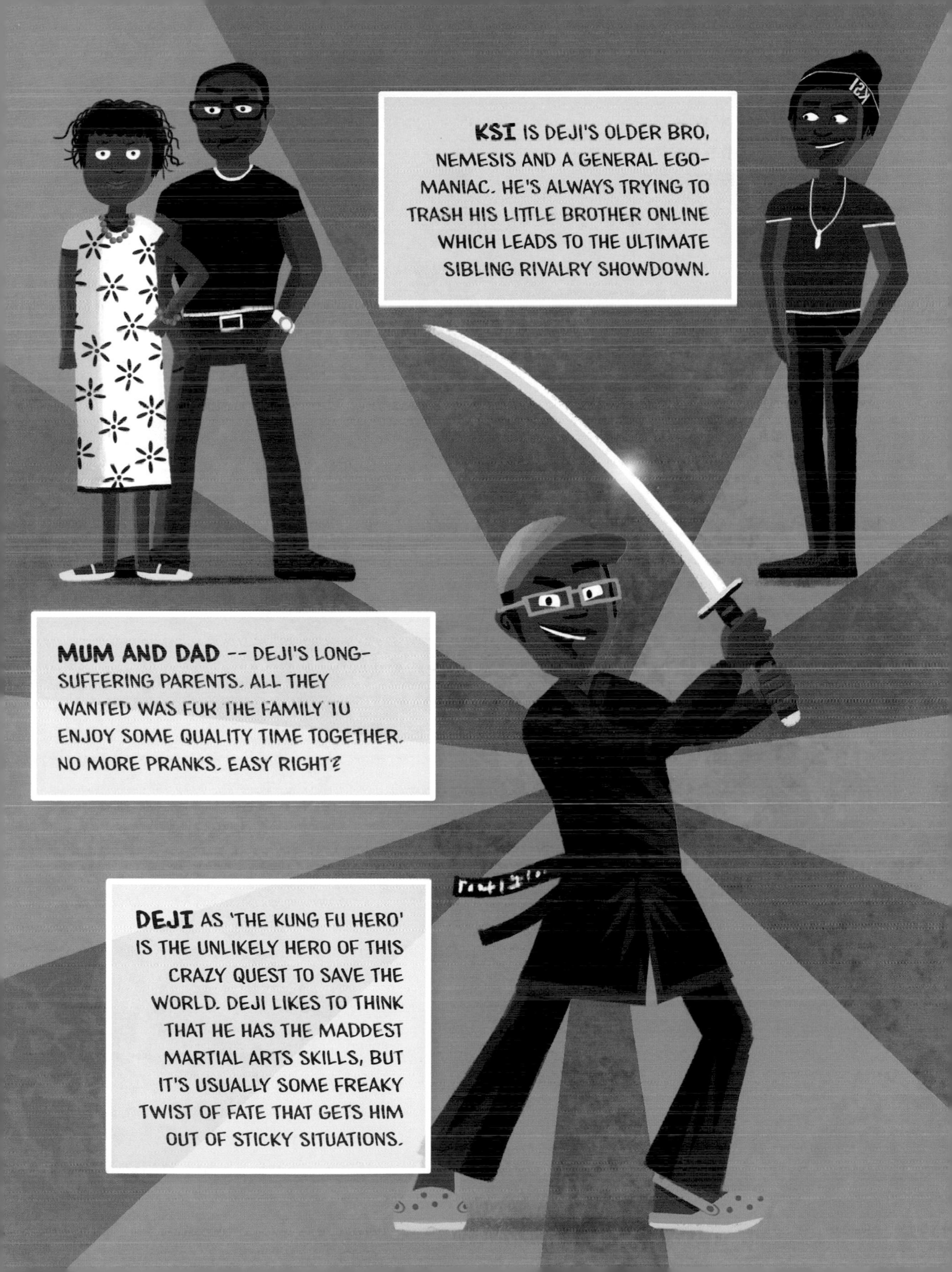
KSI IS DEJI'S OLDER BRO, NEMESIS AND A GENERAL EGO-MANIAC. HE'S ALWAYS TRYING TO TRASH HIS LITTLE BROTHER ONLINE WHICH LEADS TO THE ULTIMATE SIBLING RIVALRY SHOWDOWN.
MUM AND DAD -- DEJI'S LONG-SUFFERING PARENTS. ALL THEY WANTED WAS FOR THE FAMILY TO ENJOY SOME QUALITY TIME TOGETHER. NO MORE PRANKS. EASY RIGHT?
DEJI AS 'THE KUNG FU HERO' IS THE UNLIKELY HERO OF THIS CRAZY QUEST TO SAVE THE WORLD. DEJI LIKES TO THINK THAT HE HAS THE MADDEST MARTIAL ARTS SKILLS, BUT IT'S USUALLY SOME FREAKY TWIST OF FATE THAT GETS HIM OUT OF STICKY SITUATIONS.

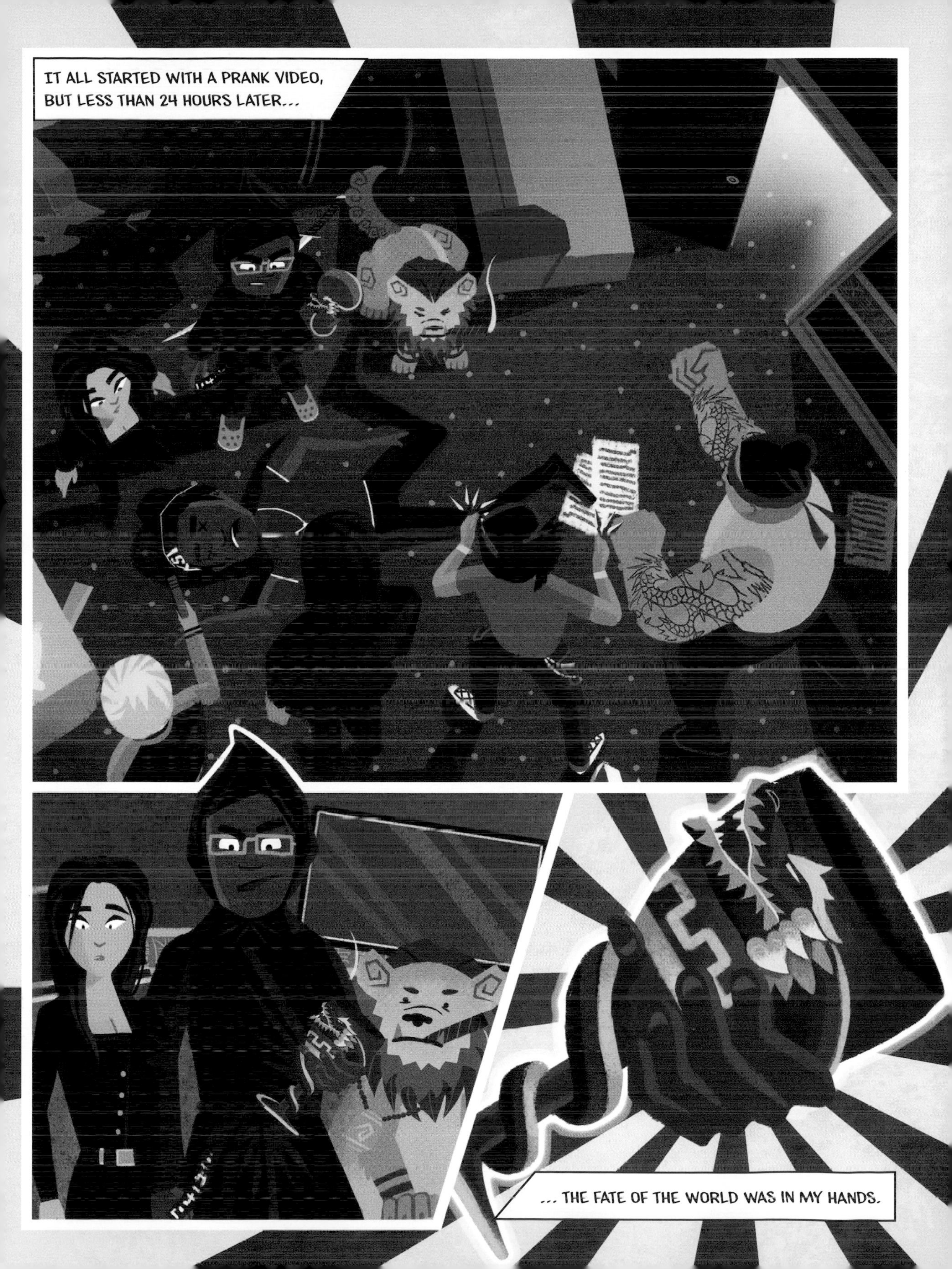
IT ALL STARTED WITH A PRANK VIDEO,
BUT LESS THAN 24 HOURS LATER...
... THE FATE OF THE WORLD WAS IN MY HANDS.

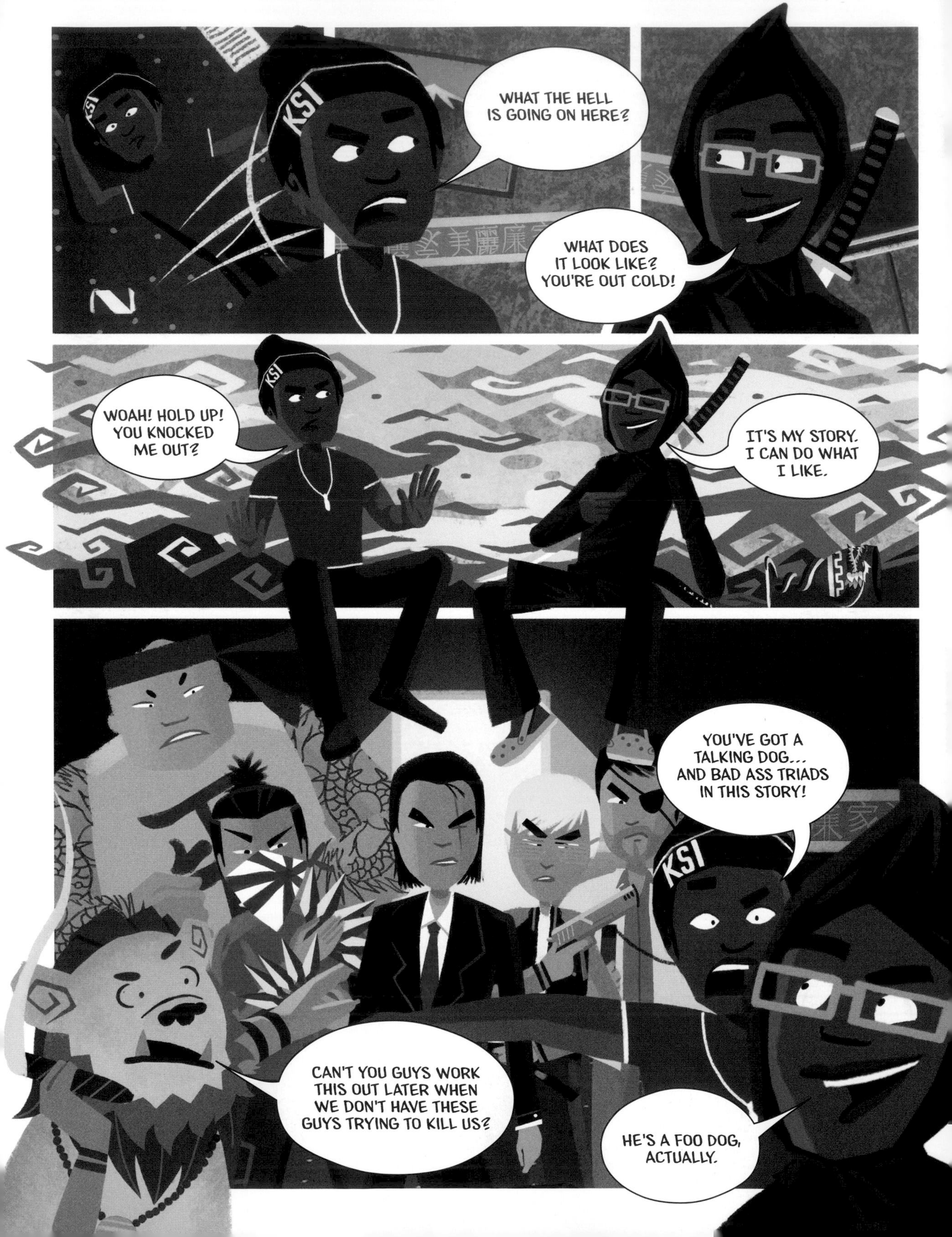
WHAT THE HELL IS GOING ON HERE?
WHAT DOES IT LOOK LIKE? YOU'RE OUT COLD!
WOAH! HOLD UP! YOU KNOCKED ME OUT?
IT'S MY STORY. I CAN DO WHAT I LIKE.
YOU'VE GOT A TALKING DOG... AND BAD ASS TRIADS IN THIS STORY!
CAN'T YOU GUYS WORK THIS OUT LATER WHEN WE DON'T HAVE THESE GUYS TRYING TO KILL US?
HE'S A FOO DOG, ACTUALLY.

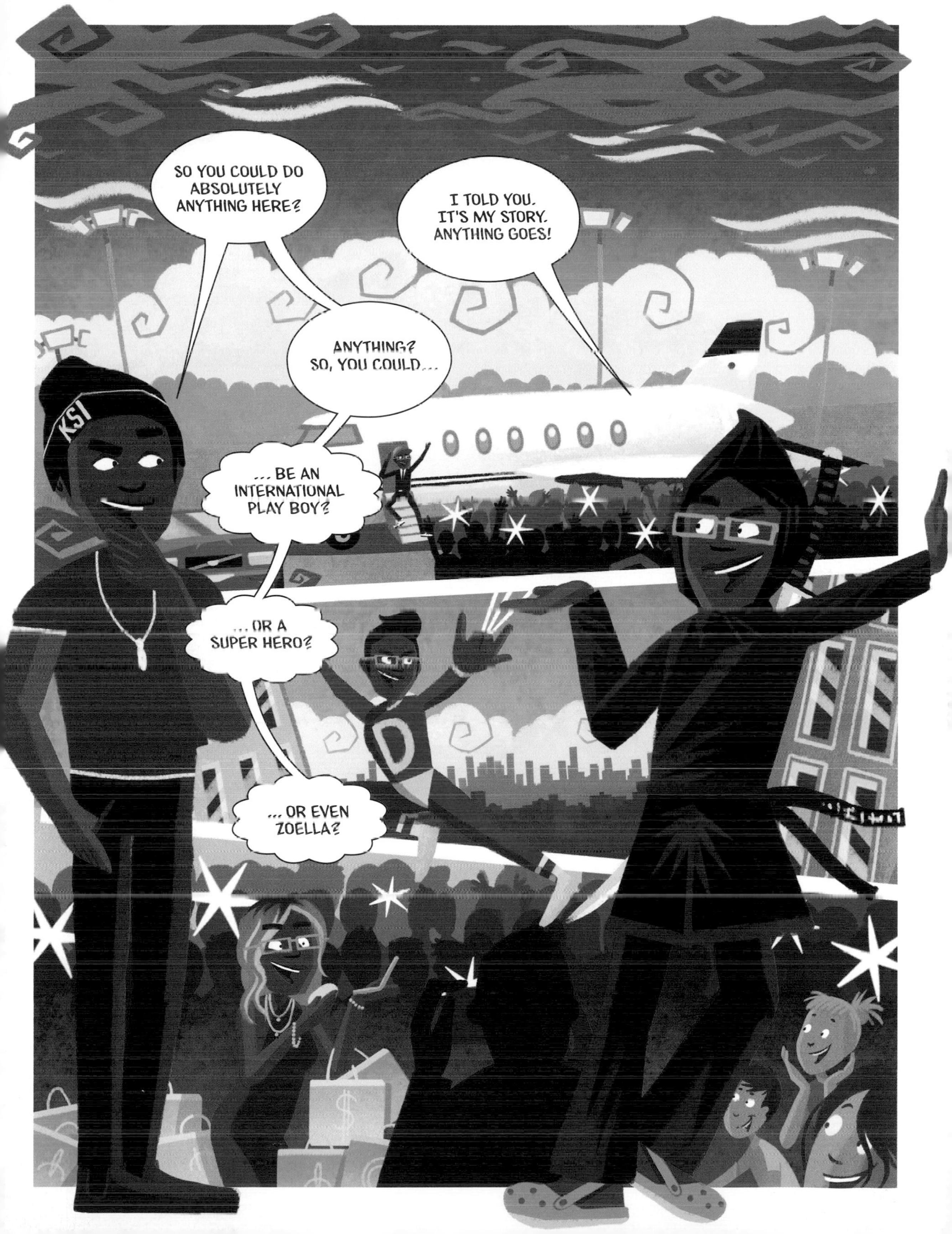
SO YOU COULD DO ABSOLUTELY ANYTHING HERE?
I TOLD YOU. IT'S MY STORY. ANYTHING GOES!
ANYTHING? SO, YOU COULD...
... BE AN INTERNATIONAL PLAY BOY?
... OR A SUPER HERO?
... OR EVEN ZOELLA?

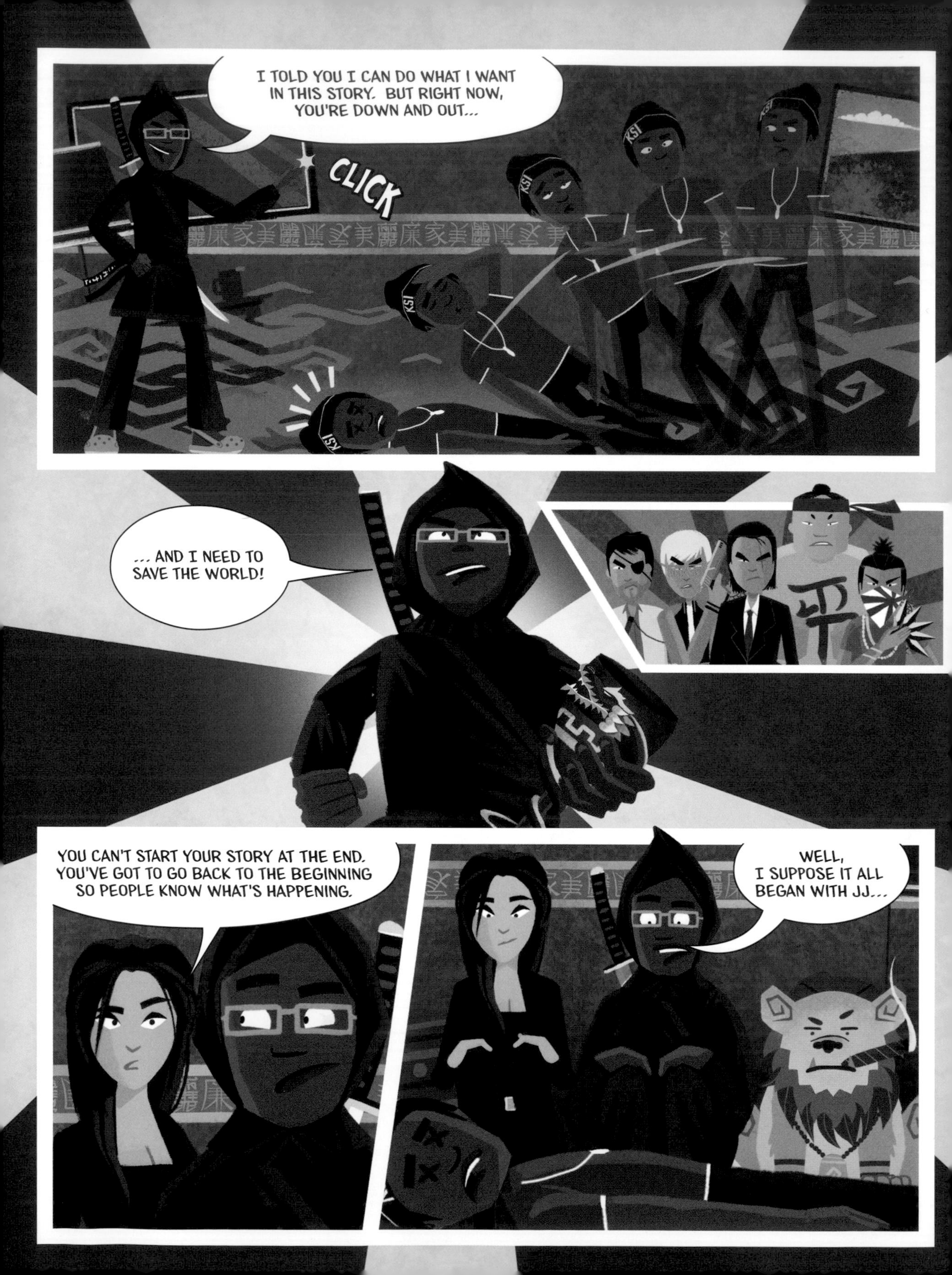
I TOLD YOU I CAN DO WHAT I WANT IN THIS STORY. BUT RIGHT NOW, YOU'RE DOWN AND OUT...
CLICK
KSI
KSI
KSI
KSI
KSI
... AND I NEED TO SAVE THE WORLD!
YOU CAN'T START YOUR STORY AT THE END. YOU'VE GOT TO GO BACK TO THE BEGINNING SO PEOPLE KNOW WHAT'S HAPPENING.
WELL, I SUPPOSE IT ALL BEGAN WITH JJ...

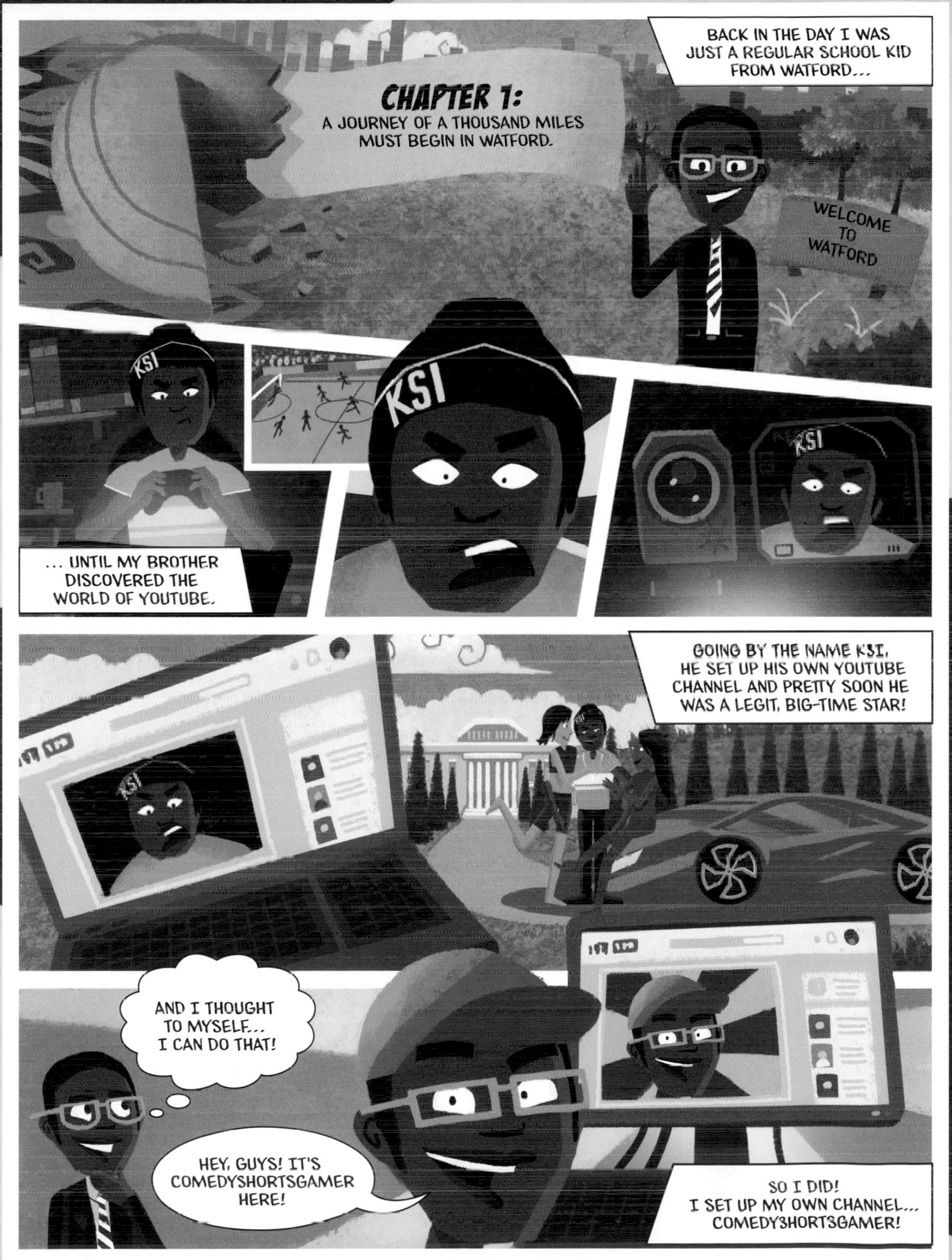
CHAPTER 1:
A JOURNEY OF A THOUSAND MILES MUST BEGIN IN WATFORD.
BACK IN THE DAY I WAS JUST A REGULAR SCHOOL KID FROM WATFORD...
WELCOME TO WATFORD
KSI
KSI
KSI
... UNTIL MY BROTHER DISCOVERED THE WORLD OF YOUTUBE.
GOING BY THE NAME KSI, HE SET UP HIS OWN YOUTUBE CHANNEL AND PRETTY SOON HE WAS A LEGIT, BIG-TIME STAR!
KSI
AND I THOUGHT TO MYSELF... I CAN DO THAT!
HEY, GUYS! IT'S COMEDYSHORTSGAMER HERE!
SO I DID! I SET UP MY OWN CHANNEL... COMEDYSHORTSGAMER!

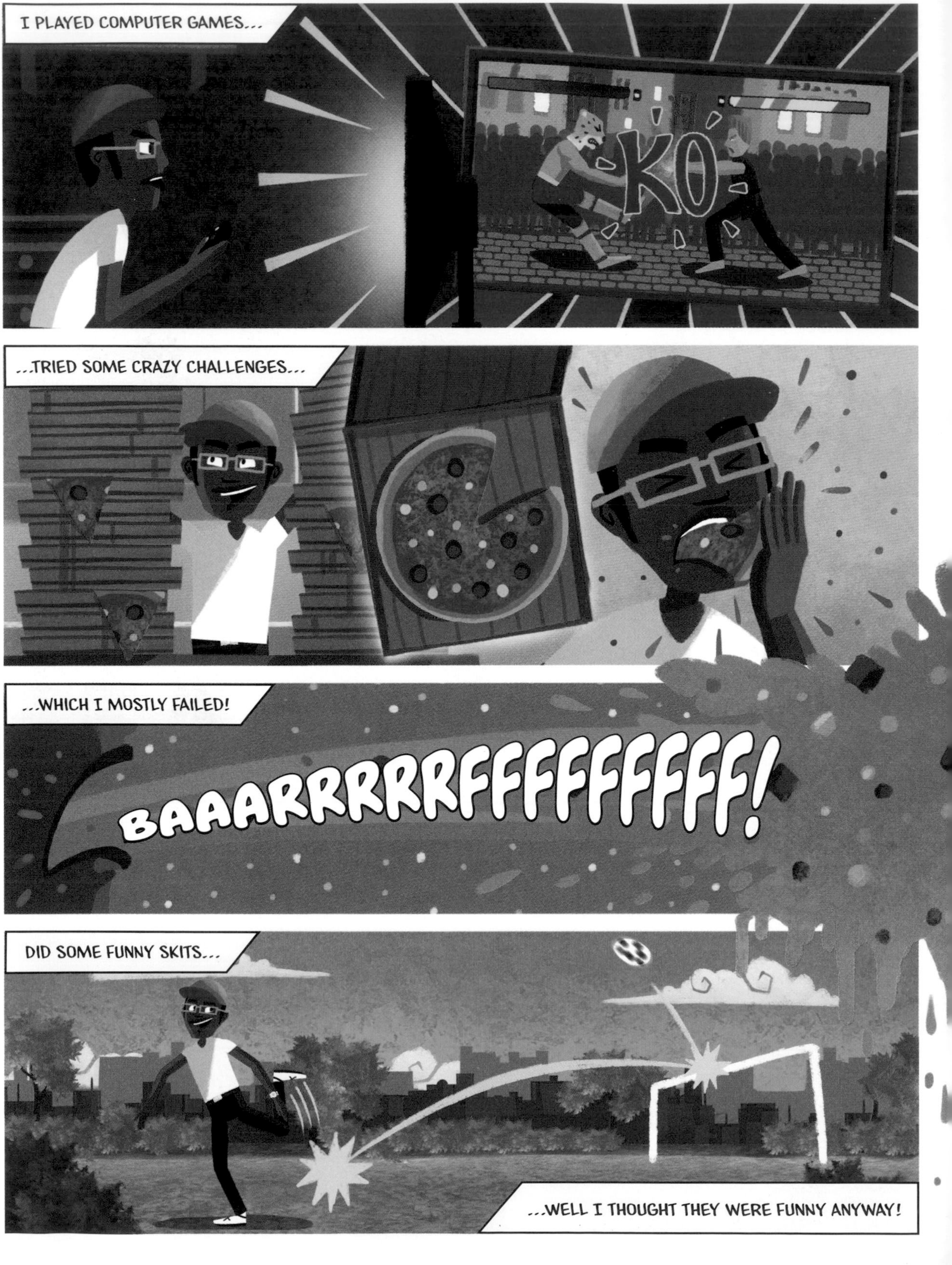
I PLAYED COMPUTER GAMES...
KO
...TRIED SOME CRAZY CHALLENGES...
...WHICH I MOSTLY FAILED!
BAAARRRRRRFFFFFFFFFF!
DID SOME FUNNY SKITS...
...WELL I THOUGHT THEY WERE FUNNY ANYWAY!

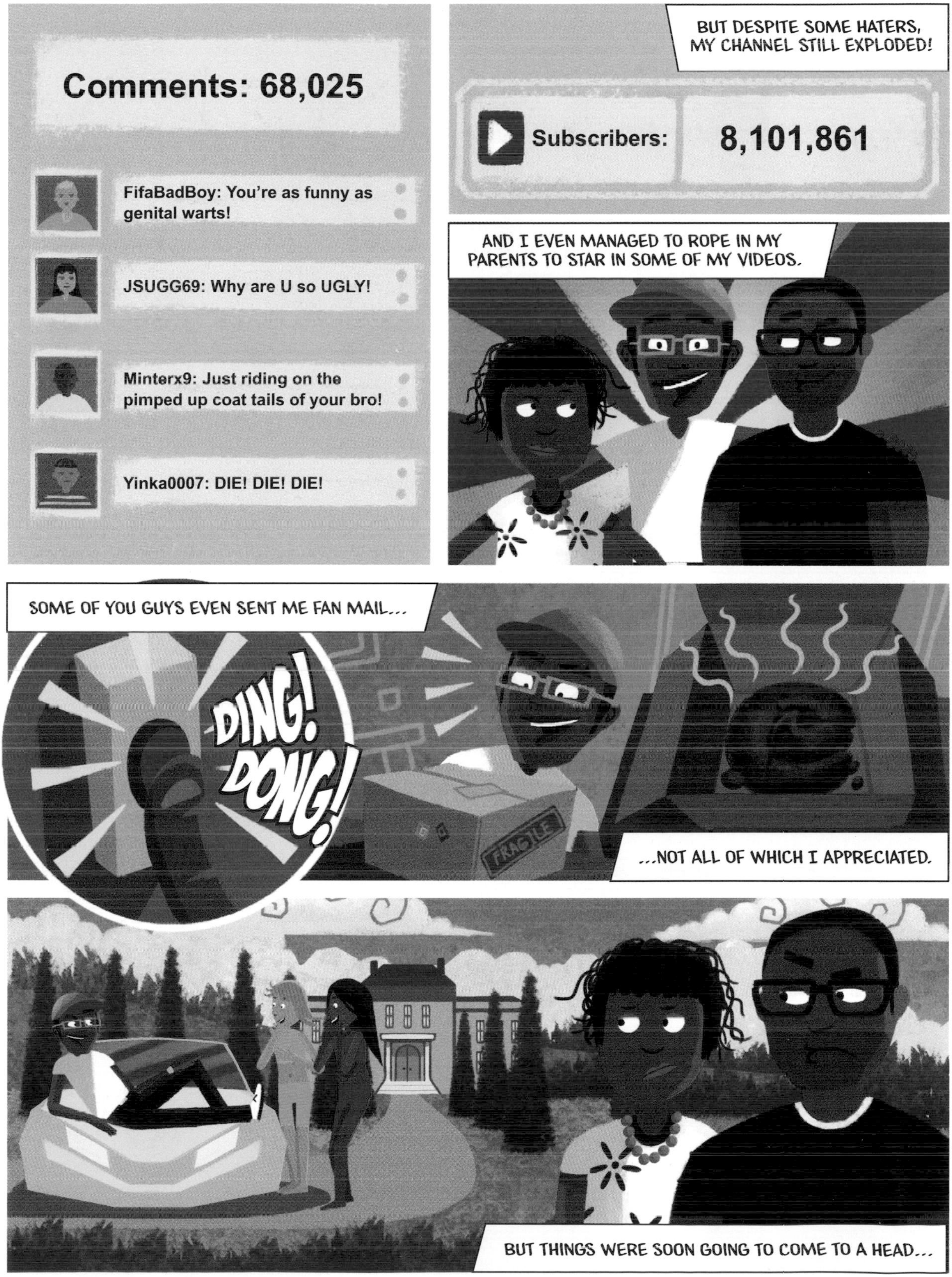
Comments: 68,025
FifaBadBoy: You're as funny as genital warts!
JSUGG69: Why are U so UGLY!
Minterx9: Just riding on the pimped up coat tails of your bro!
Yinka0007: DIE! DIE! DIE!
BUT DESPITE SOME HATERS, MY CHANNEL STILL EXPLODED!
Subscribers:
8,101,861
AND I EVEN MANAGED TO ROPE IN MY PARENTS TO STAR IN SOME OF MY VIDEOS.
SOME OF YOU GUYS EVEN SENT ME FAN MAIL...
DING! DONG!
FRAGILE
...NOT ALL OF WHICH I APPRECIATED.
BUT THINGS WERE SOON GOING TO COME TO A HEAD...

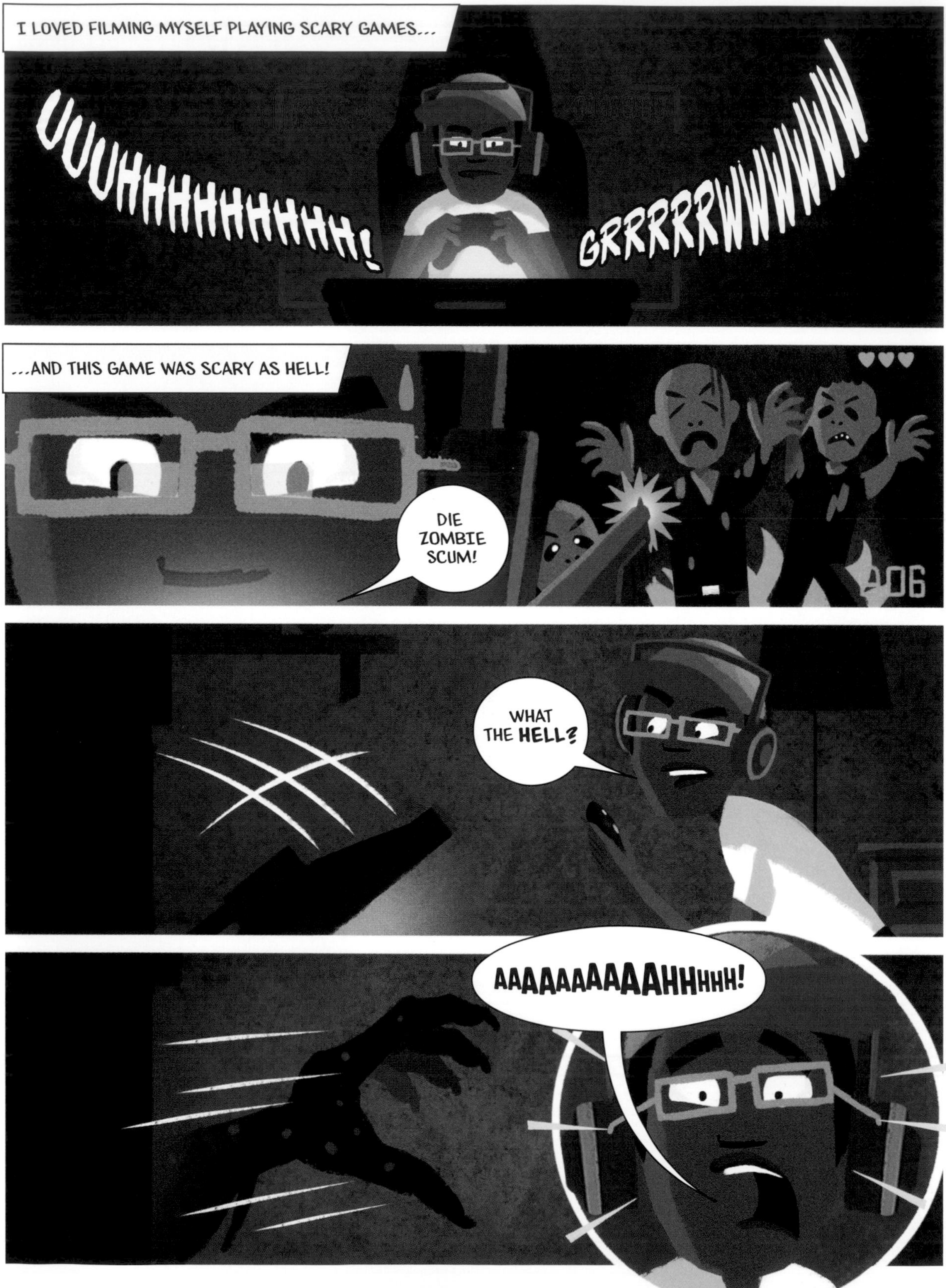
I LOVED FILMING MYSELF PLAYING SCARY GAMES...
UUUHHHHHHHHHH!
GRRRRRWWWWWW
...AND THIS GAME WAS SCARY AS HELL!
DIE ZOMBIE SCUM!
WHAT THE HELL?
AAAAAAAAAAHHHHH!

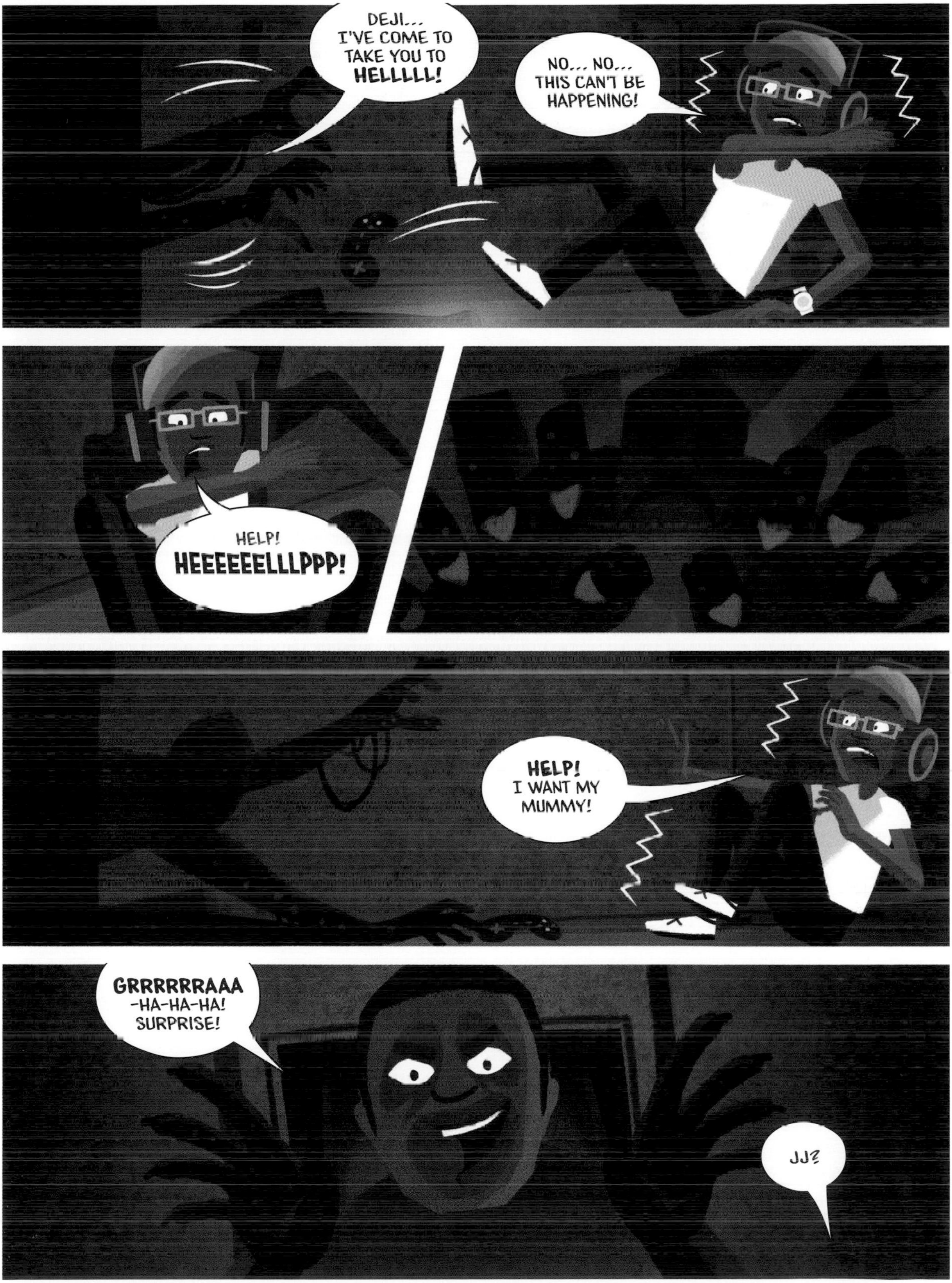
DEJI... I'VE COME TO TAKE YOU TO HELLLLL!
NO... NO... THIS CAN'T BE HAPPENING!
HELP! HEEEEEELLLPPP!
HELP! I WANT MY MUMMY!
GRRRRRRAAA -HA-HA-HA! SURPRISE!
JJ?

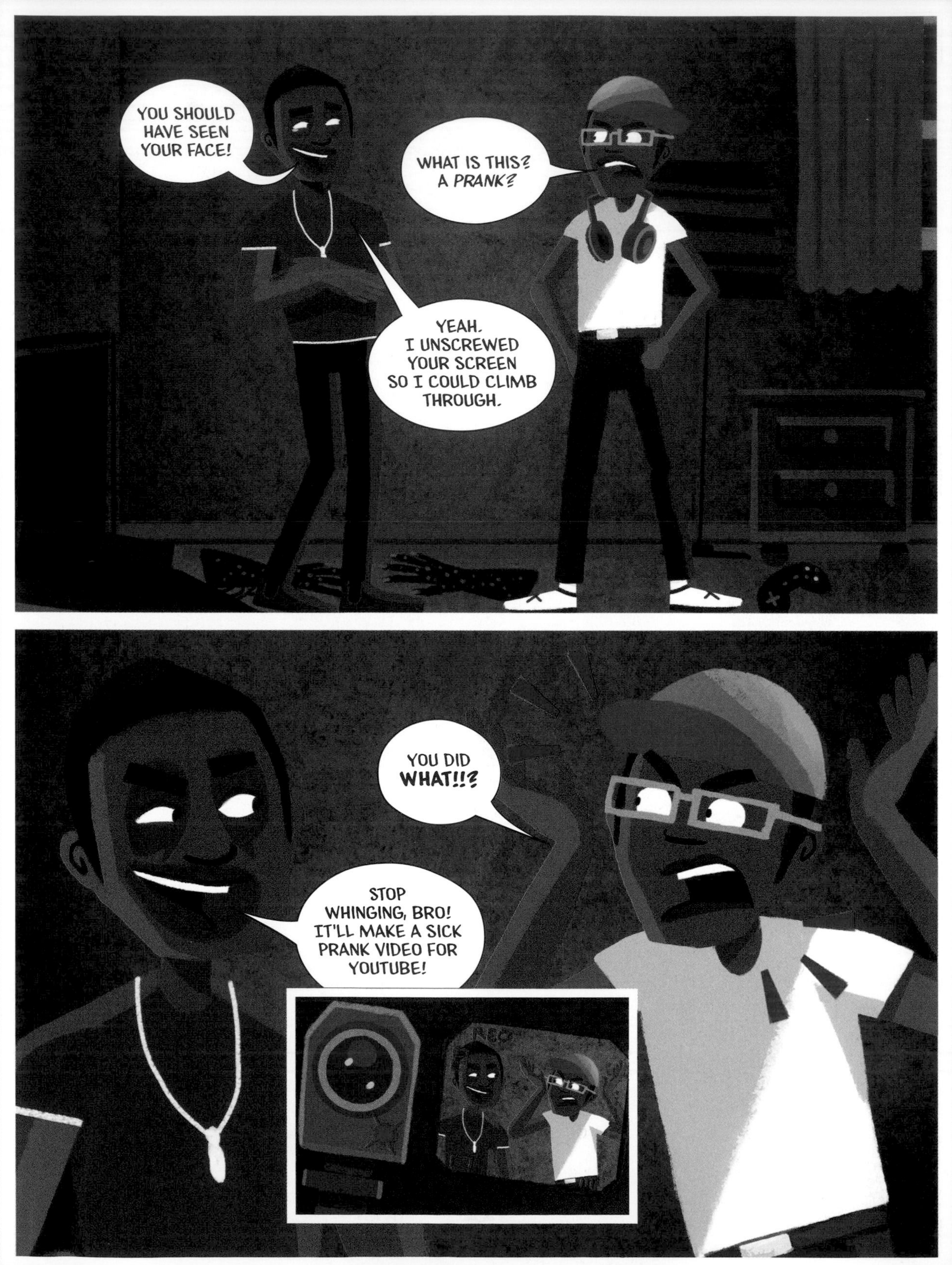
YOU SHOULD HAVE SEEN YOUR FACE!
WHAT IS THIS? A *PRANK*?
YEAH. I UNSCREWED YOUR SCREEN SO I COULD CLIMB THROUGH.
YOU DID **WHAT!!?**
STOP WHINGING, BRO! IT'LL MAKE A SICK PRANK VIDEO FOR YOUTUBE!

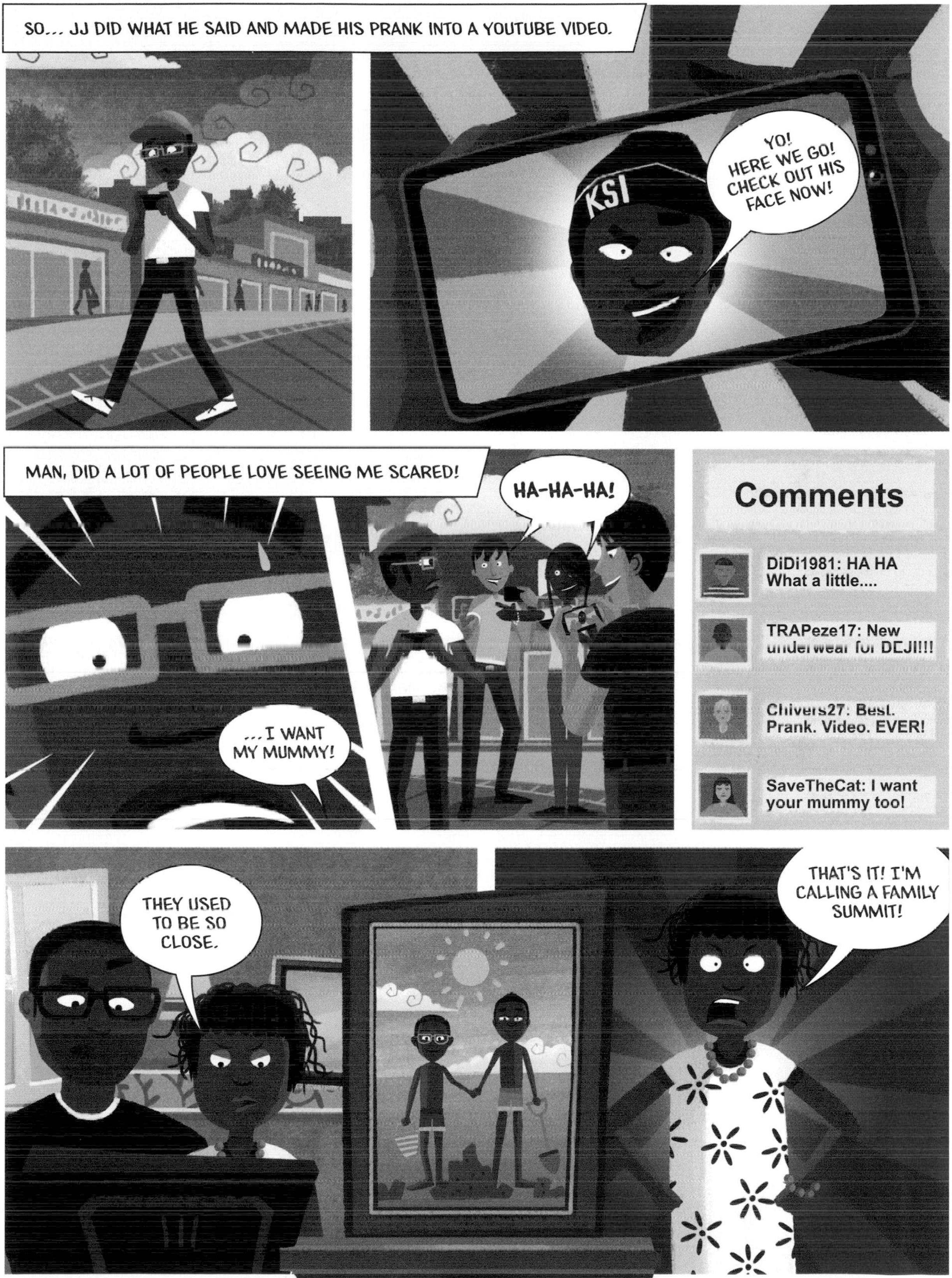
SO... JJ DID WHAT HE SAID AND MADE HIS PRANK INTO A YOUTUBE VIDEO.
YO! HERE WE GO! CHECK OUT HIS FACE NOW!
KSI
MAN, DID A LOT OF PEOPLE LOVE SEEING ME SCARED!
...I WANT MY MUMMY!
HA-HA-HA!
Comments
DiDi1981: HA HA What a little....
TRAPeze17: New underwear for DEJI!!!
Chivers27: Best. Prank. Video. EVER!
SaveTheCat: I want your mummy too!
THEY USED TO BE SO CLOSE.
THAT'S IT! I'M CALLING A FAMILY SUMMIT!

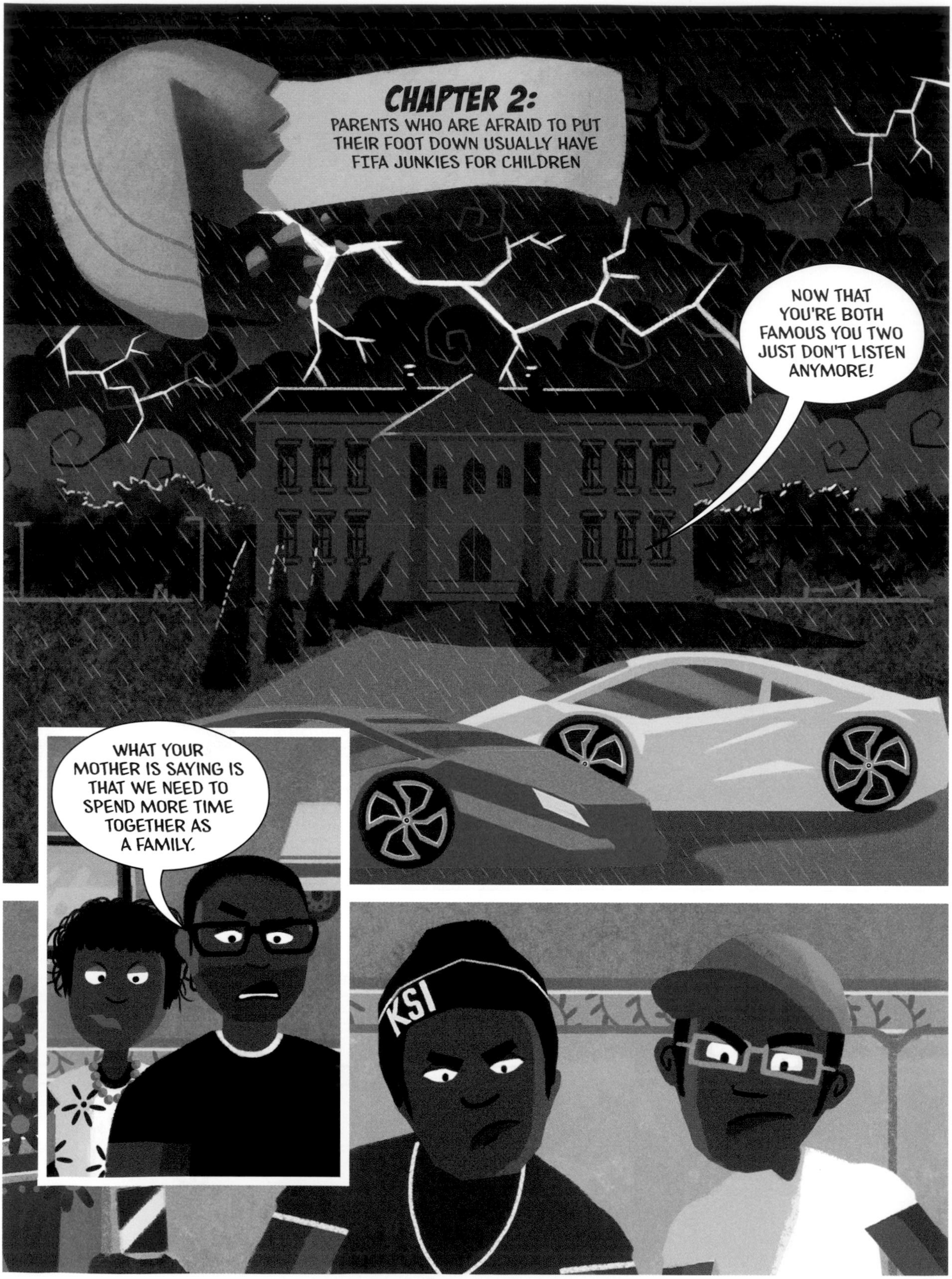
CHAPTER 2:
PARENTS WHO ARE AFRAID TO PUT THEIR FOOT DOWN USUALLY HAVE FIFA JUNKIES FOR CHILDREN
NOW THAT YOU'RE BOTH FAMOUS YOU TWO JUST DON'T LISTEN ANYMORE!
WHAT YOUR MOTHER IS SAYING IS THAT WE NEED TO SPEND MORE TIME TOGETHER AS A FAMILY.
KSI

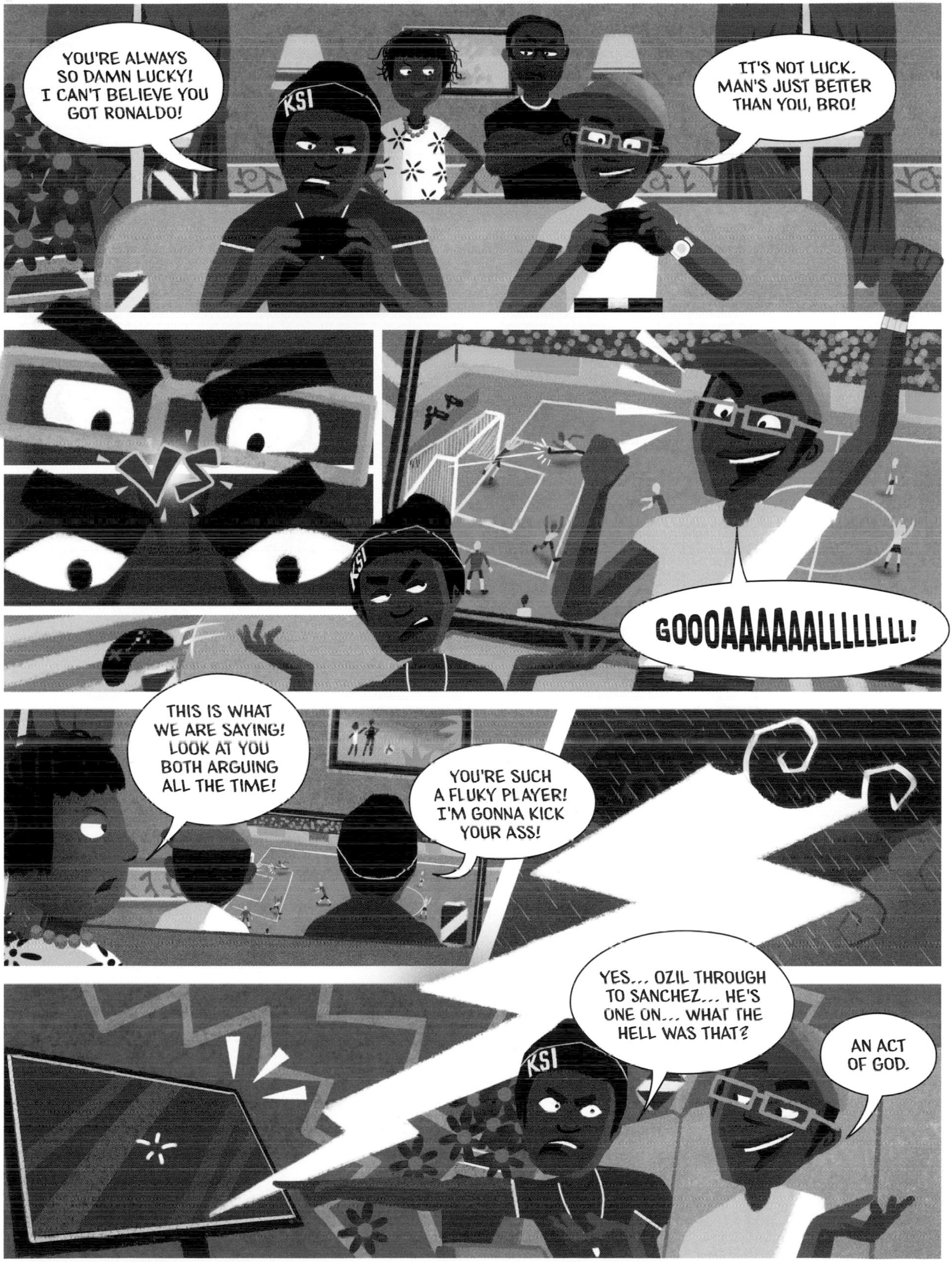
YOU'RE ALWAYS SO DAMN LUCKY! I CAN'T BELIEVE YOU GOT RONALDO!
IT'S NOT LUCK. MAN'S JUST BETTER THAN YOU, BRO!
VS
GOOOAAAAAALLLLLLLL!
THIS IS WHAT WE ARE SAYING! LOOK AT YOU BOTH ARGUING ALL THE TIME!
YOU'RE SUCH A FLUKY PLAYER! I'M GONNA KICK YOUR ASS!
YES... OZIL THROUGH TO SANCHEZ... HE'S ONE ON... WHAT THE HELL WAS THAT?
AN ACT OF GOD.

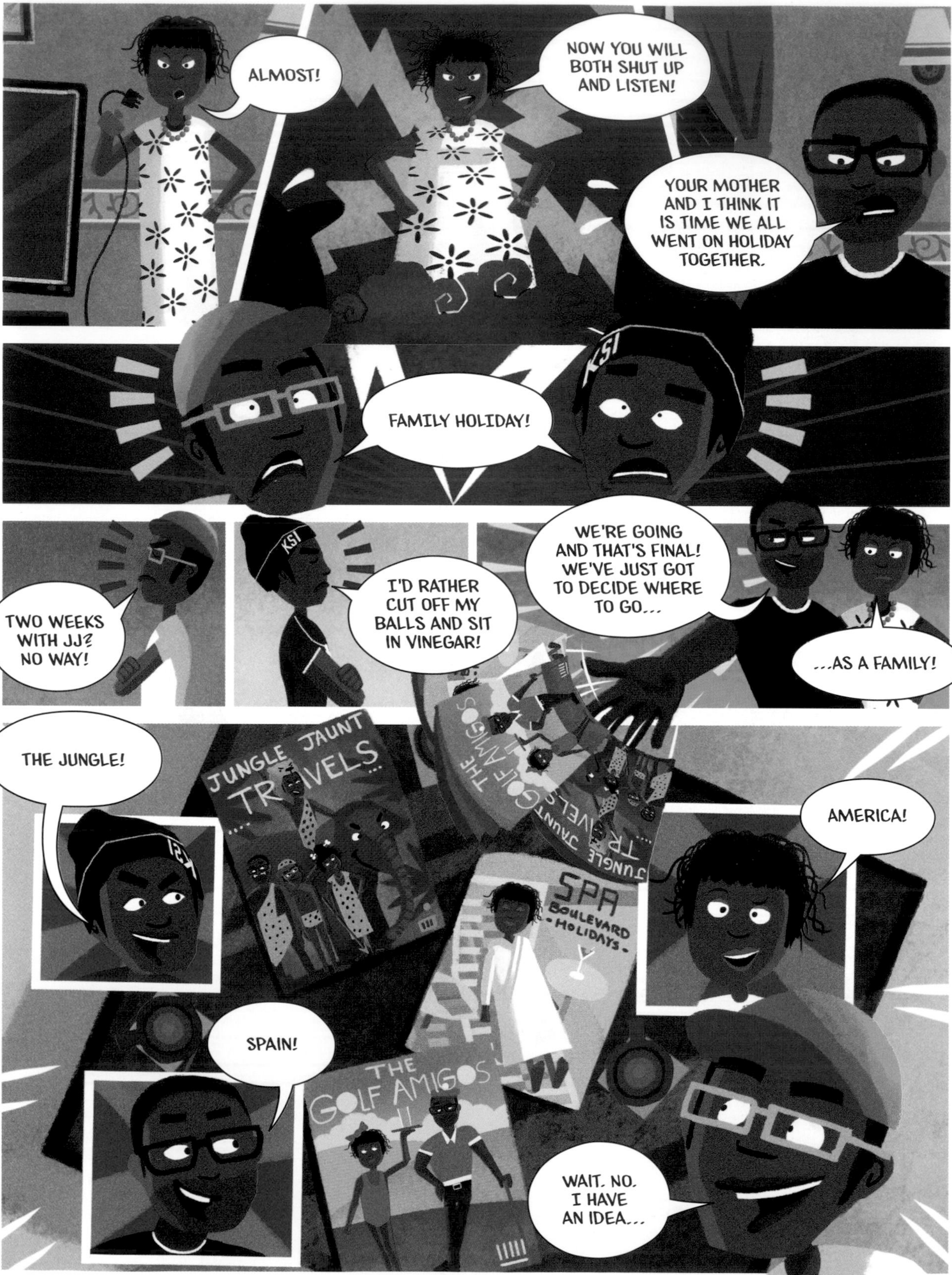
ALMOST!
NOW YOU WILL BOTH SHUT UP AND LISTEN!
YOUR MOTHER AND I THINK IT IS TIME WE ALL WENT ON HOLIDAY TOGETHER.
FAMILY HOLIDAY!
KSI
TWO WEEKS WITH JJ? NO WAY!
I'D RATHER CUT OFF MY BALLS AND SIT IN VINEGAR!
WE'RE GOING AND THAT'S FINAL! WE'VE JUST GOT TO DECIDE WHERE TO GO...
...AS A FAMILY!
THE JUNGLE!
JUNGLE JAUNT TRAVELS
AMERICA!
SPA BOULEVARD HOLIDAYS
SPAIN!
THE GOLF AMIGOS II
WAIT. NO. I HAVE AN IDEA...

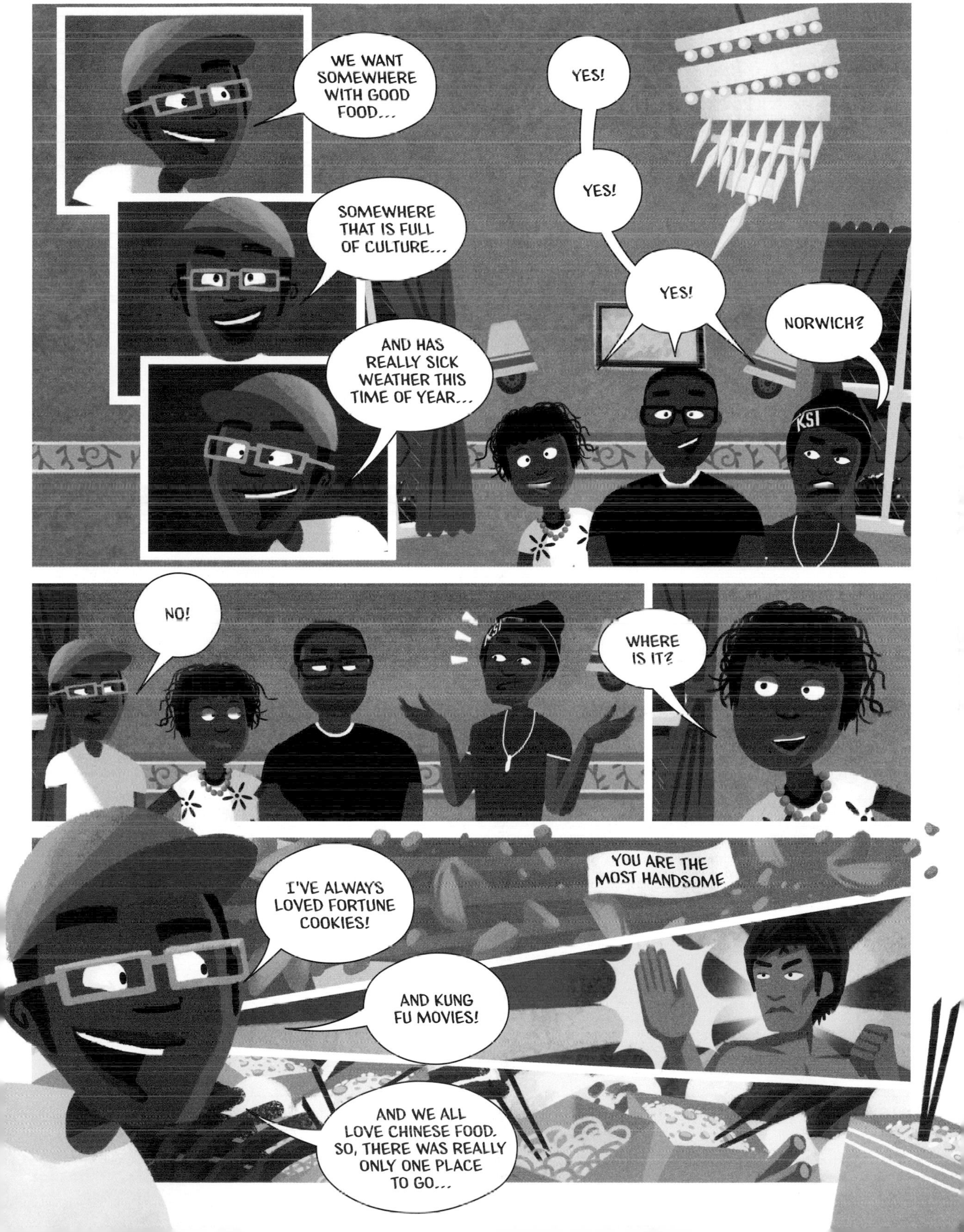
WE WANT SOMEWHERE WITH GOOD FOOD...
SOMEWHERE THAT IS FULL OF CULTURE...
AND HAS REALLY SICK WEATHER THIS TIME OF YEAR...
YES!
YES!
YES!
NORWICH?
KSI
NO!
KSI
WHERE IS IT?
I'VE ALWAYS LOVED FORTUNE COOKIES!
YOU ARE THE MOST HANDSOME
AND KUNG FU MOVIES!
AND WE ALL LOVE CHINESE FOOD. SO, THERE WAS REALLY ONLY ONE PLACE TO GO...

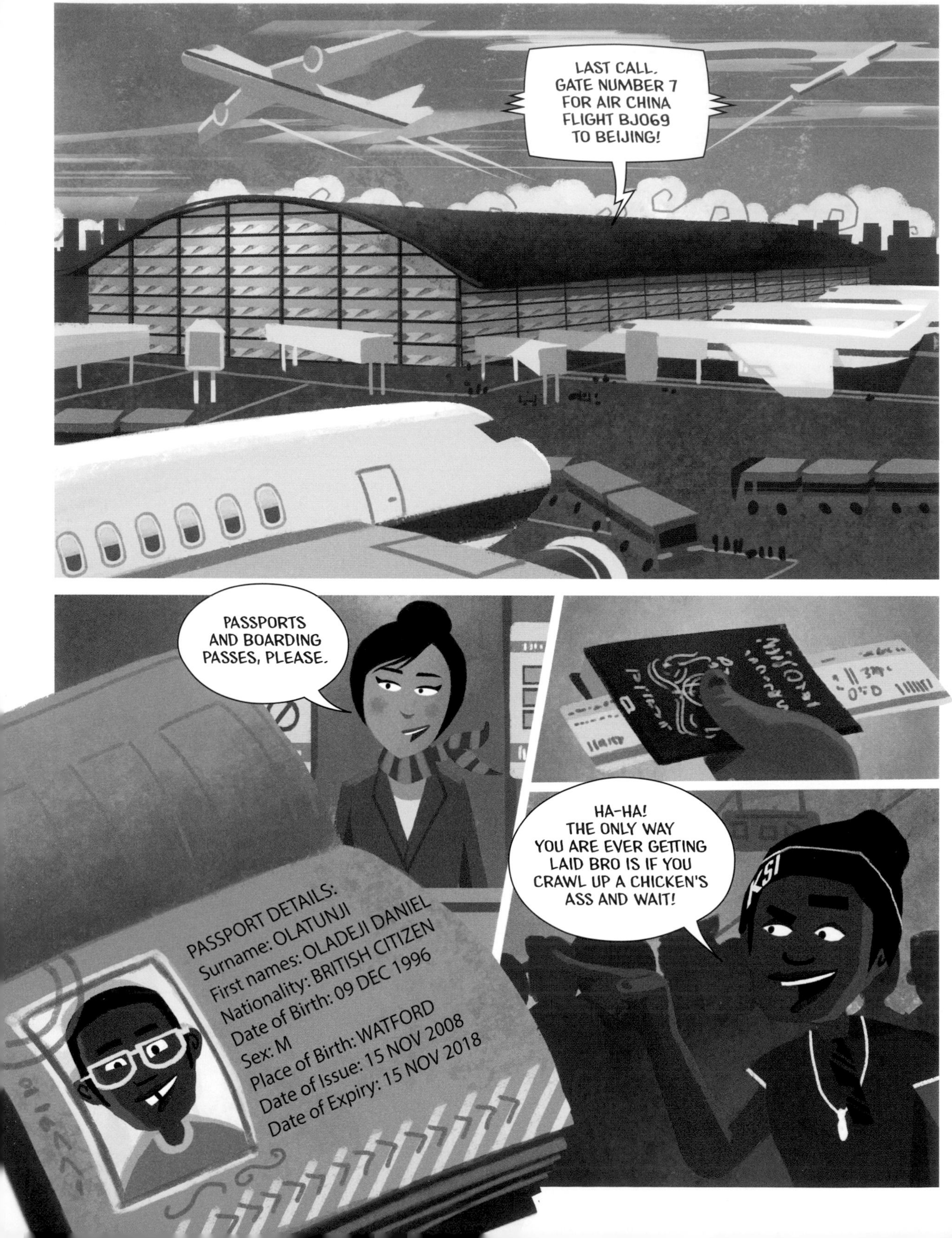
LAST CALL. GATE NUMBER 7 FOR AIR CHINA FLIGHT BJ069 TO BEIJING!
PASSPORTS AND BOARDING PASSES, PLEASE.
PASSPORT DETAILS:
Surname: OLATUNJI
First names: OLADEJI DANIEL
Nationality: BRITISH CITIZEN
Date of Birth: 09 DEC 1996
Sex: M
Place of Birth: WATFORD
Date of Issue: 15 NOV 2008
Date of Expiry: 15 NOV 2018
HA-HA! THE ONLY WAY YOU ARE EVER GETTING LAID BRO IS IF YOU CRAWL UP A CHICKEN'S ASS AND WAIT!
KSI

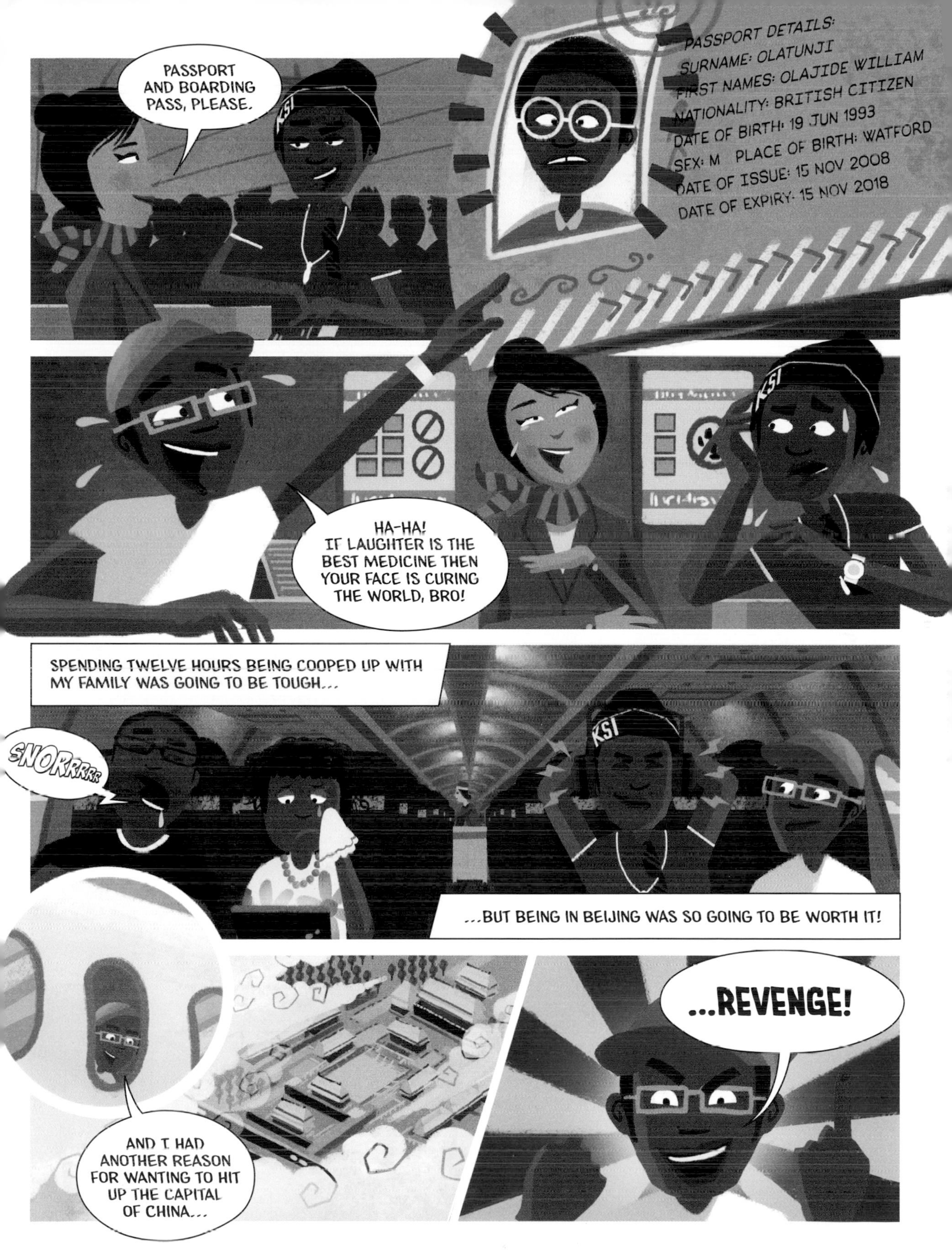

PASSPORT AND BOARDING PASS, PLEASE.
PASSPORT DETAILS:
SURNAME: OLATUNJI
FIRST NAMES: OLAJIDE WILLIAM
NATIONALITY: BRITISH CITIZEN
DATE OF BIRTH: 19 JUN 1993
SEX: M PLACE OF BIRTH: WATFORD
DATE OF ISSUE: 15 NOV 2008
DATE OF EXPIRY: 15 NOV 2018
HA-HA! IF LAUGHTER IS THE BEST MEDICINE THEN YOUR FACE IS CURING THE WORLD, BRO!
SPENDING TWELVE HOURS BEING COOPED UP WITH MY FAMILY WAS GOING TO BE TOUGH...
SNORRRRR
...BUT BEING IN BEIJING WAS SO GOING TO BE WORTH IT!
AND I HAD ANOTHER REASON FOR WANTING TO HIT UP THE CAPITAL OF CHINA...
...REVENGE!

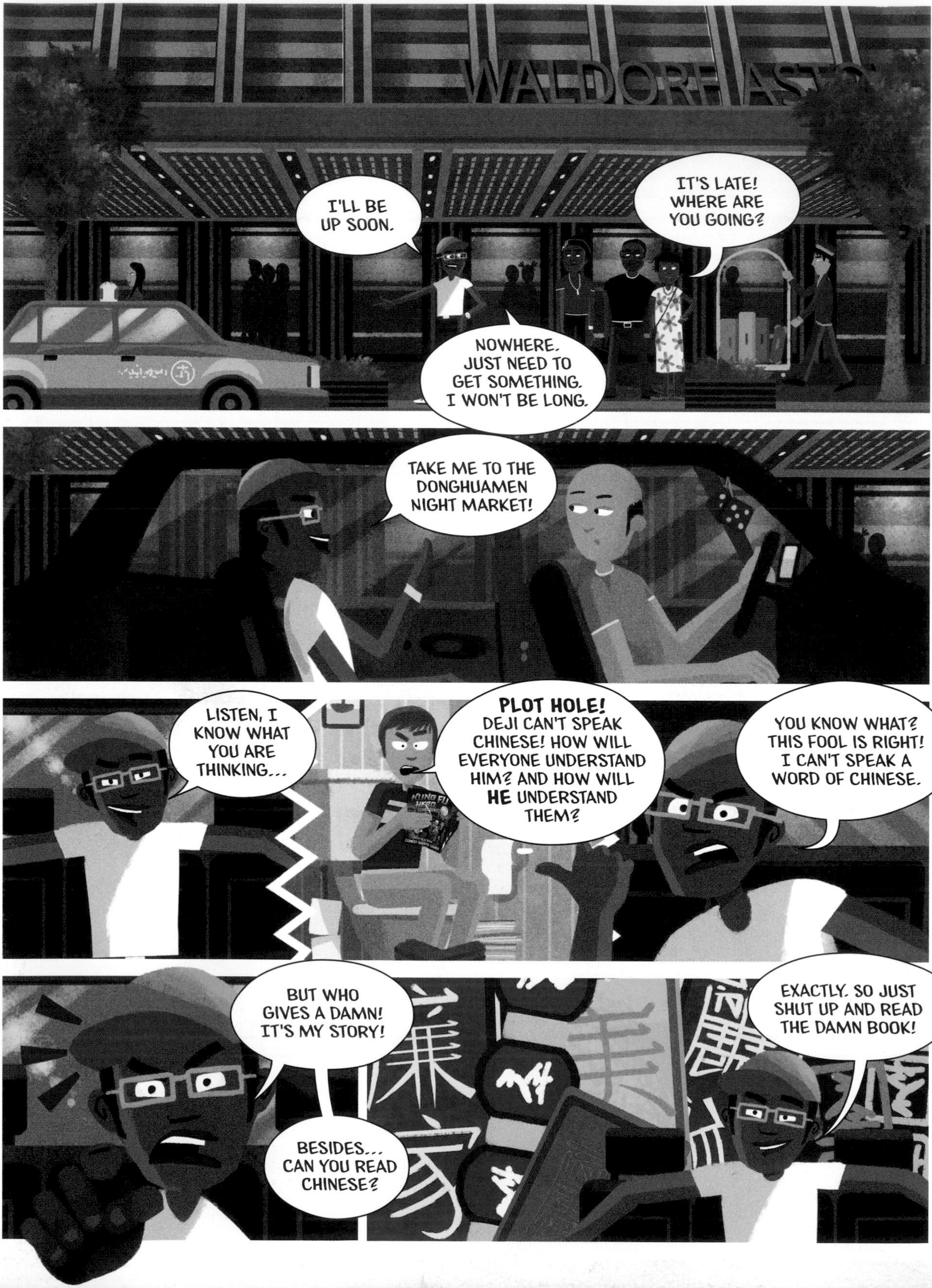
WALDORF ASTO
I'LL BE UP SOON.
IT'S LATE! WHERE ARE YOU GOING?
NOWHERE. JUST NEED TO GET SOMETHING. I WON'T BE LONG.
TAKE ME TO THE DONGHUAMEN NIGHT MARKET!
LISTEN, I KNOW WHAT YOU ARE THINKING...
PLOT HOLE! DEJI CAN'T SPEAK CHINESE! HOW WILL EVERYONE UNDERSTAND HIM? AND HOW WILL HE UNDERSTAND THEM?
YOU KNOW WHAT? THIS FOOL IS RIGHT! I CAN'T SPEAK A WORD OF CHINESE.
BUT WHO GIVES A DAMN! IT'S MY STORY!
BESIDES... CAN YOU READ CHINESE?
EXACTLY. SO JUST SHUT UP AND READ THE DAMN BOOK!

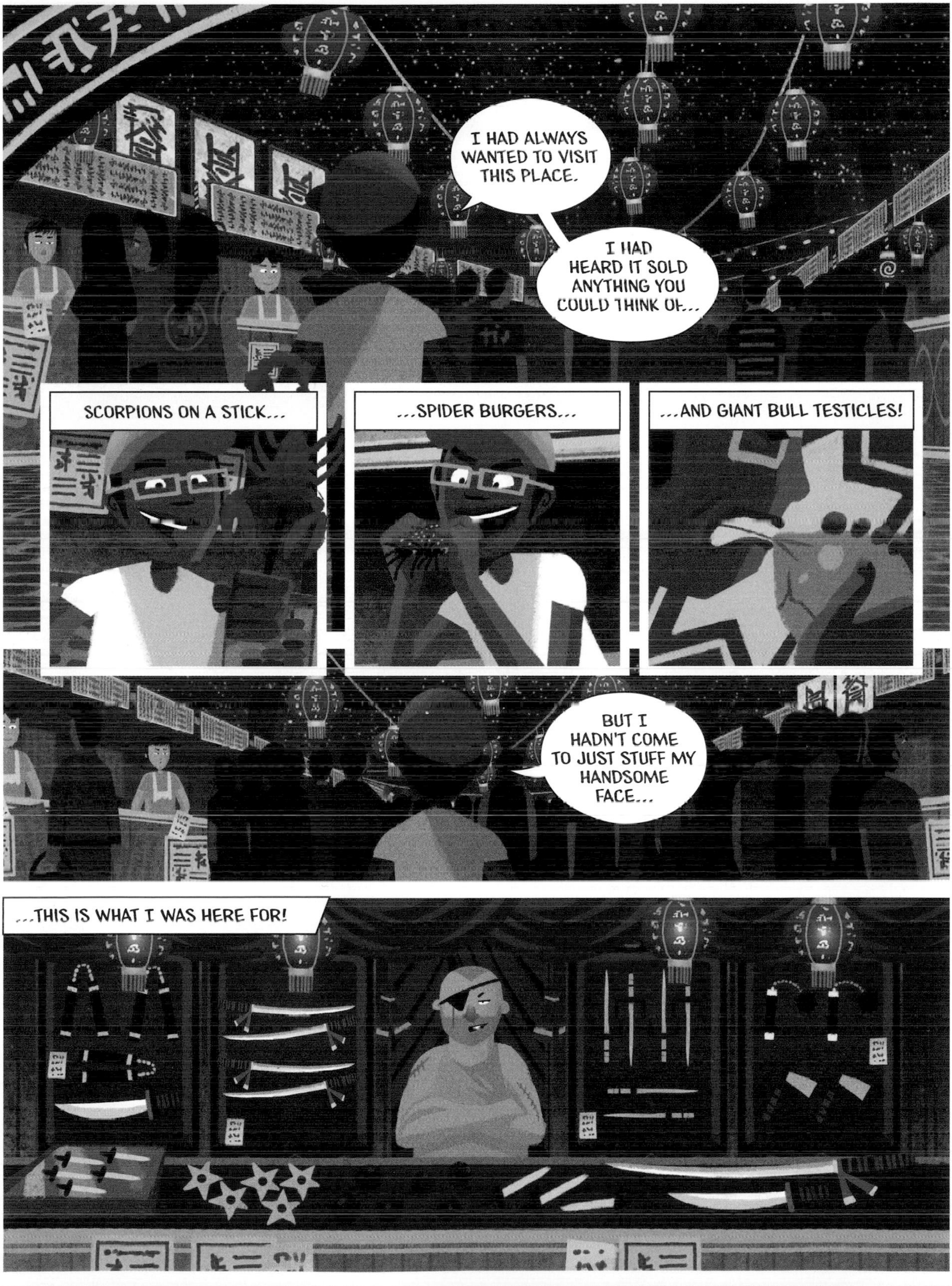
I HAD ALWAYS WANTED TO VISIT THIS PLACE.
I HAD HEARD IT SOLD ANYTHING YOU COULD THINK OF...
SCORPIONS ON A STICK...
...SPIDER BURGERS...
...AND GIANT BULL TESTICLES!
BUT I HADN'T COME TO JUST STUFF MY HANDSOME FACE...
...THIS IS WHAT I WAS HERE FOR!

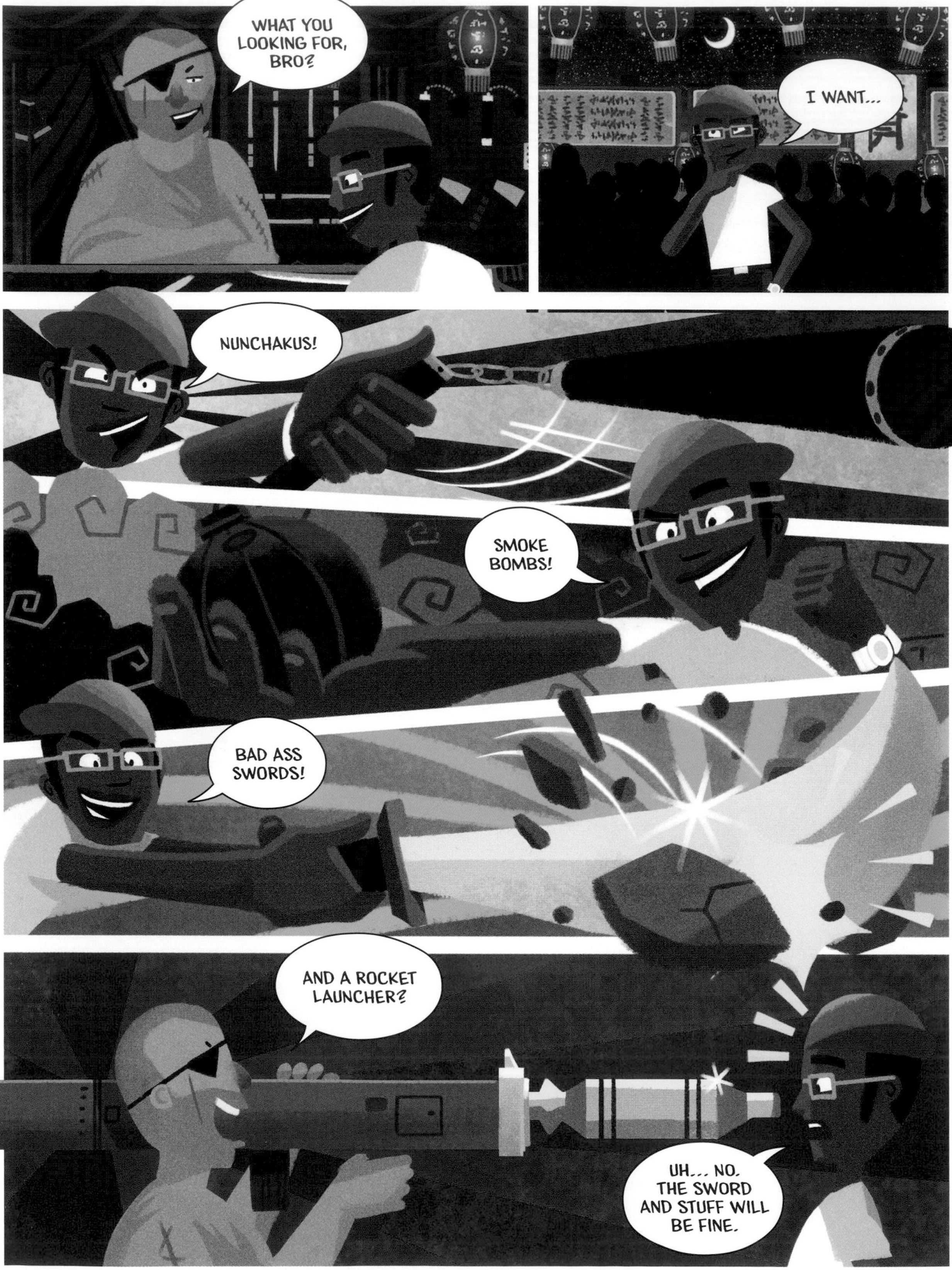
WHAT YOU LOOKING FOR, BRO?
I WANT...
NUNCHAKUS!
SMOKE BOMBS!
BAD ASS SWORDS!
AND A ROCKET LAUNCHER?
UH... NO. THE SWORD AND STUFF WILL BE FINE.

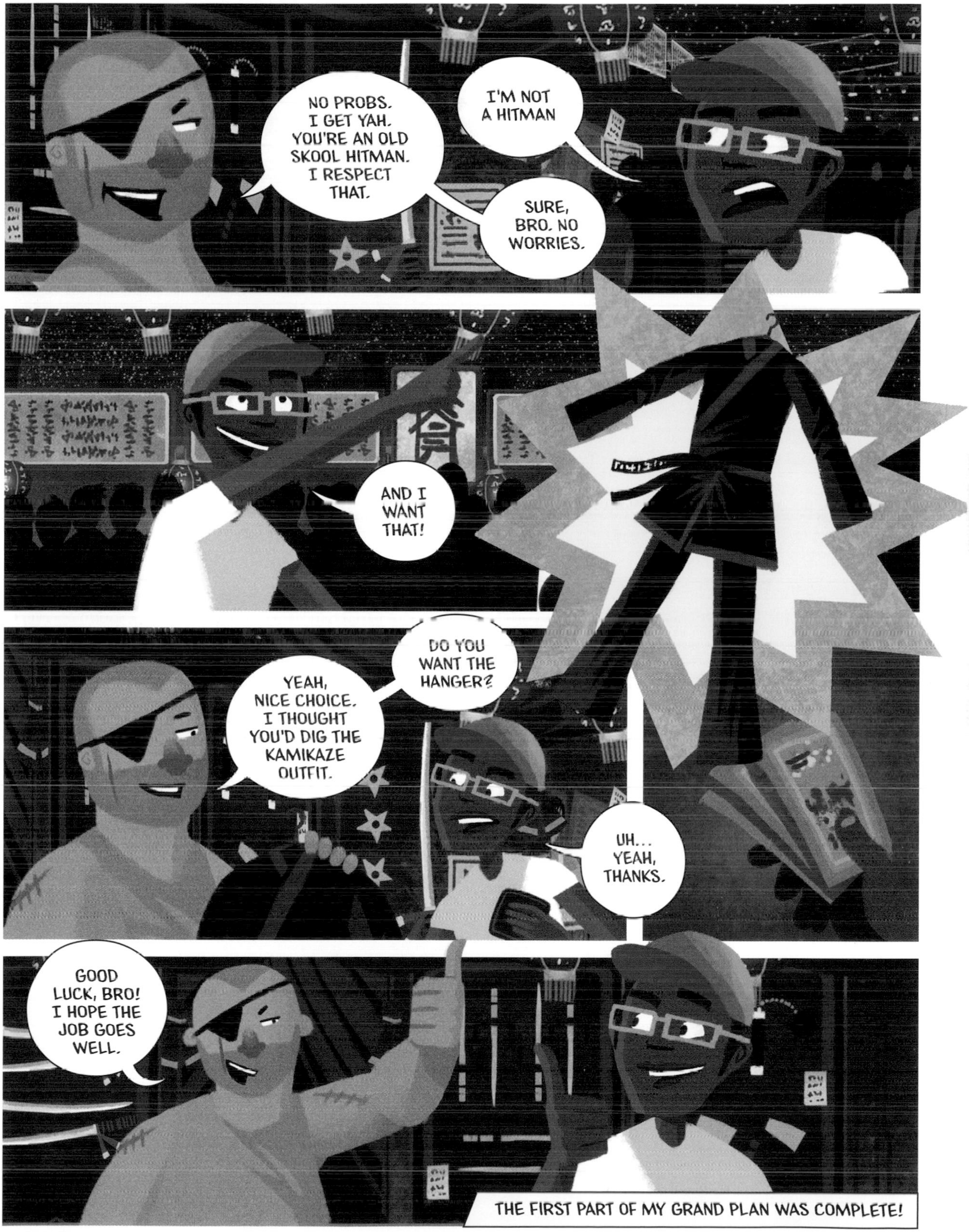
NO PROBS. I GET YAH. YOU'RE AN OLD SKOOL HITMAN. I RESPECT THAT.
I'M NOT A HITMAN
SURE, BRO. NO WORRIES.
AND I WANT THAT!
DO YOU WANT THE HANGER?
YEAH, NICE CHOICE. I THOUGHT YOU'D DIG THE KAMIKAZE OUTFIT.
UH... YEAH, THANKS.
GOOD LUCK, BRO! I HOPE THE JOB GOES WELL.
THE FIRST PART OF MY GRAND PLAN WAS COMPLETE!

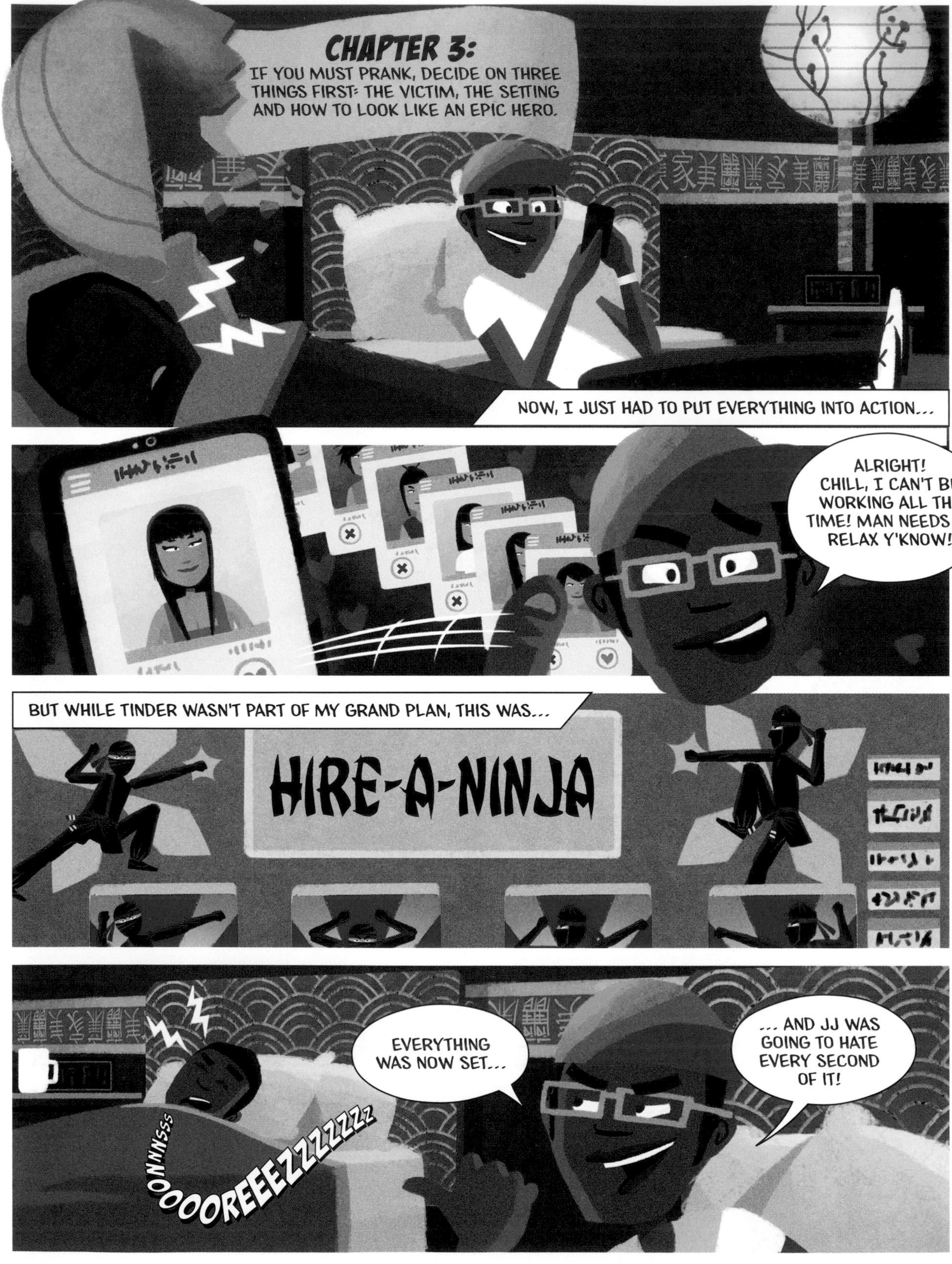
CHAPTER 3:
IF YOU MUST PRANK, DECIDE ON THREE THINGS FIRST: THE VICTIM, THE SETTING AND HOW TO LOOK LIKE AN EPIC HERO.
NOW, I JUST HAD TO PUT EVERYTHING INTO ACTION...
ALRIGHT! CHILL, I CAN'T BE WORKING ALL THE TIME! MAN NEEDS TO RELAX Y'KNOW!
BUT WHILE TINDER WASN'T PART OF MY GRAND PLAN, THIS WAS...
HIRE-A-NINJA
EVERYTHING WAS NOW SET...
... AND JJ WAS GOING TO HATE EVERY SECOND OF IT!
SNNNNOOOOOREEEZZZZZZZz

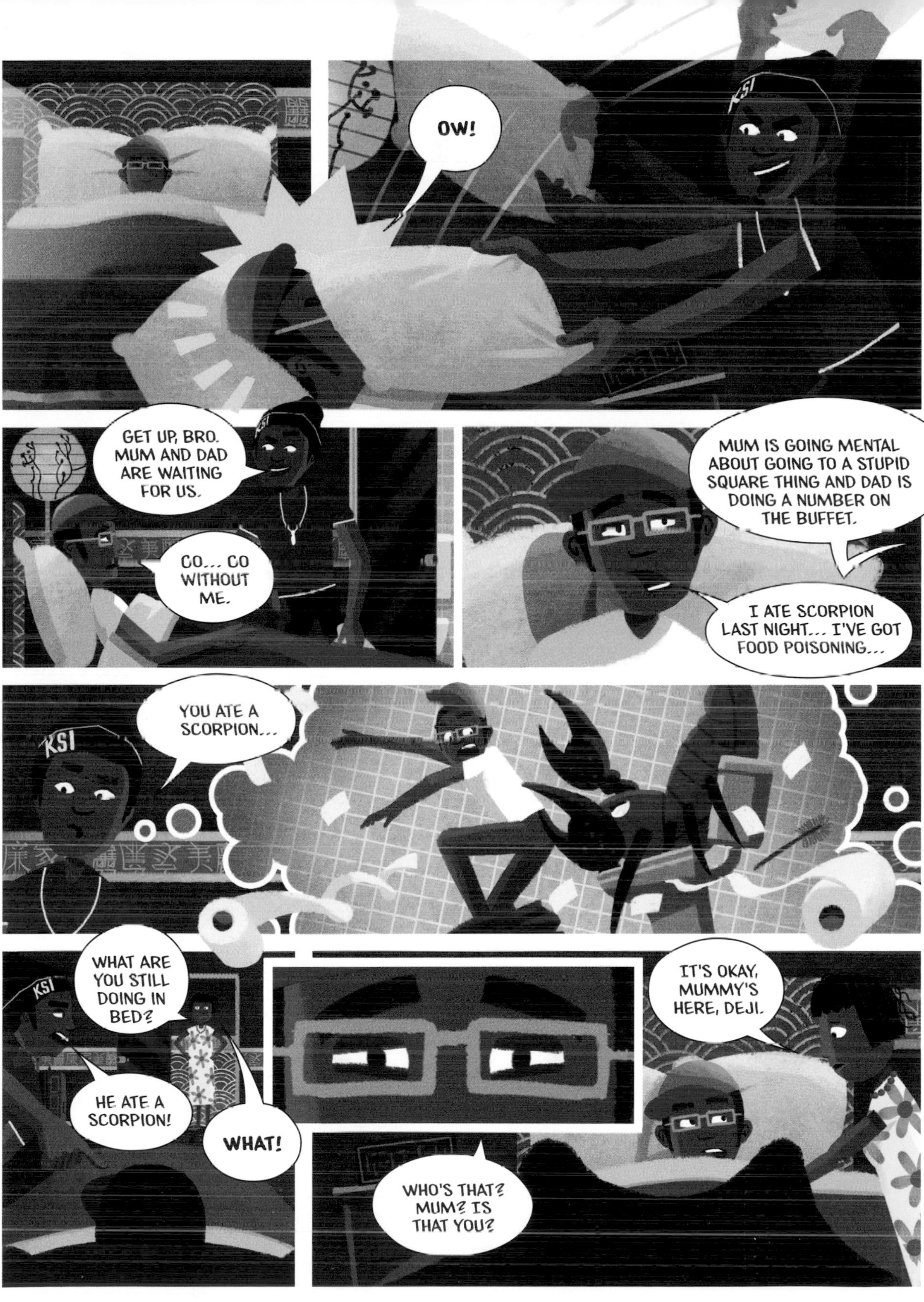

OW!
GET UP, BRO. MUM AND DAD ARE WAITING FOR US.
GO... GO WITHOUT ME.
MUM IS GOING MENTAL ABOUT GOING TO A STUPID SQUARE THING AND DAD IS DOING A NUMBER ON THE BUFFET.
I ATE SCORPION LAST NIGHT... I'VE GOT FOOD POISONING...
YOU ATE A SCORPION...
WHAT ARE YOU STILL DOING IN BED?
HE ATE A SCORPION!
WHAT!
WHO'S THAT? MUM? IS THAT YOU?
IT'S OKAY, MUMMY'S HERE, DEJI.

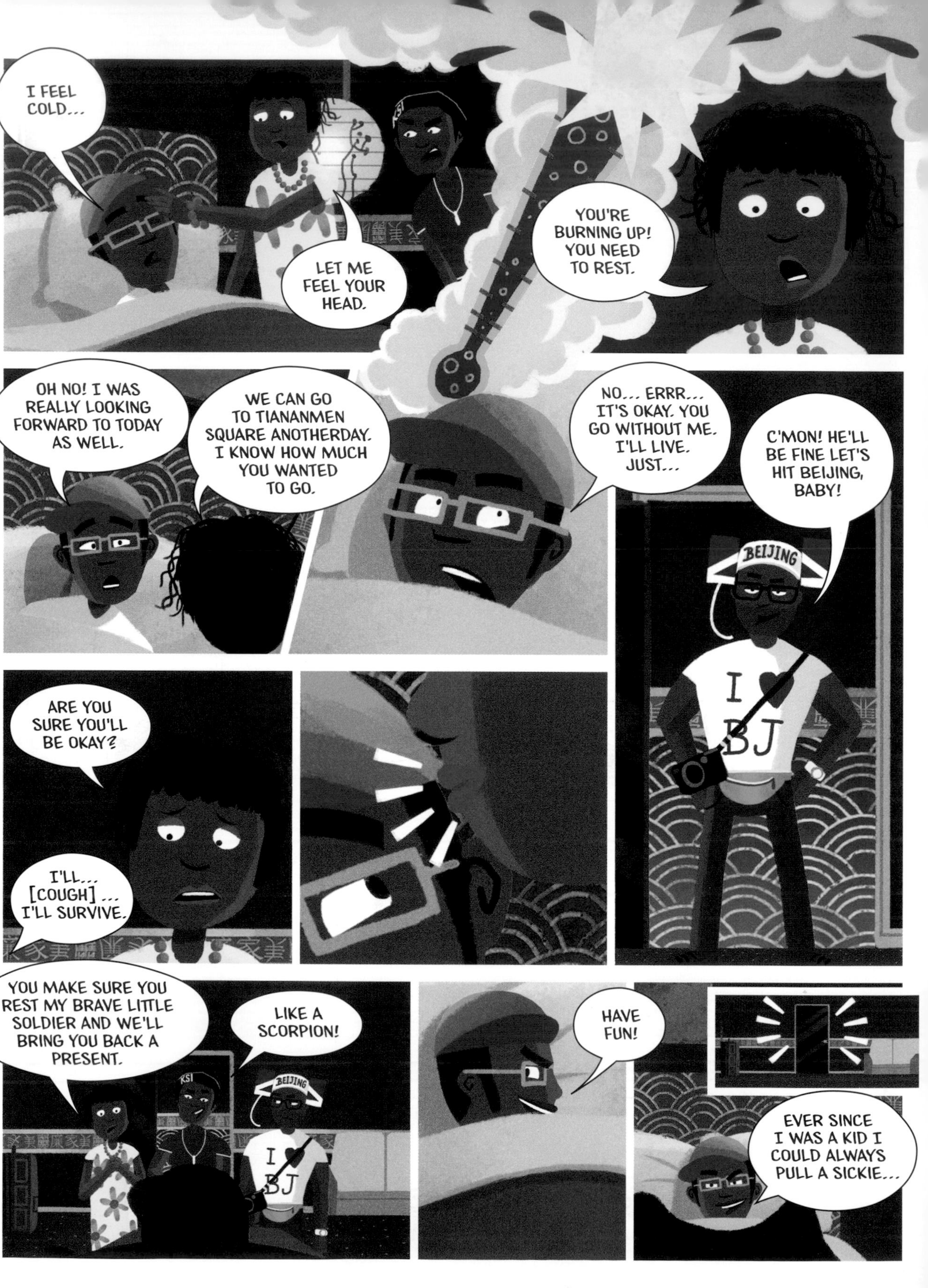
I FEEL COLD...
LET ME FEEL YOUR HEAD.
YOU'RE BURNING UP! YOU NEED TO REST.
OH NO! I WAS REALLY LOOKING FORWARD TO TODAY AS WELL.
WE CAN GO TO TIANANMEN SQUARE ANOTHERDAY. I KNOW HOW MUCH YOU WANTED TO GO.
NO... ERRR... IT'S OKAY. YOU GO WITHOUT ME. I'LL LIVE. JUST...
C'MON! HE'LL BE FINE LET'S HIT BEIJING, BABY!
BEIJING
I BJ
ARE YOU SURE YOU'LL BE OKAY?
I'LL... [COUGH] ... I'LL SURVIVE.
YOU MAKE SURE YOU REST MY BRAVE LITTLE SOLDIER AND WE'LL BRING YOU BACK A PRESENT.
LIKE A SCORPION!
HAVE FUN!
EVER SINCE I WAS A KID I COULD ALWAYS PULL A SICKIE...

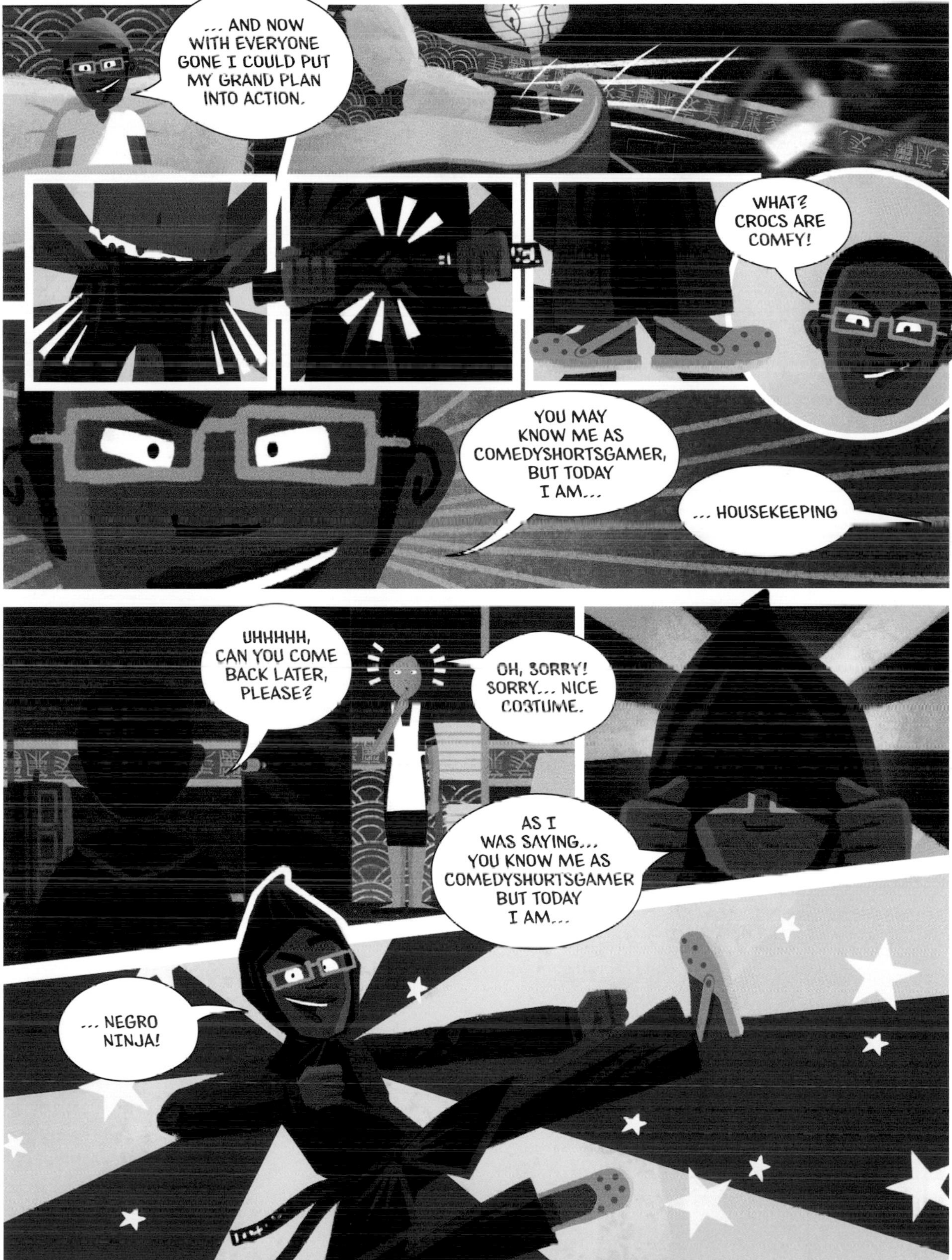
... AND NOW WITH EVERYONE GONE I COULD PUT MY GRAND PLAN INTO ACTION.
WHAT? CROCS ARE COMFY!
YOU MAY KNOW ME AS COMEDYSHORTSGAMER, BUT TODAY I AM...
... HOUSEKEEPING
UHHHHH, CAN YOU COME BACK LATER, PLEASE?
OH, SORRY! SORRY... NICE COSTUME.
AS I WAS SAYING... YOU KNOW ME AS COMEDYSHORTSGAMER BUT TODAY I AM...
... NEGRO NINJA!

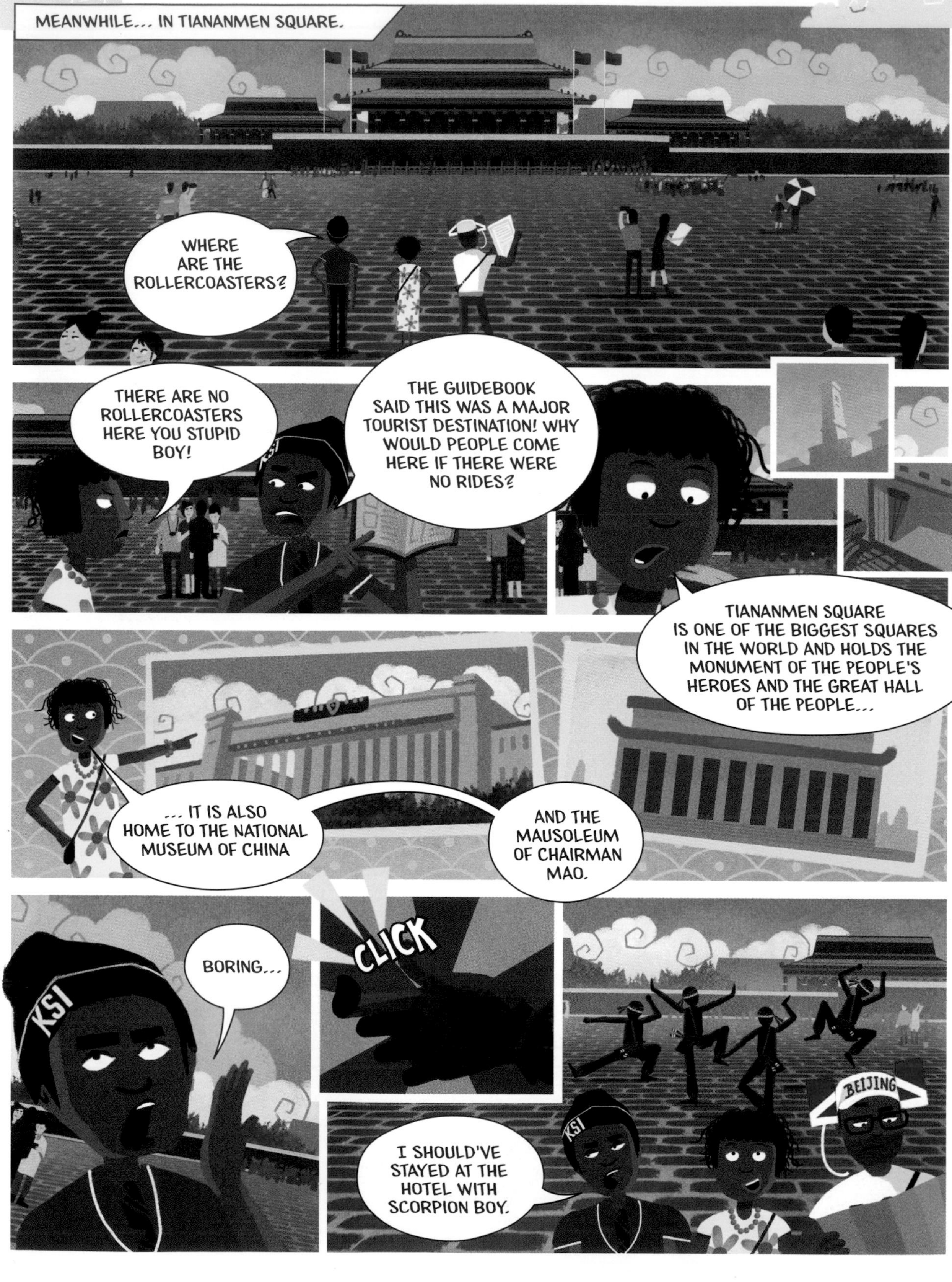
MEANWHILE... IN TIANANMEN SQUARE.
WHERE ARE THE ROLLERCOASTERS?
THERE ARE NO ROLLERCOASTERS HERE YOU STUPID BOY!
KSI
THE GUIDEBOOK SAID THIS WAS A MAJOR TOURIST DESTINATION! WHY WOULD PEOPLE COME HERE IF THERE WERE NO RIDES?
TIANANMEN SQUARE IS ONE OF THE BIGGEST SQUARES IN THE WORLD AND HOLDS THE MONUMENT OF THE PEOPLE'S HEROES AND THE GREAT HALL OF THE PEOPLE...
... IT IS ALSO HOME TO THE NATIONAL MUSEUM OF CHINA
AND THE MAUSOLEUM OF CHAIRMAN MAO.
KSI
BORING...
CLICK
KSI
BEIJING
I SHOULD'VE STAYED AT THE HOTEL WITH SCORPION BOY.

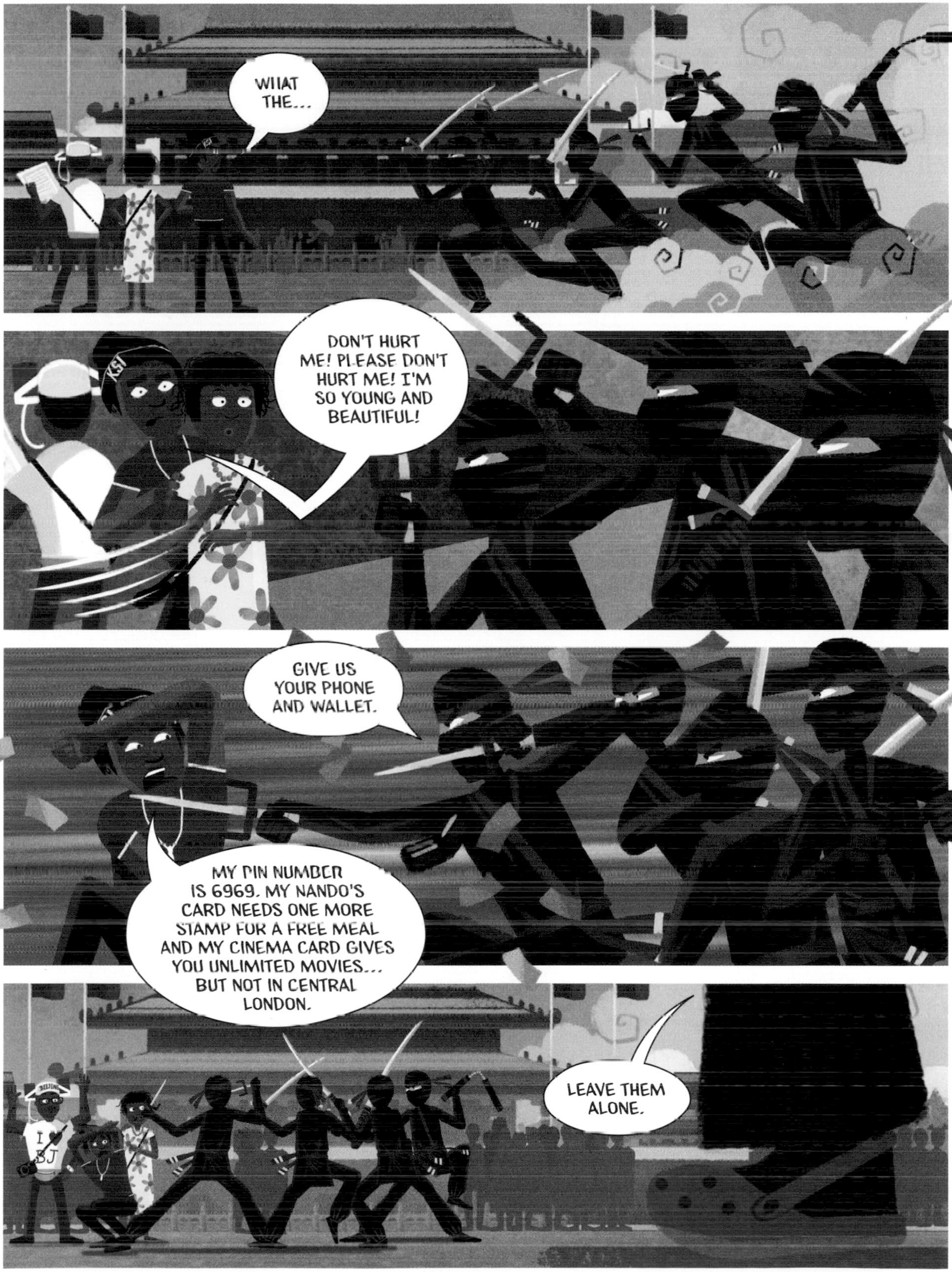
WHAT THE...
DON'T HURT ME! PLEASE DON'T HURT ME! I'M SO YOUNG AND BEAUTIFUL!
KSI
GIVE US YOUR PHONE AND WALLET.
MY PIN NUMBER IS 6969. MY NANDO'S CARD NEEDS ONE MORE STAMP FOR A FREE MEAL AND MY CINEMA CARD GIVES YOU UNLIMITED MOVIES... BUT NOT IN CENTRAL LONDON.
BEIJING
I BJ
LEAVE THEM ALONE.

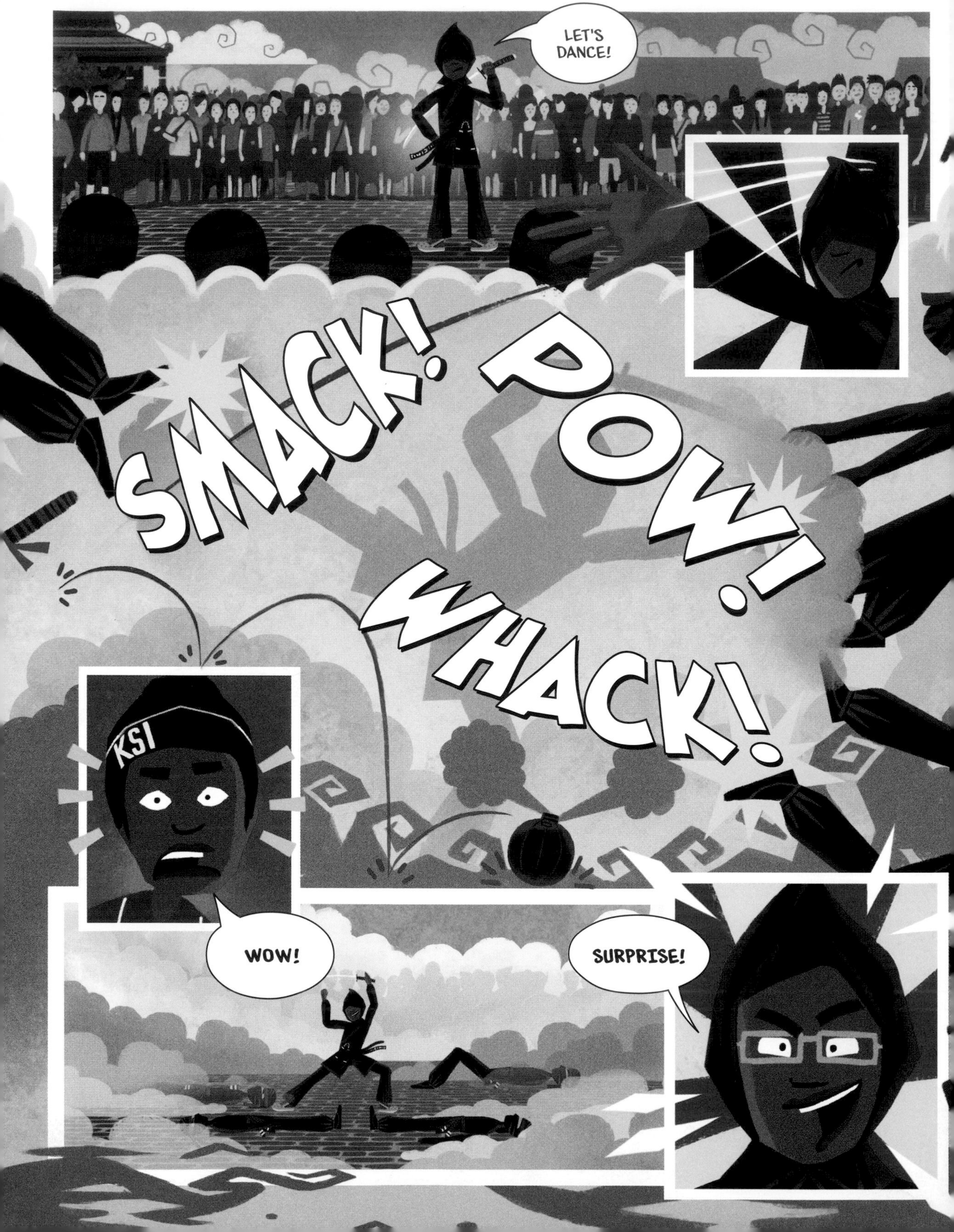
LET'S DANCE!
SMACK!
POW!
WHACK!
KSI
WOW!
SURPRISE!

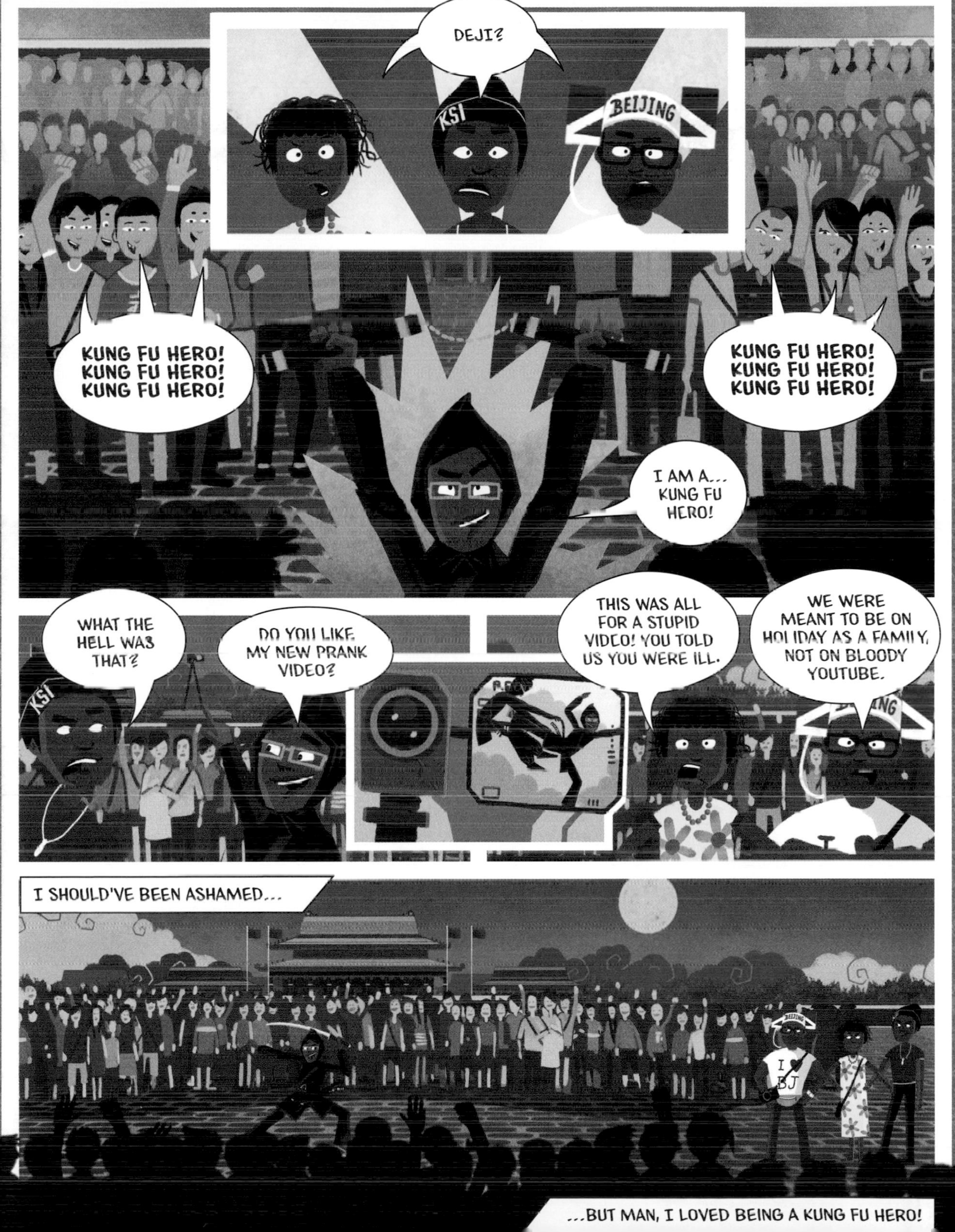
DEJI?
BEIJING
KSI
KUNG FU HERO! KUNG FU HERO! KUNG FU HERO!
KUNG FU HERO! KUNG FU HERO! KUNG FU HERO!
I AM A... KUNG FU HERO!
WHAT THE HELL WAS THAT?
DO YOU LIKE MY NEW PRANK VIDEO?
THIS WAS ALL FOR A STUPID VIDEO! YOU TOLD US YOU WERE ILL.
WE WERE MEANT TO BE ON HOLIDAY AS A FAMILY, NOT ON BLOODY YOUTUBE.
I SHOULD'VE BEEN ASHAMED...
...BUT MAN, I LOVED BEING A KUNG FU HERO!

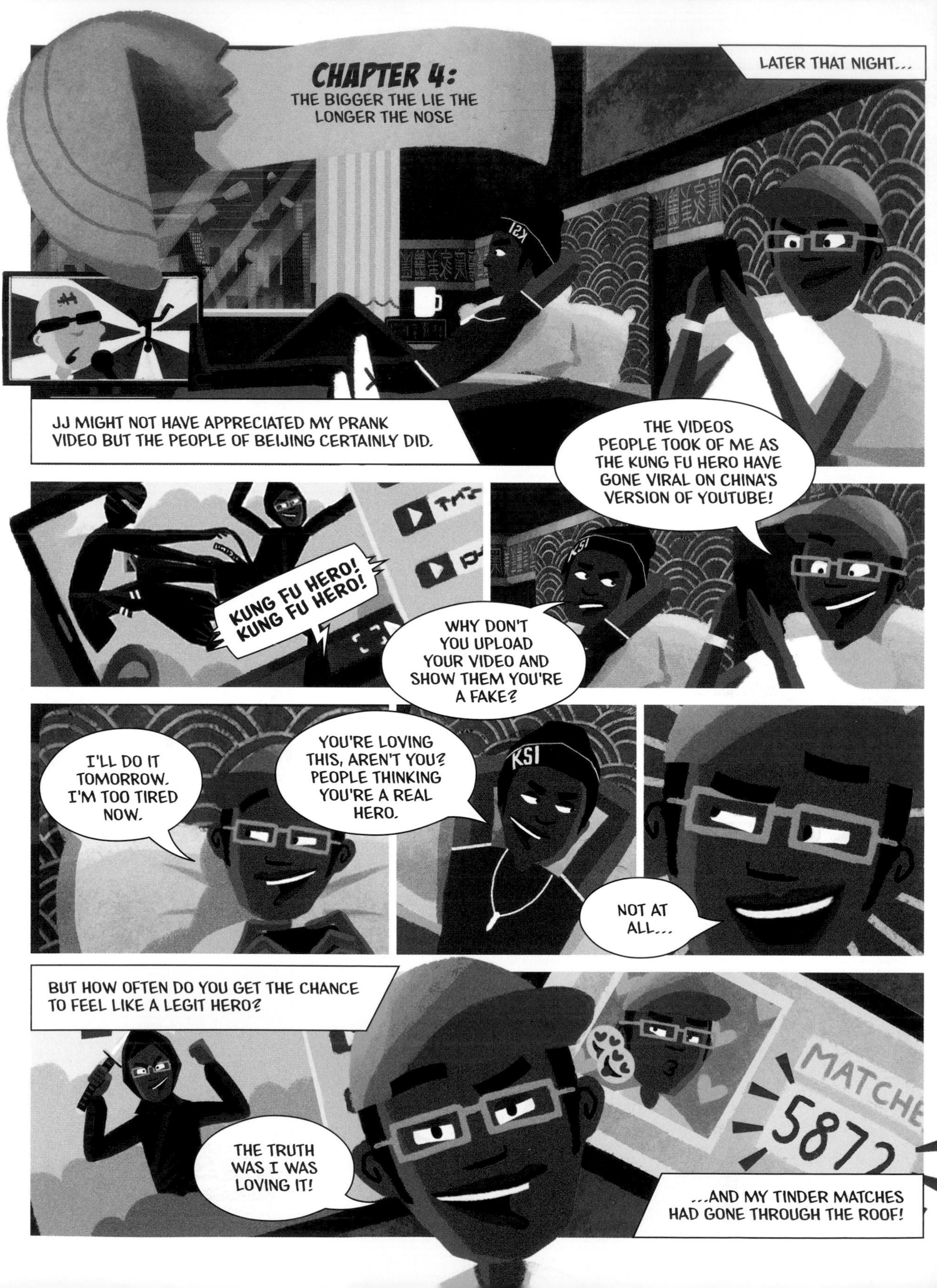
CHAPTER 4:
THE BIGGER THE LIE THE LONGER THE NOSE
LATER THAT NIGHT...
JJ MIGHT NOT HAVE APPRECIATED MY PRANK VIDEO BUT THE PEOPLE OF BEIJING CERTAINLY DID.
THE VIDEOS PEOPLE TOOK OF ME AS THE KUNG FU HERO HAVE GONE VIRAL ON CHINA'S VERSION OF YOUTUBE!
KUNG FU HERO! KUNG FU HERO!
WHY DON'T YOU UPLOAD YOUR VIDEO AND SHOW THEM YOU'RE A FAKE?
I'LL DO IT TOMORROW. I'M TOO TIRED NOW.
YOU'RE LOVING THIS, AREN'T YOU? PEOPLE THINKING YOU'RE A REAL HERO.
NOT AT ALL...
BUT HOW OFTEN DO YOU GET THE CHANCE TO FEEL LIKE A LEGIT HERO?
THE TRUTH WAS I WAS LOVING IT!
MATCHES
5872
...AND MY TINDER MATCHES HAD GONE THROUGH THE ROOF!

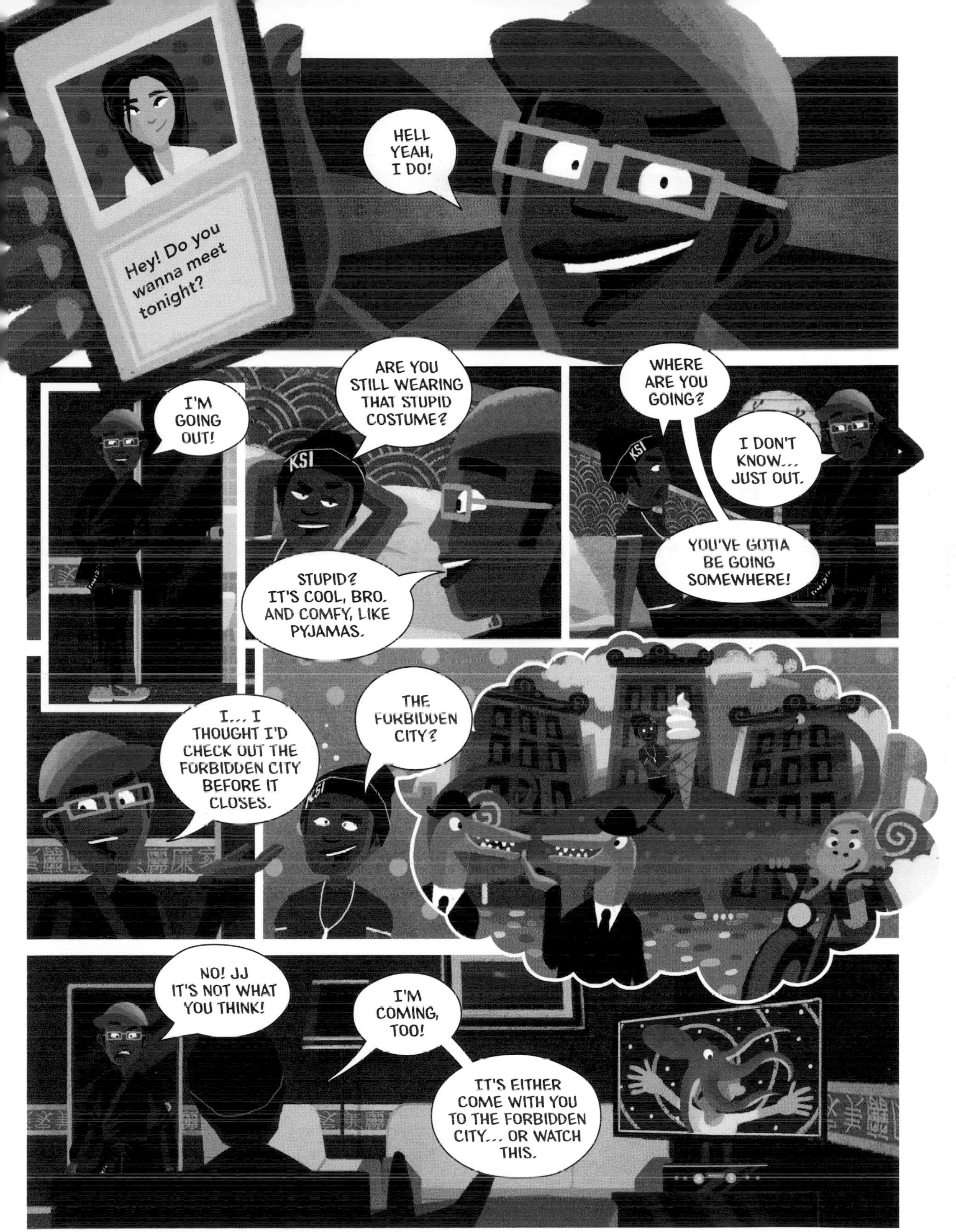
Hey! Do you wanna meet tonight?
HELL YEAH, I DO!
I'M GOING OUT!
ARE YOU STILL WEARING THAT STUPID COSTUME?
STUPID? IT'S COOL, BRO. AND COMFY, LIKE PYJAMAS.
WHERE ARE YOU GOING?
I DON'T KNOW... JUST OUT.
YOU'VE GOTTA BE GOING SOMEWHERE!
I... I THOUGHT I'D CHECK OUT THE FORBIDDEN CITY BEFORE IT CLOSES.
THE FORBIDDEN CITY?
NO! JJ IT'S NOT WHAT YOU THINK!
I'M COMING, TOO!
IT'S EITHER COME WITH YOU TO THE FORBIDDEN CITY... OR WATCH THIS.

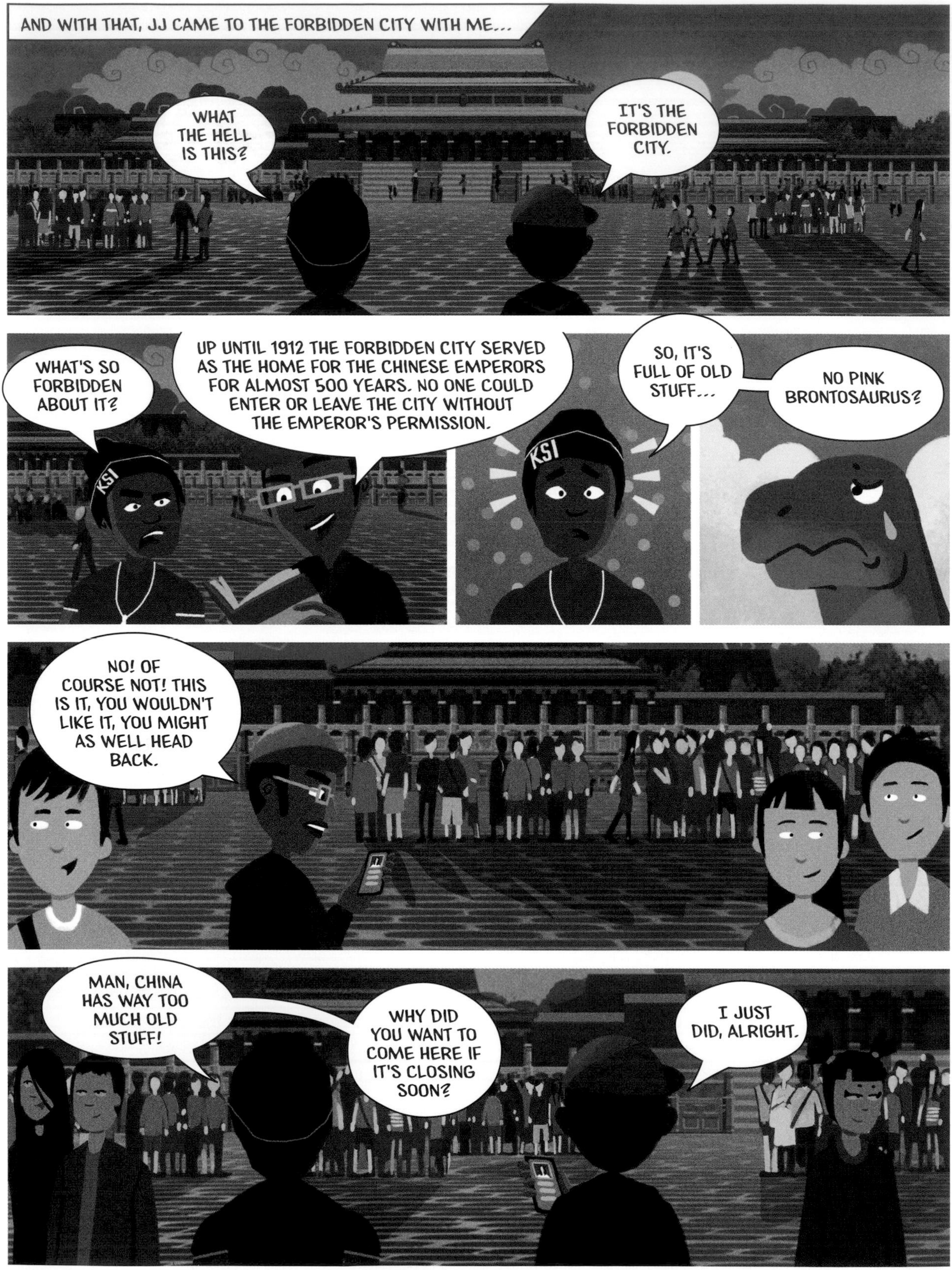
AND WITH THAT, JJ CAME TO THE FORBIDDEN CITY WITH ME...
WHAT THE HELL IS THIS?
IT'S THE FORBIDDEN CITY.
WHAT'S SO FORBIDDEN ABOUT IT?
UP UNTIL 1912 THE FORBIDDEN CITY SERVED AS THE HOME FOR THE CHINESE EMPERORS FOR ALMOST 500 YEARS. NO ONE COULD ENTER OR LEAVE THE CITY WITHOUT THE EMPEROR'S PERMISSION.
SO, IT'S FULL OF OLD STUFF...
NO PINK BRONTOSAURUS?
KSI
NO! OF COURSE NOT! THIS IS IT, YOU WOULDN'T LIKE IT, YOU MIGHT AS WELL HEAD BACK.
MAN, CHINA HAS WAY TOO MUCH OLD STUFF!
WHY DID YOU WANT TO COME HERE IF IT'S CLOSING SOON?
I JUST DID, ALRIGHT.

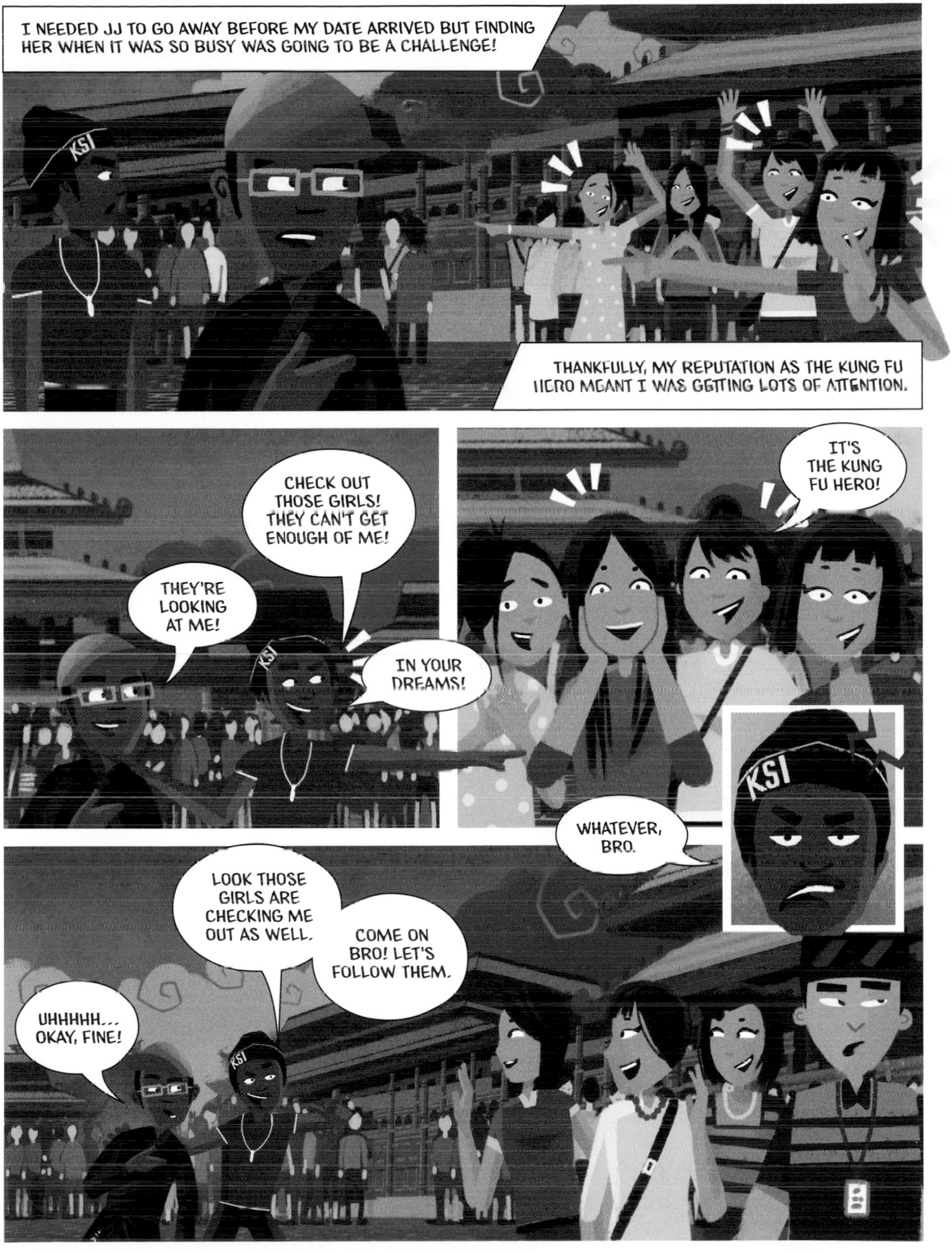
I NEEDED JJ TO GO AWAY BEFORE MY DATE ARRIVED BUT FINDING HER WHEN IT WAS SO BUSY WAS GOING TO BE A CHALLENGE!
THANKFULLY, MY REPUTATION AS THE KUNG FU HERO MEANT I WAS GETTING LOTS OF ATTENTION.
CHECK OUT THOSE GIRLS! THEY CAN'T GET ENOUGH OF ME!
THEY'RE LOOKING AT ME!
IN YOUR DREAMS!
IT'S THE KUNG FU HERO!
WHATEVER, BRO.
LOOK THOSE GIRLS ARE CHECKING ME OUT AS WELL.
COME ON BRO! LET'S FOLLOW THEM.
UHHHHH... OKAY, FINE!

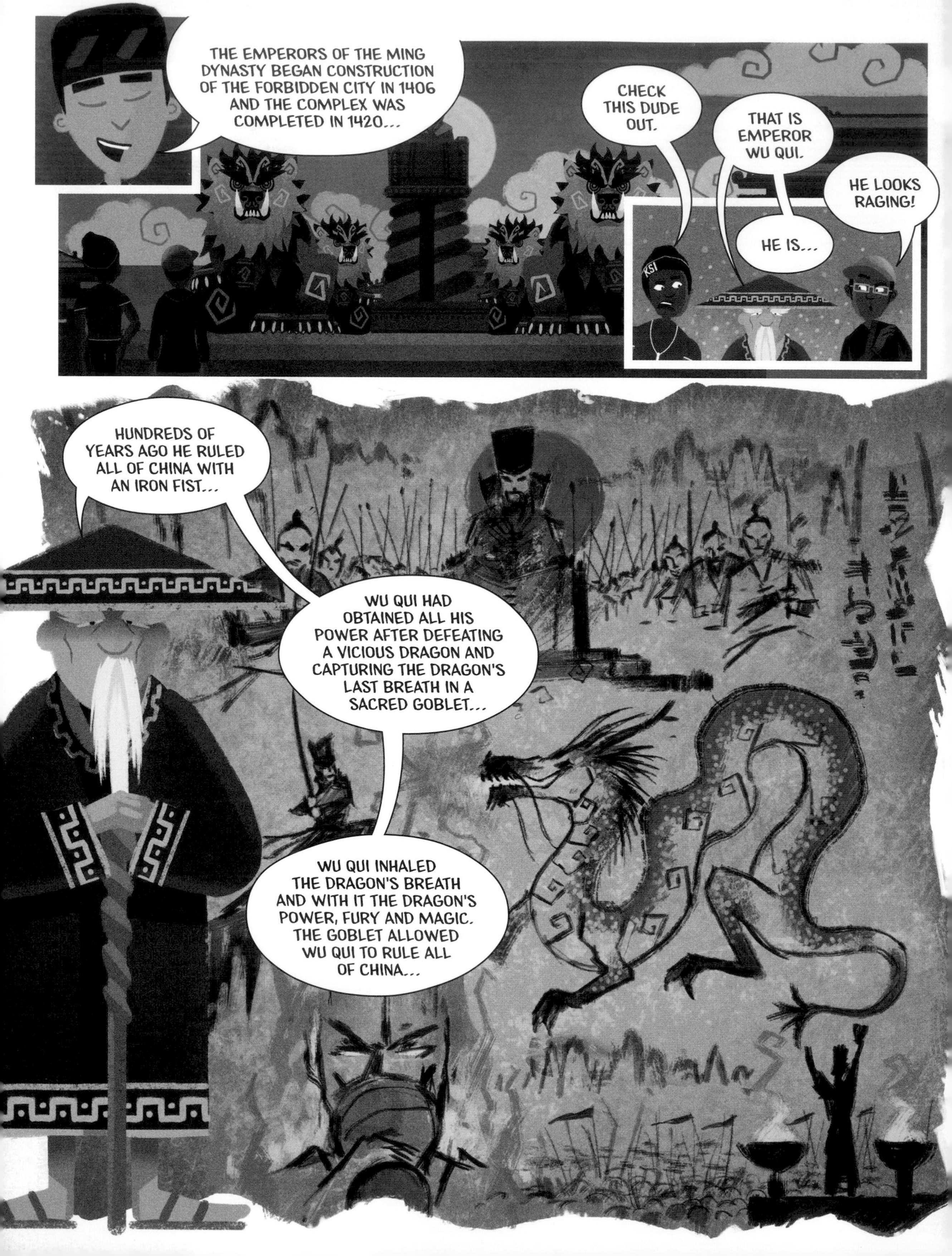
THE EMPERORS OF THE MING DYNASTY BEGAN CONSTRUCTION OF THE FORBIDDEN CITY IN 1406 AND THE COMPLEX WAS COMPLETED IN 1420...
CHECK THIS DUDE OUT.
THAT IS EMPEROR WU QUI.
HE LOOKS RAGING!
HE IS...
KSI
HUNDREDS OF YEARS AGO HE RULED ALL OF CHINA WITH AN IRON FIST...
WU QUI HAD OBTAINED ALL HIS POWER AFTER DEFEATING A VICIOUS DRAGON AND CAPTURING THE DRAGON'S LAST BREATH IN A SACRED GOBLET...
WU QUI INHALED THE DRAGON'S BREATH AND WITH IT THE DRAGON'S POWER, FURY AND MAGIC. THE GOBLET ALLOWED WU QUI TO RULE ALL OF CHINA...

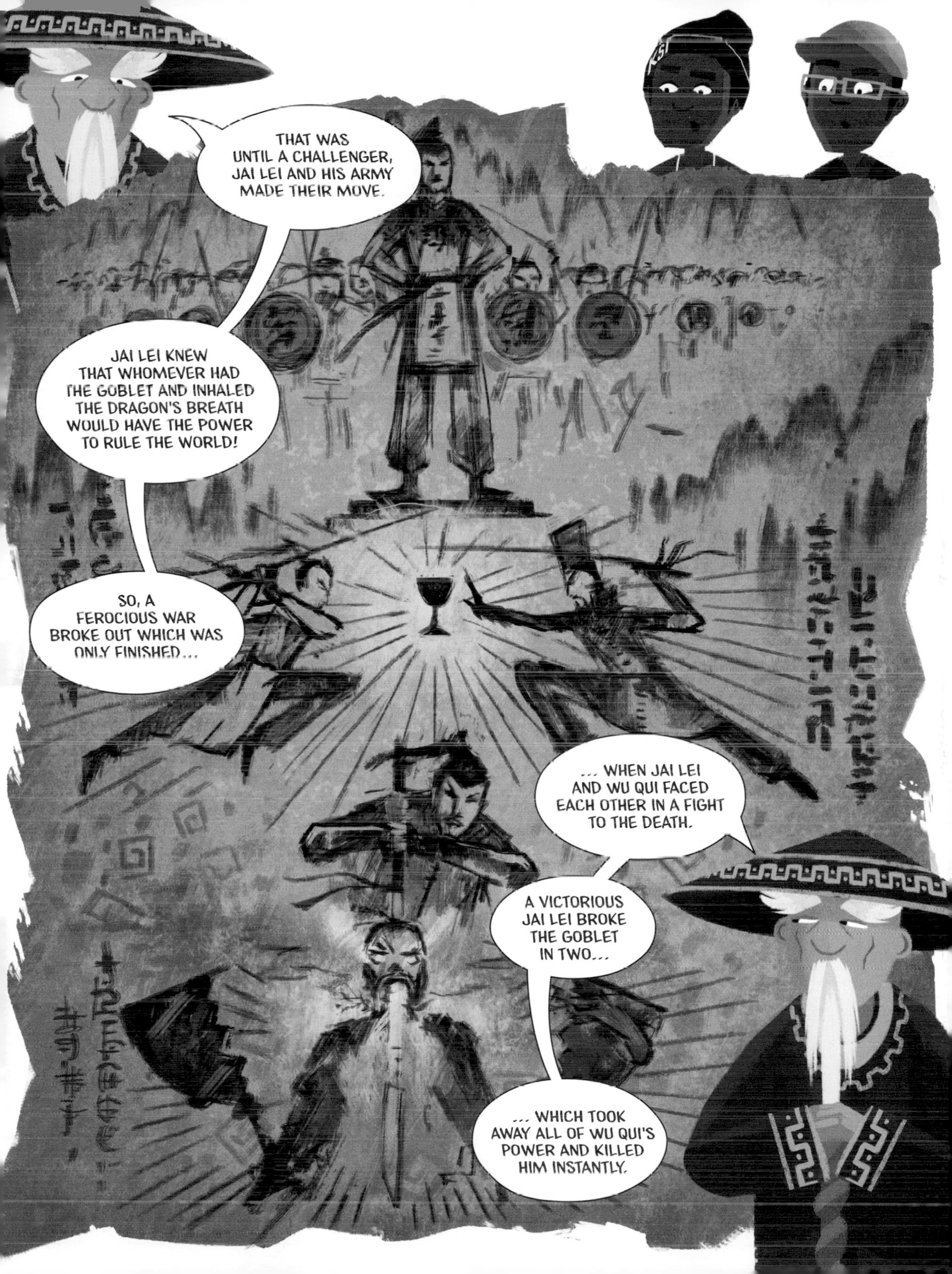
THAT WAS UNTIL A CHALLENGER, JAI LEI AND HIS ARMY MADE THEIR MOVE.
JAI LEI KNEW THAT WHOMEVER HAD THE GOBLET AND INHALED THE DRAGON'S BREATH WOULD HAVE THE POWER TO RULE THE WORLD!
SO, A FEROCIOUS WAR BROKE OUT WHICH WAS ONLY FINISHED...
... WHEN JAI LEI AND WU QUI FACED EACH OTHER IN A FIGHT TO THE DEATH.
A VICTORIOUS JAI LEI BROKE THE GOBLET IN TWO...
... WHICH TOOK AWAY ALL OF WU QUI'S POWER AND KILLED HIM INSTANTLY.

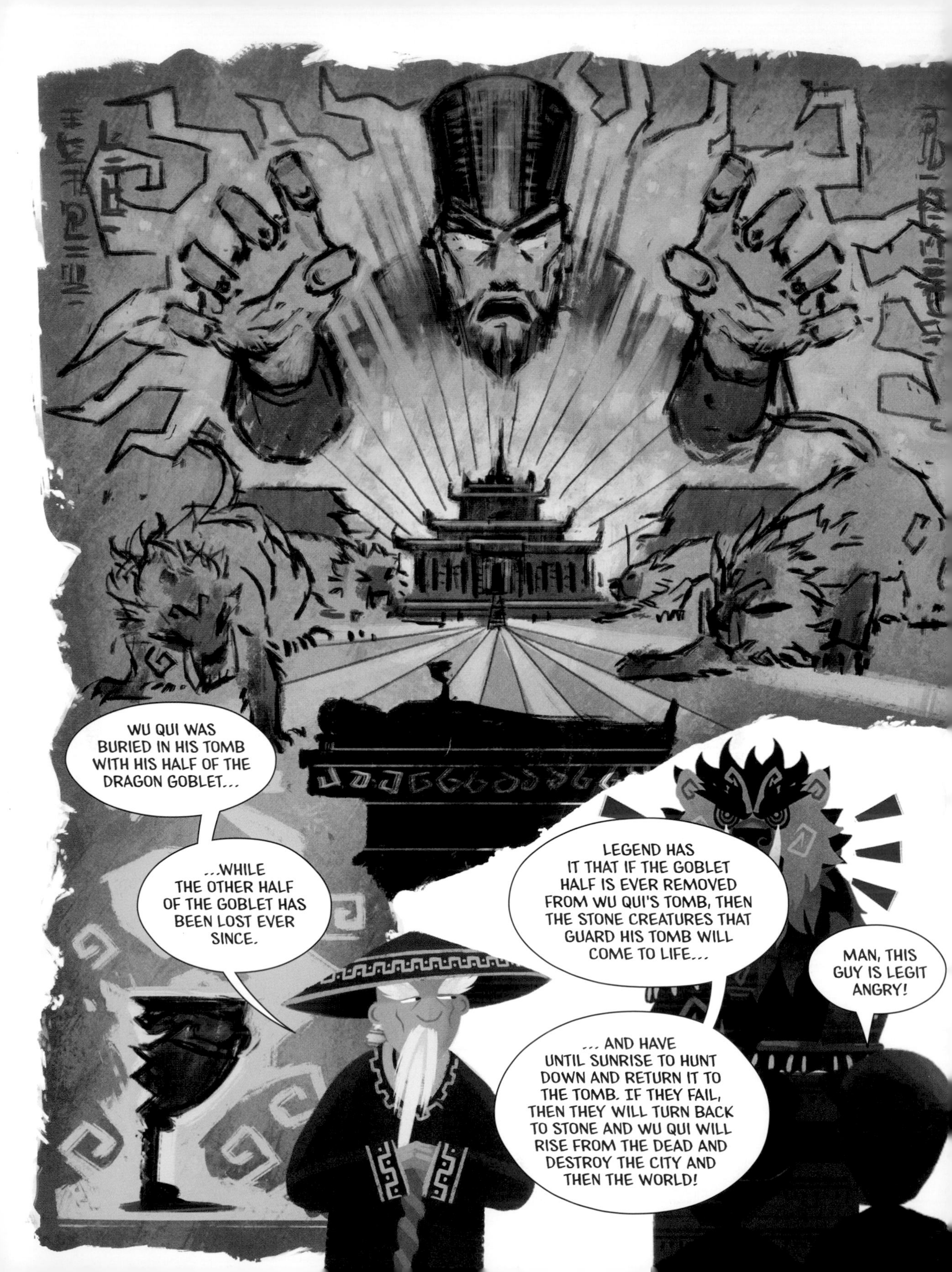
WU QUI WAS BURIED IN HIS TOMB WITH HIS HALF OF THE DRAGON GOBLET...
...WHILE THE OTHER HALF OF THE GOBLET HAS BEEN LOST EVER SINCE.
LEGEND HAS IT THAT IF THE GOBLET HALF IS EVER REMOVED FROM WU QUI'S TOMB, THEN THE STONE CREATURES THAT GUARD HIS TOMB WILL COME TO LIFE...
... AND HAVE UNTIL SUNRISE TO HUNT DOWN AND RETURN IT TO THE TOMB. IF THEY FAIL, THEN THEY WILL TURN BACK TO STONE AND WU QUI WILL RISE FROM THE DEAD AND DESTROY THE CITY AND THEN THE WORLD!
MAN, THIS GUY IS LEGIT ANGRY!

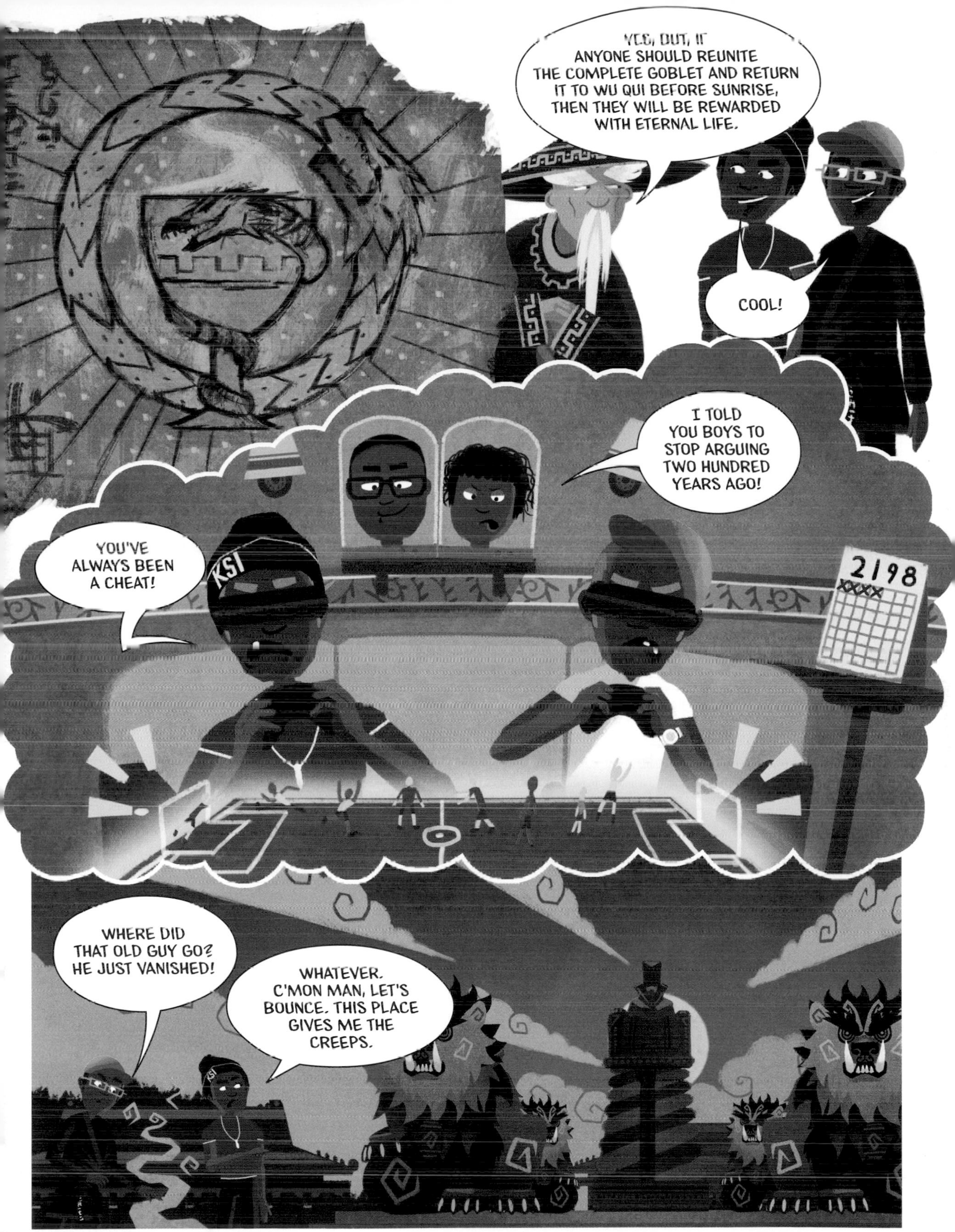
YES, BUT, IF ANYONE SHOULD REUNITE THE COMPLETE GOBLET AND RETURN IT TO WU QUI BEFORE SUNRISE, THEN THEY WILL BE REWARDED WITH ETERNAL LIFE.
COOL!
I TOLD YOU BOYS TO STOP ARGUING TWO HUNDRED YEARS AGO!
YOU'VE ALWAYS BEEN A CHEAT!
KSI
2198
WHERE DID THAT OLD GUY GO? HE JUST VANISHED!
WHATEVER. C'MON MAN, LET'S BOUNCE. THIS PLACE GIVES ME THE CREEPS.

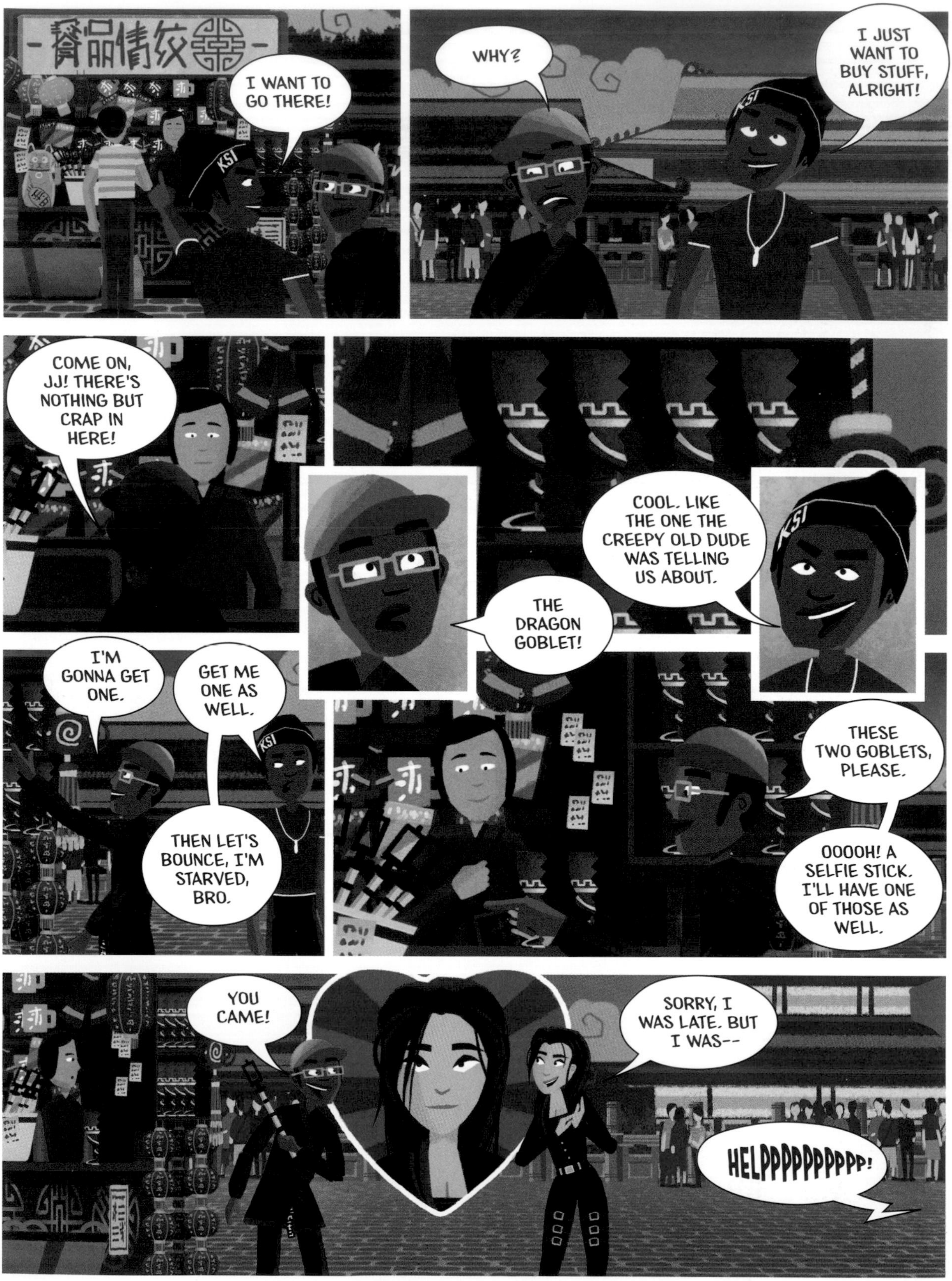
I WANT TO GO THERE!
WHY?
I JUST WANT TO BUY STUFF, ALRIGHT!
COME ON, JJ! THERE'S NOTHING BUT CRAP IN HERE!
THE DRAGON GOBLET!
COOL. LIKE THE ONE THE CREEPY OLD DUDE WAS TELLING US ABOUT.
I'M GONNA GET ONE.
GET ME ONE AS WELL.
THEN LET'S BOUNCE, I'M STARVED, BRO.
THESE TWO GOBLETS, PLEASE.
OOOOH! A SELFIE STICK. I'LL HAVE ONE OF THOSE AS WELL.
YOU CAME!
SORRY, I WAS LATE. BUT I WAS--
HELPPPPPPPPPP!

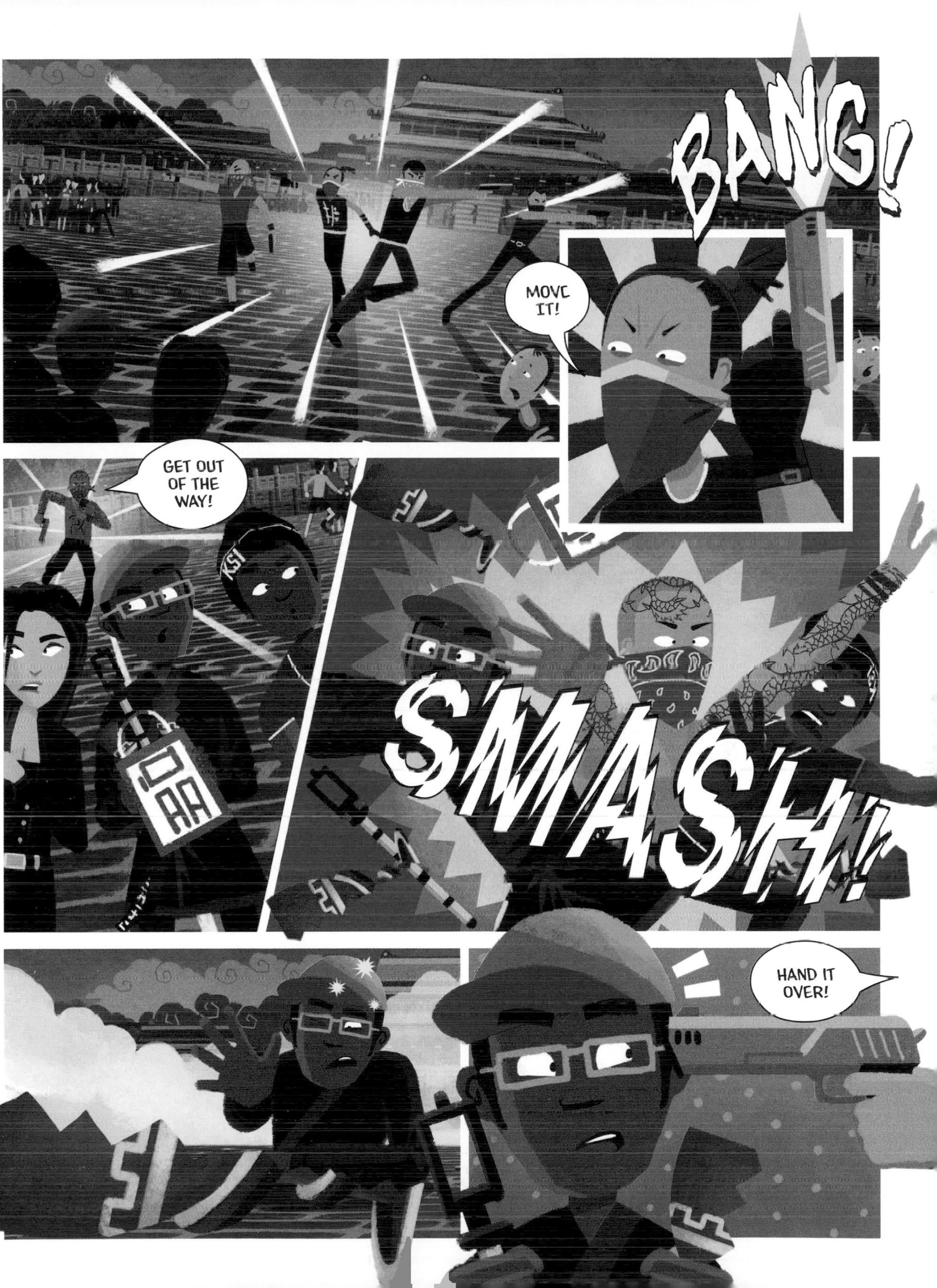
BANG!
MOVE IT!
GET OUT OF THE WAY!
SMASH!!
HAND IT OVER!

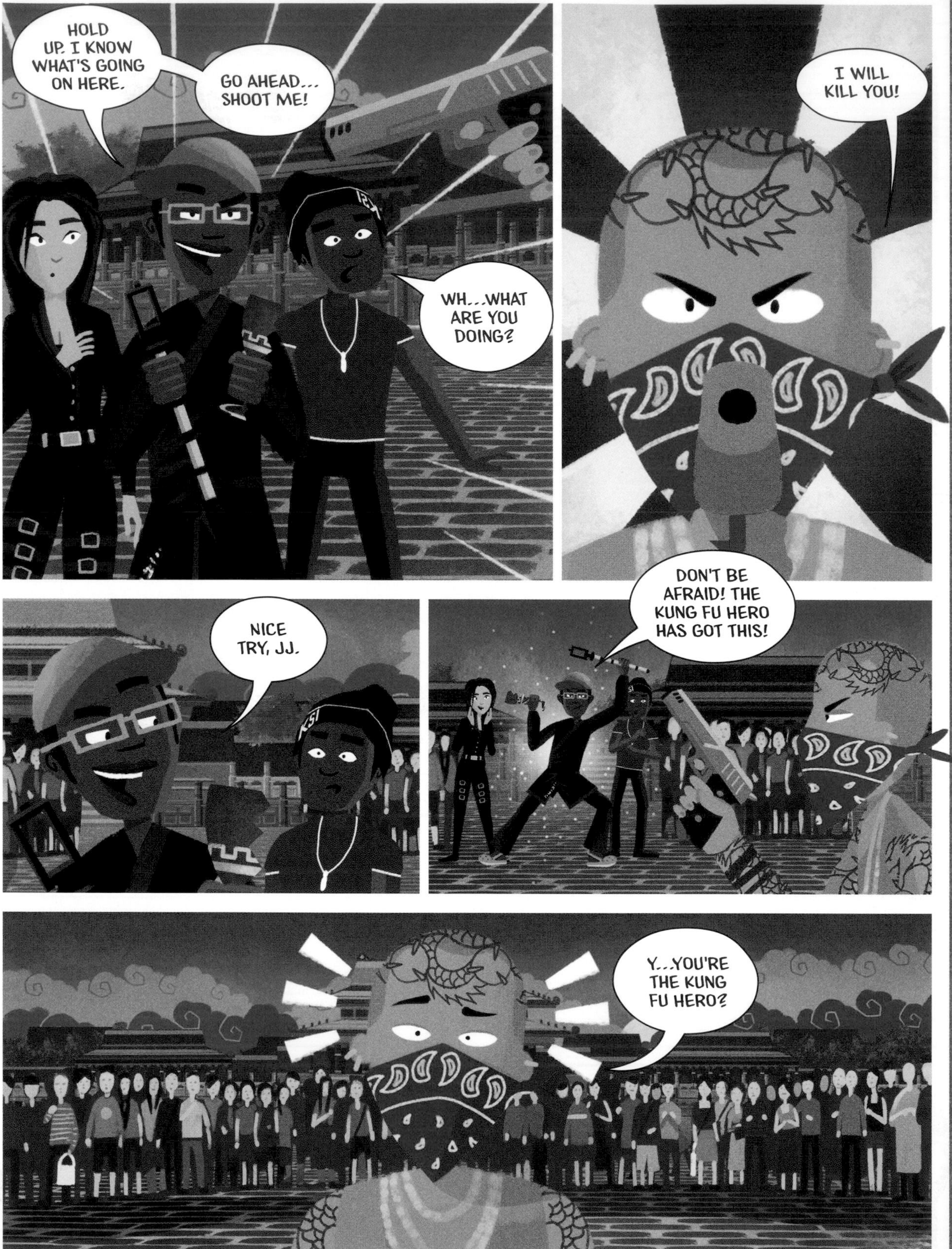
HOLD UP. I KNOW WHAT'S GOING ON HERE.
GO AHEAD... SHOOT ME!
WH...WHAT ARE YOU DOING?
I WILL KILL YOU!
NICE TRY, JJ.
DON'T BE AFRAID! THE KUNG FU HERO HAS GOT THIS!
Y...YOU'RE THE KUNG FU HERO?

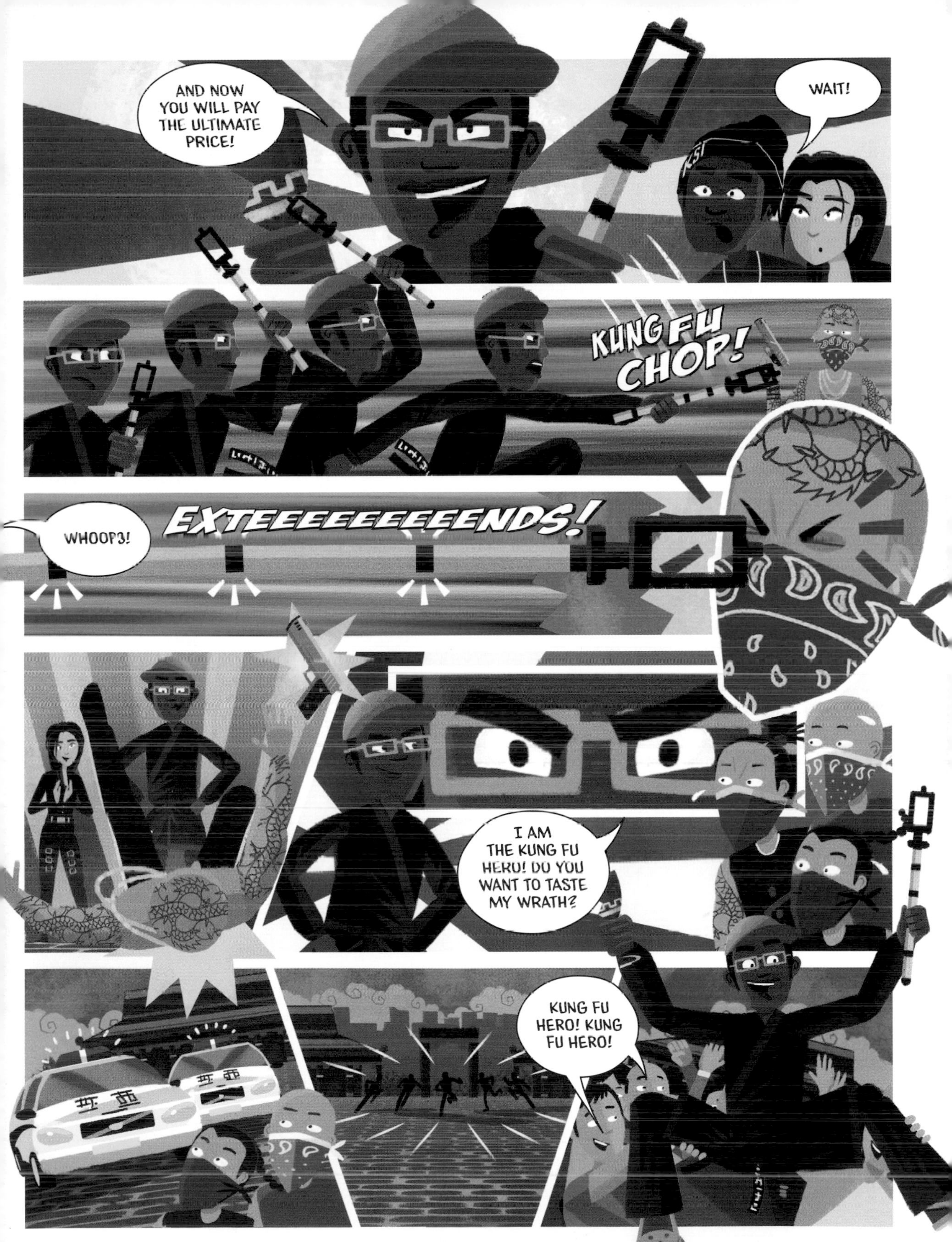
AND NOW YOU WILL PAY THE ULTIMATE PRICE!
WAIT!
KUNG FU CHOP!
WHOOPS!
EXTEEEEEEEEEEENDS!
I AM THE KUNG FU HERO! DO YOU WANT TO TASTE MY WRATH?
KUNG FU HERO! KUNG FU HERO!

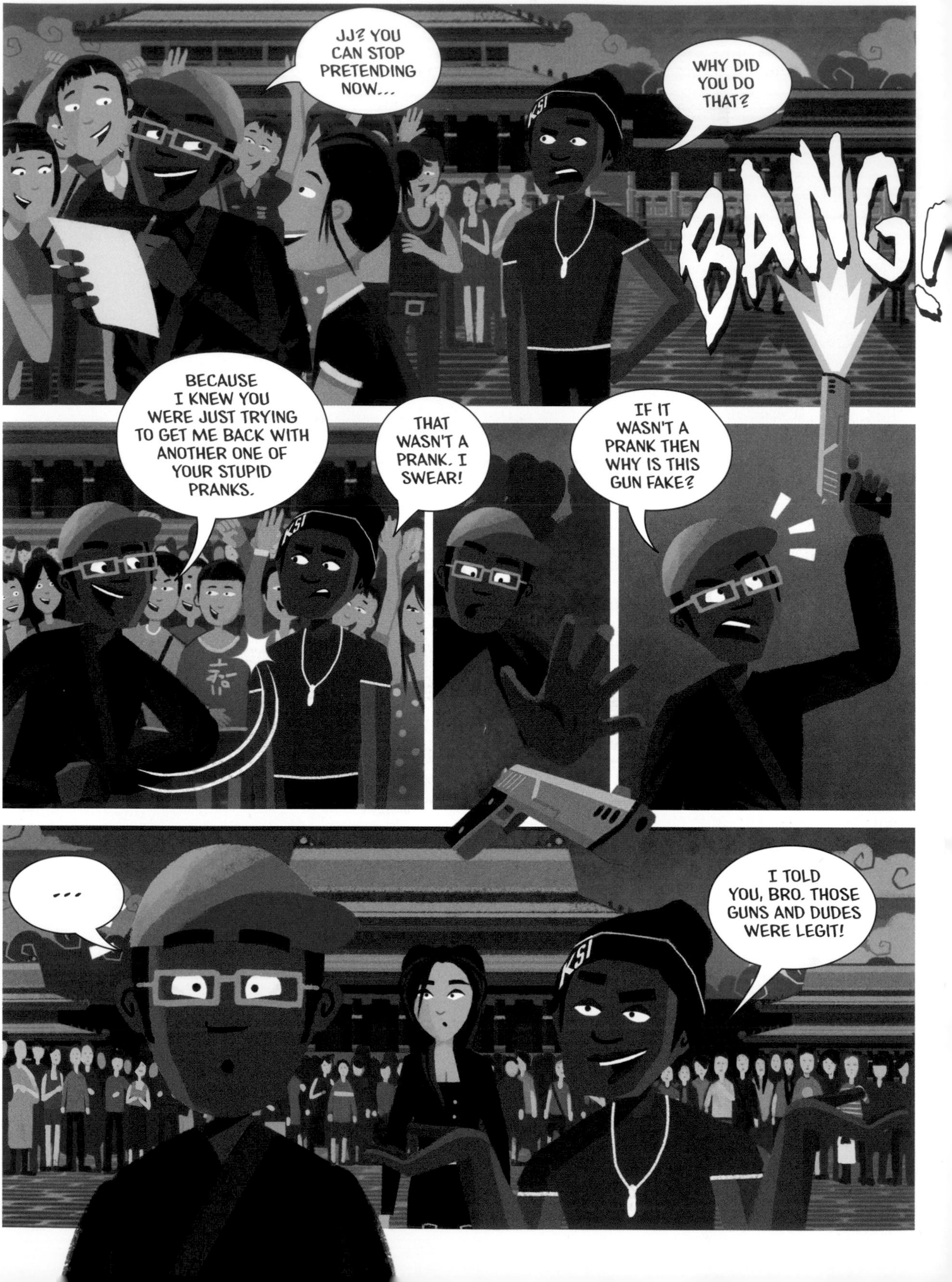
JJ? YOU CAN STOP PRETENDING NOW...
WHY DID YOU DO THAT?
BANG!
KSI
BECAUSE I KNEW YOU WERE JUST TRYING TO GET ME BACK WITH ANOTHER ONE OF YOUR STUPID PRANKS.
THAT WASN'T A PRANK. I SWEAR!
IF IT WASN'T A PRANK THEN WHY IS THIS GUN FAKE?
...
I TOLD YOU, BRO. THOSE GUNS AND DUDES WERE LEGIT!

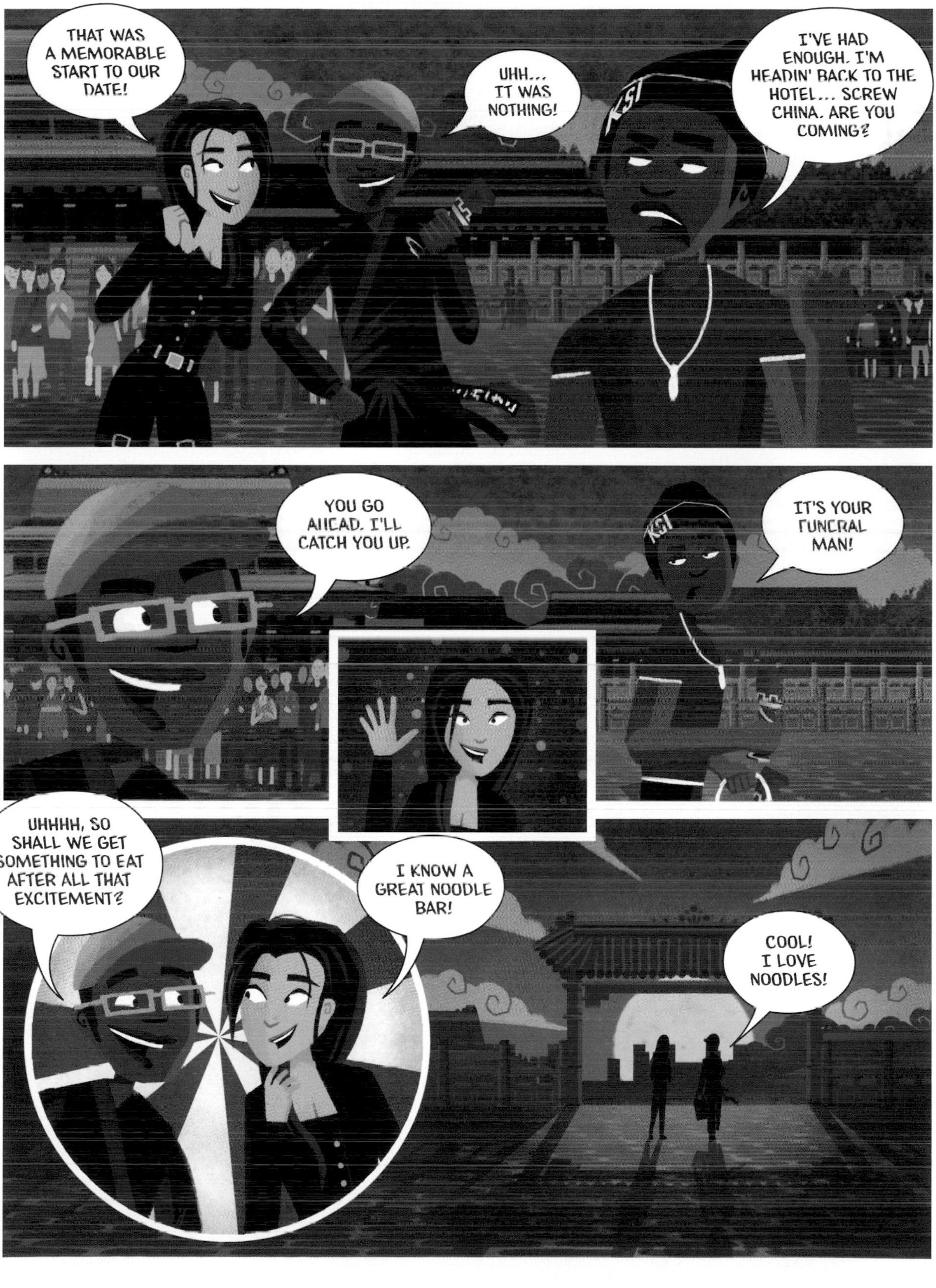
THAT WAS A MEMORABLE START TO OUR DATE!
UHH... IT WAS NOTHING!
I'VE HAD ENOUGH. I'M HEADIN' BACK TO THE HOTEL... SCREW CHINA. ARE YOU COMING?
KSI
YOU GO AHEAD. I'LL CATCH YOU UP.
IT'S YOUR FUNERAL MAN!
KSI
UHHHH, SO SHALL WE GET SOMETHING TO EAT AFTER ALL THAT EXCITEMENT?
I KNOW A GREAT NOODLE BAR!
COOL! I LOVE NOODLES!

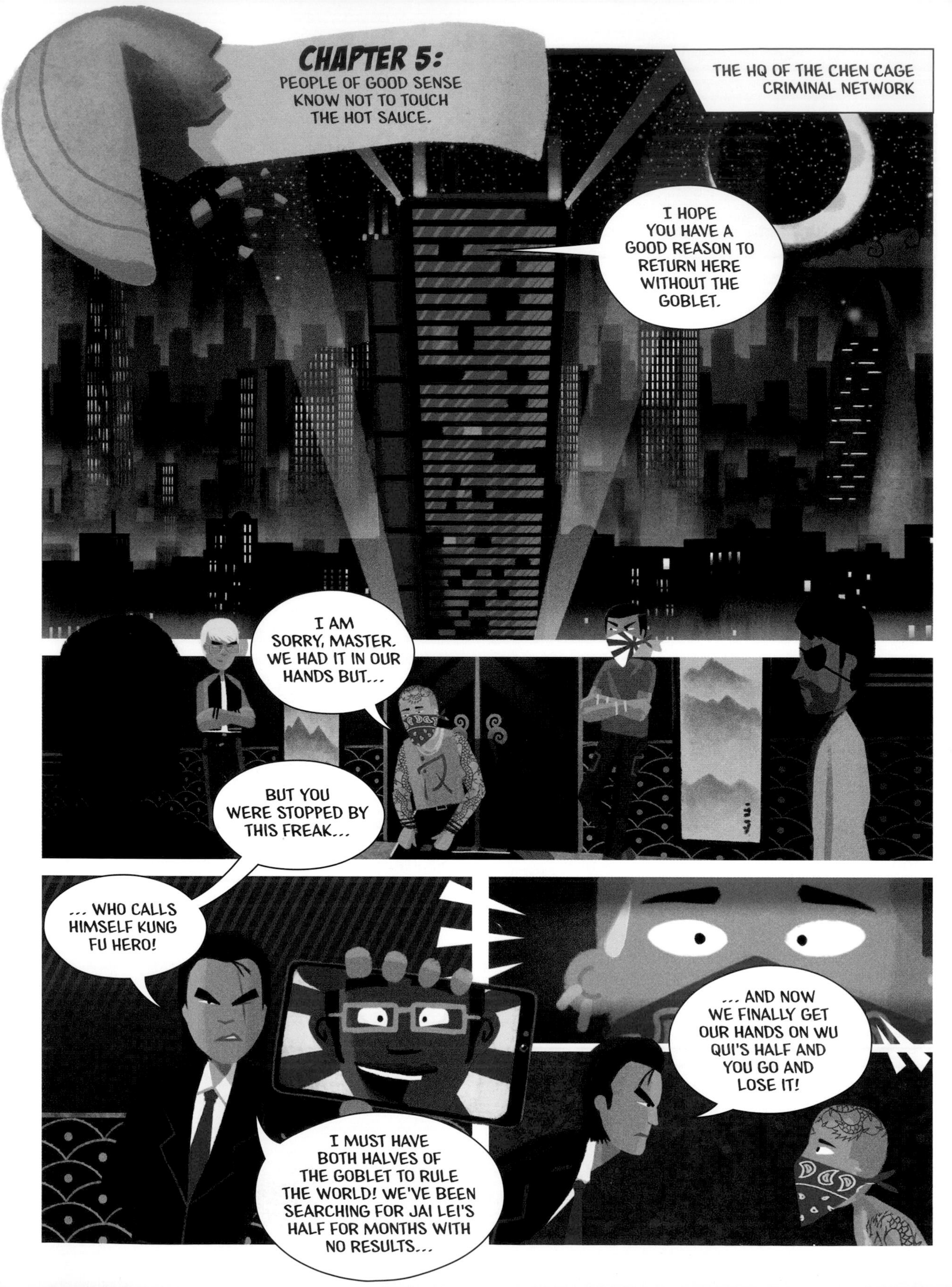
CHAPTER 5:
PEOPLE OF GOOD SENSE KNOW NOT TO TOUCH THE HOT SAUCE.
THE HQ OF THE CHEN CAGE CRIMINAL NETWORK
I HOPE YOU HAVE A GOOD REASON TO RETURN HERE WITHOUT THE GOBLET.
I AM SORRY, MASTER. WE HAD IT IN OUR HANDS BUT...
BUT YOU WERE STOPPED BY THIS FREAK...
... WHO CALLS HIMSELF KUNG FU HERO!
... AND NOW WE FINALLY GET OUR HANDS ON WU QUI'S HALF AND YOU GO AND LOSE IT!
I MUST HAVE BOTH HALVES OF THE GOBLET TO RULE THE WORLD! WE'VE BEEN SEARCHING FOR JAI LEI'S HALF FOR MONTHS WITH NO RESULTS...

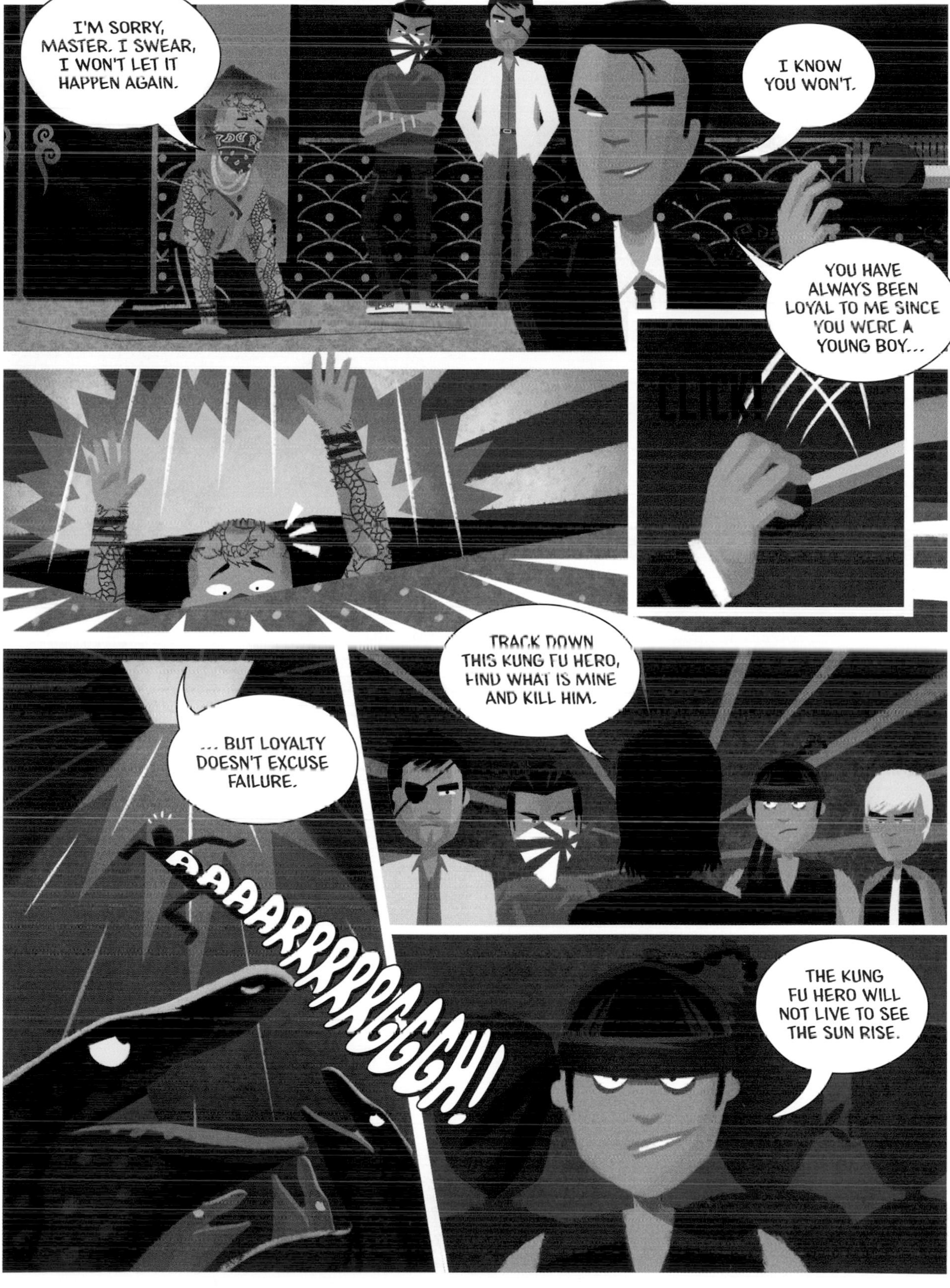
I'M SORRY, MASTER. I SWEAR, I WON'T LET IT HAPPEN AGAIN.
I KNOW YOU WON'T.
YOU HAVE ALWAYS BEEN LOYAL TO ME SINCE YOU WERE A YOUNG BOY...
CLICK!
... BUT LOYALTY DOESN'T EXCUSE FAILURE.
AAAARRRRRRGGGH!
TRACK DOWN THIS KUNG FU HERO, FIND WHAT IS MINE AND KILL HIM.
THE KUNG FU HERO WILL NOT LIVE TO SEE THE SUN RISE.

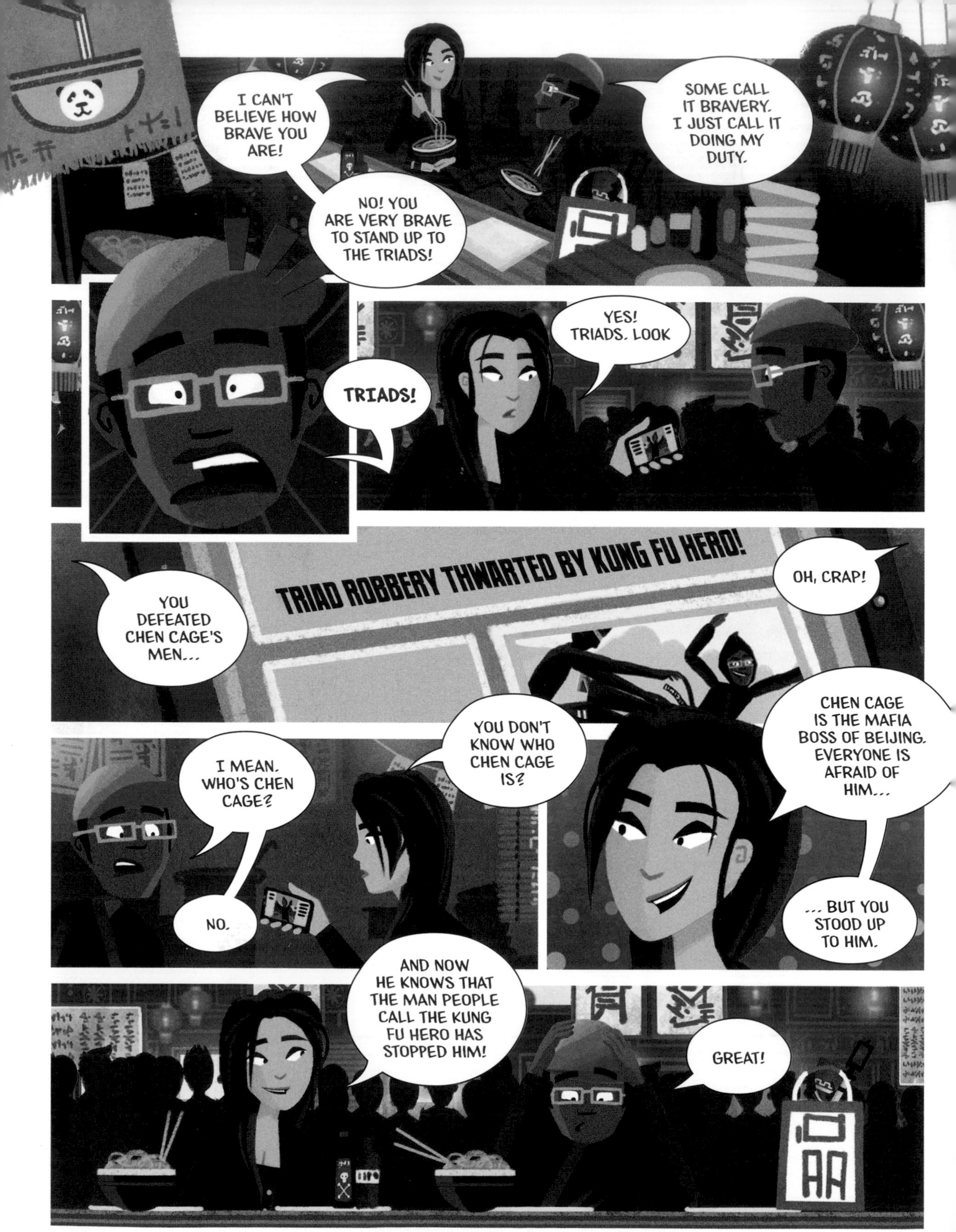

I CAN'T BELIEVE HOW BRAVE YOU ARE!
SOME CALL IT BRAVERY. I JUST CALL IT DOING MY DUTY.
NO! YOU ARE VERY BRAVE TO STAND UP TO THE TRIADS!
TRIADS!
YES! TRIADS. LOOK
TRIAD ROBBERY THWARTED BY KUNG FU HERO!
YOU DEFEATED CHEN CAGE'S MEN...
OH, CRAP!
I MEAN. WHO'S CHEN CAGE?
YOU DON'T KNOW WHO CHEN CAGE IS?
NO.
CHEN CAGE IS THE MAFIA BOSS OF BEIJING. EVERYONE IS AFRAID OF HIM...
... BUT YOU STOOD UP TO HIM.
AND NOW HE KNOWS THAT THE MAN PEOPLE CALL THE KUNG FU HERO HAS STOPPED HIM!
GREAT!

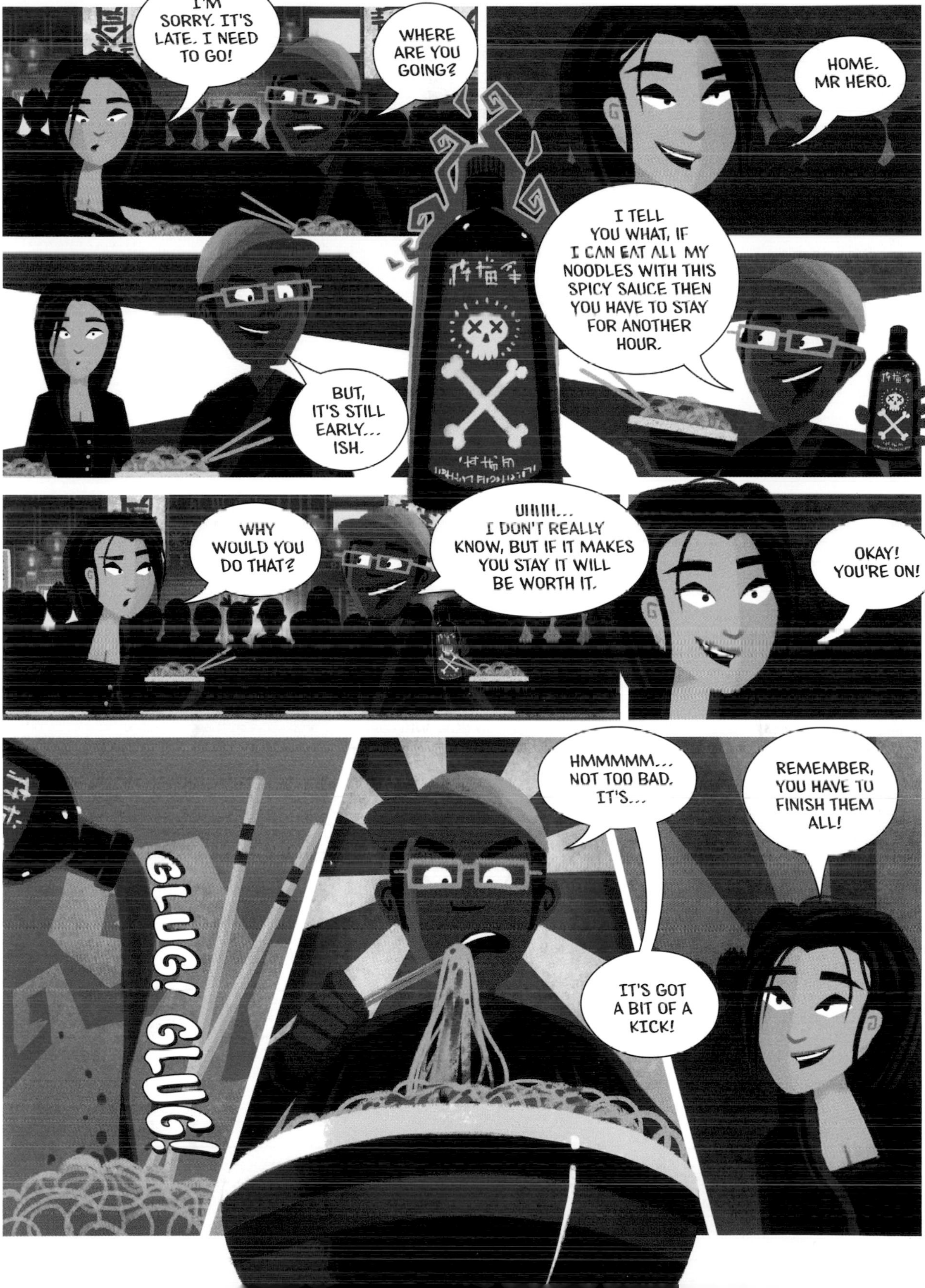
I'M SORRY. IT'S LATE. I NEED TO GO!
WHERE ARE YOU GOING?
HOME. MR HERO.
BUT, IT'S STILL EARLY... ISH.
I TELL YOU WHAT, IF I CAN EAT ALL MY NOODLES WITH THIS SPICY SAUCE THEN YOU HAVE TO STAY FOR ANOTHER HOUR.
WHY WOULD YOU DO THAT?
UHHH... I DON'T REALLY KNOW, BUT IF IT MAKES YOU STAY IT WILL BE WORTH IT.
OKAY! YOU'RE ON!
GLUG! GLUG! GLUG!
HMMMMM... NOT TOO BAD. IT'S...
IT'S GOT A BIT OF A KICK!
REMEMBER, YOU HAVE TO FINISH THEM ALL!

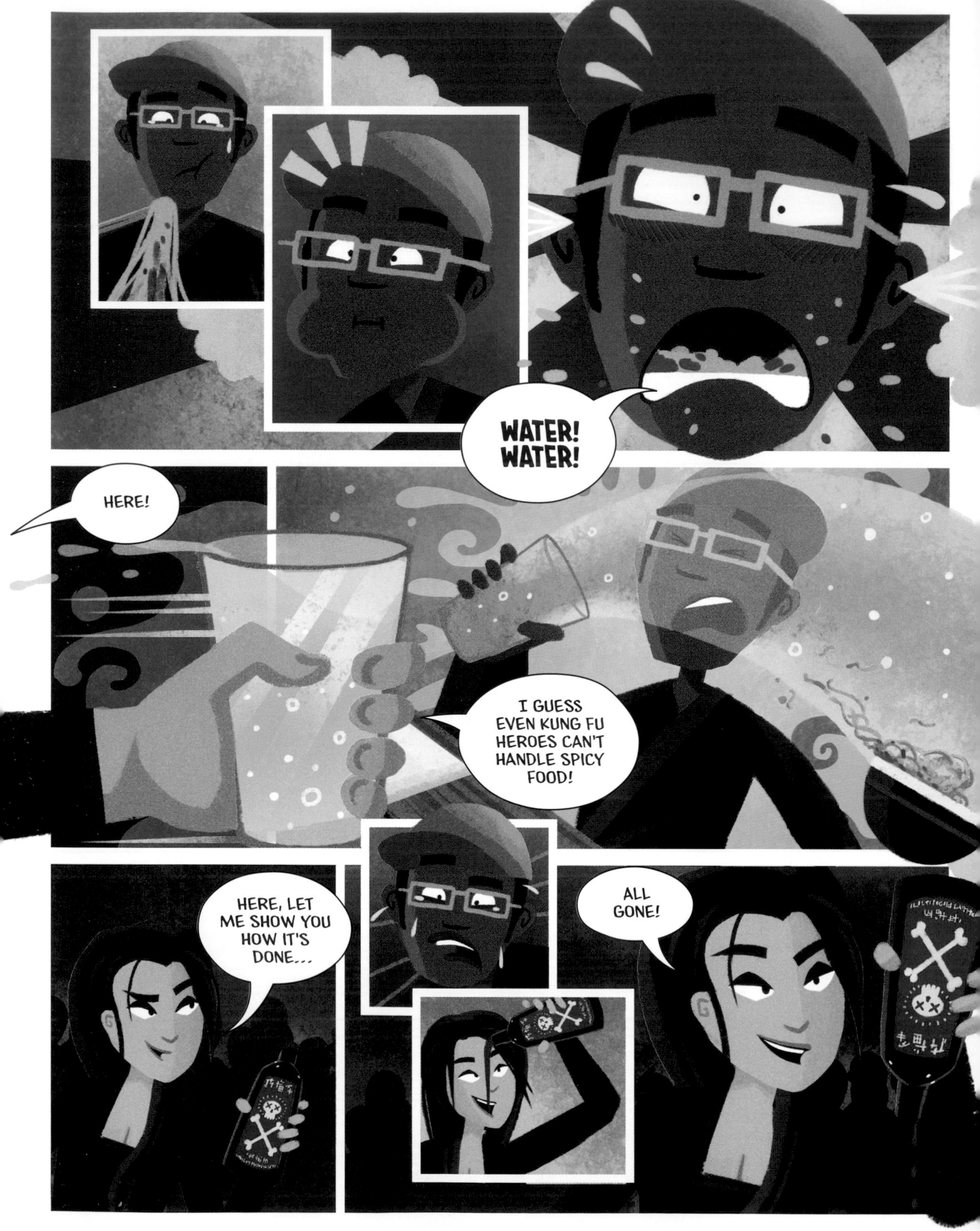
WATER! WATER!
HERE!
I GUESS EVEN KUNG FU HEROES CAN'T HANDLE SPICY FOOD!
HERE, LET ME SHOW YOU HOW IT'S DONE...
ALL GONE!

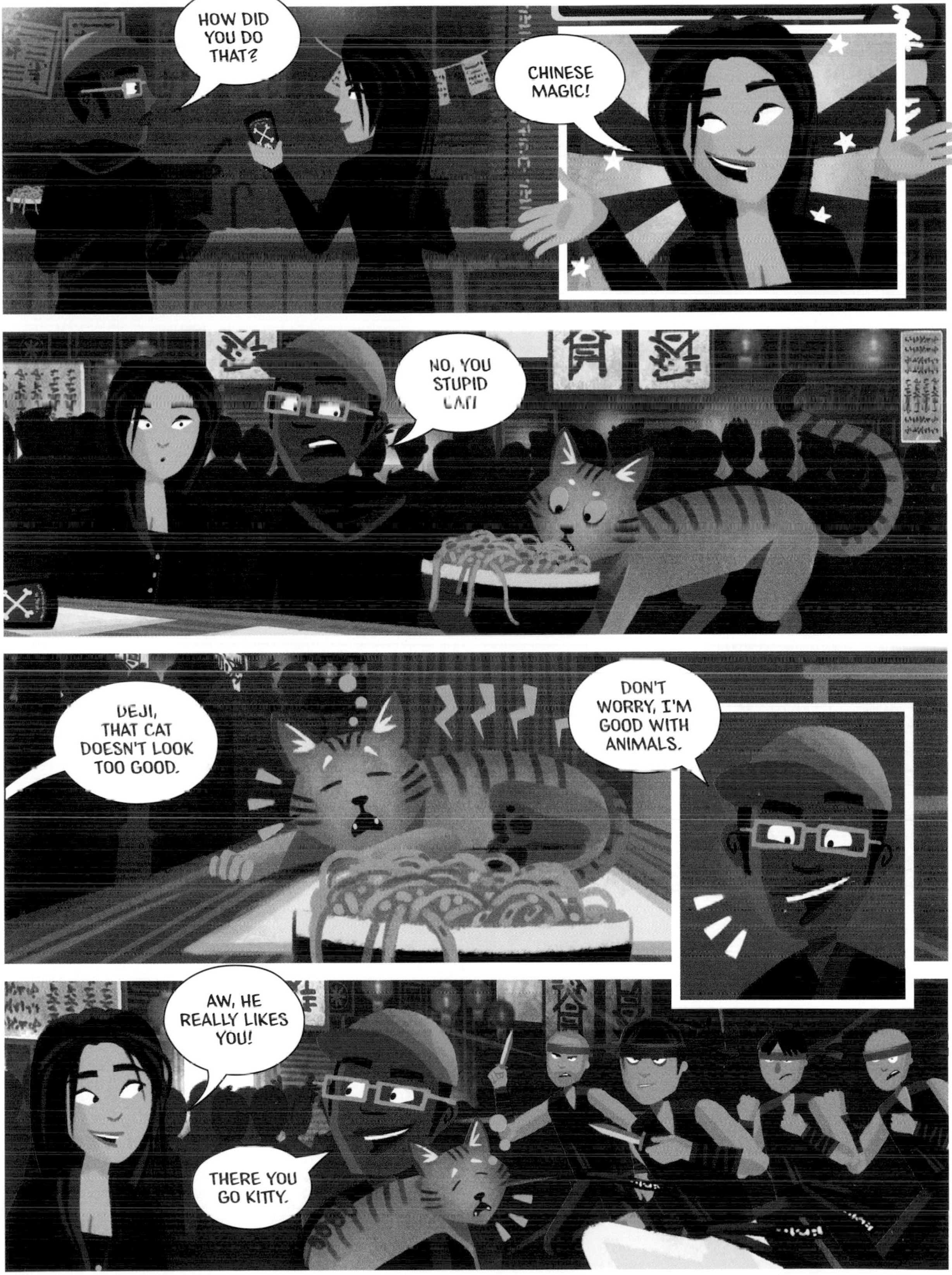
HOW DID YOU DO THAT?
CHINESE MAGIC!
NO, YOU STUPID
DEJI, THAT CAT DOESN'T LOOK TOO GOOD.
DON'T WORRY, I'M GOOD WITH ANIMALS.
AW, HE REALLY LIKES YOU!
THERE YOU GO KITTY.

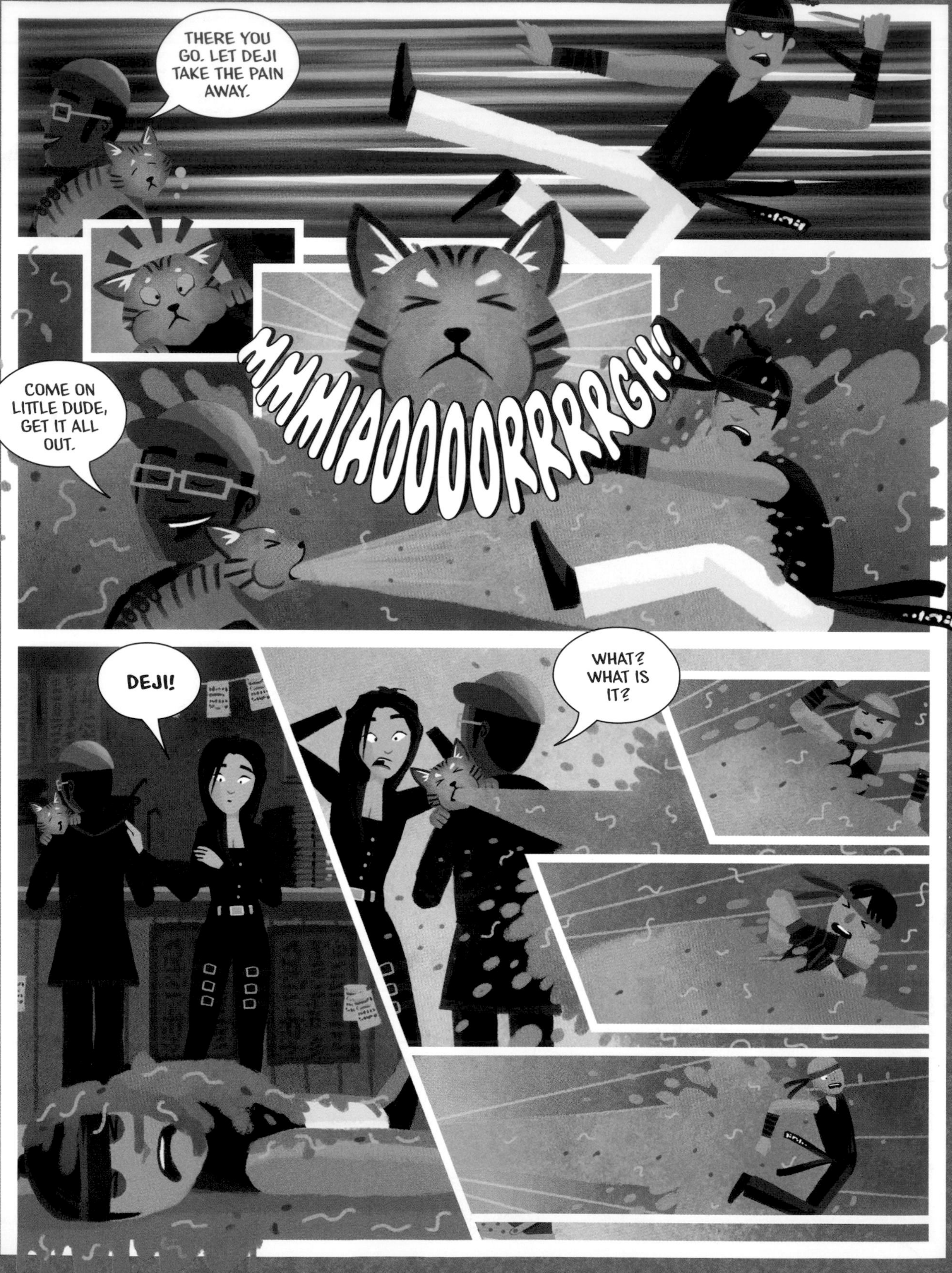
THERE YOU GO. LET DEJI TAKE THE PAIN AWAY.
MMMIAOOOORRRRGH!
COME ON LITTLE DUDE, GET IT ALL OUT.
DEJI!
WHAT? WHAT IS IT?

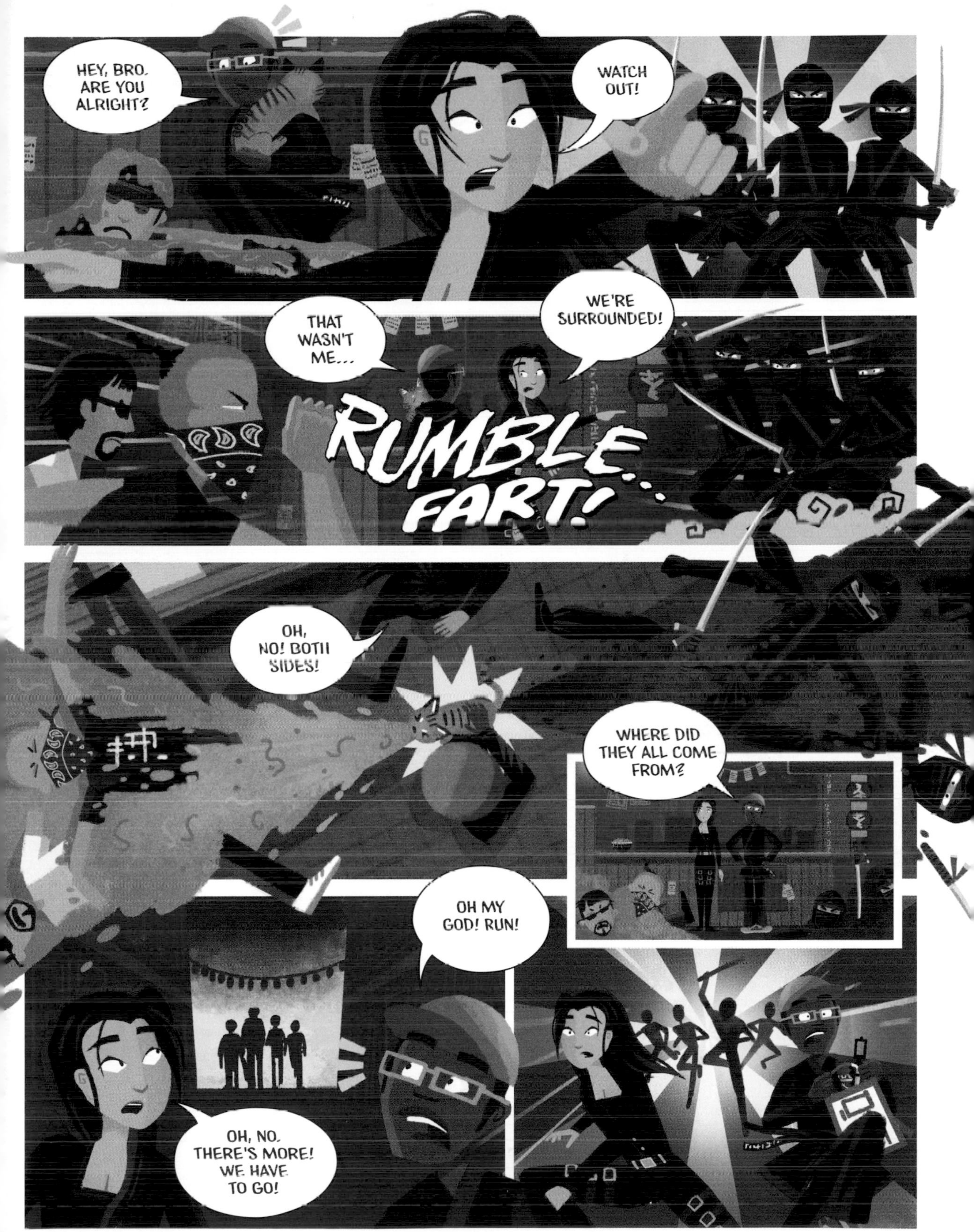
HEY, BRO. ARE YOU ALRIGHT?
WATCH OUT!
THAT WASN'T ME...
WE'RE SURROUNDED!
RUMBLE... FART!
OH, NO! BOTH SIDES!
WHERE DID THEY ALL COME FROM?
OH, NO. THERE'S MORE! WE HAVE TO GO!
OH MY GOD! RUN!

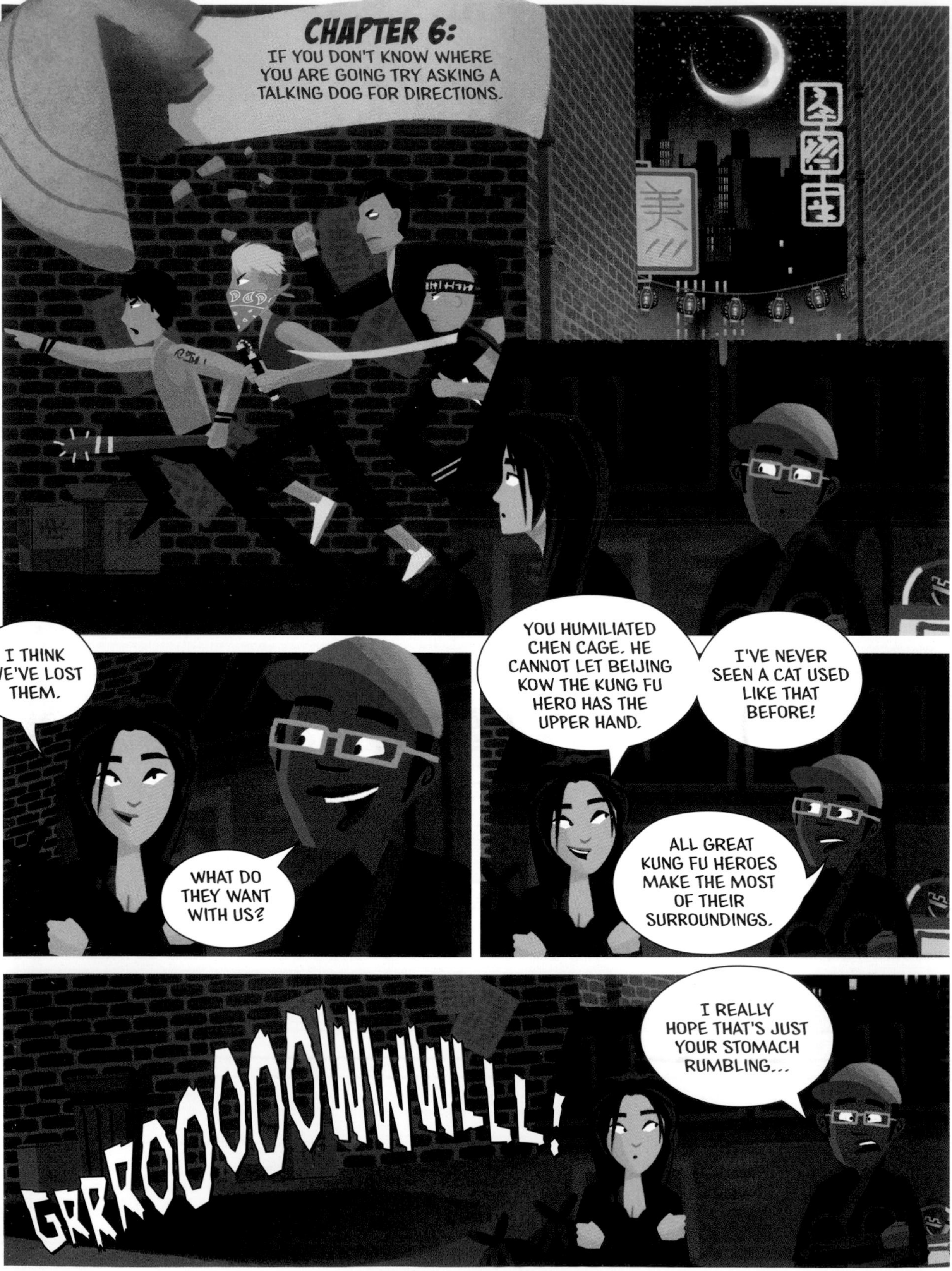
CHAPTER 6:
IF YOU DON'T KNOW WHERE YOU ARE GOING TRY ASKING A TALKING DOG FOR DIRECTIONS.
I THINK WE'VE LOST THEM.
WHAT DO THEY WANT WITH US?
YOU HUMILIATED CHEN CAGE. HE CANNOT LET BEIJING KOW THE KUNG FU HERO HAS THE UPPER HAND.
I'VE NEVER SEEN A CAT USED LIKE THAT BEFORE!
ALL GREAT KUNG FU HEROES MAKE THE MOST OF THEIR SURROUNDINGS.
GRRROOOOOWWWLLL!
I REALLY HOPE THAT'S JUST YOUR STOMACH RUMBLING...

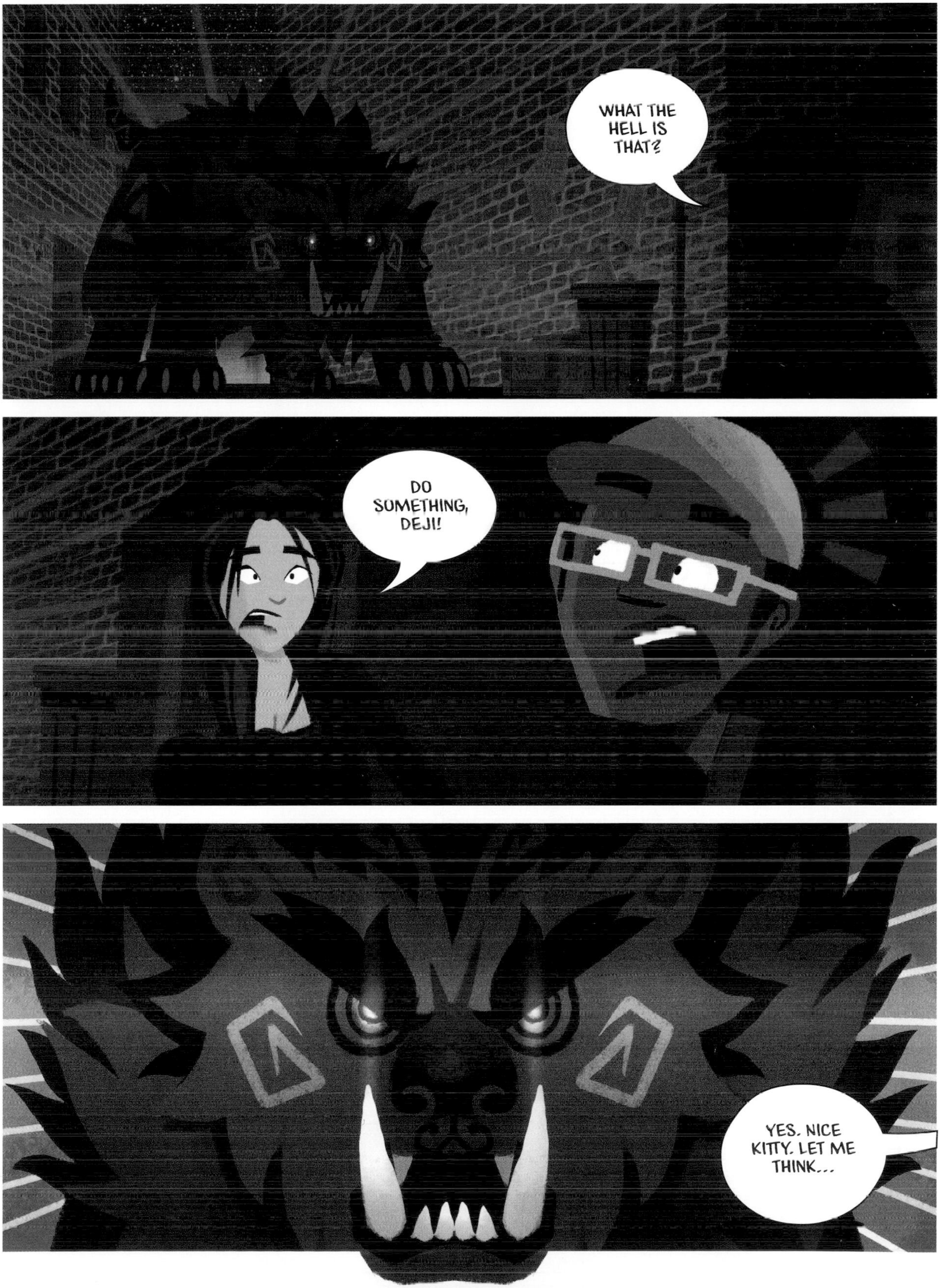
WHAT THE HELL IS THAT?
DO SOMETHING, DEJI!
YES. NICE KITTY. LET ME THINK...

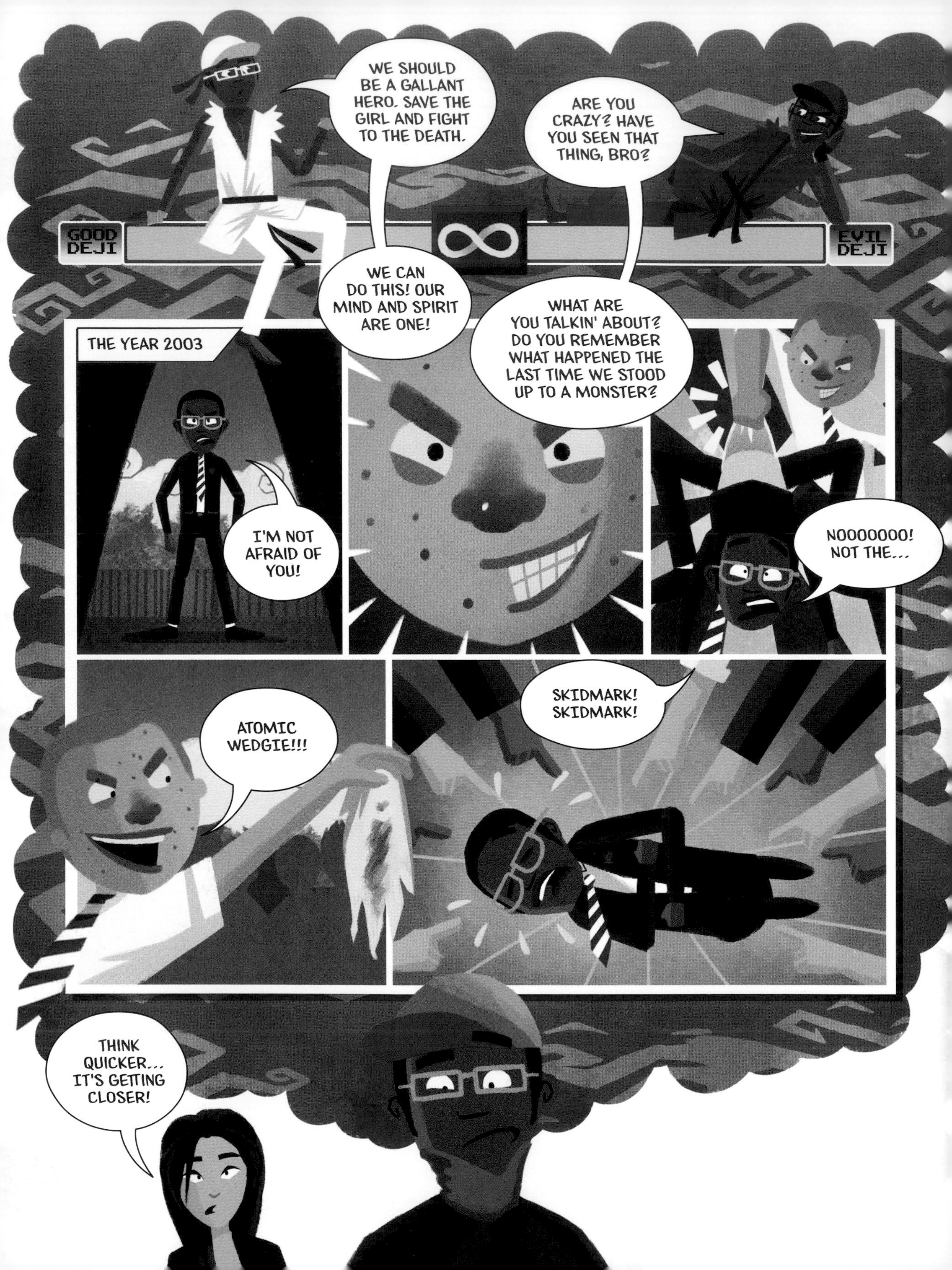
WE SHOULD BE A GALLANT HERO. SAVE THE GIRL AND FIGHT TO THE DEATH.
ARE YOU CRAZY? HAVE YOU SEEN THAT THING, BRO?
GOOD DEJI
EVIL DEJI
WE CAN DO THIS! OUR MIND AND SPIRIT ARE ONE!
WHAT ARE YOU TALKIN' ABOUT? DO YOU REMEMBER WHAT HAPPENED THE LAST TIME WE STOOD UP TO A MONSTER?
THE YEAR 2003
I'M NOT AFRAID OF YOU!
NOOOOOOO! NOT THE...
ATOMIC WEDGIE!!!
SKIDMARK! SKIDMARK!
THINK QUICKER... IT'S GETTING CLOSER!

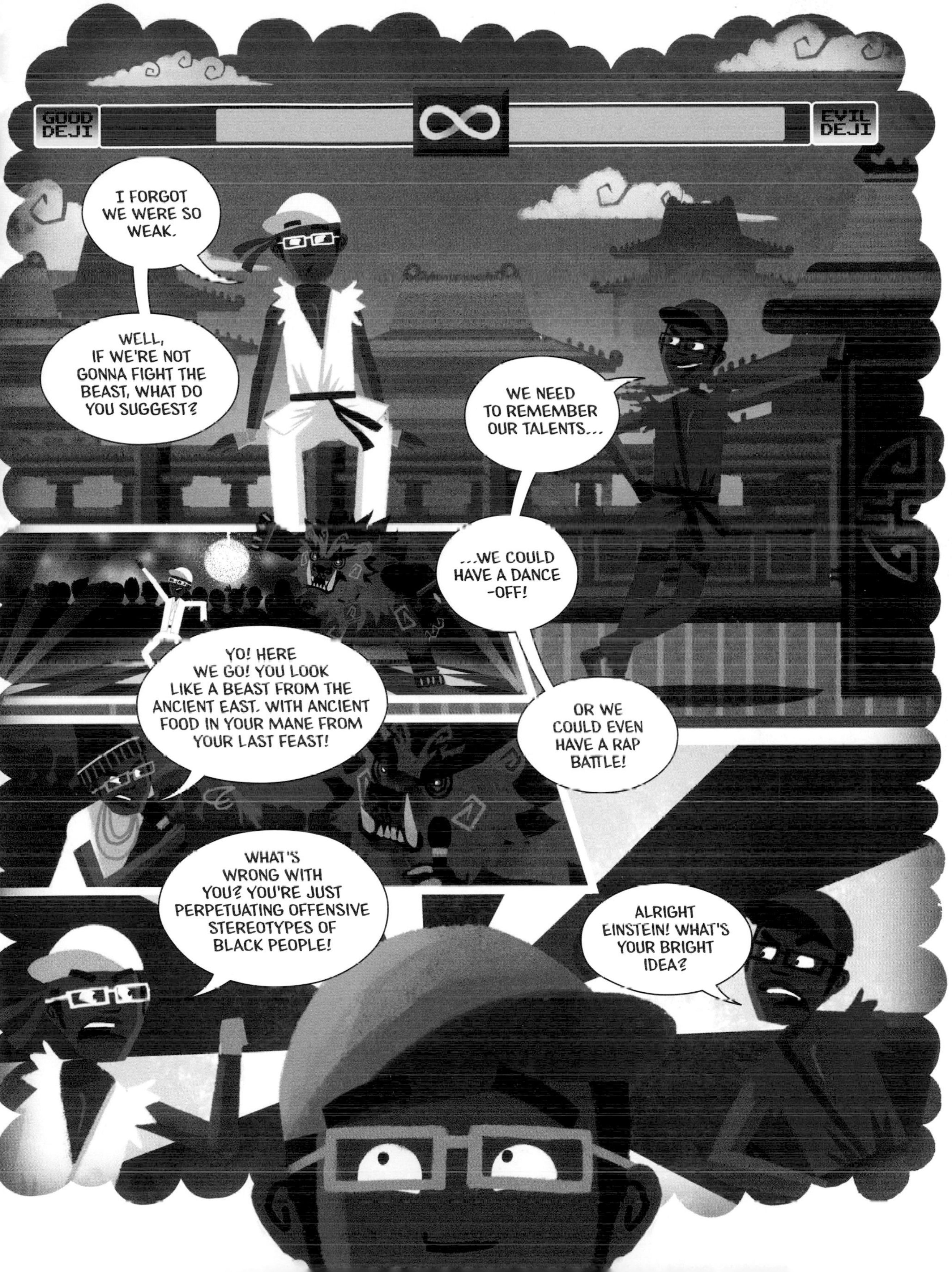
GOOD DEJI
EVIL DEJI
I FORGOT WE WERE SO WEAK.
WELL, IF WE'RE NOT GONNA FIGHT THE BEAST, WHAT DO YOU SUGGEST?
WE NEED TO REMEMBER OUR TALENTS...
...WE COULD HAVE A DANCE -OFF!
OR WE COULD EVEN HAVE A RAP BATTLE!
YO! HERE WE GO! YOU LOOK LIKE A BEAST FROM THE ANCIENT EAST. WITH ANCIENT FOOD IN YOUR MANE FROM YOUR LAST FEAST!
WHAT'S WRONG WITH YOU? YOU'RE JUST PERPETUATING OFFENSIVE STEREOTYPES OF BLACK PEOPLE!
ALRIGHT EINSTEIN! WHAT'S YOUR BRIGHT IDEA?

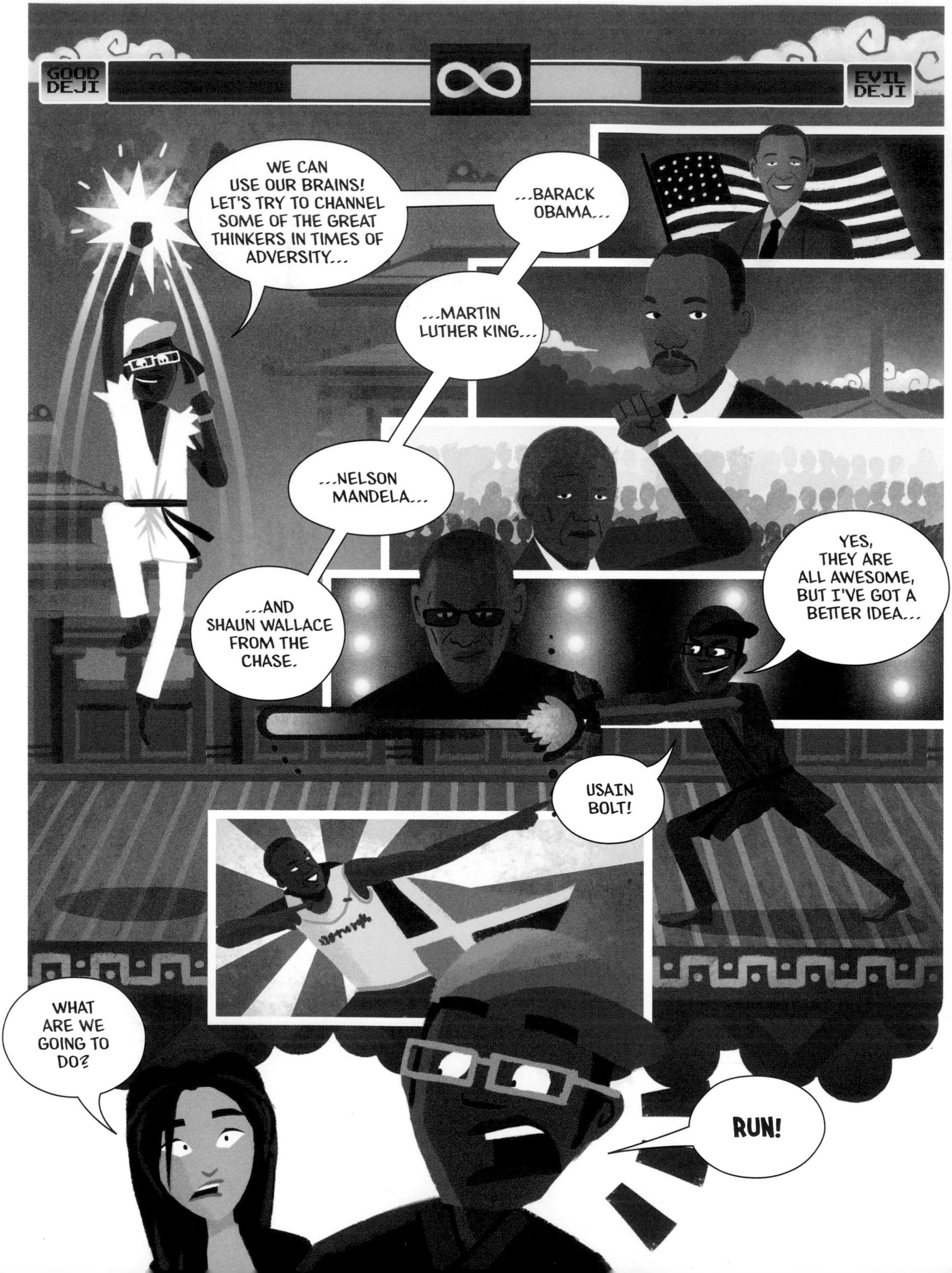
GOOD DEJI
EVIL DEJI
WE CAN USE OUR BRAINS! LET'S TRY TO CHANNEL SOME OF THE GREAT THINKERS IN TIMES OF ADVERSITY...
...BARACK OBAMA...
...MARTIN LUTHER KING...
...NELSON MANDELA...
...AND SHAUN WALLACE FROM THE CHASE.
YES, THEY ARE ALL AWESOME, BUT I'VE GOT A BETTER IDEA...
USAIN BOLT!
WHAT ARE WE GOING TO DO?
RUN!

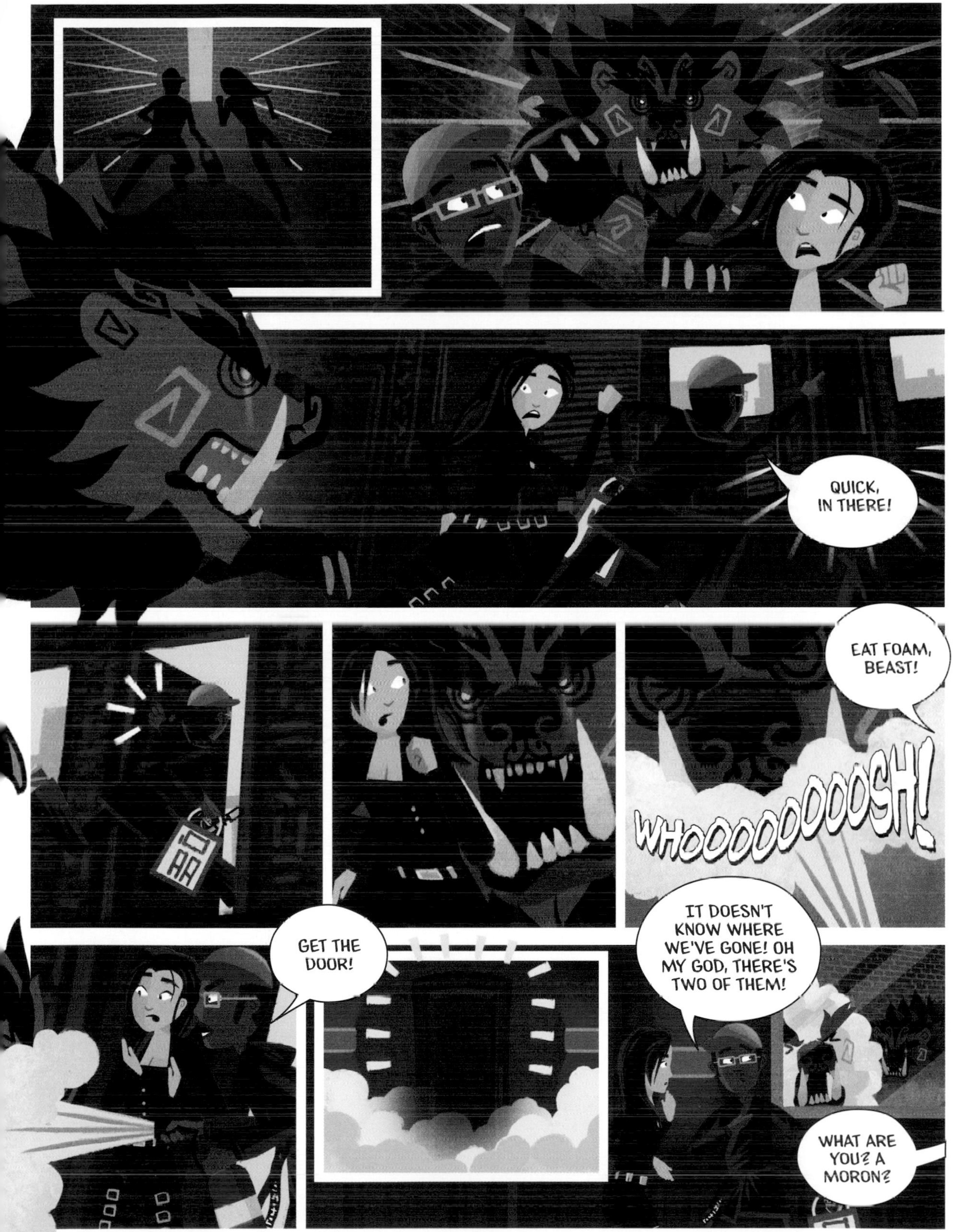
QUICK, IN THERE!
EAT FOAM, BEAST!
WHOOOOOOOOOSH!
GET THE DOOR!
IT DOESN'T KNOW WHERE WE'VE GONE! OH MY GOD, THERE'S TWO OF THEM!
WHAT ARE YOU? A MORON?

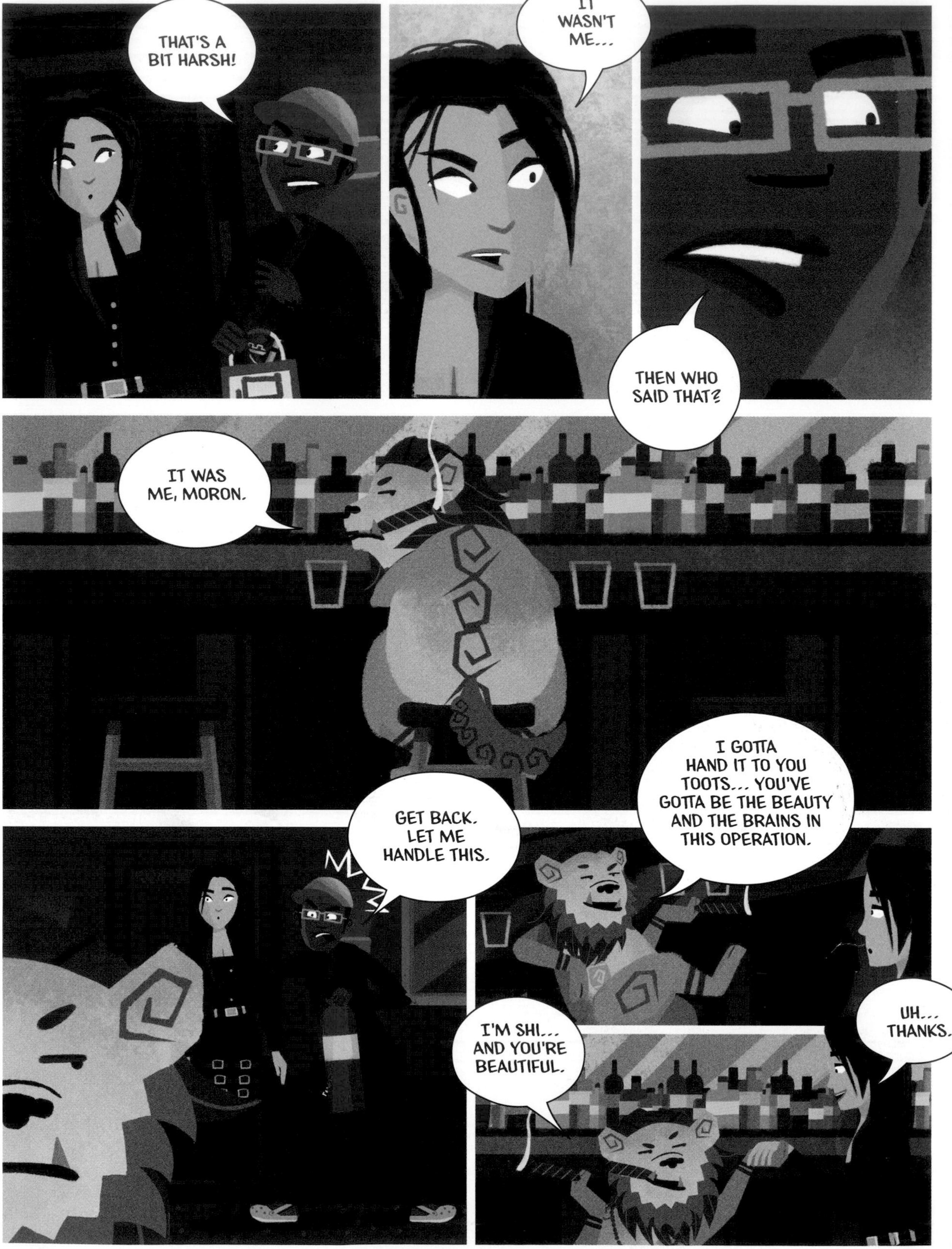
THAT'S A BIT HARSH!
IT WASN'T ME...
THEN WHO SAID THAT?
IT WAS ME, MORON.
GET BACK. LET ME HANDLE THIS.
I GOTTA HAND IT TO YOU TOOTS... YOU'VE GOTTA BE THE BEAUTY AND THE BRAINS IN THIS OPERATION.
I'M SHI... AND YOU'RE BEAUTIFUL.
UH... THANKS.

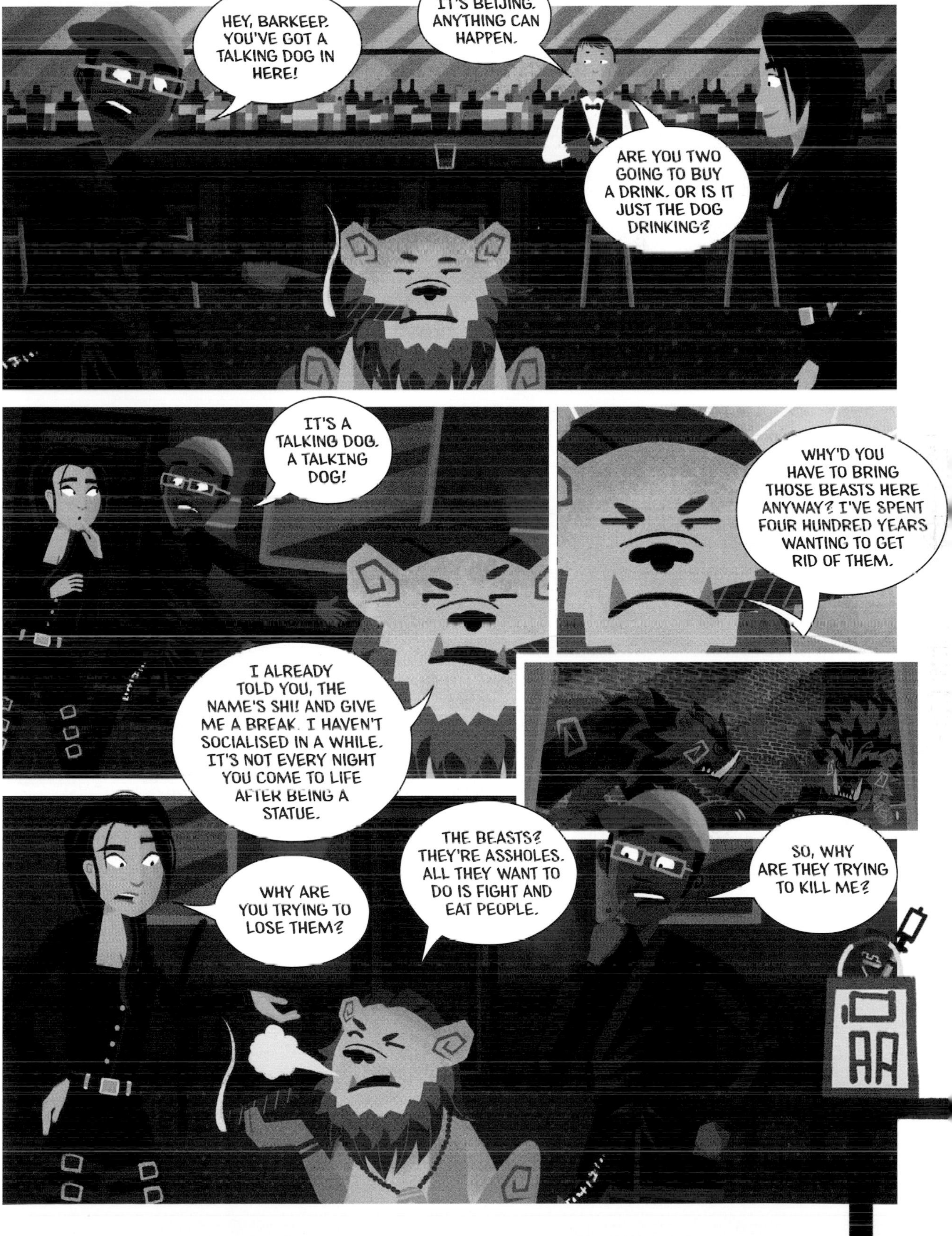
HEY, BARKEEP. YOU'VE GOT A TALKING DOG IN HERE!
IT'S BEIJING. ANYTHING CAN HAPPEN.
ARE YOU TWO GOING TO BUY A DRINK, OR IS IT JUST THE DOG DRINKING?
IT'S A TALKING DOG. A TALKING DOG!
WHY'D YOU HAVE TO BRING THOSE BEASTS HERE ANYWAY? I'VE SPENT FOUR HUNDRED YEARS WANTING TO GET RID OF THEM.
I ALREADY TOLD YOU, THE NAME'S SHI! AND GIVE ME A BREAK. I HAVEN'T SOCIALISED IN A WHILE. IT'S NOT EVERY NIGHT YOU COME TO LIFE AFTER BEING A STATUE.
WHY ARE YOU TRYING TO LOSE THEM?
THE BEASTS? THEY'RE ASSHOLES. ALL THEY WANT TO DO IS FIGHT AND EAT PEOPLE.
SO, WHY ARE THEY TRYING TO KILL ME?

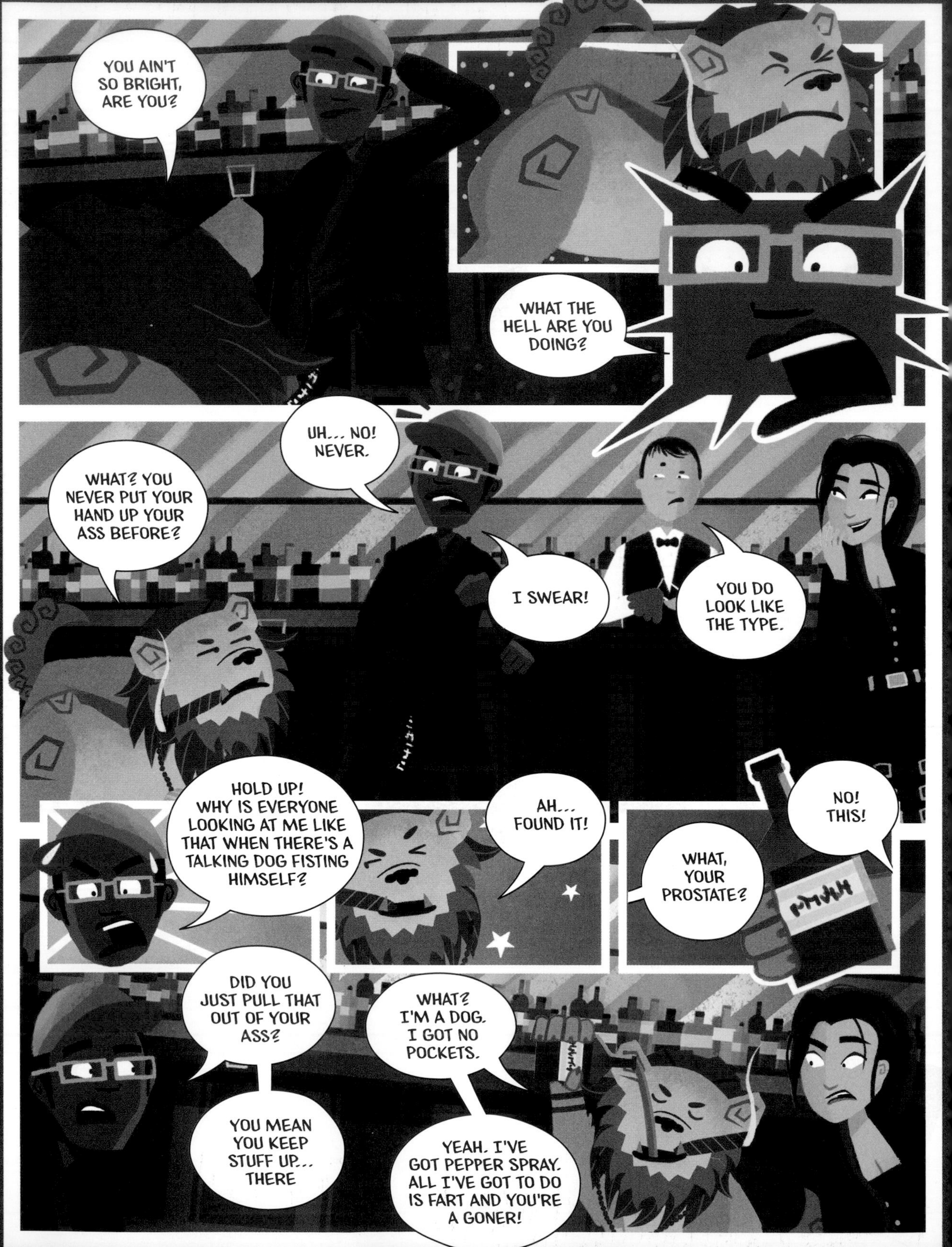
YOU AIN'T SO BRIGHT, ARE YOU?
WHAT THE HELL ARE YOU DOING?
UH... NO! NEVER.
WHAT? YOU NEVER PUT YOUR HAND UP YOUR ASS BEFORE?
I SWEAR!
YOU DO LOOK LIKE THE TYPE.
HOLD UP! WHY IS EVERYONE LOOKING AT ME LIKE THAT WHEN THERE'S A TALKING DOG FISTING HIMSELF?
AH... FOUND IT!
WHAT, YOUR PROSTATE?
NO! THIS!
DID YOU JUST PULL THAT OUT OF YOUR ASS?
YOU MEAN YOU KEEP STUFF UP... THERE
WHAT? I'M A DOG. I GOT NO POCKETS.
YEAH. I'VE GOT PEPPER SPRAY. ALL I'VE GOT TO DO IS FART AND YOU'RE A GONER!

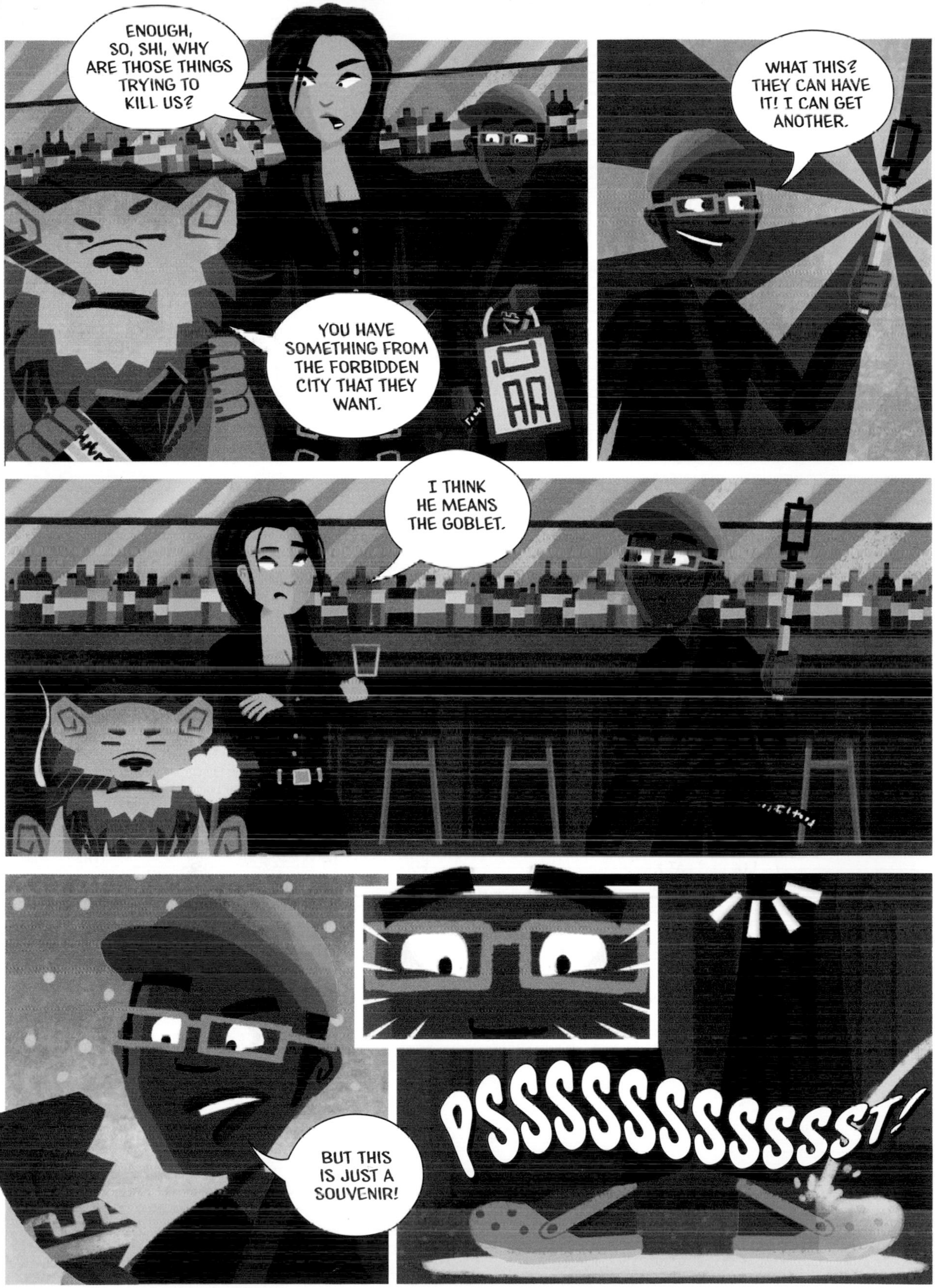
ENOUGH, SO, SHI, WHY ARE THOSE THINGS TRYING TO KILL US?
YOU HAVE SOMETHING FROM THE FORBIDDEN CITY THAT THEY WANT.
WHAT THIS? THEY CAN HAVE IT! I CAN GET ANOTHER.
I THINK HE MEANS THE GOBLET.
BUT THIS IS JUST A SOUVENIR!
PSSSSSSSSSSSST!

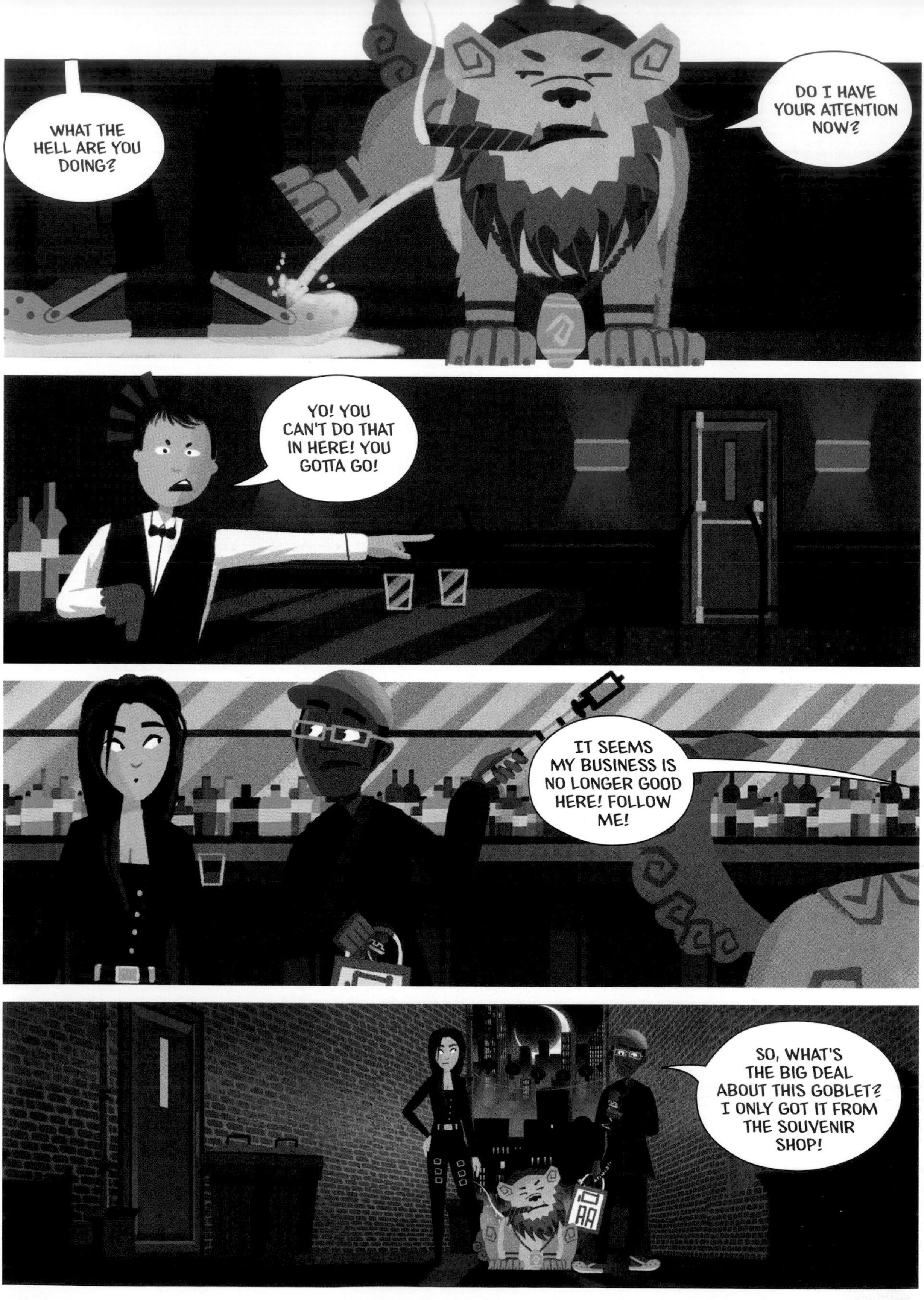
WHAT THE HELL ARE YOU DOING?
DO I HAVE YOUR ATTENTION NOW?
YO! YOU CAN'T DO THAT IN HERE! YOU GOTTA GO!
IT SEEMS MY BUSINESS IS NO LONGER GOOD HERE! FOLLOW ME!
SO, WHAT'S THE BIG DEAL ABOUT THIS GOBLET? I ONLY GOT IT FROM THE SOUVENIR SHOP!

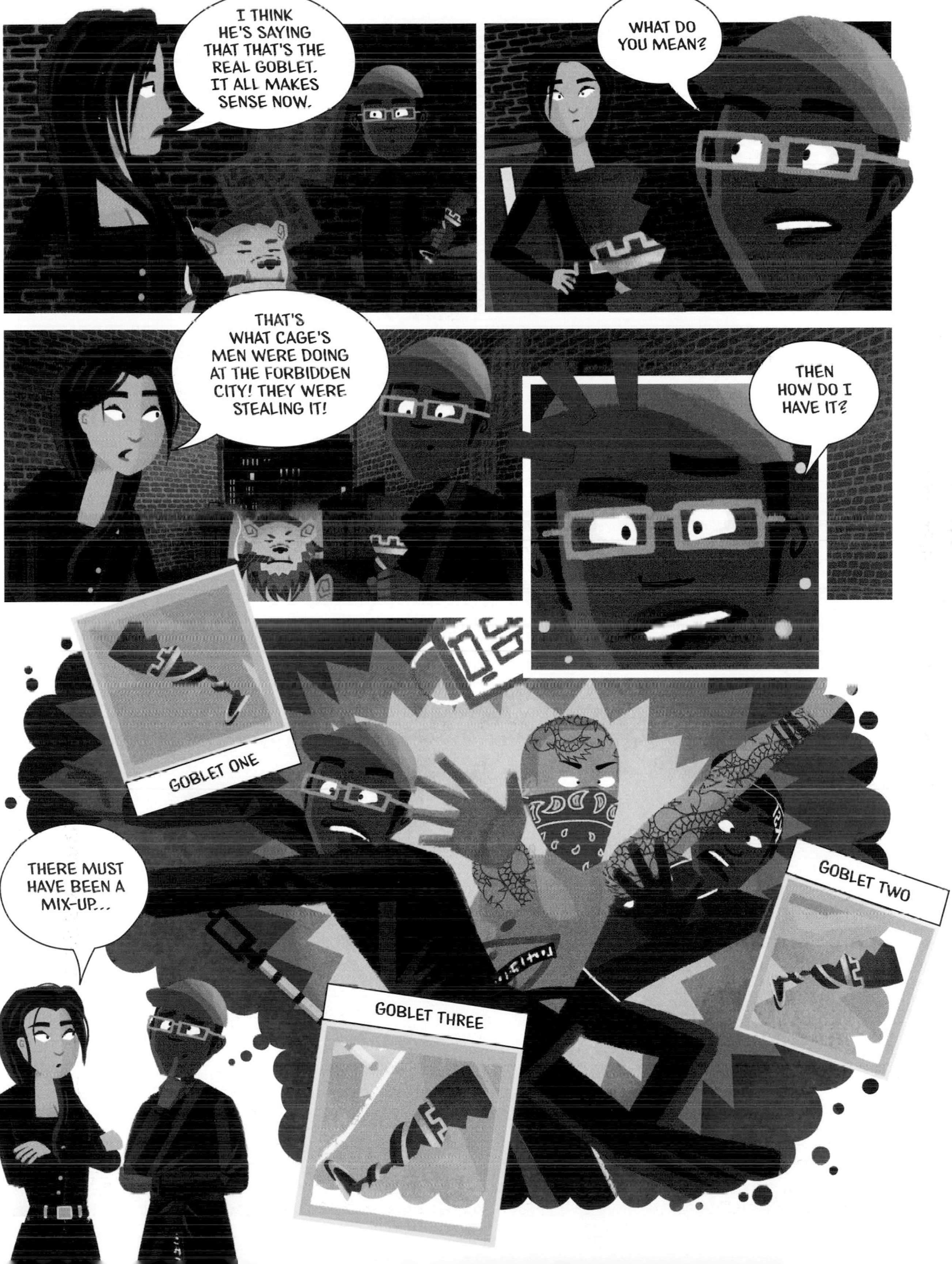

I THINK HE'S SAYING THAT THAT'S THE REAL GOBLET. IT ALL MAKES SENSE NOW.
WHAT DO YOU MEAN?
THAT'S WHAT CAGE'S MEN WERE DOING AT THE FORBIDDEN CITY! THEY WERE STEALING IT!
THEN HOW DO I HAVE IT?
GOBLET ONE
THERE MUST HAVE BEEN A MIX-UP...
GOBLET TWO
GOBLET THREE

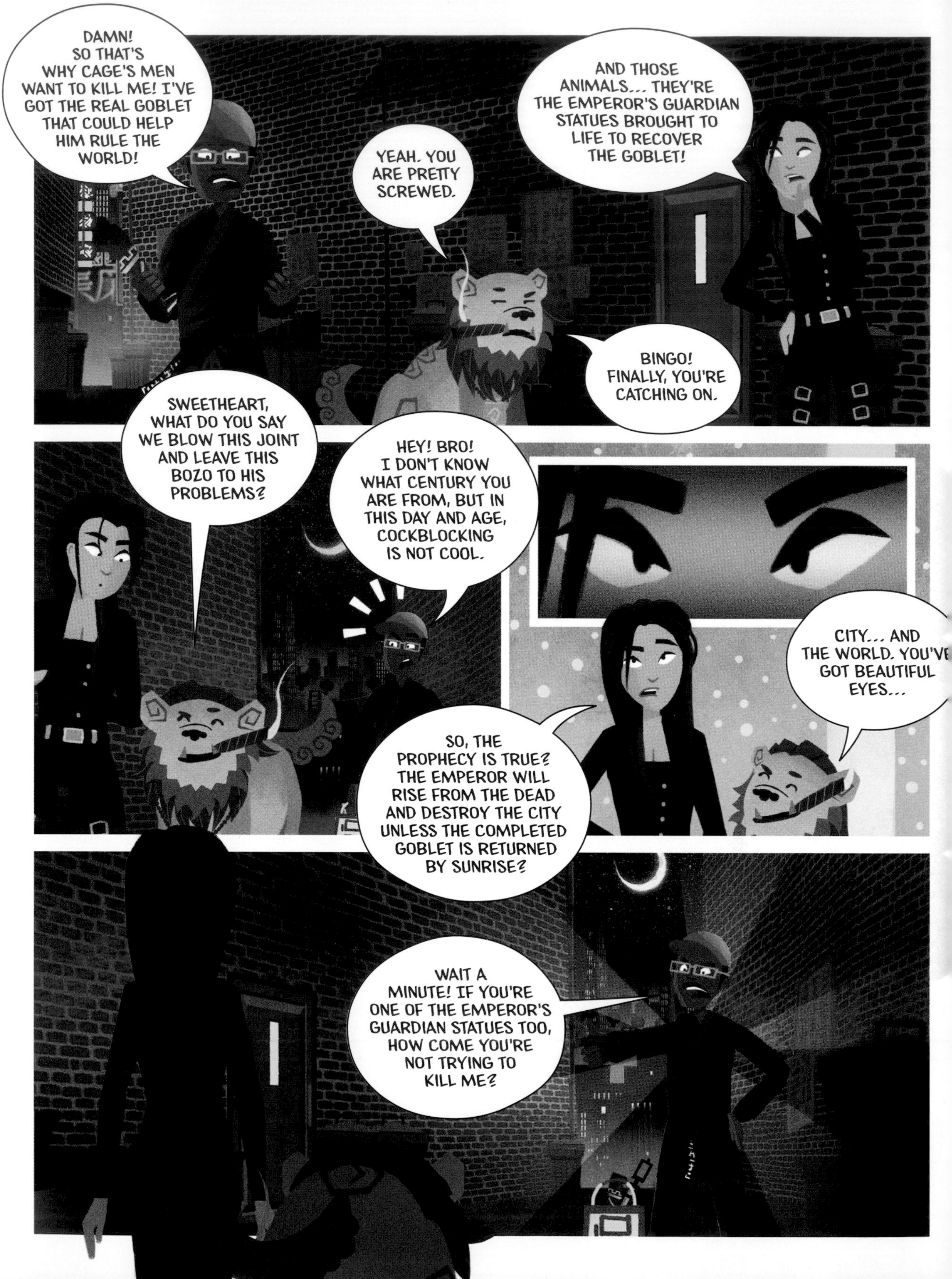
DAMN! SO THAT'S WHY CAGE'S MEN WANT TO KILL ME! I'VE GOT THE REAL GOBLET THAT COULD HELP HIM RULE THE WORLD!
YEAH. YOU ARE PRETTY SCREWED.
AND THOSE ANIMALS... THEY'RE THE EMPEROR'S GUARDIAN STATUES BROUGHT TO LIFE TO RECOVER THE GOBLET!
BINGO! FINALLY, YOU'RE CATCHING ON.
SWEETHEART, WHAT DO YOU SAY WE BLOW THIS JOINT AND LEAVE THIS BOZO TO HIS PROBLEMS?
HEY! BRO! I DON'T KNOW WHAT CENTURY YOU ARE FROM, BUT IN THIS DAY AND AGE, COCKBLOCKING IS NOT COOL.
SO, THE PROPHECY IS TRUE? THE EMPEROR WILL RISE FROM THE DEAD AND DESTROY THE CITY UNLESS THE COMPLETED GOBLET IS RETURNED BY SUNRISE?
CITY... AND THE WORLD. YOU'VE GOT BEAUTIFUL EYES...
WAIT A MINUTE! IF YOU'RE ONE OF THE EMPEROR'S GUARDIAN STATUES TOO, HOW COME YOU'RE NOT TRYING TO KILL ME?

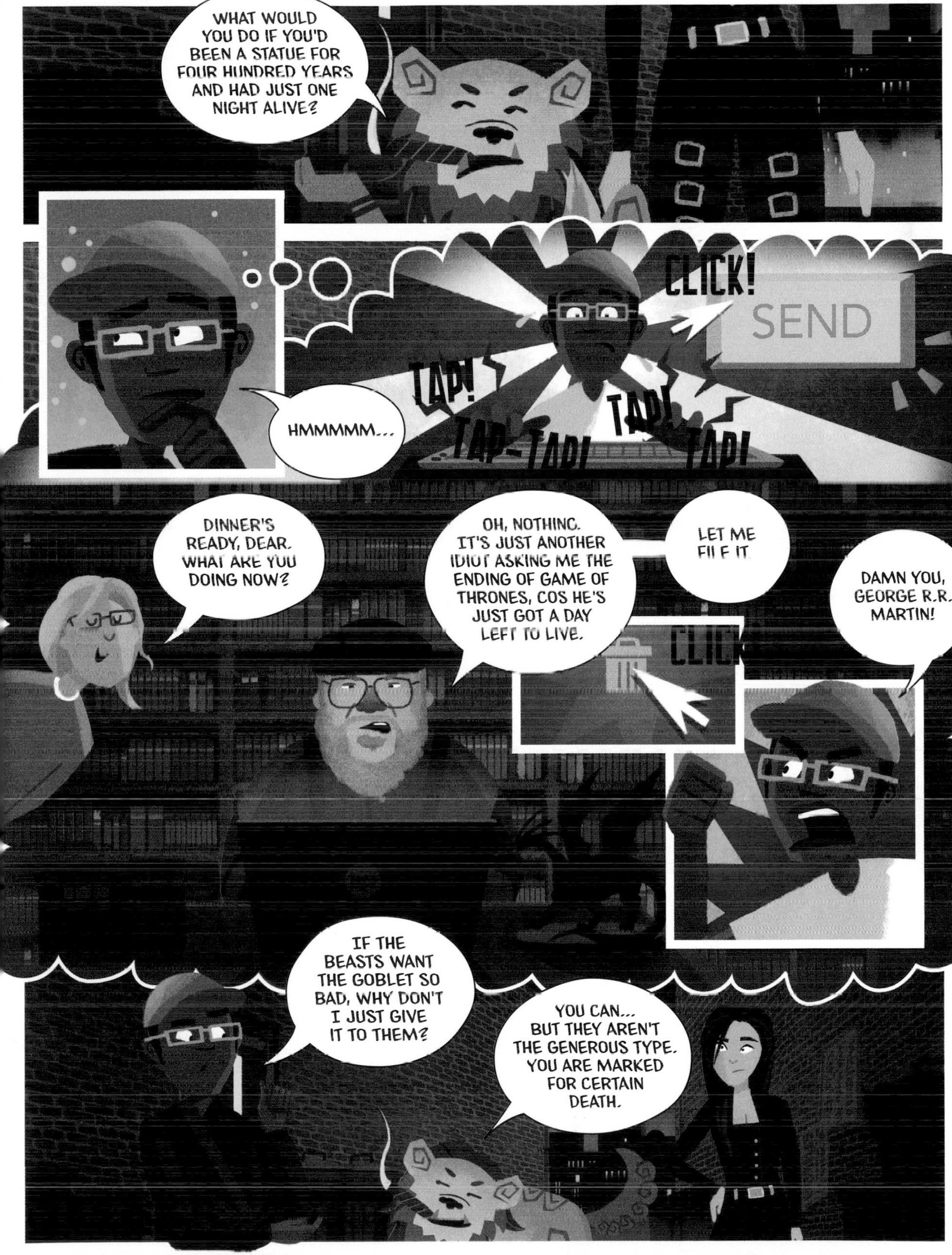
WHAT WOULD YOU DO IF YOU'D BEEN A STATUE FOR FOUR HUNDRED YEARS AND HAD JUST ONE NIGHT ALIVE?
HMMMMM...
TAP!
TAP-TAP!
TAP!
TAP!
CLICK!
SEND
DINNER'S READY, DEAR. WHAT ARE YOU DOING NOW?
OH, NOTHING. IT'S JUST ANOTHER IDIOT ASKING ME THE ENDING OF GAME OF THRONES, COS HE'S JUST GOT A DAY LEFT TO LIVE.
LET ME FILE IT.
CLICK
DAMN YOU, GEORGE R.R. MARTIN!
IF THE BEASTS WANT THE GOBLET SO BAD, WHY DON'T I JUST GIVE IT TO THEM?
YOU CAN... BUT THEY AREN'T THE GENEROUS TYPE. YOU ARE MARKED FOR CERTAIN DEATH.

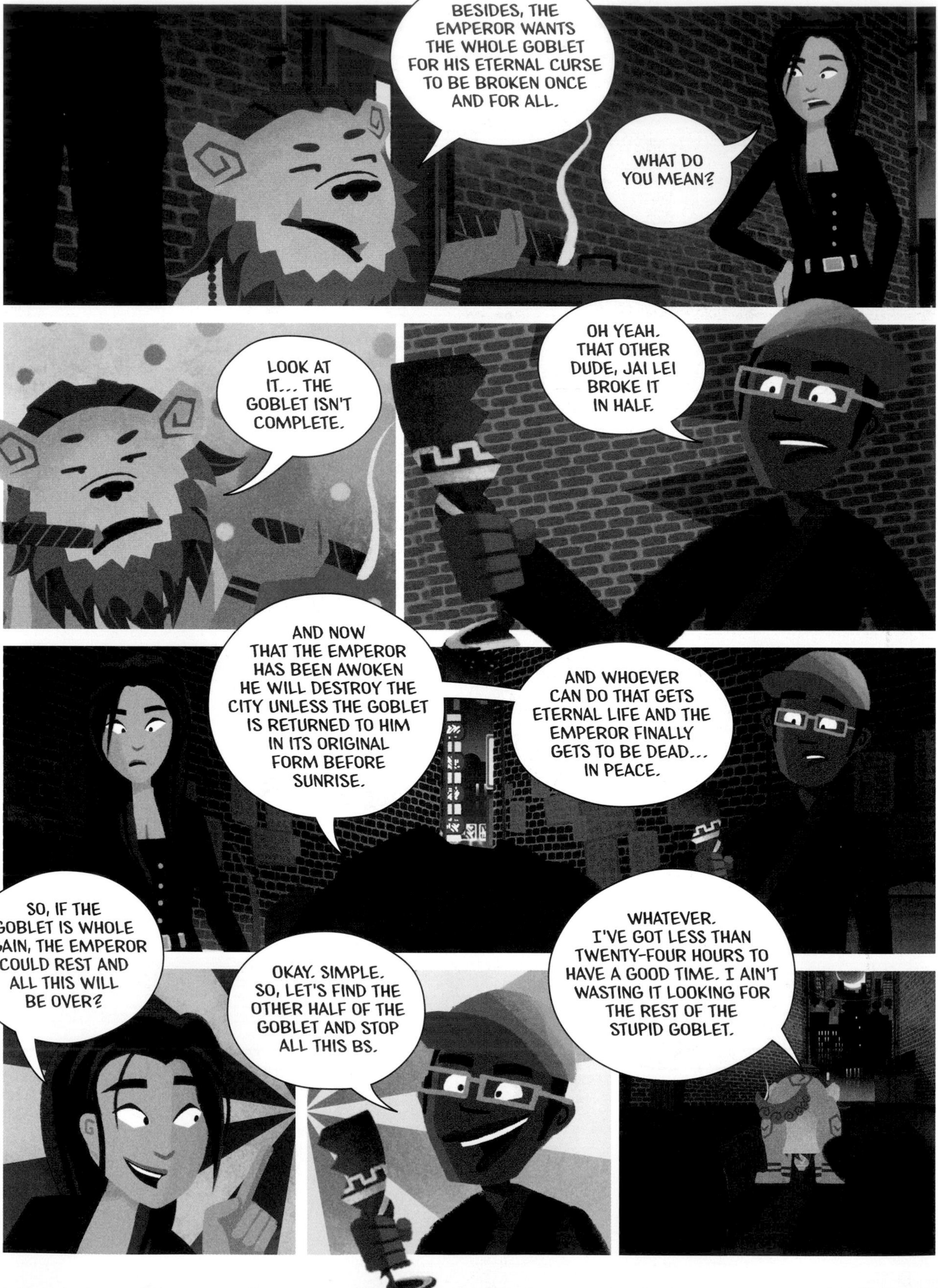
BESIDES, THE EMPEROR WANTS THE WHOLE GOBLET FOR HIS ETERNAL CURSE TO BE BROKEN ONCE AND FOR ALL.
WHAT DO YOU MEAN?
LOOK AT IT... THE GOBLET ISN'T COMPLETE.
OH YEAH. THAT OTHER DUDE, JAI LEI BROKE IT IN HALF.
AND NOW THAT THE EMPEROR HAS BEEN AWOKEN HE WILL DESTROY THE CITY UNLESS THE GOBLET IS RETURNED TO HIM IN ITS ORIGINAL FORM BEFORE SUNRISE.
AND WHOEVER CAN DO THAT GETS ETERNAL LIFE AND THE EMPEROR FINALLY GETS TO BE DEAD... IN PEACE.
SO, IF THE GOBLET IS WHOLE AGAIN, THE EMPEROR COULD REST AND ALL THIS WILL BE OVER?
OKAY. SIMPLE. SO, LET'S FIND THE OTHER HALF OF THE GOBLET AND STOP ALL THIS BS.
WHATEVER. I'VE GOT LESS THAN TWENTY-FOUR HOURS TO HAVE A GOOD TIME. I AIN'T WASTING IT LOOKING FOR THE REST OF THE STUPID GOBLET.

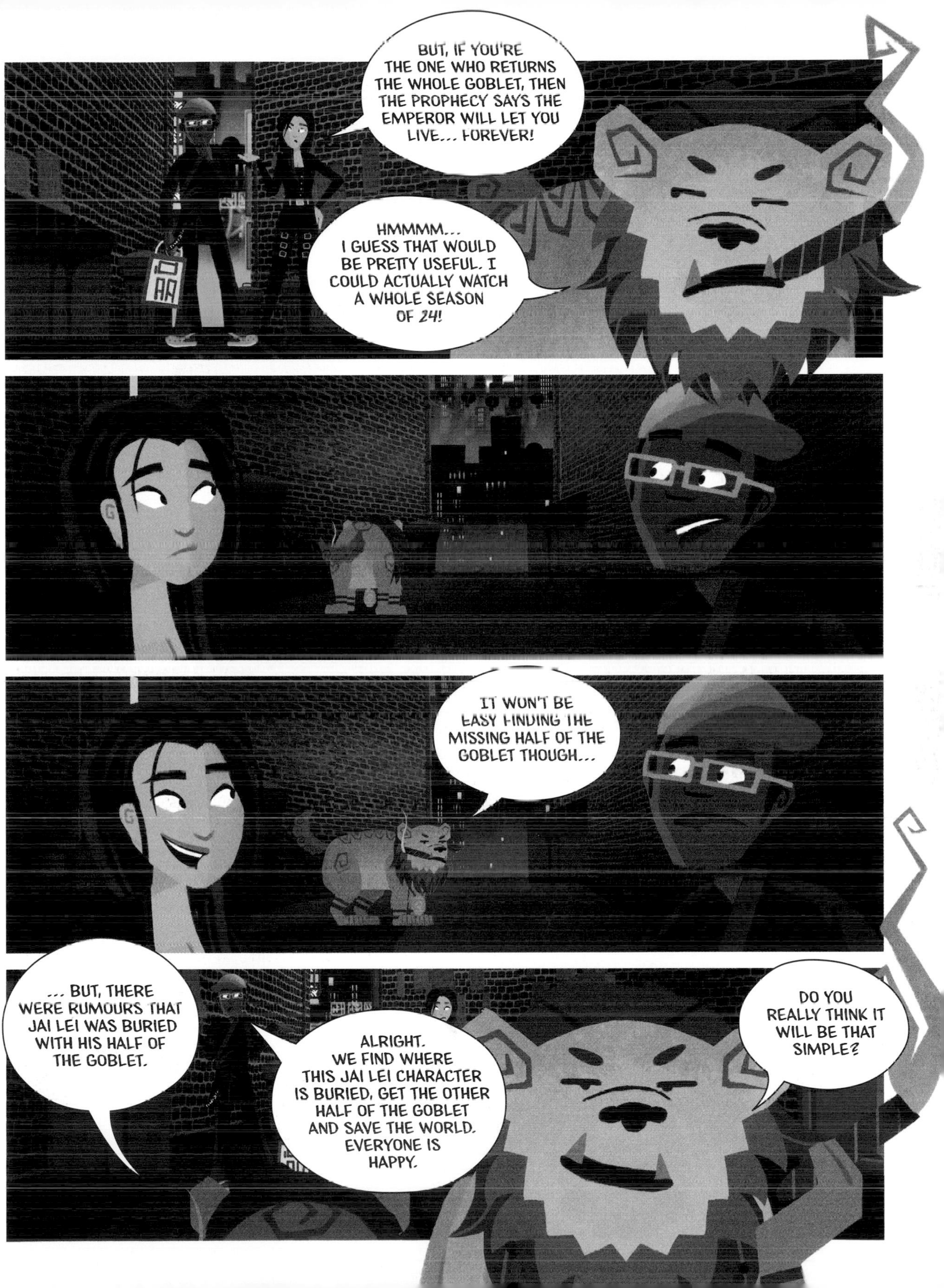
BUT, IF YOU'RE THE ONE WHO RETURNS THE WHOLE GOBLET, THEN THE PROPHECY SAYS THE EMPEROR WILL LET YOU LIVE... FOREVER!
HMMMM... I GUESS THAT WOULD BE PRETTY USEFUL. I COULD ACTUALLY WATCH A WHOLE SEASON OF *24*!
IT WON'T BE EASY FINDING THE MISSING HALF OF THE GOBLET THOUGH...
... BUT, THERE WERE RUMOURS THAT JAI LEI WAS BURIED WITH HIS HALF OF THE GOBLET.
ALRIGHT. WE FIND WHERE THIS JAI LEI CHARACTER IS BURIED, GET THE OTHER HALF OF THE GOBLET AND SAVE THE WORLD. EVERYONE IS HAPPY.
DO YOU REALLY THINK IT WILL BE THAT SIMPLE?

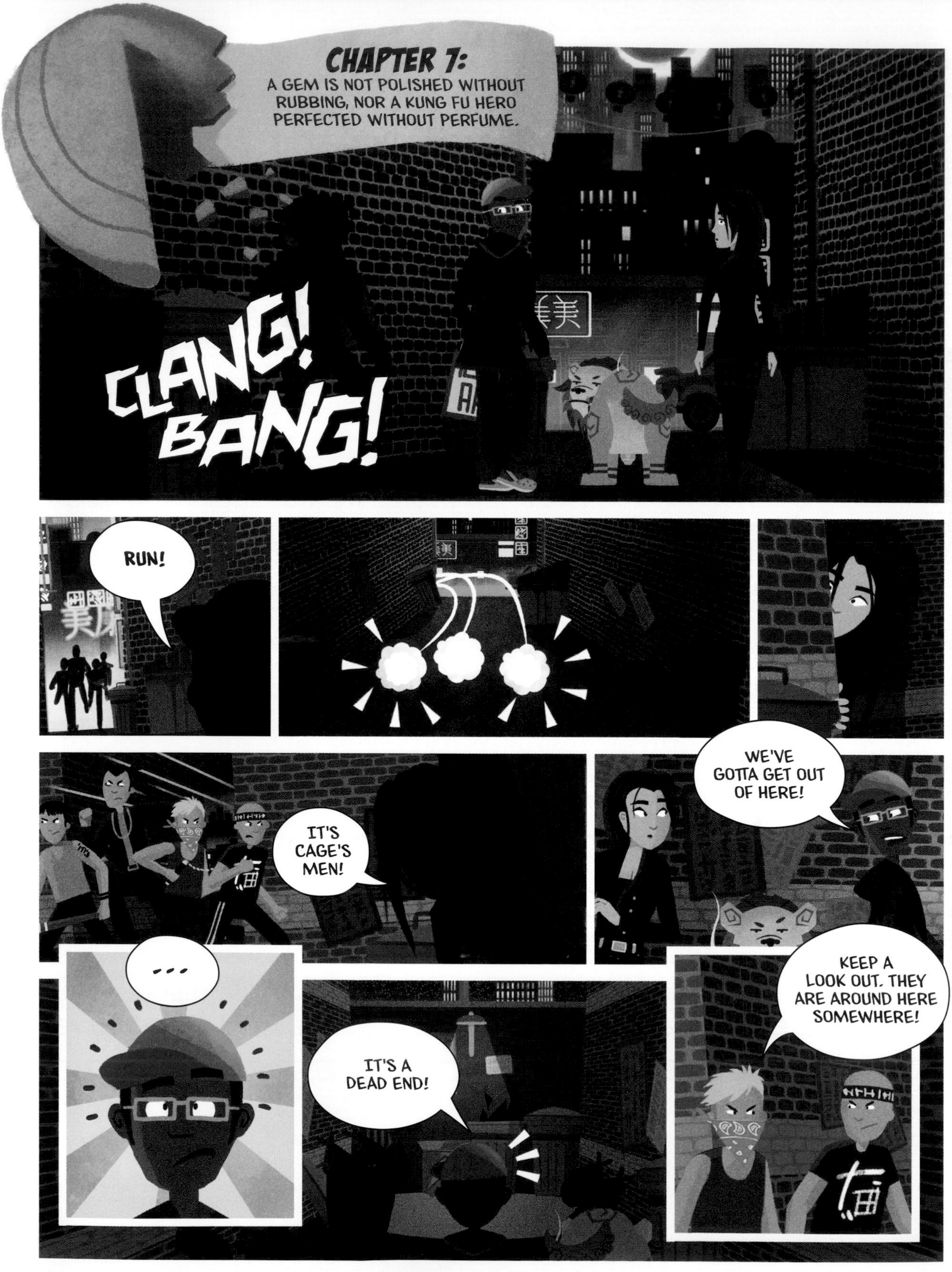
CHAPTER 7:
A GEM IS NOT POLISHED WITHOUT RUBBING, NOR A KUNG FU HERO PERFECTED WITHOUT PERFUME.
CLANG! BANG!
RUN!
IT'S CAGE'S MEN!
WE'VE GOTTA GET OUT OF HERE!
...
IT'S A DEAD END!
KEEP A LOOK OUT. THEY ARE AROUND HERE SOMEWHERE!

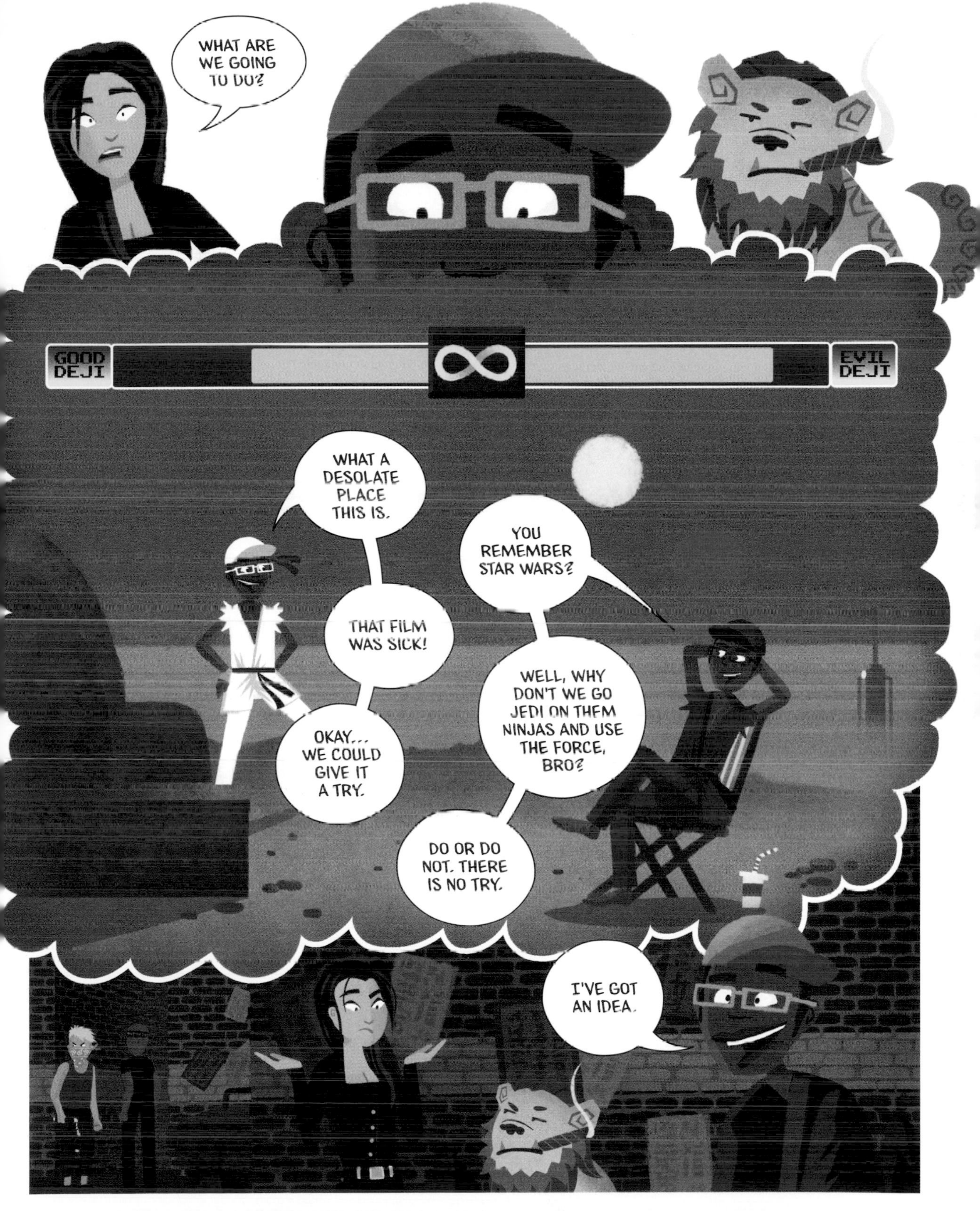
WHAT ARE WE GOING TO DO?
GOOD DEJI
EVIL DEJI
WHAT A DESOLATE PLACE THIS IS.
YOU REMEMBER STAR WARS?
THAT FILM WAS SICK!
WELL, WHY DON'T WE GO JEDI ON THEM NINJAS AND USE THE FORCE, BRO?
OKAY... WE COULD GIVE IT A TRY.
DO OR DO NOT. THERE IS NO TRY.
I'VE GOT AN IDEA.

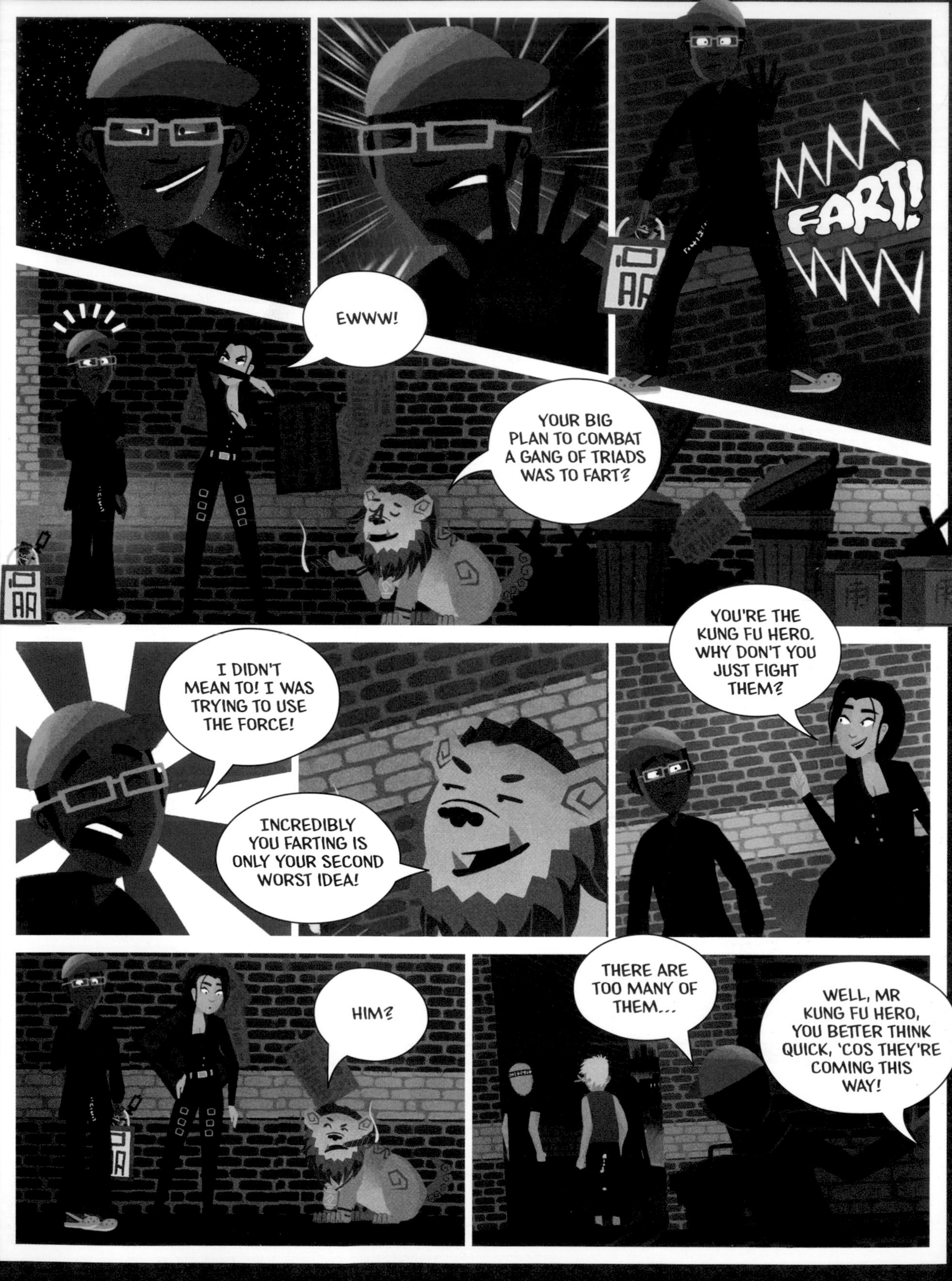
FART!
EWWW!
YOUR BIG PLAN TO COMBAT A GANG OF TRIADS WAS TO FART?
I DIDN'T MEAN TO! I WAS TRYING TO USE THE FORCE!
INCREDIBLY YOU FARTING IS ONLY YOUR SECOND WORST IDEA!
YOU'RE THE KUNG FU HERO. WHY DON'T YOU JUST FIGHT THEM?
HIM?
THERE ARE TOO MANY OF THEM...
WELL, MR KUNG FU HERO, YOU BETTER THINK QUICK, 'COS THEY'RE COMING THIS WAY!

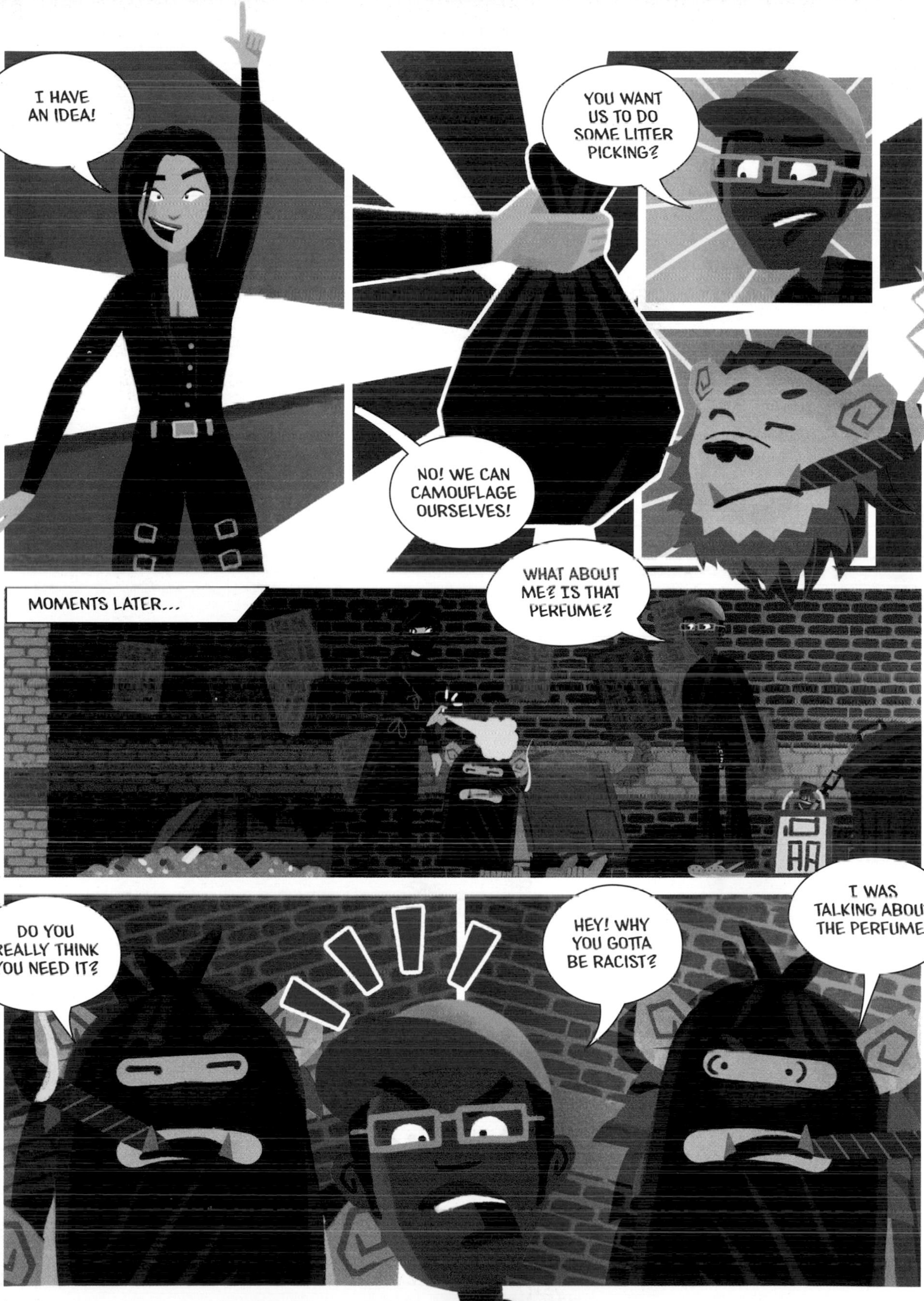

I HAVE AN IDEA!
YOU WANT US TO DO SOME LITTER PICKING?
NO! WE CAN CAMOUFLAGE OURSELVES!
MOMENTS LATER...
WHAT ABOUT ME? IS THAT PERFUME?
DO YOU REALLY THINK YOU NEED IT?
HEY! WHY YOU GOTTA BE RACIST?
I WAS TALKING ABOUT THE PERFUME.

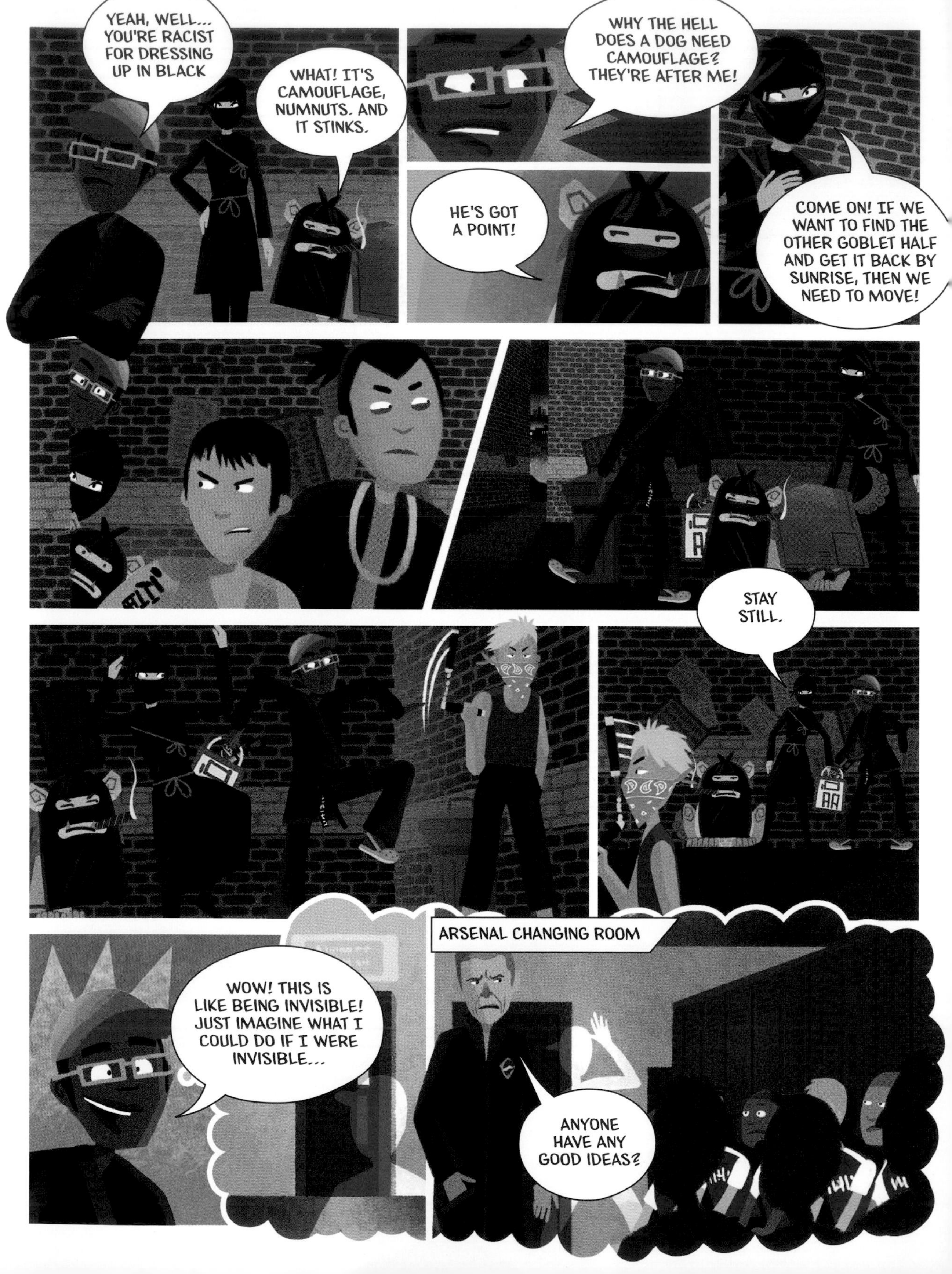
YEAH, WELL... YOU'RE RACIST FOR DRESSING UP IN BLACK
WHAT! IT'S CAMOUFLAGE, NUMNUTS. AND IT STINKS.
WHY THE HELL DOES A DOG NEED CAMOUFLAGE? THEY'RE AFTER ME!
HE'S GOT A POINT!
COME ON! IF WE WANT TO FIND THE OTHER GOBLET HALF AND GET IT BACK BY SUNRISE, THEN WE NEED TO MOVE!
STAY STILL.
WOW! THIS IS LIKE BEING INVISIBLE! JUST IMAGINE WHAT I COULD DO IF I WERE INVISIBLE...
ARSENAL CHANGING ROOM
ANYONE HAVE ANY GOOD IDEAS?

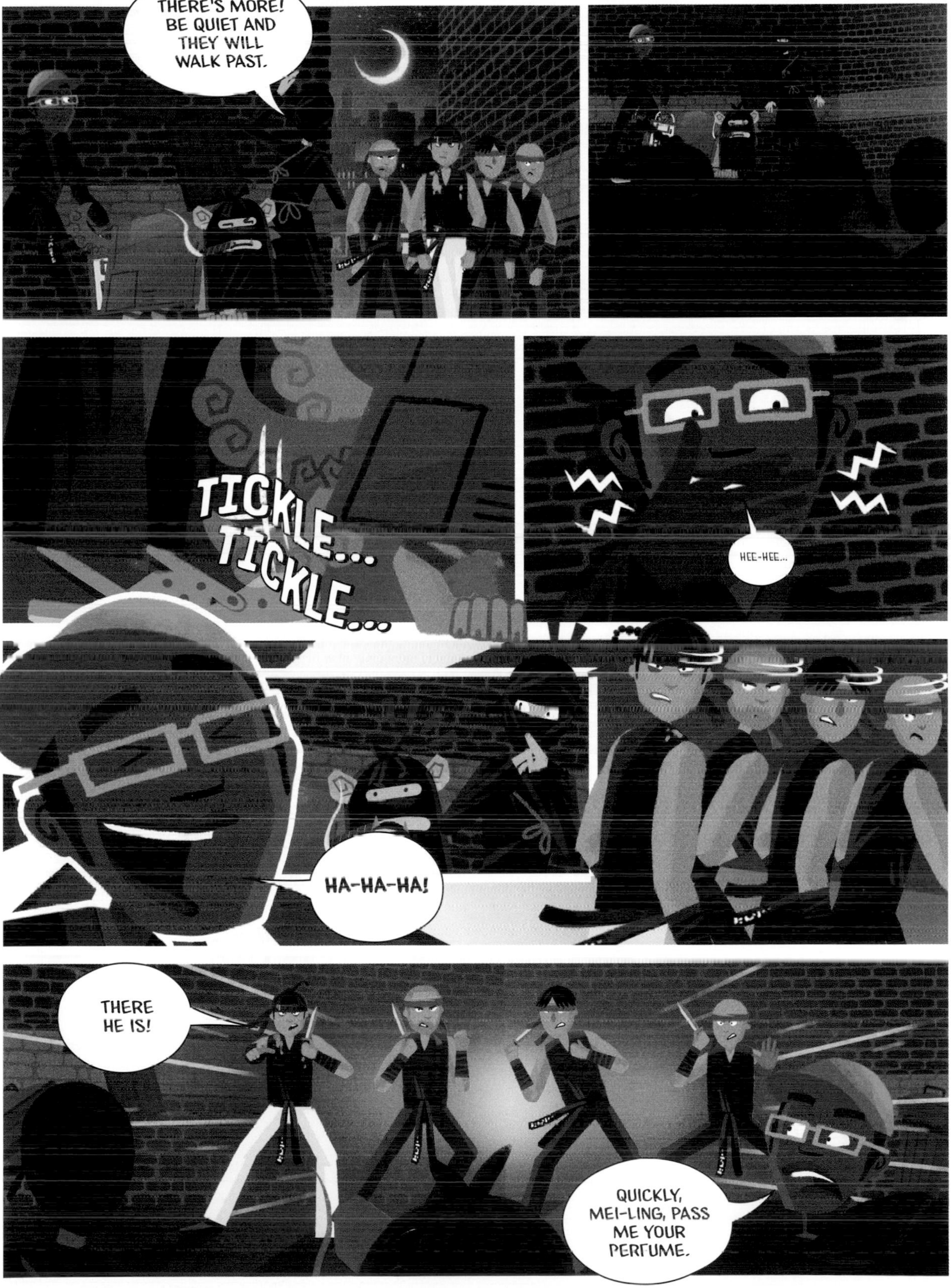
THERE'S MORE! BE QUIET AND THEY WILL WALK PAST.
TICKLE... TICKLE...
HEE-HEE...
HA-HA-HA!
THERE HE IS!
QUICKLY, MEI-LING, PASS ME YOUR PERFUME.

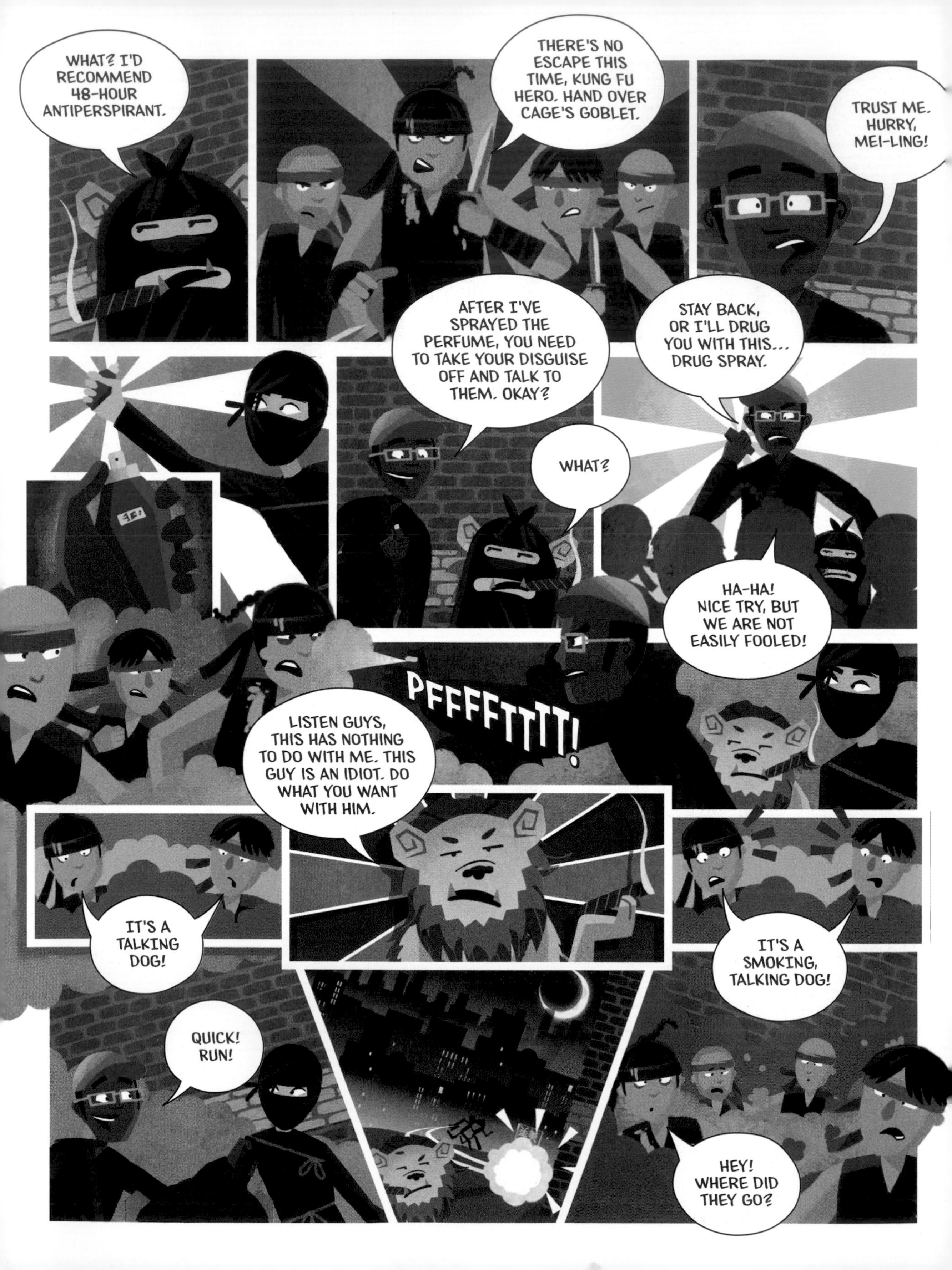
WHAT? I'D RECOMMEND 48-HOUR ANTIPERSPIRANT.
THERE'S NO ESCAPE THIS TIME, KUNG FU HERO. HAND OVER CAGE'S GOBLET.
TRUST ME. HURRY, MEI-LING!
AFTER I'VE SPRAYED THE PERFUME, YOU NEED TO TAKE YOUR DISGUISE OFF AND TALK TO THEM. OKAY?
WHAT?
STAY BACK, OR I'LL DRUG YOU WITH THIS... DRUG SPRAY.
HA-HA! NICE TRY, BUT WE ARE NOT EASILY FOOLED!
PFFFFTTTT!
LISTEN GUYS, THIS HAS NOTHING TO DO WITH ME. THIS GUY IS AN IDIOT. DO WHAT YOU WANT WITH HIM.
IT'S A TALKING DOG!
IT'S A SMOKING, TALKING DOG!
QUICK! RUN!
HEY! WHERE DID THEY GO?

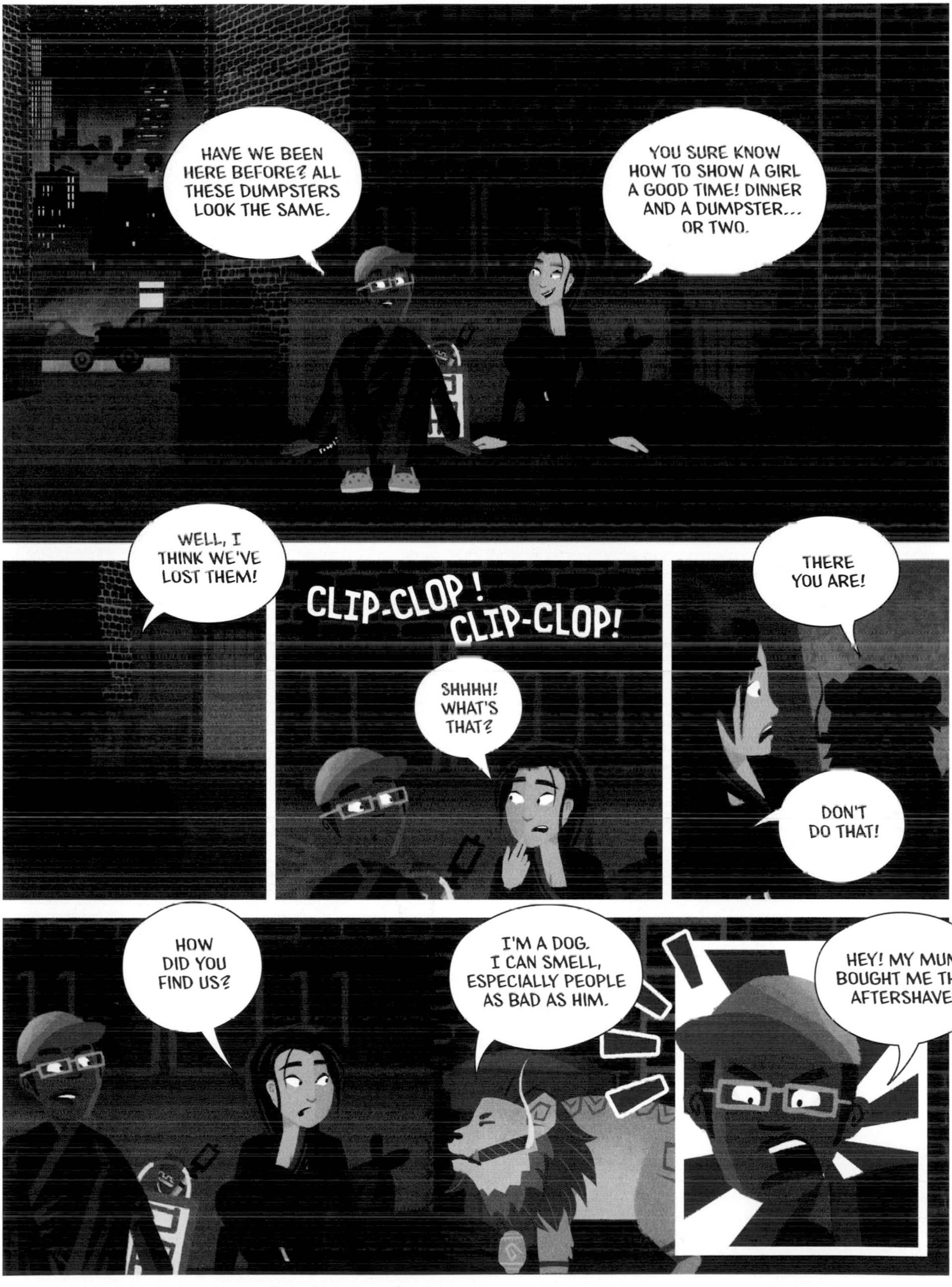
HAVE WE BEEN HERE BEFORE? ALL THESE DUMPSTERS LOOK THE SAME.
YOU SURE KNOW HOW TO SHOW A GIRL A GOOD TIME! DINNER AND A DUMPSTER... OR TWO.
WELL, I THINK WE'VE LOST THEM!
CLIP-CLOP! CLIP-CLOP!
SHHHH! WHAT'S THAT?
THERE YOU ARE!
DON'T DO THAT!
HOW DID YOU FIND US?
I'M A DOG. I CAN SMELL, ESPECIALLY PEOPLE AS BAD AS HIM.
HEY! MY MUM BOUGHT ME THIS AFTERSHAVE.

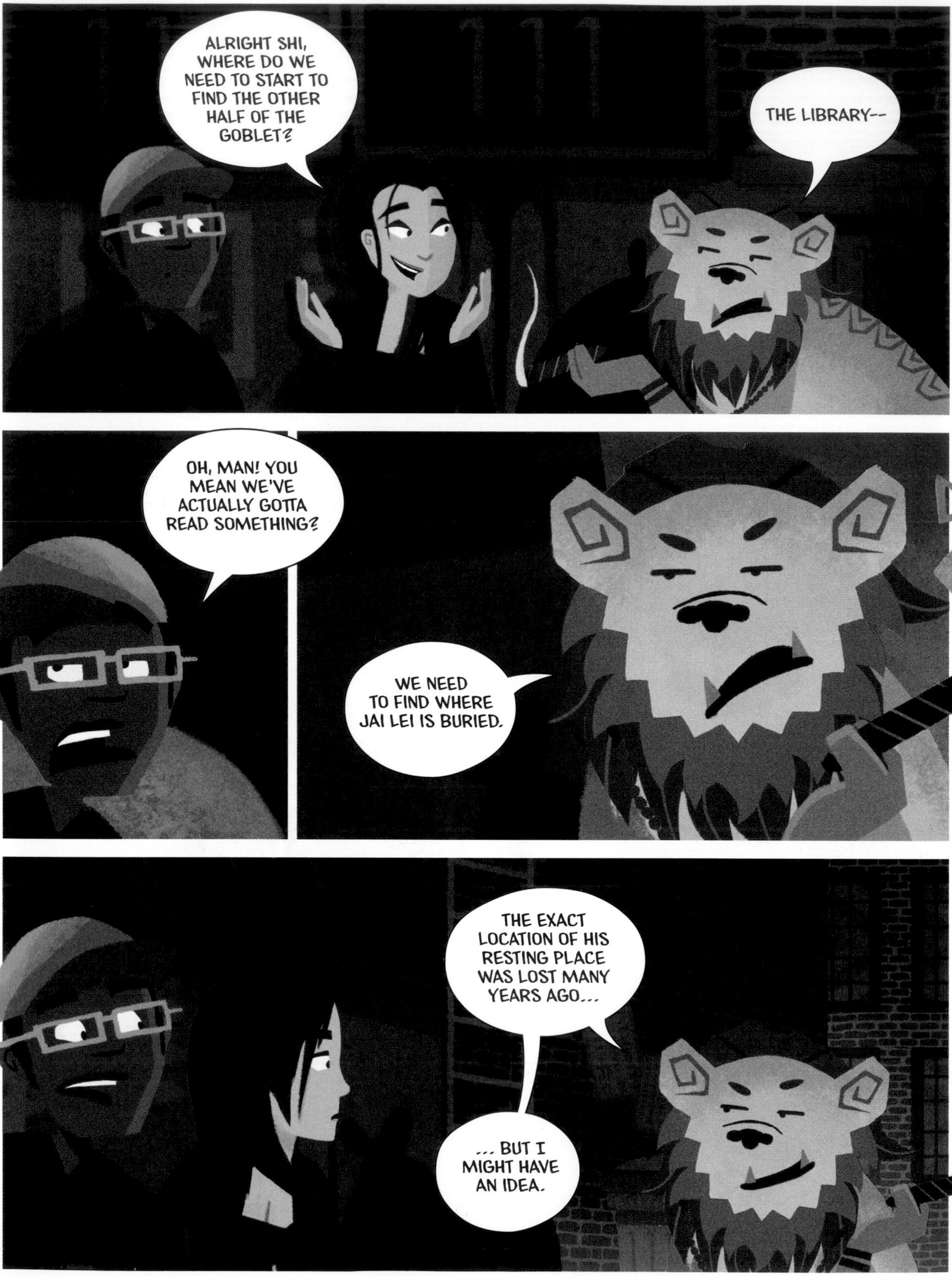
ALRIGHT SHI, WHERE DO WE NEED TO START TO FIND THE OTHER HALF OF THE GOBLET?
THE LIBRARY--
OH, MAN! YOU MEAN WE'VE ACTUALLY GOTTA READ SOMETHING?
WE NEED TO FIND WHERE JAI LEI IS BURIED.
THE EXACT LOCATION OF HIS RESTING PLACE WAS LOST MANY YEARS AGO...
... BUT I MIGHT HAVE AN IDEA.

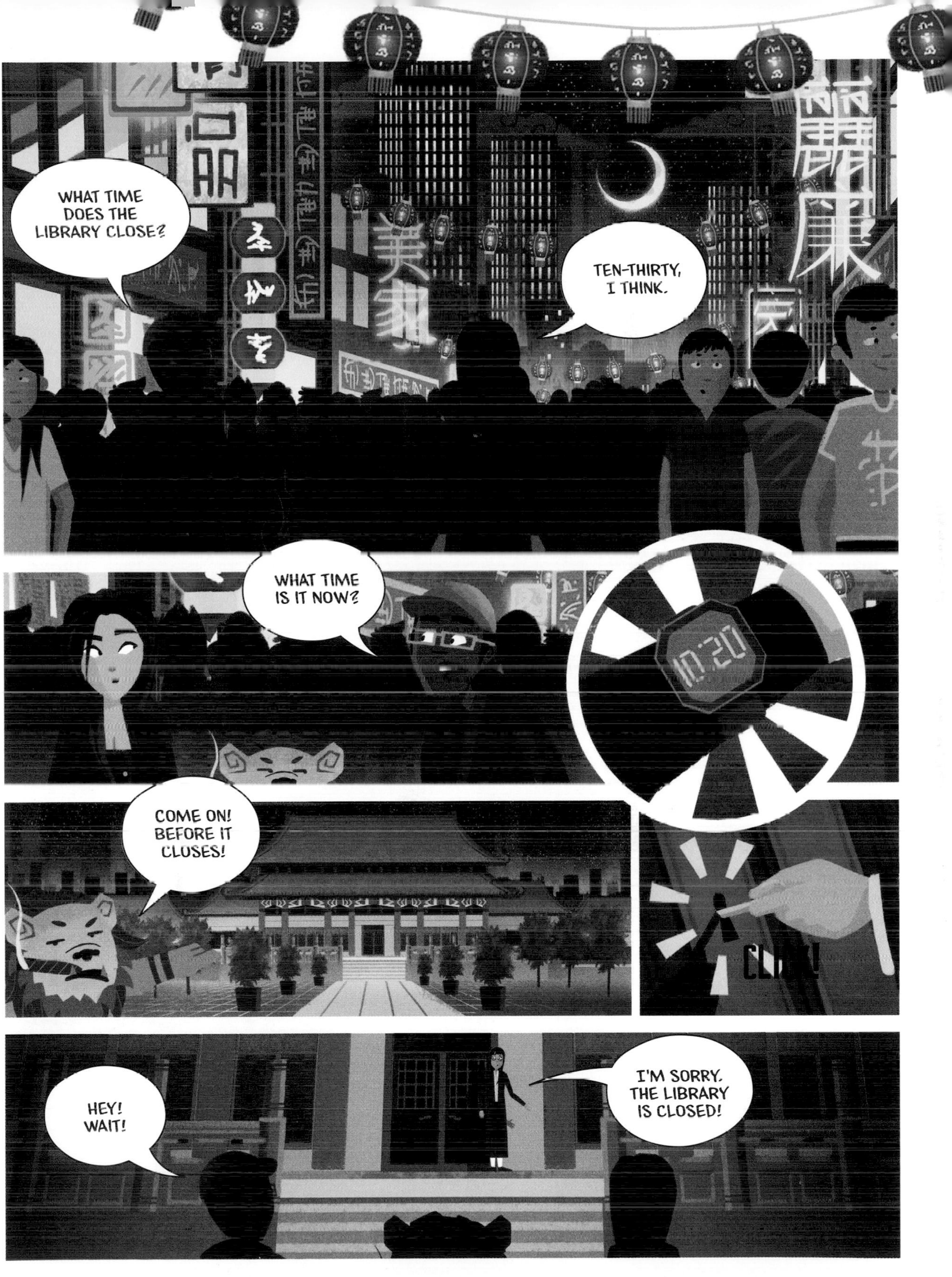
WHAT TIME DOES THE LIBRARY CLOSE?
TEN-THIRTY, I THINK.
WHAT TIME IS IT NOW?
10:20
COME ON! BEFORE IT CLOSES!
HEY! WAIT!
I'M SORRY. THE LIBRARY IS CLOSED!

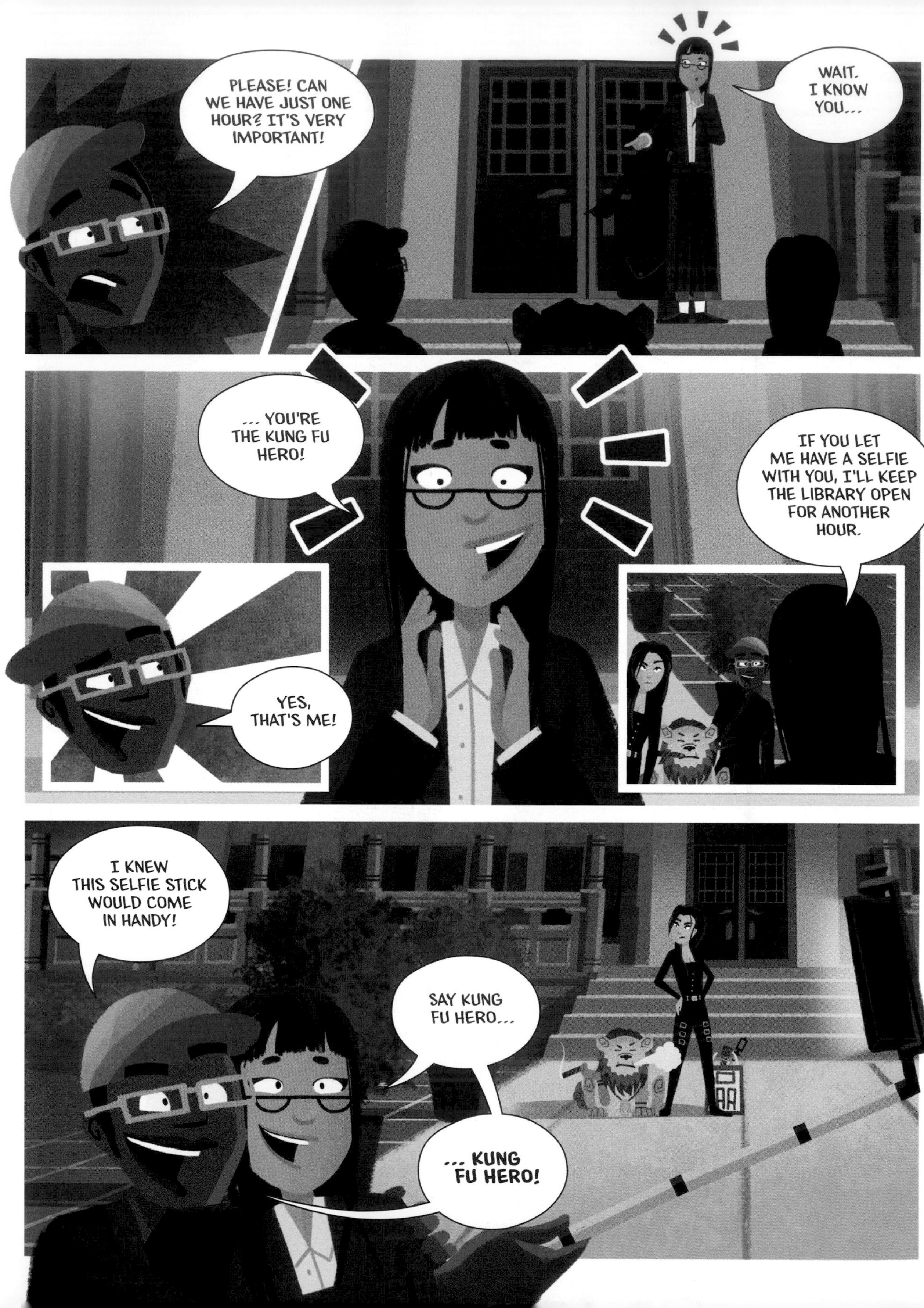
PLEASE! CAN WE HAVE JUST ONE HOUR? IT'S VERY IMPORTANT!
WAIT. I KNOW YOU...
... YOU'RE THE KUNG FU HERO!
YES, THAT'S ME!
IF YOU LET ME HAVE A SELFIE WITH YOU, I'LL KEEP THE LIBRARY OPEN FOR ANOTHER HOUR.
I KNEW THIS SELFIE STICK WOULD COME IN HANDY!
SAY KUNG FU HERO...
... KUNG FU HERO!

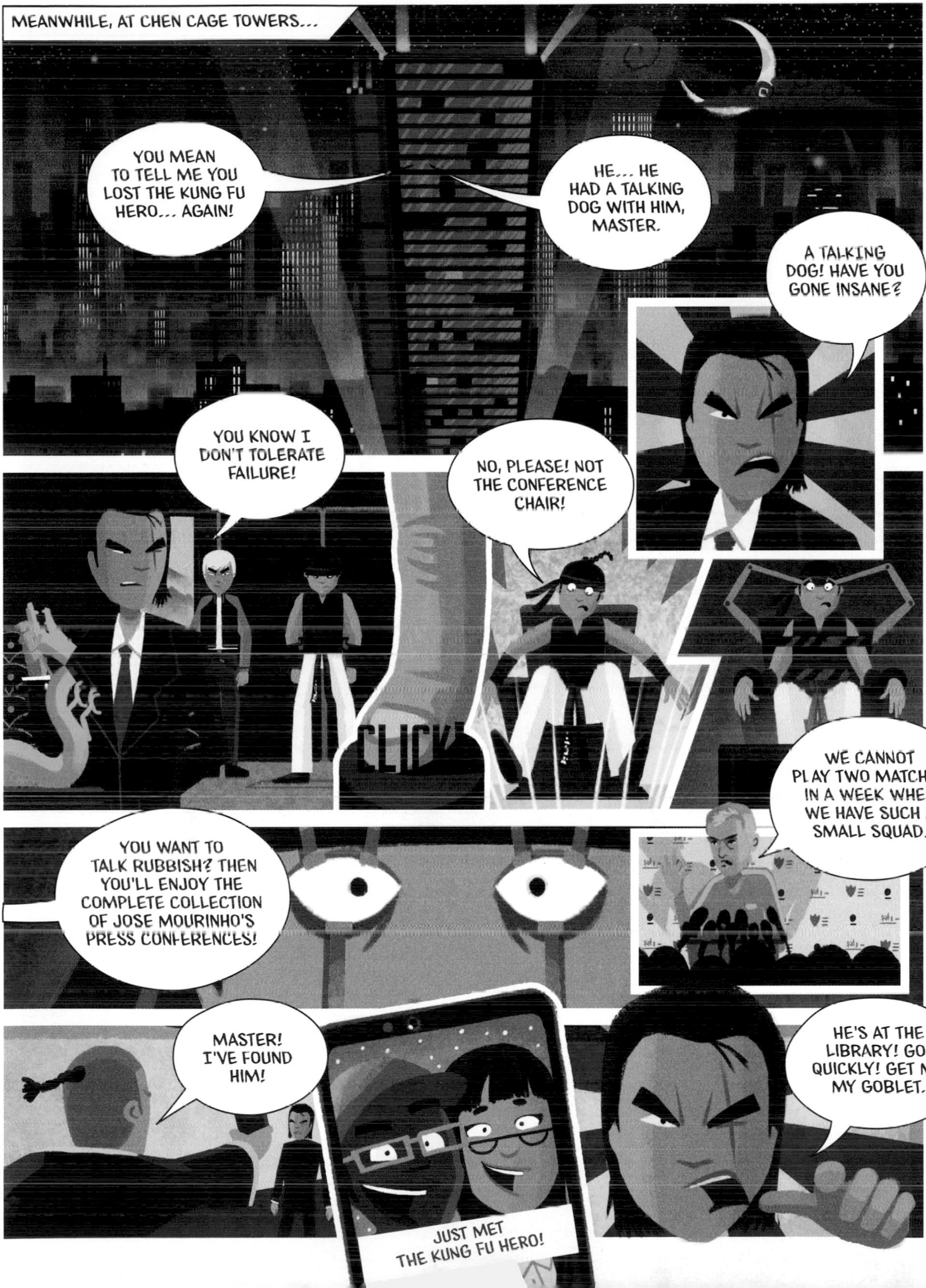
MEANWHILE, AT CHEN CAGE TOWERS...
YOU MEAN TO TELL ME YOU LOST THE KUNG FU HERO... AGAIN!
HE... HE HAD A TALKING DOG WITH HIM, MASTER.
A TALKING DOG! HAVE YOU GONE INSANE?
YOU KNOW I DON'T TOLERATE FAILURE!
NO, PLEASE! NOT THE CONFERENCE CHAIR!
CLICK
WE CANNOT PLAY TWO MATCHES IN A WEEK WHEN WE HAVE SUCH A SMALL SQUAD...
YOU WANT TO TALK RUBBISH? THEN YOU'LL ENJOY THE COMPLETE COLLECTION OF JOSE MOURINHO'S PRESS CONFERENCES!
MASTER! I'VE FOUND HIM!
JUST MET THE KUNG FU HERO!
HE'S AT THE LIBRARY! GO! QUICKLY! GET ME MY GOBLET.

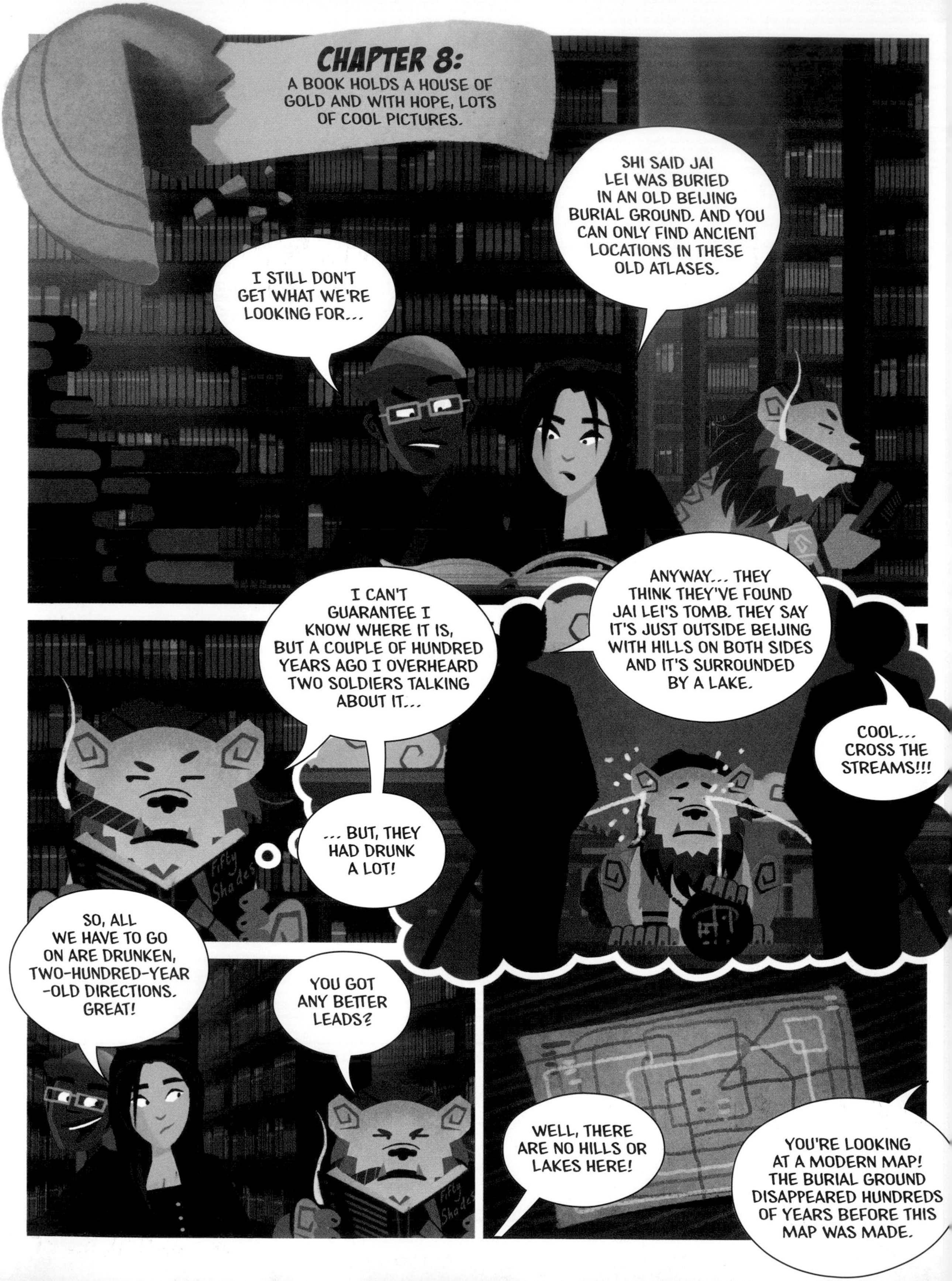
CHAPTER 8:
A BOOK HOLDS A HOUSE OF GOLD AND WITH HOPE, LOTS OF COOL PICTURES.
I STILL DON'T GET WHAT WE'RE LOOKING FOR...
SHI SAID JAI LEI WAS BURIED IN AN OLD BEIJING BURIAL GROUND. AND YOU CAN ONLY FIND ANCIENT LOCATIONS IN THESE OLD ATLASES.
I CAN'T GUARANTEE I KNOW WHERE IT IS, BUT A COUPLE OF HUNDRED YEARS AGO I OVERHEARD TWO SOLDIERS TALKING ABOUT IT...
... BUT, THEY HAD DRUNK A LOT!
ANYWAY... THEY THINK THEY'VE FOUND JAI LEI'S TOMB. THEY SAY IT'S JUST OUTSIDE BEIJING WITH HILLS ON BOTH SIDES AND IT'S SURROUNDED BY A LAKE.
COOL... CROSS THE STREAMS!!!
Fifty Shades
SO, ALL WE HAVE TO GO ON ARE DRUNKEN, TWO-HUNDRED-YEAR-OLD DIRECTIONS. GREAT!
YOU GOT ANY BETTER LEADS?
Fifty Shades
WELL, THERE ARE NO HILLS OR LAKES HERE!
YOU'RE LOOKING AT A MODERN MAP! THE BURIAL GROUND DISAPPEARED HUNDREDS OF YEARS BEFORE THIS MAP WAS MADE.

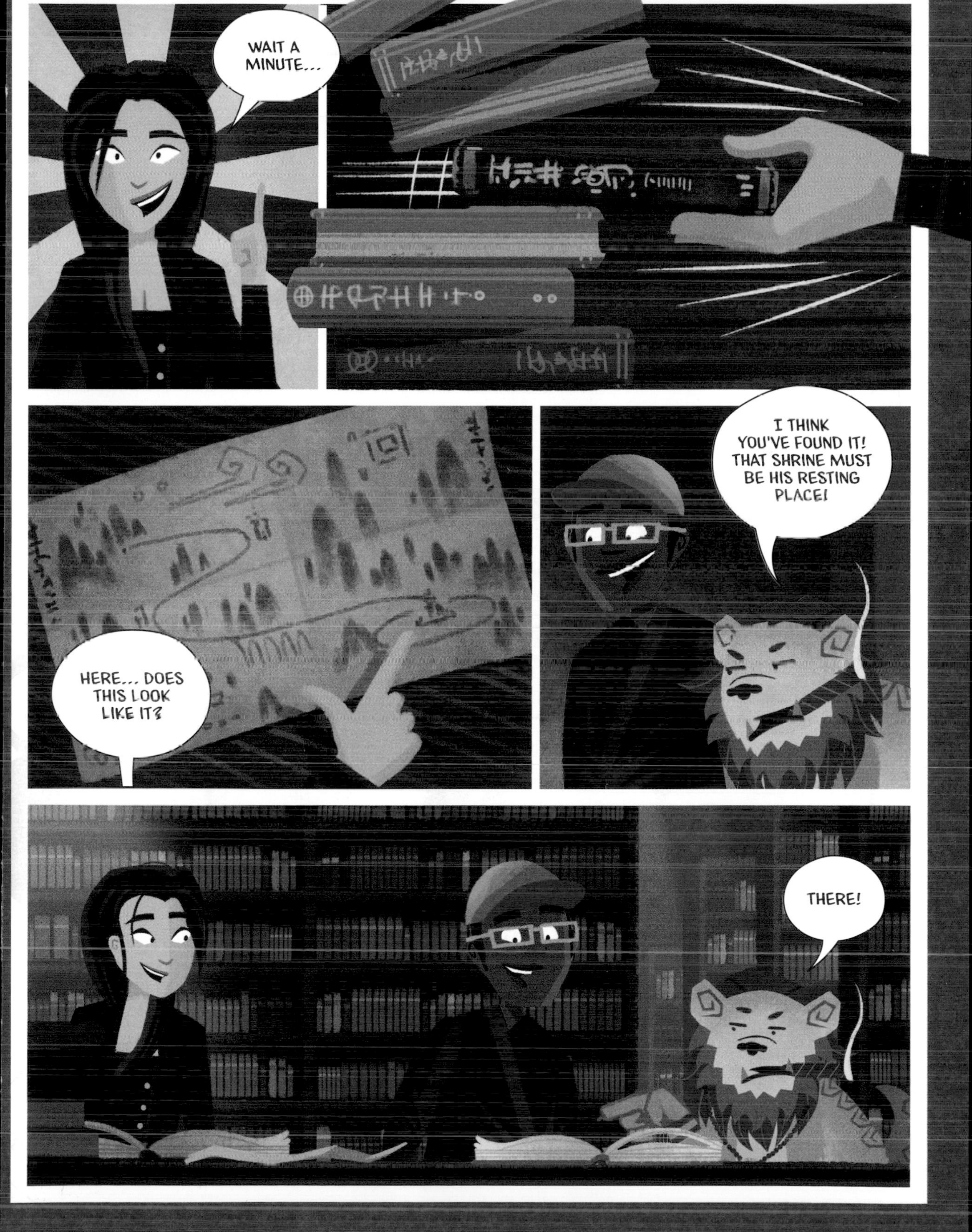
WAIT A MINUTE...
HERE... DOES THIS LOOK LIKE IT?
I THINK YOU'VE FOUND IT! THAT SHRINE MUST BE HIS RESTING PLACE!
THERE!

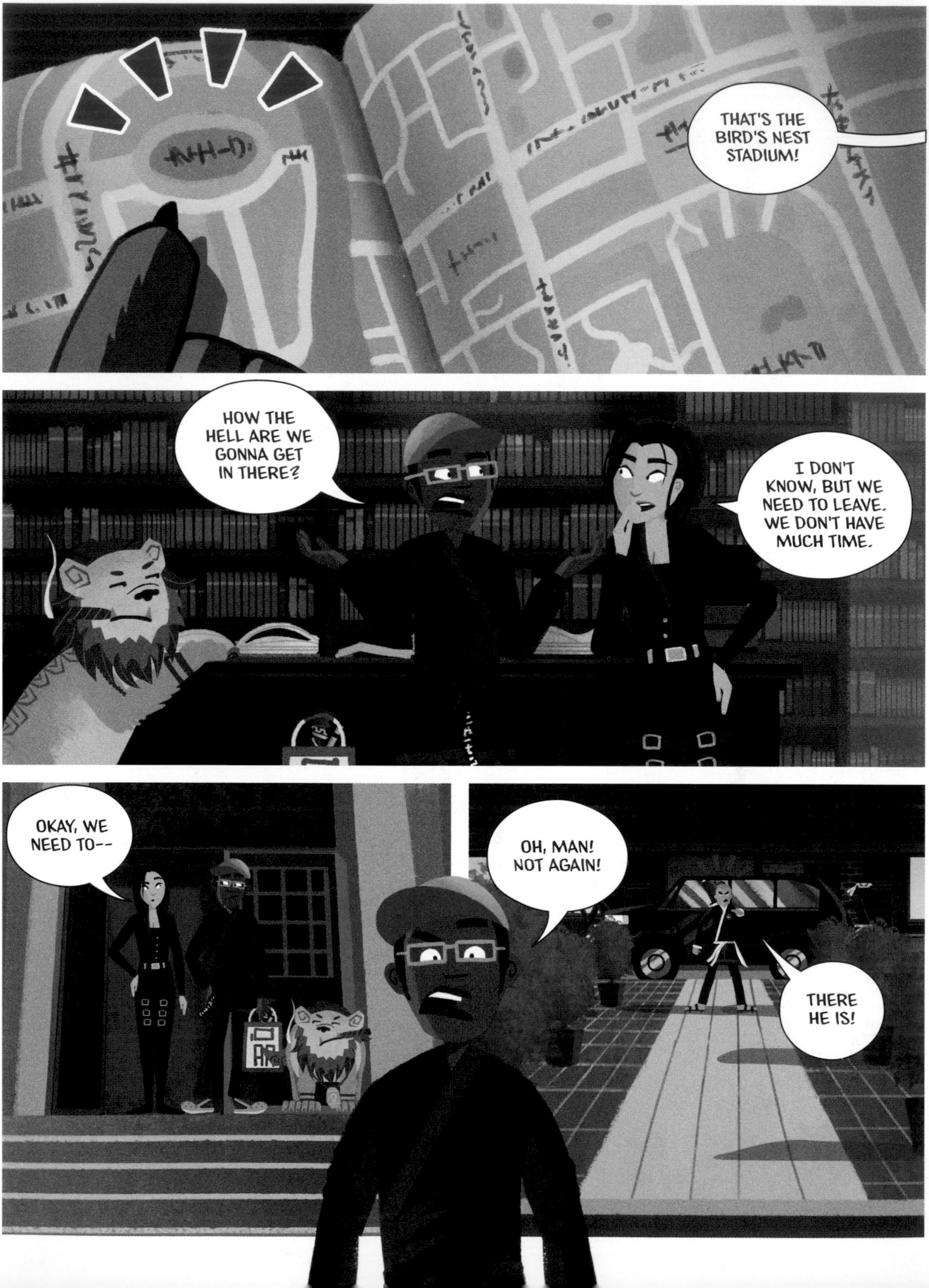
THAT'S THE BIRD'S NEST STADIUM!
HOW THE HELL ARE WE GONNA GET IN THERE?
I DON'T KNOW, BUT WE NEED TO LEAVE. WE DON'T HAVE MUCH TIME.
OKAY, WE NEED TO--
OH, MAN! NOT AGAIN!
THERE HE IS!

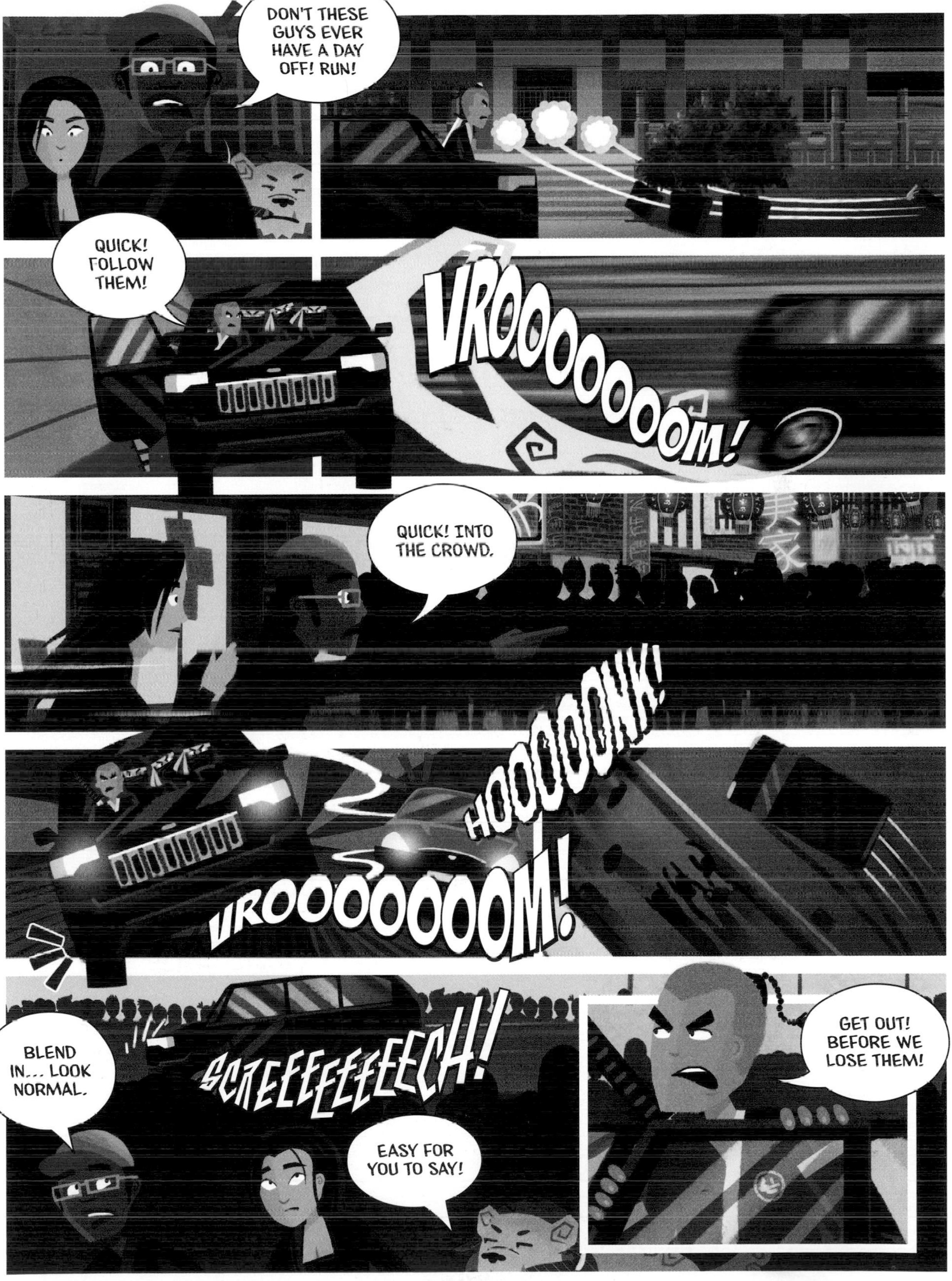
DON'T THESE GUYS EVER HAVE A DAY OFF! RUN!
QUICK! FOLLOW THEM!
VROOOOOOOOM!
QUICK! INTO THE CROWD.
HOOOOOONK!
VROOOOOOOOM!
BLEND IN... LOOK NORMAL.
SCREEEEEEEEECH!
EASY FOR YOU TO SAY!
GET OUT! BEFORE WE LOSE THEM!

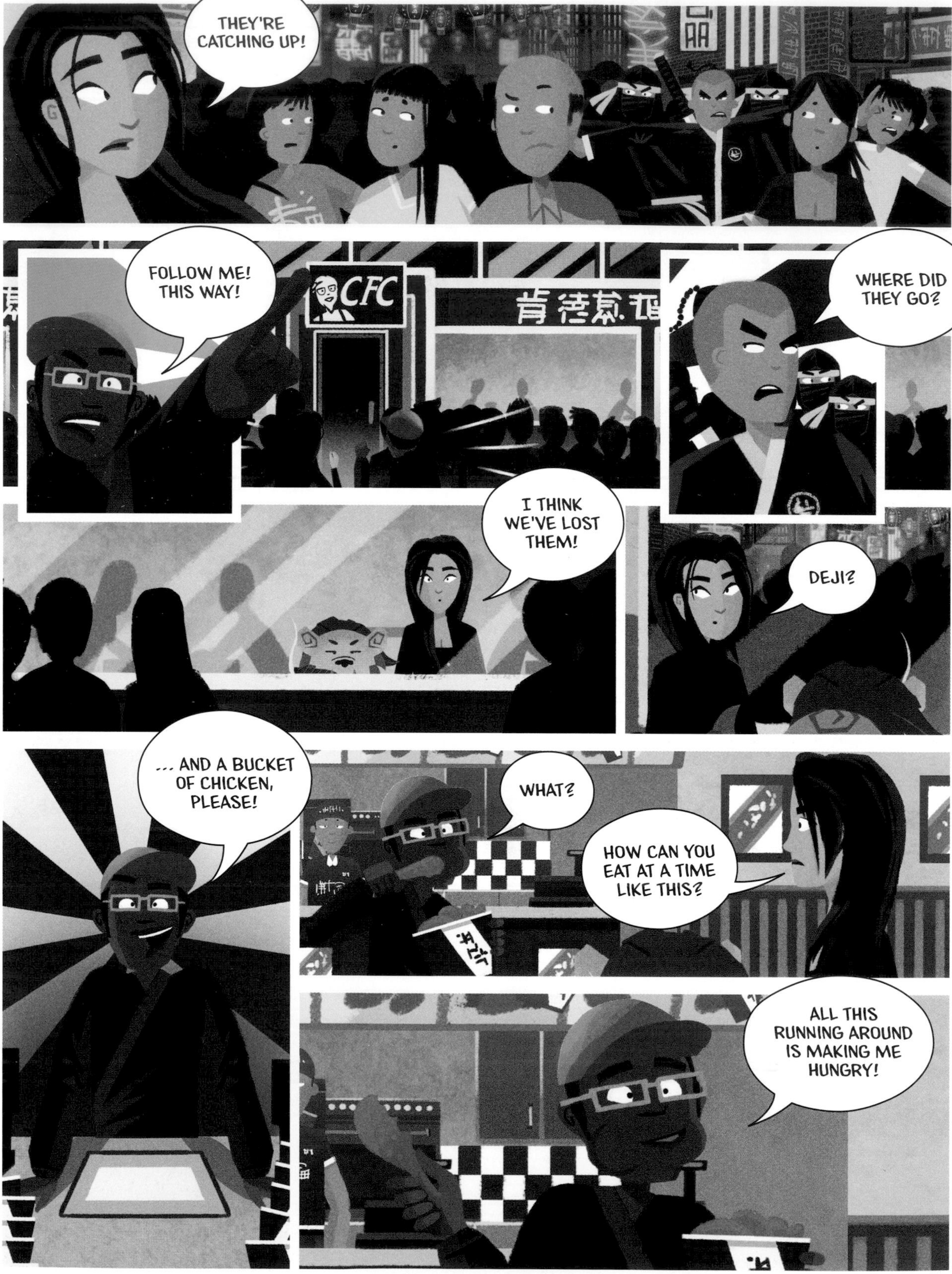
THEY'RE CATCHING UP!
FOLLOW ME! THIS WAY!
CFC
WHERE DID THEY GO?
I THINK WE'VE LOST THEM!
DEJI?
... AND A BUCKET OF CHICKEN, PLEASE!
WHAT?
HOW CAN YOU EAT AT A TIME LIKE THIS?
ALL THIS RUNNING AROUND IS MAKING ME HUNGRY!

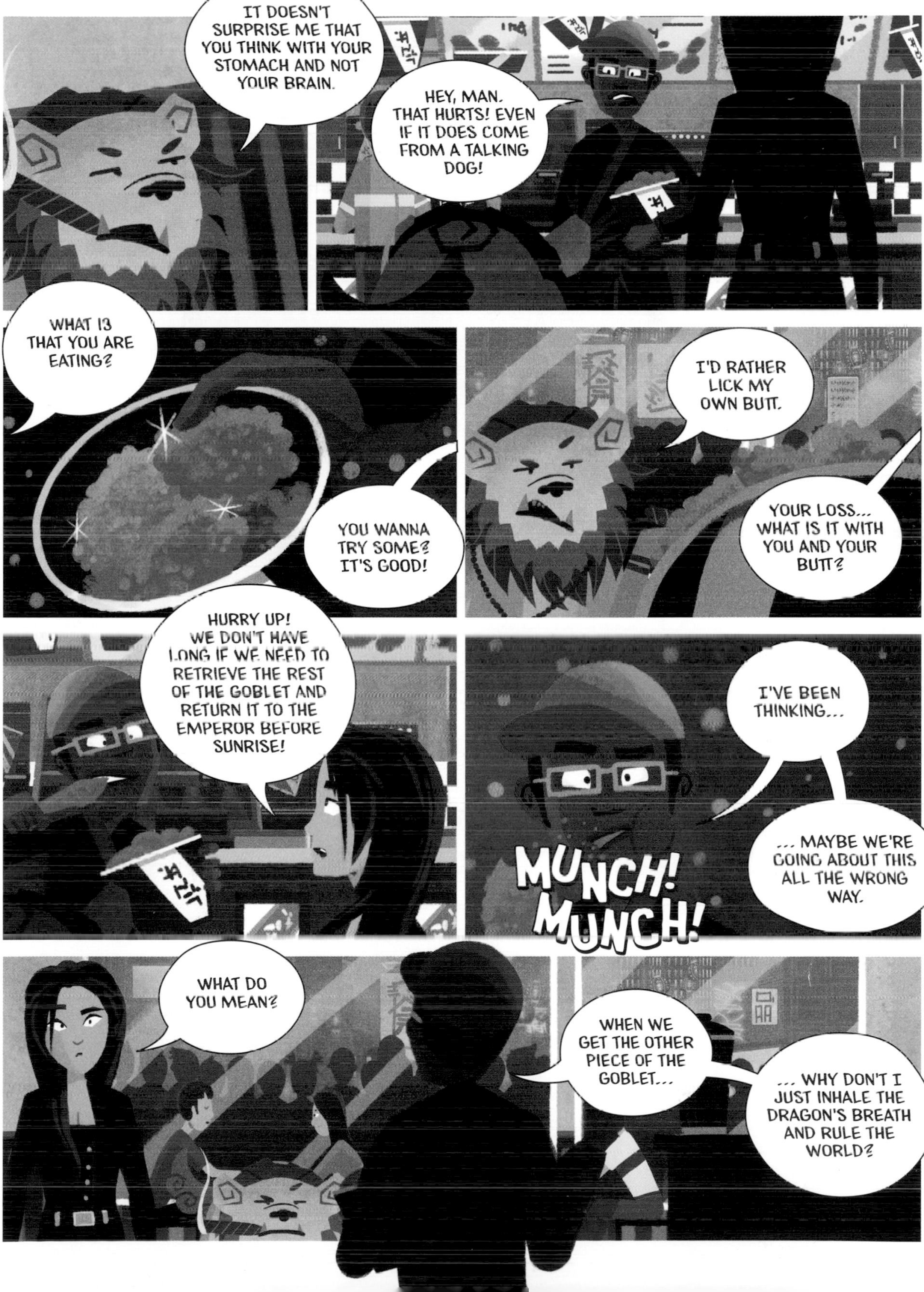
IT DOESN'T SURPRISE ME THAT YOU THINK WITH YOUR STOMACH AND NOT YOUR BRAIN.
HEY, MAN. THAT HURTS! EVEN IF IT DOES COME FROM A TALKING DOG!
WHAT IS THAT YOU ARE EATING?
YOU WANNA TRY SOME? IT'S GOOD!
I'D RATHER LICK MY OWN BUTT.
YOUR LOSS... WHAT IS IT WITH YOU AND YOUR BUTT?
HURRY UP! WE DON'T HAVE LONG IF WE NEED TO RETRIEVE THE REST OF THE GOBLET AND RETURN IT TO THE EMPEROR BEFORE SUNRISE!
I'VE BEEN THINKING...
... MAYBE WE'RE GOING ABOUT THIS ALL THE WRONG WAY.
MUNCH! MUNCH!
WHAT DO YOU MEAN?
WHEN WE GET THE OTHER PIECE OF THE GOBLET...
... WHY DON'T I JUST INHALE THE DRAGON'S BREATH AND RULE THE WORLD?

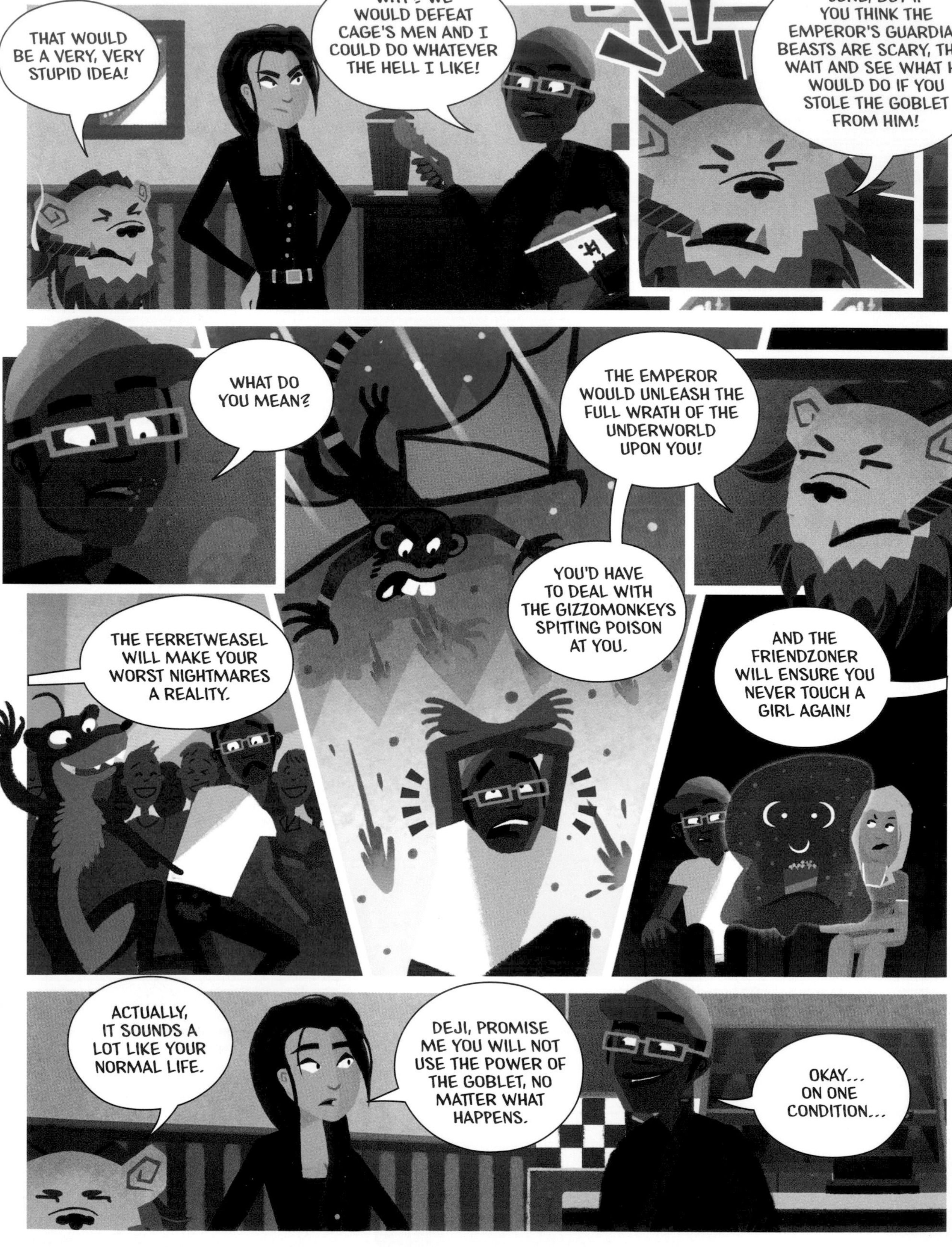
THAT WOULD BE A VERY, VERY STUPID IDEA!
WHY? WE WOULD DEFEAT CAGE'S MEN AND I COULD DO WHATEVER THE HELL I LIKE!
SURE, BUT IF YOU THINK THE EMPEROR'S GUARDIAN BEASTS ARE SCARY, THE WAIT AND SEE WHAT HE WOULD DO IF YOU STOLE THE GOBLET FROM HIM!
WHAT DO YOU MEAN?
THE EMPEROR WOULD UNLEASH THE FULL WRATH OF THE UNDERWORLD UPON YOU!
THE FERRETWEASEL WILL MAKE YOUR WORST NIGHTMARES A REALITY.
YOU'D HAVE TO DEAL WITH THE GIZZOMONKEYS SPITTING POISON AT YOU.
AND THE FRIENDZONER WILL ENSURE YOU NEVER TOUCH A GIRL AGAIN!
ACTUALLY, IT SOUNDS A LOT LIKE YOUR NORMAL LIFE.
DEJI, PROMISE ME YOU WILL NOT USE THE POWER OF THE GOBLET, NO MATTER WHAT HAPPENS.
OKAY... ON ONE CONDITION...

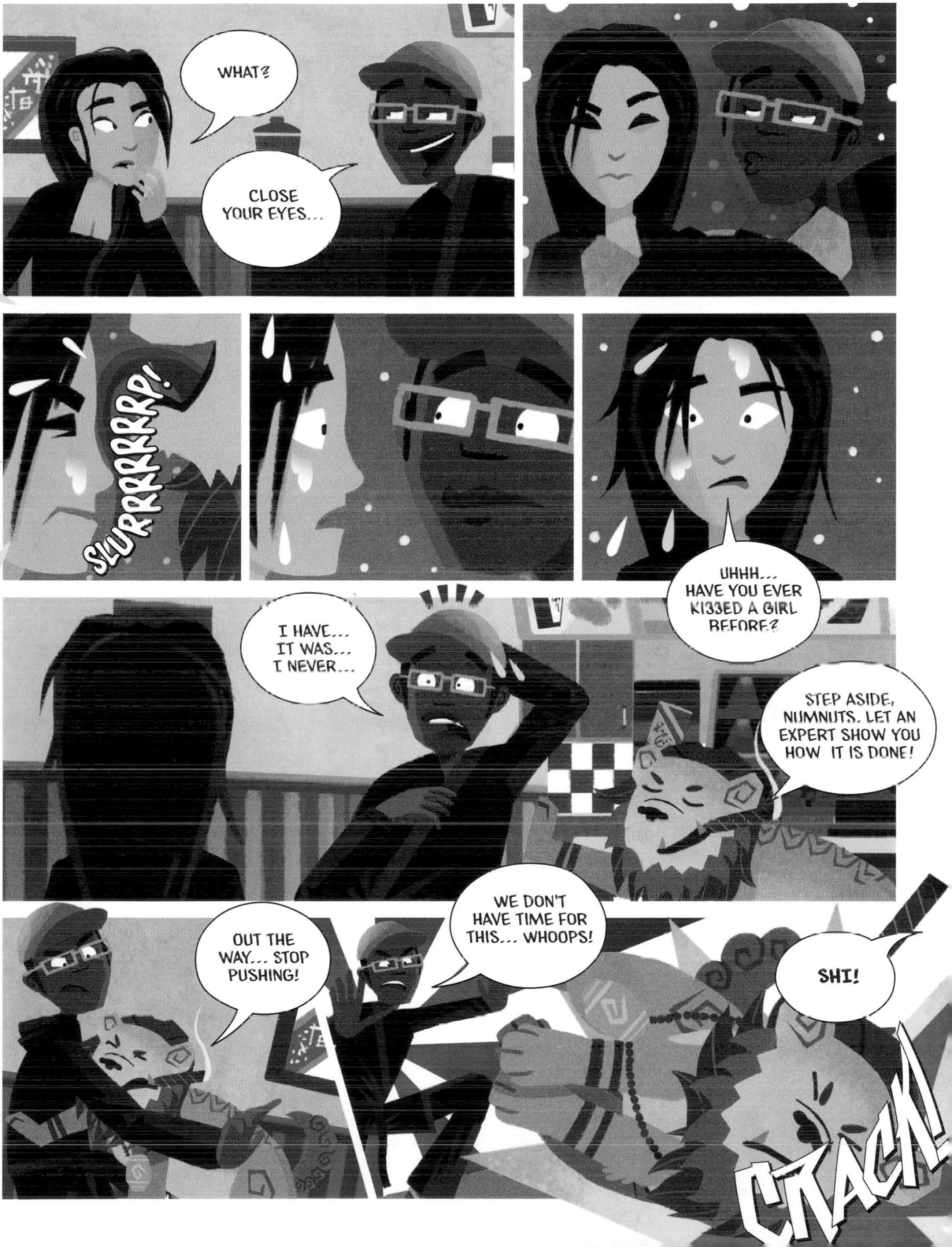
WHAT?
CLOSE YOUR EYES...
SLURRRRRRRP!
UHHH... HAVE YOU EVER KISSED A GIRL BEFORE?
I HAVE... IT WAS... I NEVER...
STEP ASIDE, NUMNUTS. LET AN EXPERT SHOW YOU HOW IT IS DONE!
OUT THE WAY... STOP PUSHING!
WE DON'T HAVE TIME FOR THIS... WHOOPS!
SHI!
CRACK!

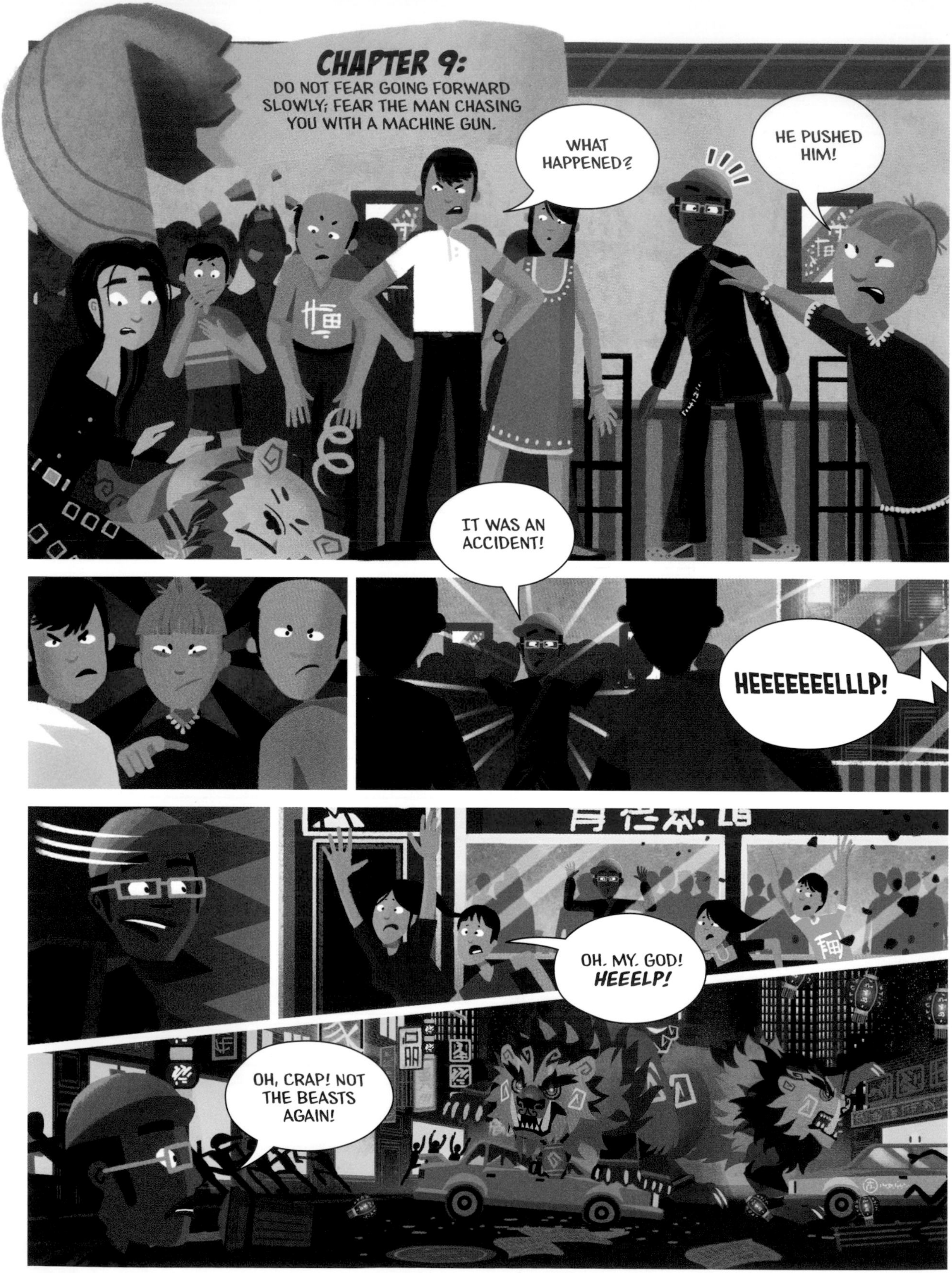
CHAPTER 9:
DO NOT FEAR GOING FORWARD SLOWLY; FEAR THE MAN CHASING YOU WITH A MACHINE GUN.
WHAT HAPPENED?
HE PUSHED HIM!
IT WAS AN ACCIDENT!
HEEEEEEELLLLP!
OH. MY. GOD! HEEELP!
OH, CRAP! NOT THE BEASTS AGAIN!

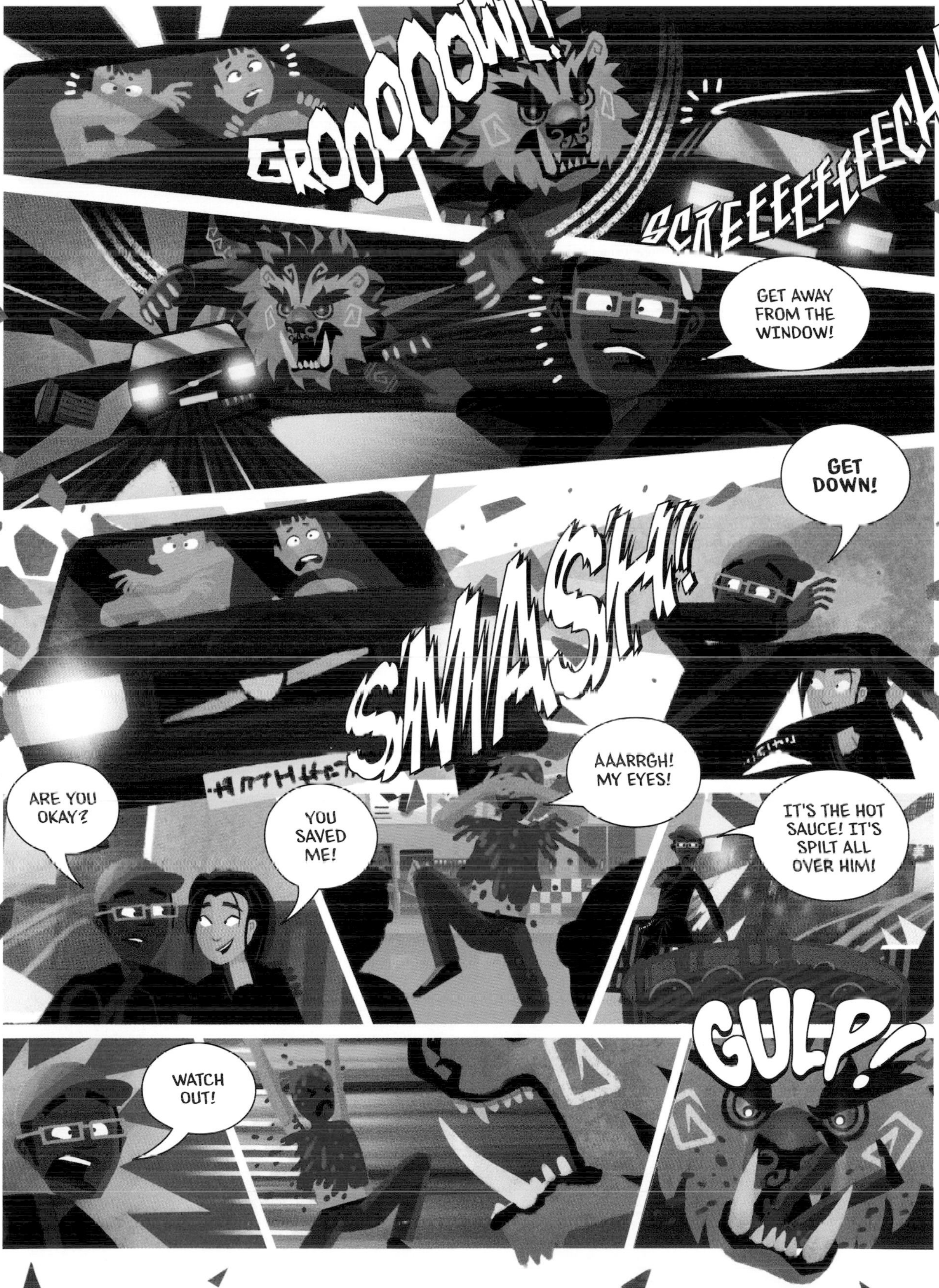
GROOOOOOWL!
SCREEEEEEEECH!
GET AWAY FROM THE WINDOW!
GET DOWN!
SMASH!
ARE YOU OKAY?
YOU SAVED ME!
AAARRGH! MY EYES!
IT'S THE HOT SAUCE! IT'S SPILT ALL OVER HIM!
WATCH OUT!
GULP!

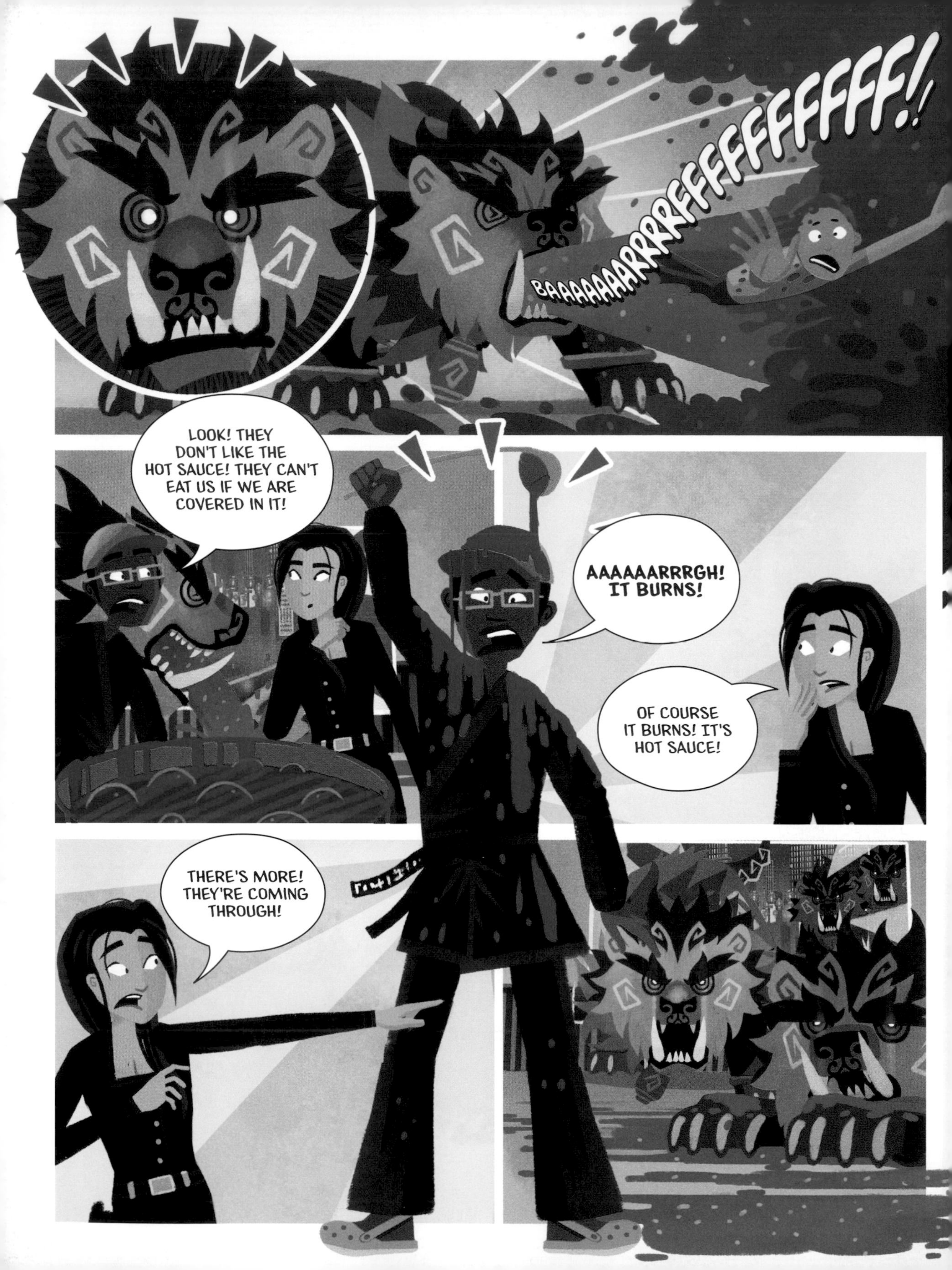

BAAAAAAARRRRFFFFFFFFFFF!
LOOK! THEY DON'T LIKE THE HOT SAUCE! THEY CAN'T EAT US IF WE ARE COVERED IN IT!
AAAAAARRRGH! IT BURNS!
OF COURSE IT BURNS! IT'S HOT SAUCE!
THERE'S MORE! THEY'RE COMING THROUGH!

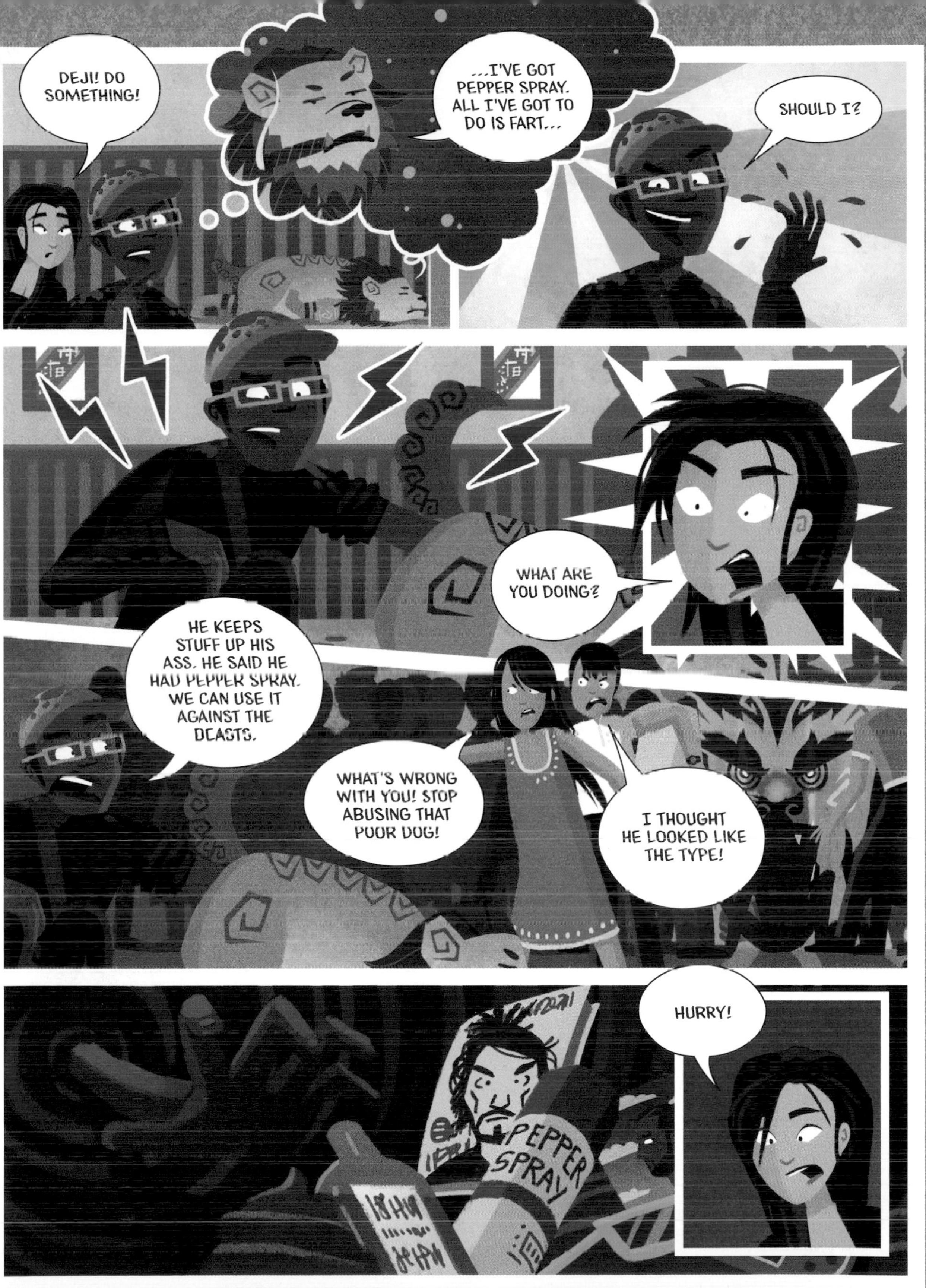
DEJI! DO SOMETHING!
...I'VE GOT PEPPER SPRAY. ALL I'VE GOT TO DO IS FART...
SHOULD I?
WHAT ARE YOU DOING?
HE KEEPS STUFF UP HIS ASS. HE SAID HE HAD PEPPER SPRAY. WE CAN USE IT AGAINST THE BEASTS.
WHAT'S WRONG WITH YOU! STOP ABUSING THAT POOR DOG!
I THOUGHT HE LOOKED LIKE THE TYPE!
HURRY!
PEPPER SPRAY

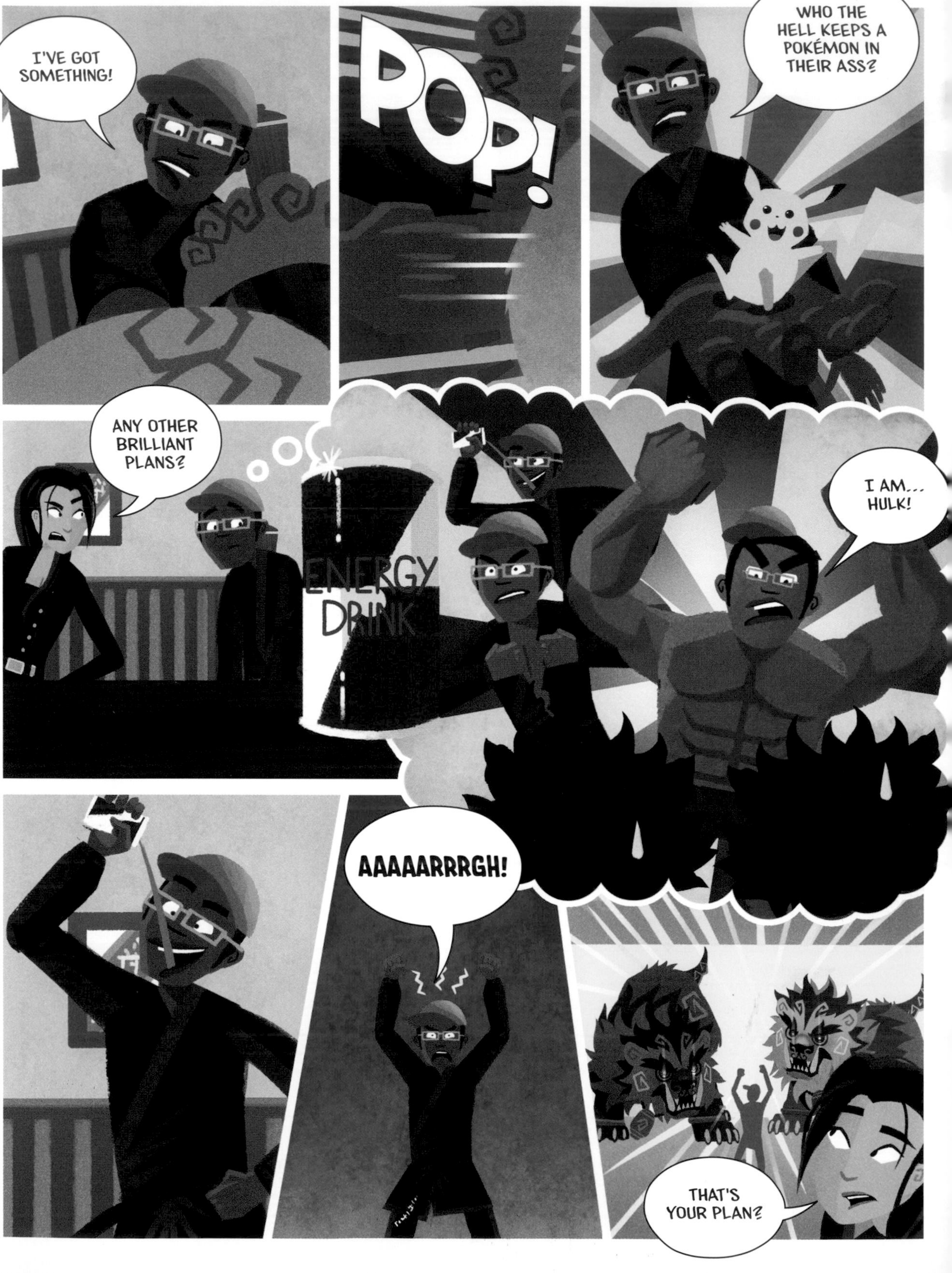
I'VE GOT SOMETHING!
POP!
WHO THE HELL KEEPS A POKÉMON IN THEIR ASS?
ANY OTHER BRILLIANT PLANS?
ENERGY DRINK
I AM... HULK!
AAAAARRRGH!
THAT'S YOUR PLAN?

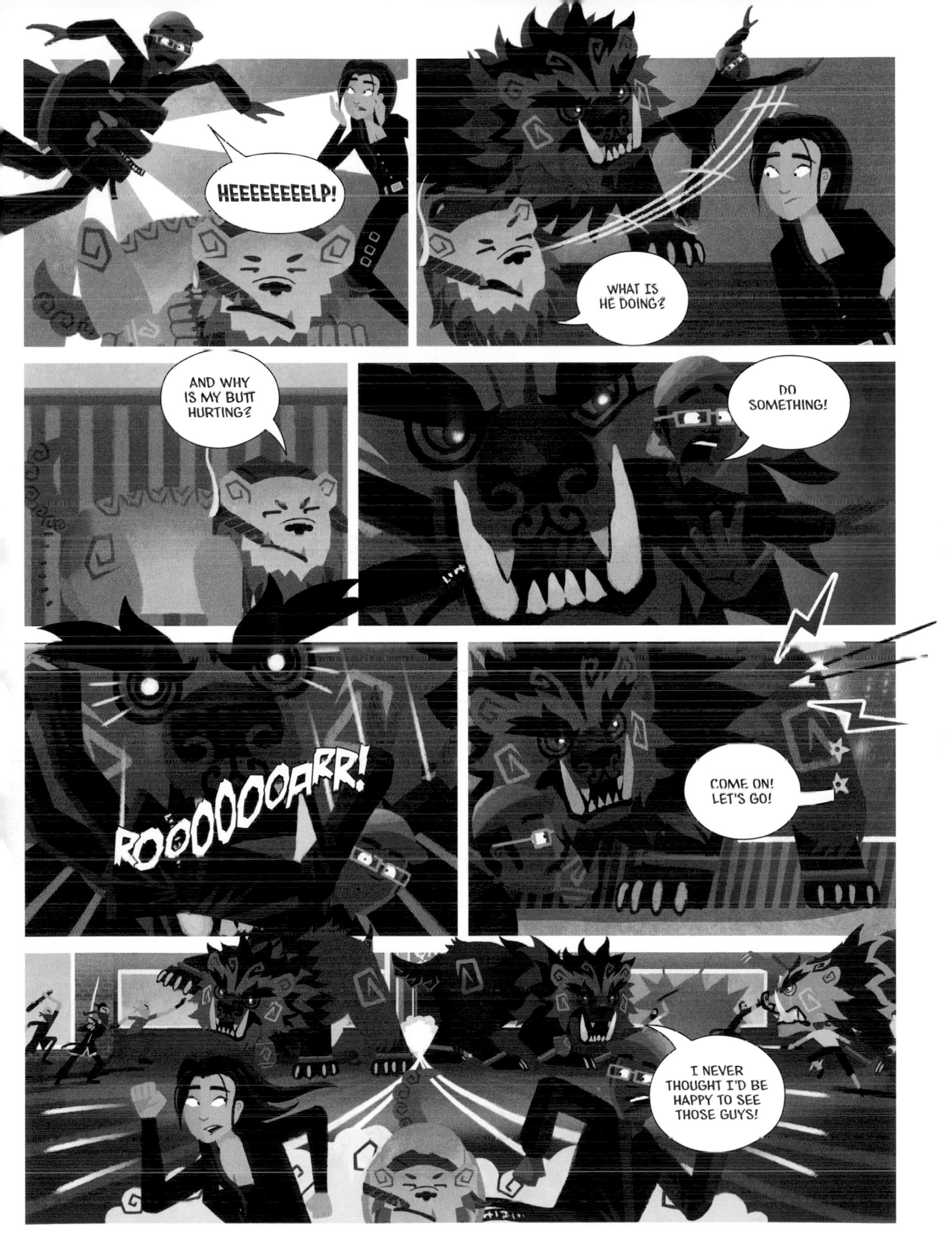
HEEEEEEEELP!
WHAT IS HE DOING?
AND WHY IS MY BUTT HURTING?
DO SOMETHING!
ROOOOOOOARR!
COME ON! LET'S GO!
I NEVER THOUGHT I'D BE HAPPY TO SEE THOSE GUYS!

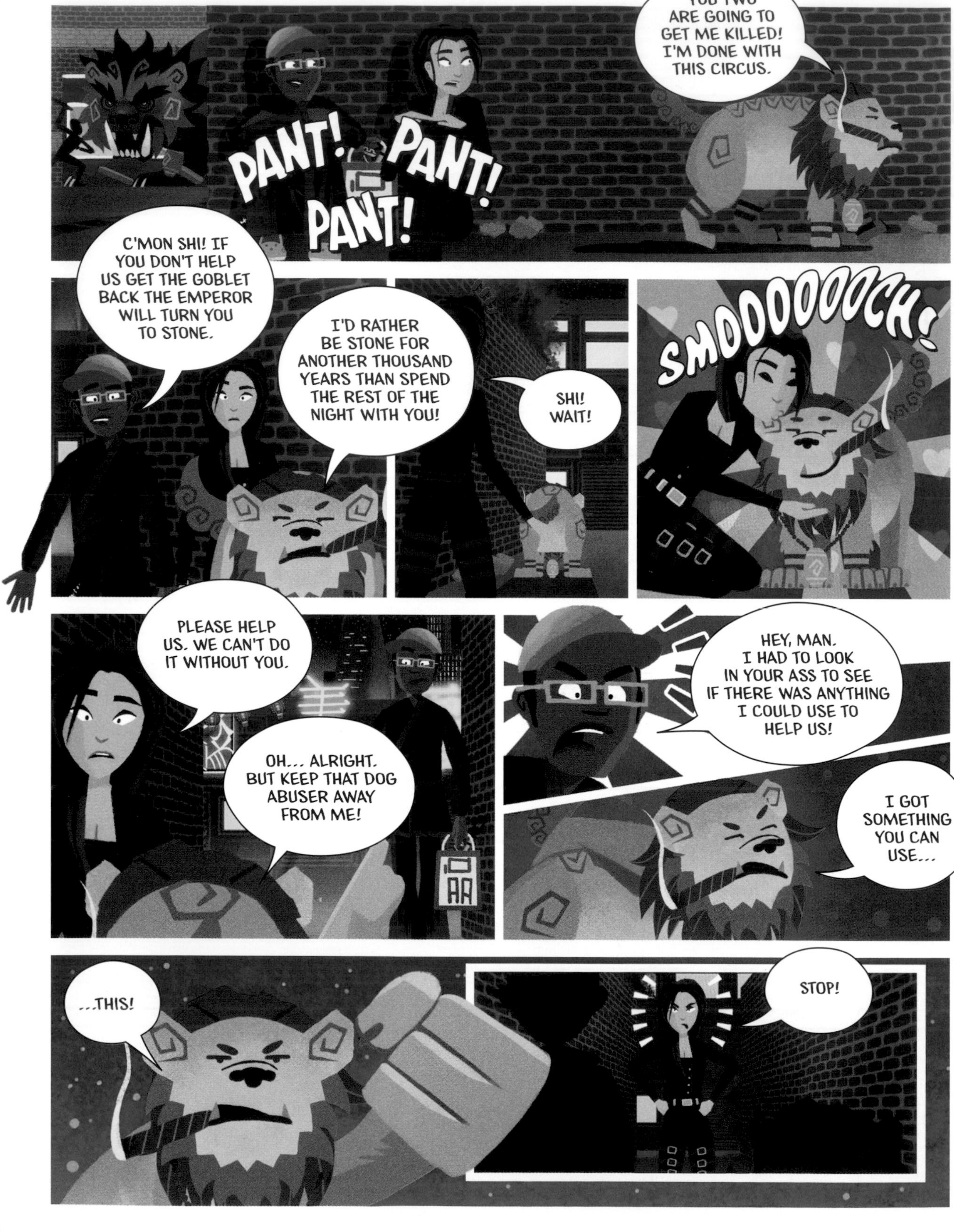
YOU TWO ARE GOING TO GET ME KILLED! I'M DONE WITH THIS CIRCUS.
PANT! PANT! PANT!
C'MON SHI! IF YOU DON'T HELP US GET THE GOBLET BACK THE EMPEROR WILL TURN YOU TO STONE.
I'D RATHER BE STONE FOR ANOTHER THOUSAND YEARS THAN SPEND THE REST OF THE NIGHT WITH YOU!
SHI! WAIT!
SMOOOOOOCH!
PLEASE HELP US. WE CAN'T DO IT WITHOUT YOU.
OH... ALRIGHT. BUT KEEP THAT DOG ABUSER AWAY FROM ME!
HEY, MAN. I HAD TO LOOK IN YOUR ASS TO SEE IF THERE WAS ANYTHING I COULD USE TO HELP US!
I GOT SOMETHING YOU CAN USE...
...THIS!
STOP!

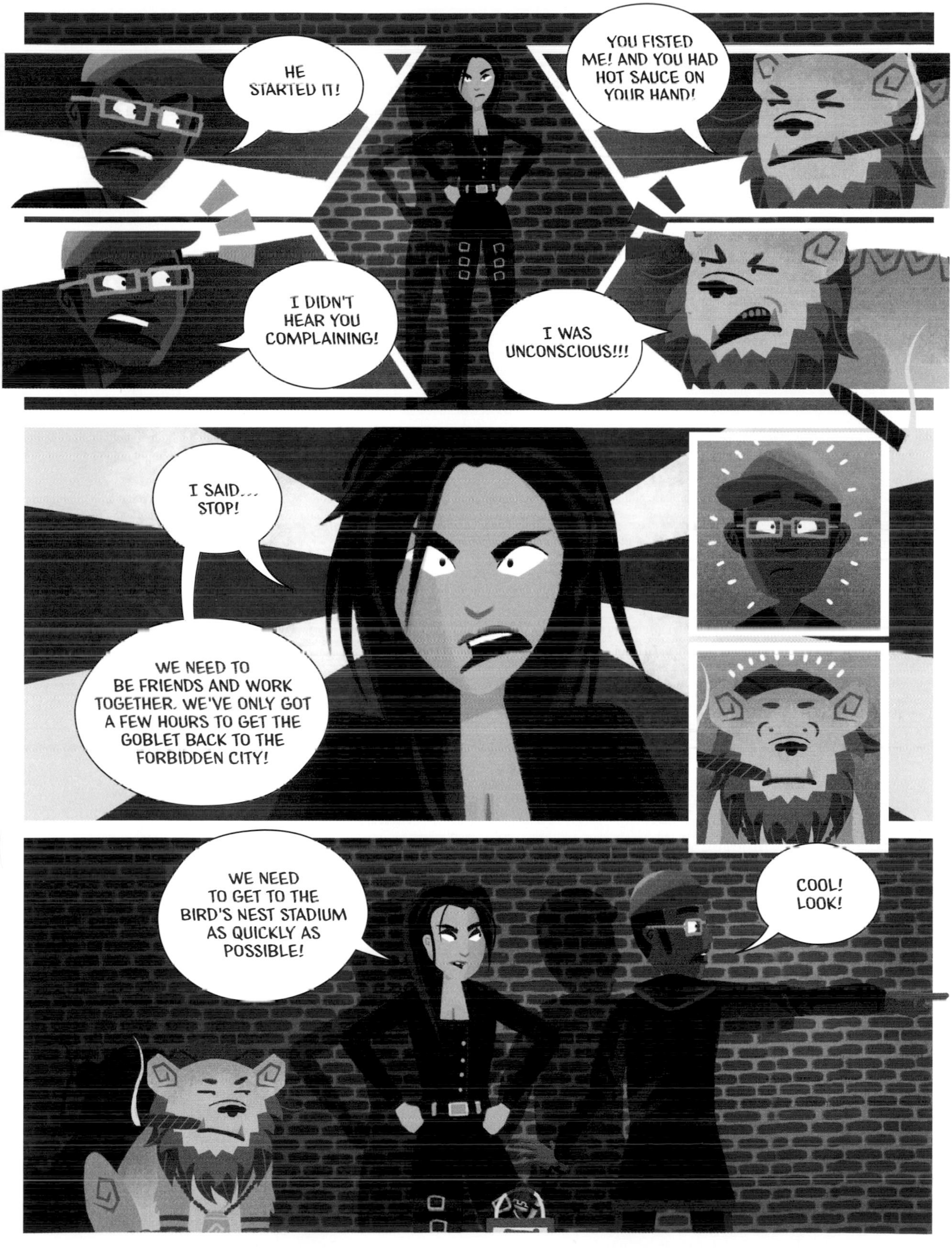
HE STARTED IT!
YOU FISTED ME! AND YOU HAD HOT SAUCE ON YOUR HAND!
I DIDN'T HEAR YOU COMPLAINING!
I WAS UNCONSCIOUS!!!
I SAID... STOP!
WE NEED TO BE FRIENDS AND WORK TOGETHER. WE'VE ONLY GOT A FEW HOURS TO GET THE GOBLET BACK TO THE FORBIDDEN CITY!
WE NEED TO GET TO THE BIRD'S NEST STADIUM AS QUICKLY AS POSSIBLE!
COOL! LOOK!

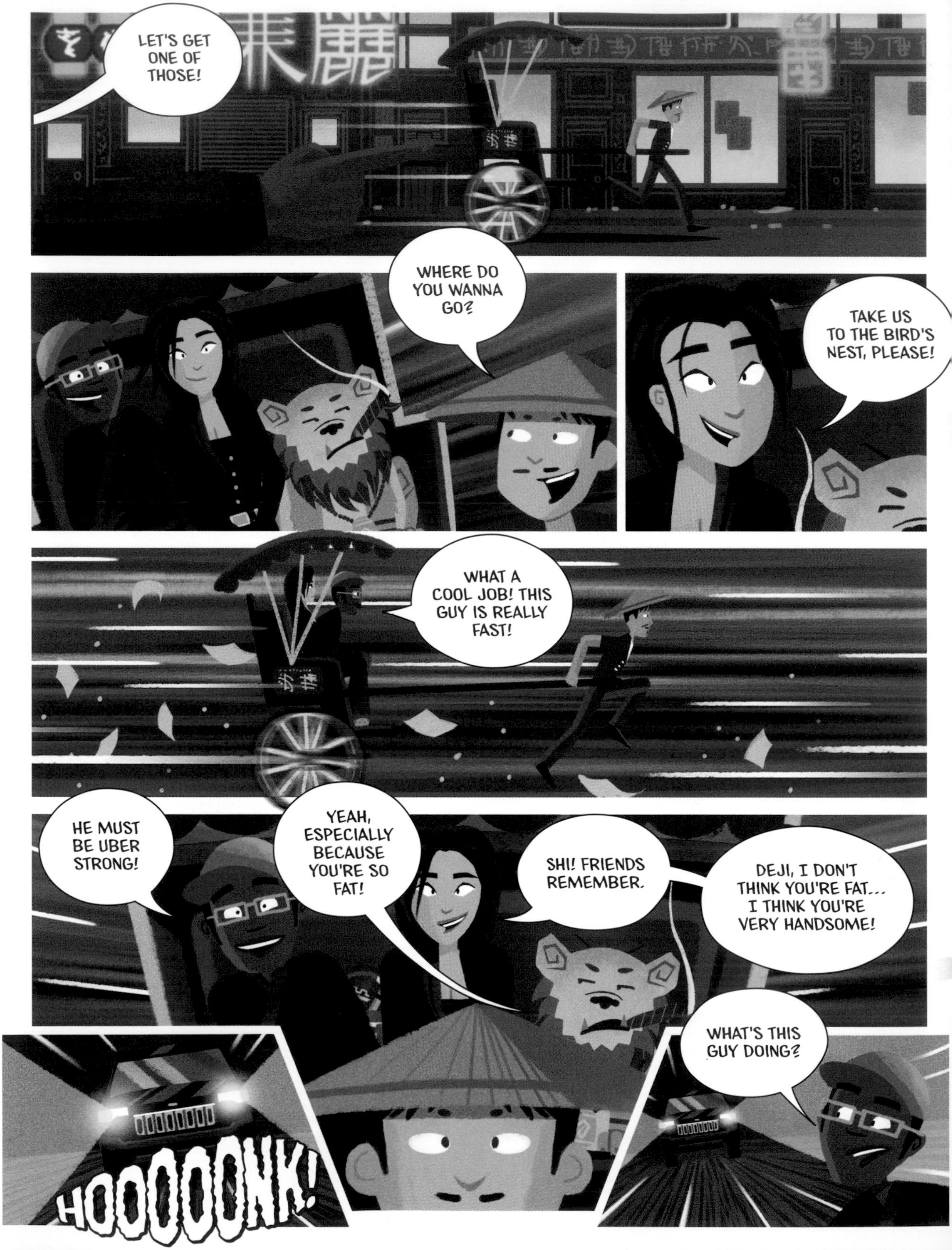
LET'S GET ONE OF THOSE!
WHERE DO YOU WANNA GO?
TAKE US TO THE BIRD'S NEST, PLEASE!
WHAT A COOL JOB! THIS GUY IS REALLY FAST!
HE MUST BE UBER STRONG!
YEAH, ESPECIALLY BECAUSE YOU'RE SO FAT!
SHI! FRIENDS REMEMBER.
DEJI, I DON'T THINK YOU'RE FAT... I THINK YOU'RE VERY HANDSOME!
HOOOOOONK!
WHAT'S THIS GUY DOING?

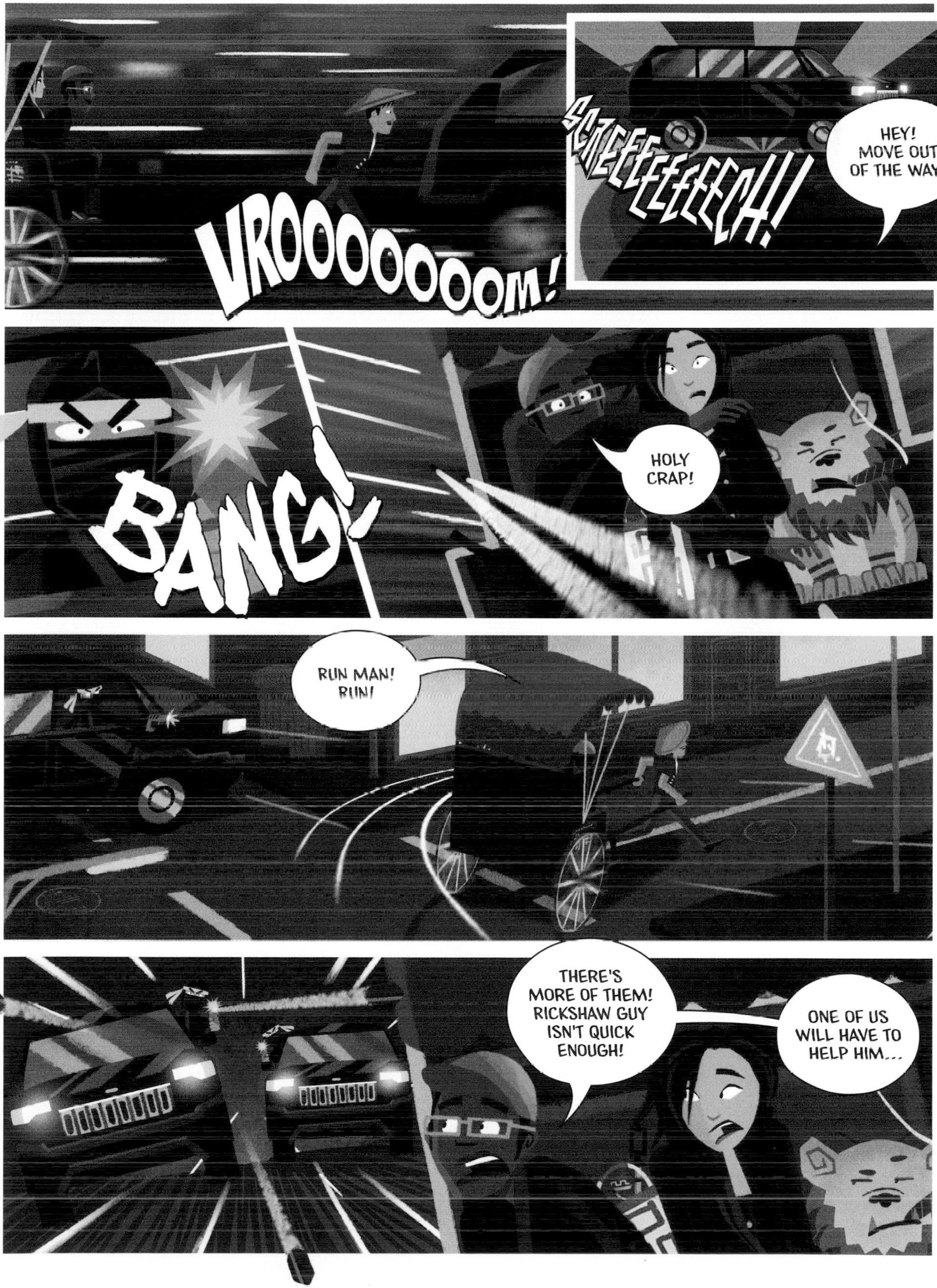
VROOOOOOOM!
SCREEEEEEEECH!
HEY! MOVE OUT OF THE WAY!
BANG!
HOLY CRAP!
RUN MAN! RUN!
THERE'S MORE OF THEM! RICKSHAW GUY ISN'T QUICK ENOUGH!
ONE OF US WILL HAVE TO HELP HIM...

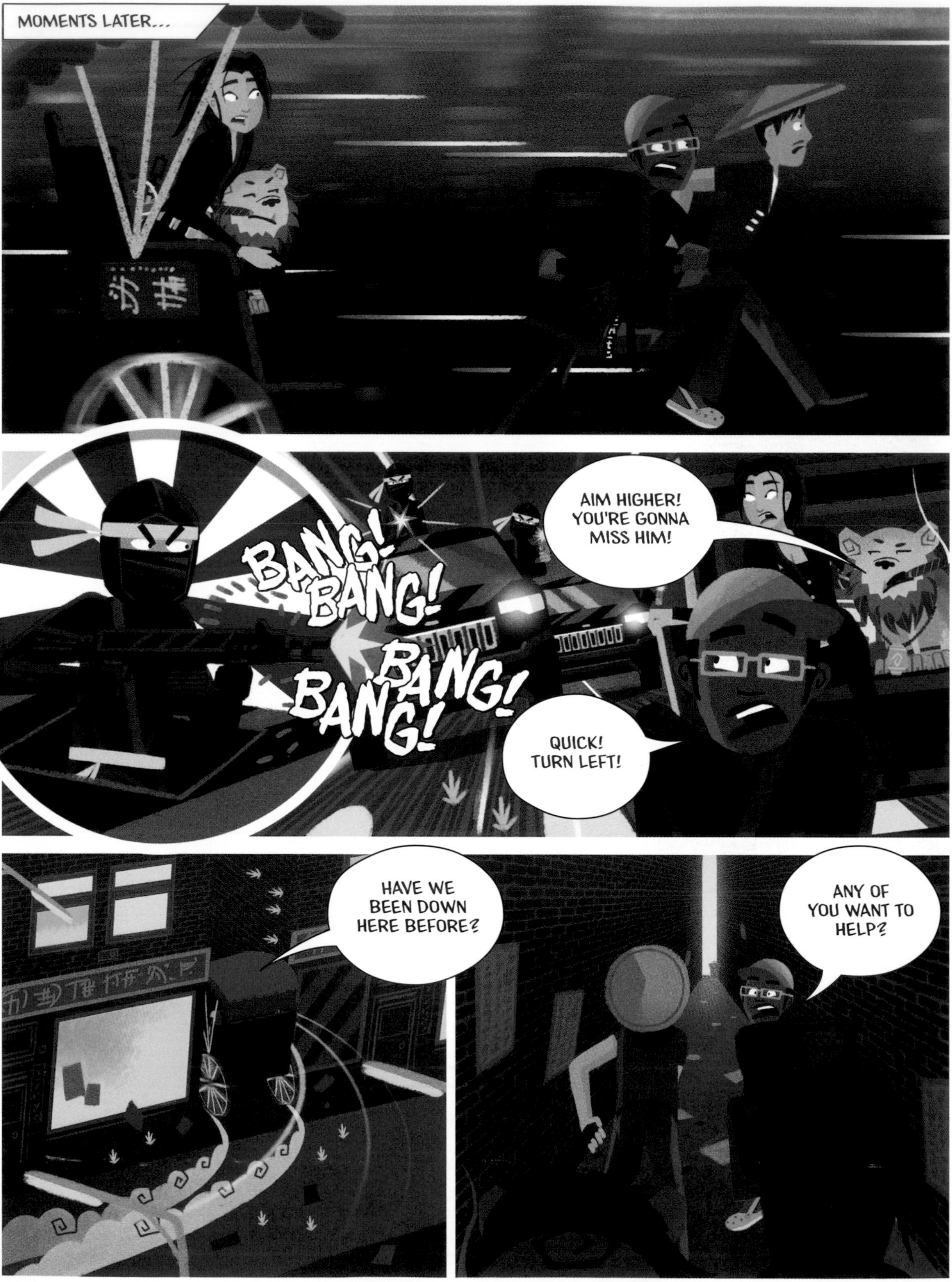
MOMENTS LATER...
BANG! BANG!
BANG! BANG!
AIM HIGHER! YOU'RE GONNA MISS HIM!
QUICK! TURN LEFT!
HAVE WE BEEN DOWN HERE BEFORE?
ANY OF YOU WANT TO HELP?

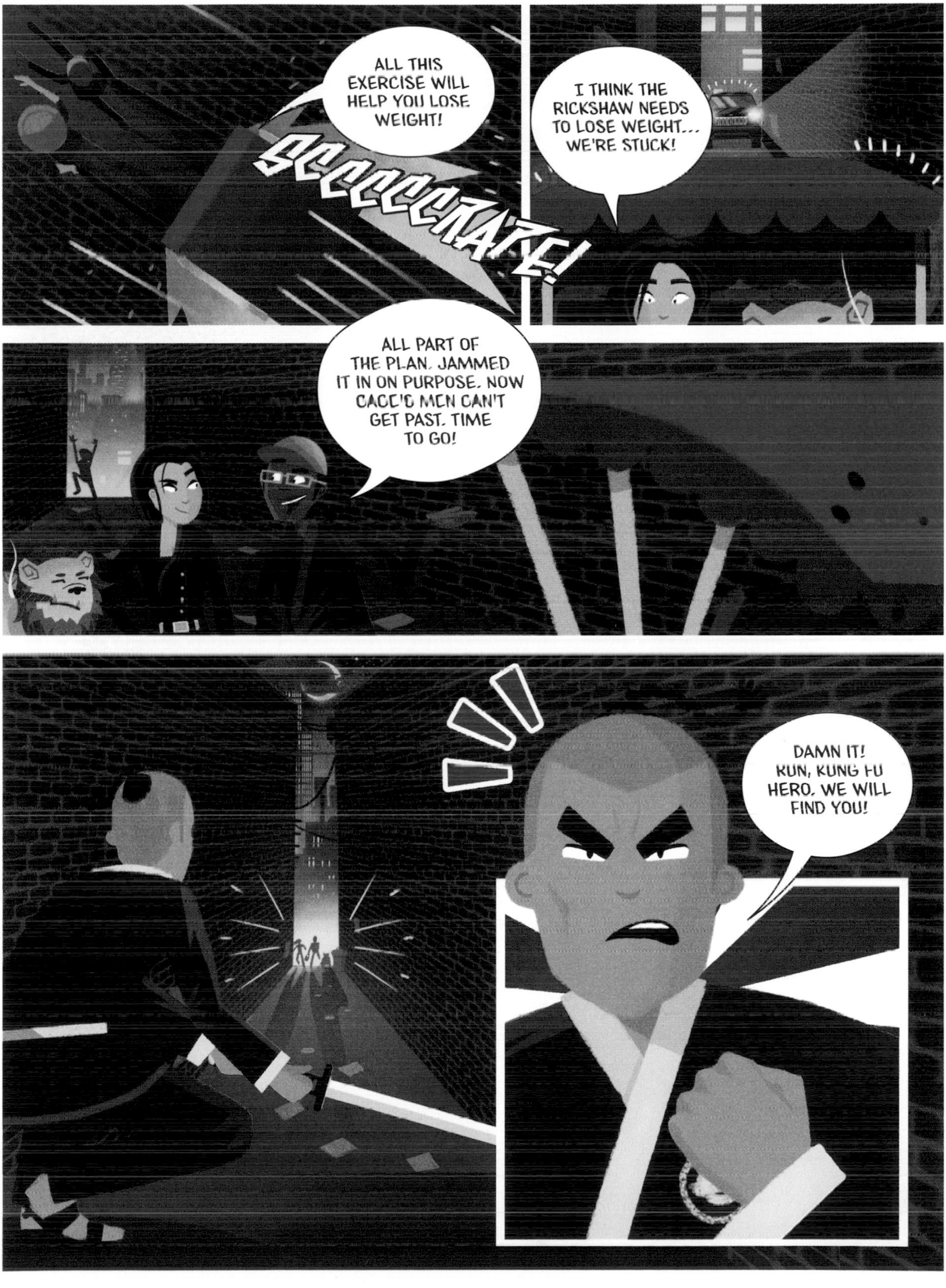
ALL THIS EXERCISE WILL HELP YOU LOSE WEIGHT!
SCCCCCRAPE!
I THINK THE RICKSHAW NEEDS TO LOSE WEIGHT... WE'RE STUCK!
ALL PART OF THE PLAN. JAMMED IT IN ON PURPOSE. NOW CAGE'S MEN CAN'T GET PAST. TIME TO GO!
DAMN IT! RUN, KUNG FU HERO. WE WILL FIND YOU!

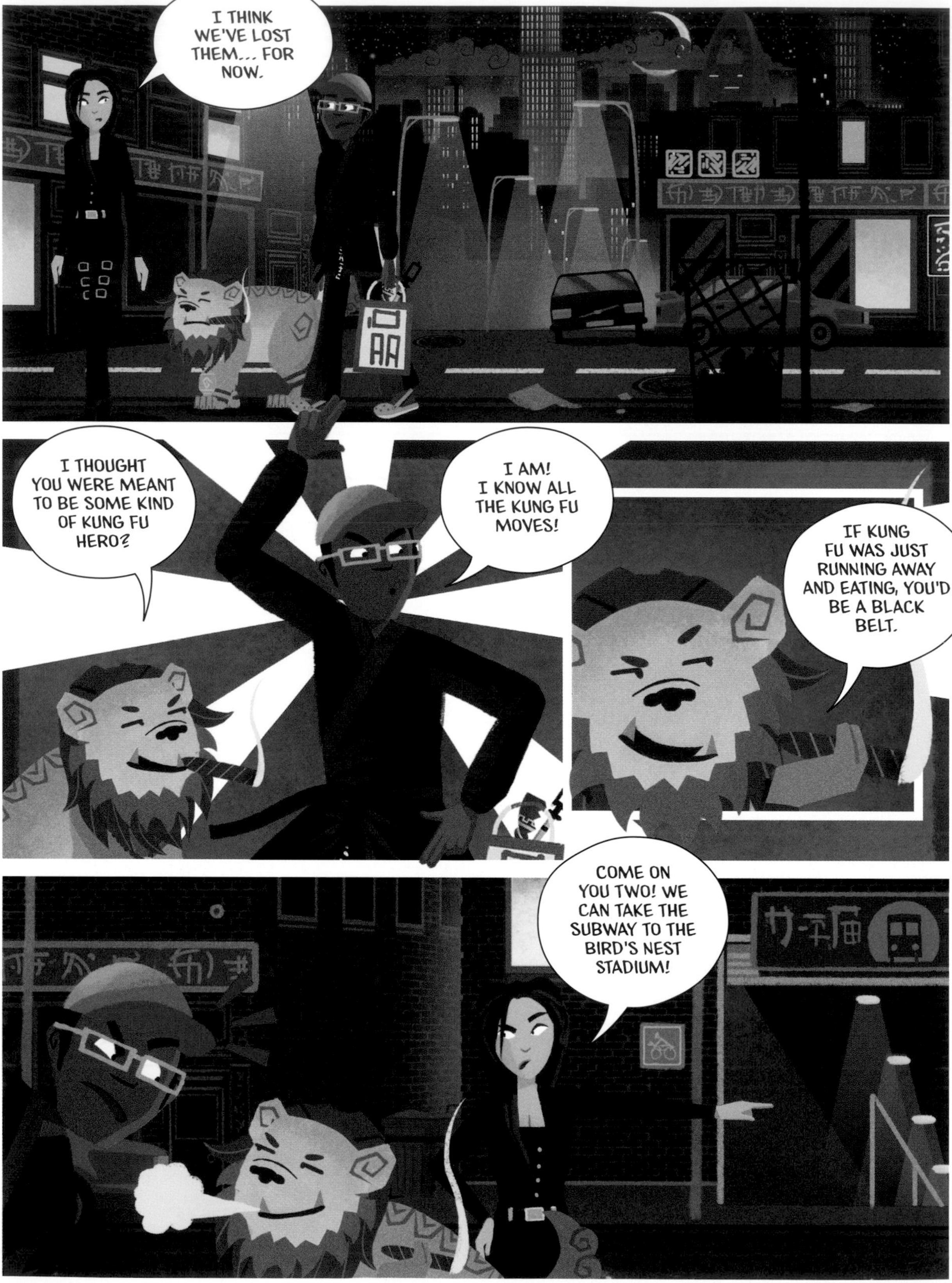

I THINK WE'VE LOST THEM... FOR NOW.
I THOUGHT YOU WERE MEANT TO BE SOME KIND OF KUNG FU HERO?
I AM! I KNOW ALL THE KUNG FU MOVES!
IF KUNG FU WAS JUST RUNNING AWAY AND EATING, YOU'D BE A BLACK BELT.
COME ON YOU TWO! WE CAN TAKE THE SUBWAY TO THE BIRD'S NEST STADIUM!

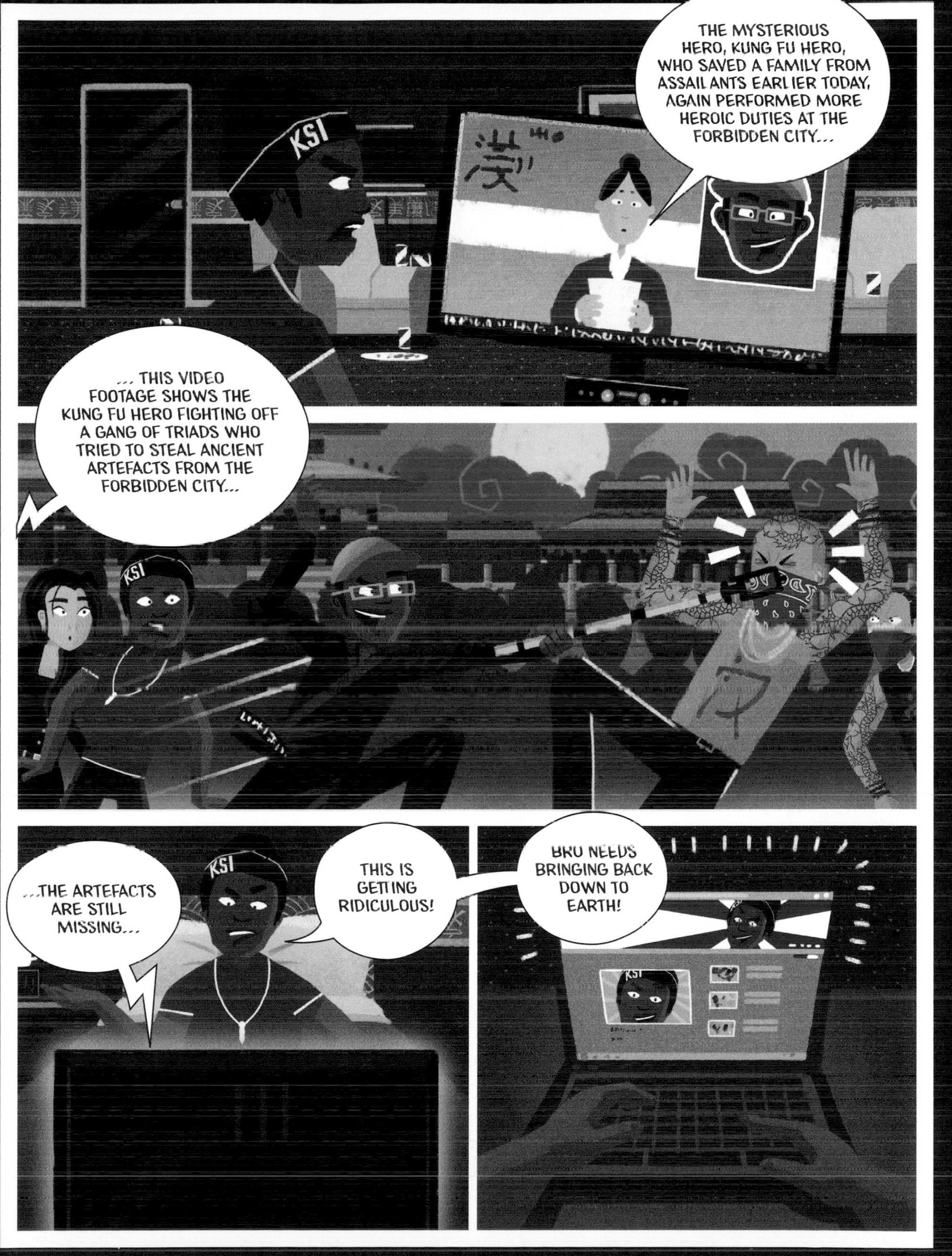
THE MYSTERIOUS HERO, KUNG FU HERO, WHO SAVED A FAMILY FROM ASSAILANTS EARLIER TODAY, AGAIN PERFORMED MORE HEROIC DUTIES AT THE FORBIDDEN CITY...
KSI
... THIS VIDEO FOOTAGE SHOWS THE KUNG FU HERO FIGHTING OFF A GANG OF TRIADS WHO TRIED TO STEAL ANCIENT ARTEFACTS FROM THE FORBIDDEN CITY...
KSI
...THE ARTEFACTS ARE STILL MISSING...
KSI
THIS IS GETTING RIDICULOUS!
BRO NEEDS BRINGING BACK DOWN TO EARTH!
KSI

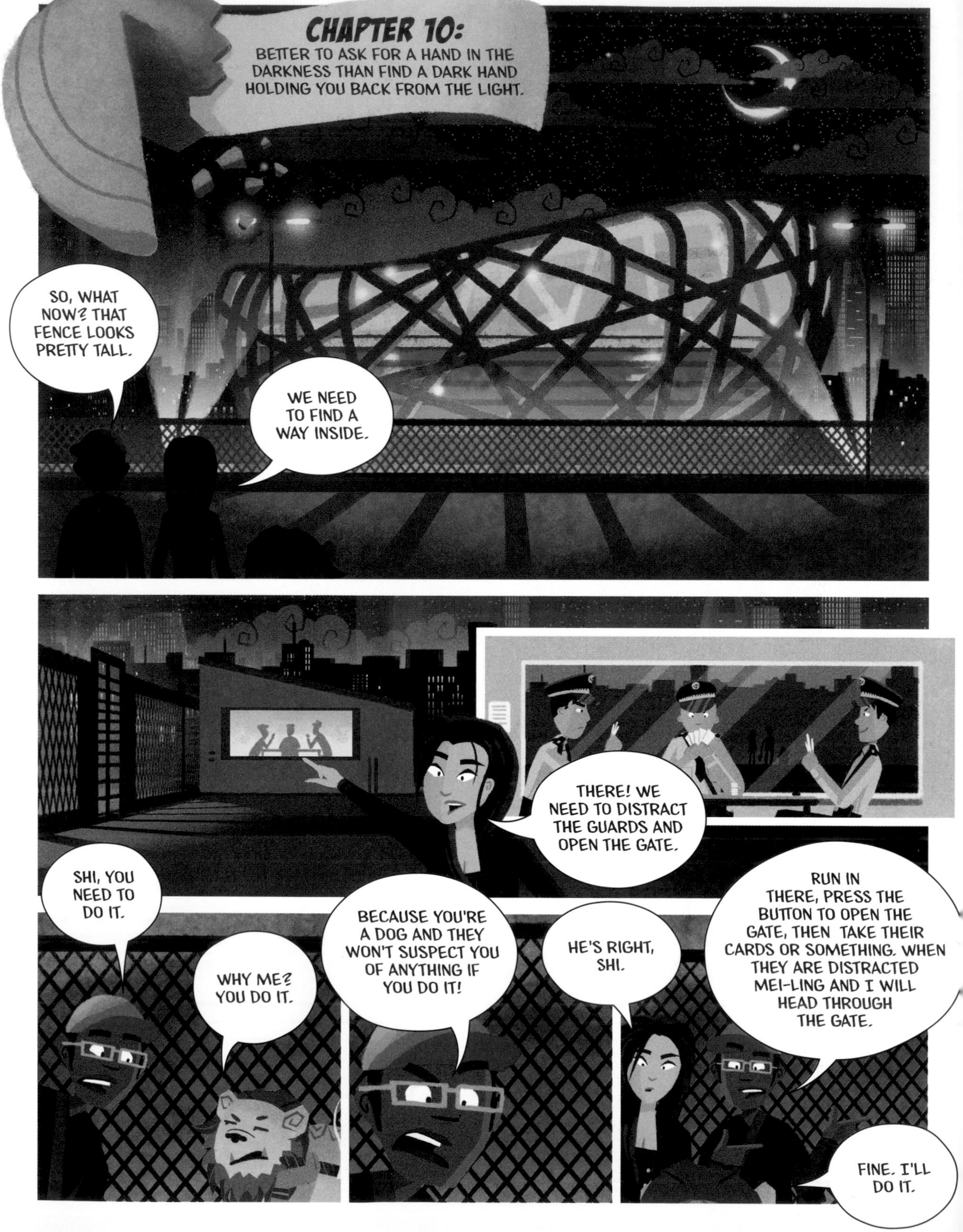
CHAPTER 10:
BETTER TO ASK FOR A HAND IN THE DARKNESS THAN FIND A DARK HAND HOLDING YOU BACK FROM THE LIGHT.
SO, WHAT NOW? THAT FENCE LOOKS PRETTY TALL.
WE NEED TO FIND A WAY INSIDE.
THERE! WE NEED TO DISTRACT THE GUARDS AND OPEN THE GATE.
SHI, YOU NEED TO DO IT.
WHY ME? YOU DO IT.
BECAUSE YOU'RE A DOG AND THEY WON'T SUSPECT YOU OF ANYTHING IF YOU DO IT!
HE'S RIGHT, SHI.
RUN IN THERE, PRESS THE BUTTON TO OPEN THE GATE, THEN TAKE THEIR CARDS OR SOMETHING. WHEN THEY ARE DISTRACTED MEI-LING AND I WILL HEAD THROUGH THE GATE.
FINE. I'LL DO IT.

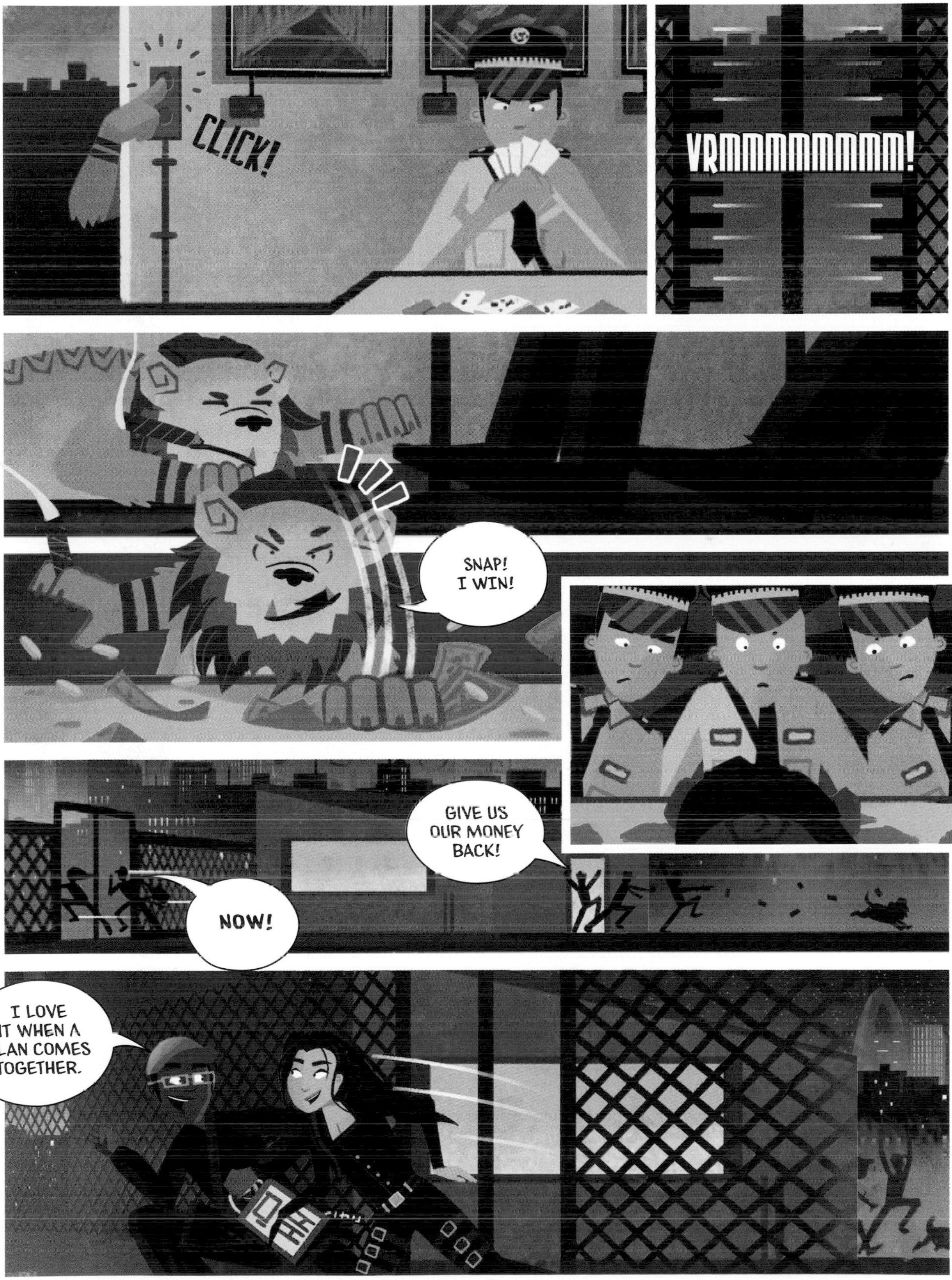
CLICK!
VRMMMMMMMM!
SNAP! I WIN!
GIVE US OUR MONEY BACK!
NOW!
I LOVE IT WHEN A PLAN COMES TOGETHER.

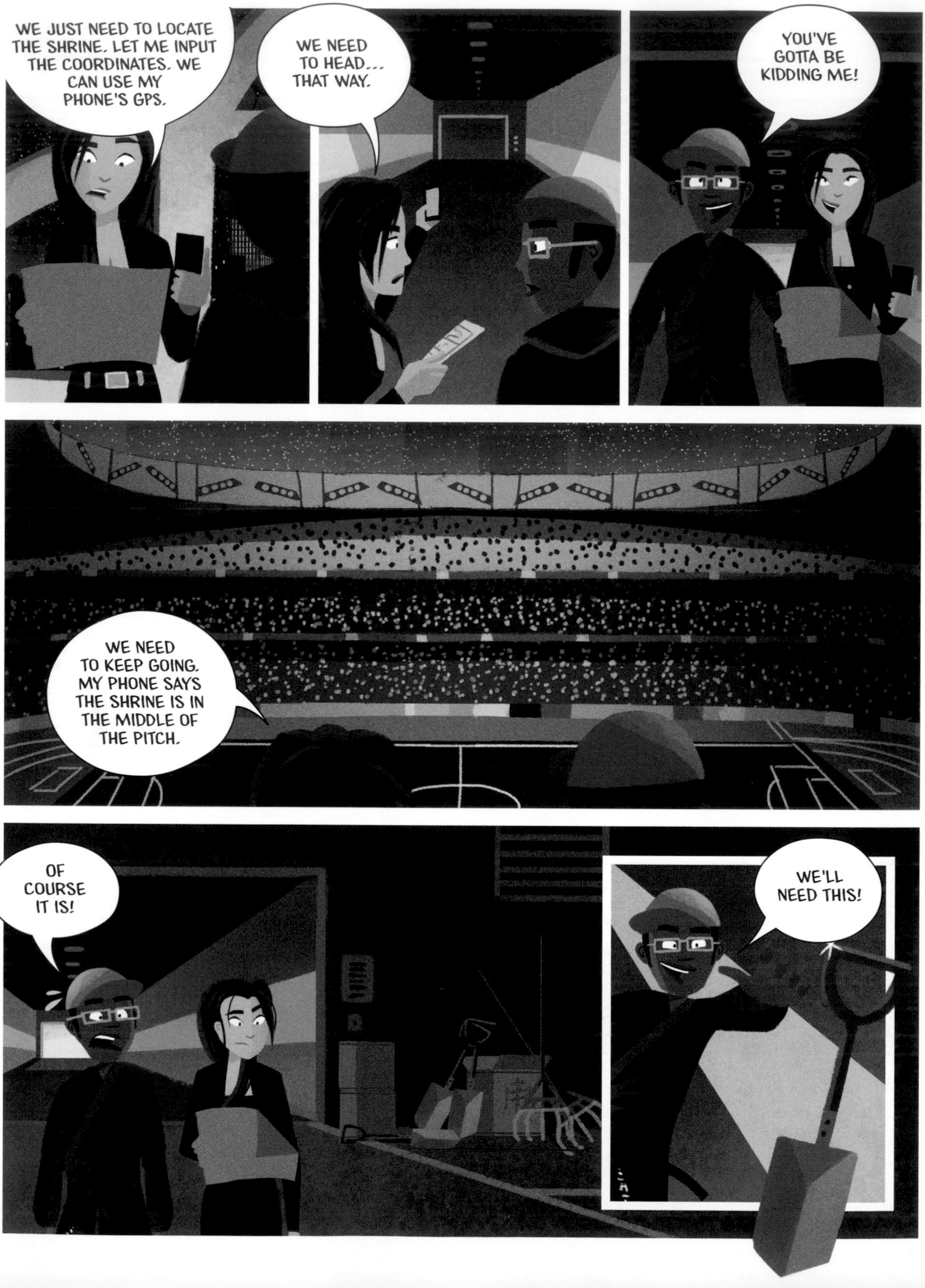
WE JUST NEED TO LOCATE THE SHRINE. LET ME INPUT THE COORDINATES. WE CAN USE MY PHONE'S GPS.
WE NEED TO HEAD... THAT WAY.
YOU'VE GOTTA BE KIDDING ME!
WE NEED TO KEEP GOING. MY PHONE SAYS THE SHRINE IS IN THE MIDDLE OF THE PITCH.
OF COURSE IT IS!
WE'LL NEED THIS!

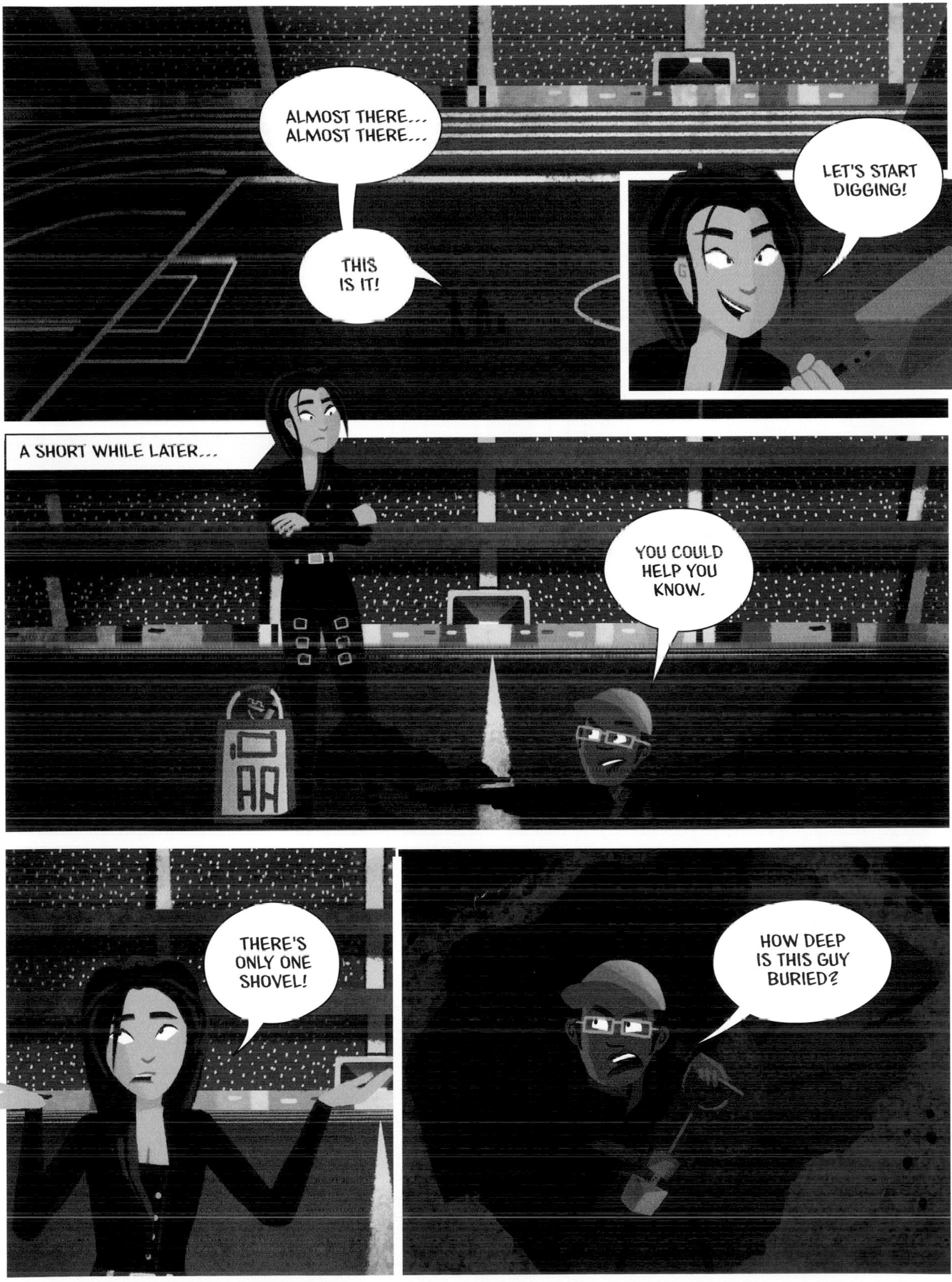
ALMOST THERE... ALMOST THERE...
THIS IS IT!
LET'S START DIGGING!
A SHORT WHILE LATER...
YOU COULD HELP YOU KNOW.
THERE'S ONLY ONE SHOVEL!
HOW DEEP IS THIS GUY BURIED?

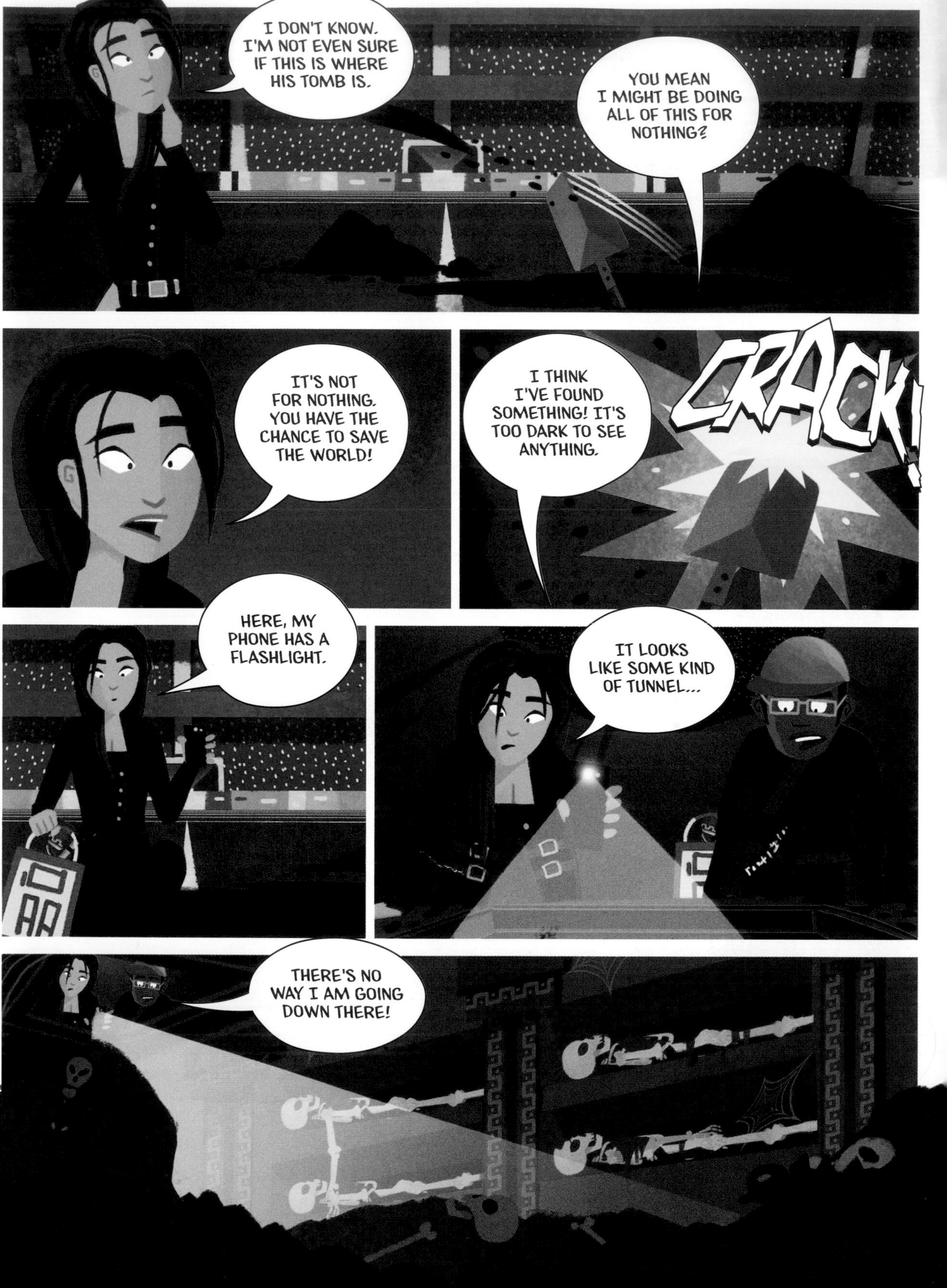
I DON'T KNOW. I'M NOT EVEN SURE IF THIS IS WHERE HIS TOMB IS.
YOU MEAN I MIGHT BE DOING ALL OF THIS FOR NOTHING?
IT'S NOT FOR NOTHING. YOU HAVE THE CHANCE TO SAVE THE WORLD!
CRACK!
I THINK I'VE FOUND SOMETHING! IT'S TOO DARK TO SEE ANYTHING.
HERE, MY PHONE HAS A FLASHLIGHT.
IT LOOKS LIKE SOME KIND OF TUNNEL...
THERE'S NO WAY I AM GOING DOWN THERE!

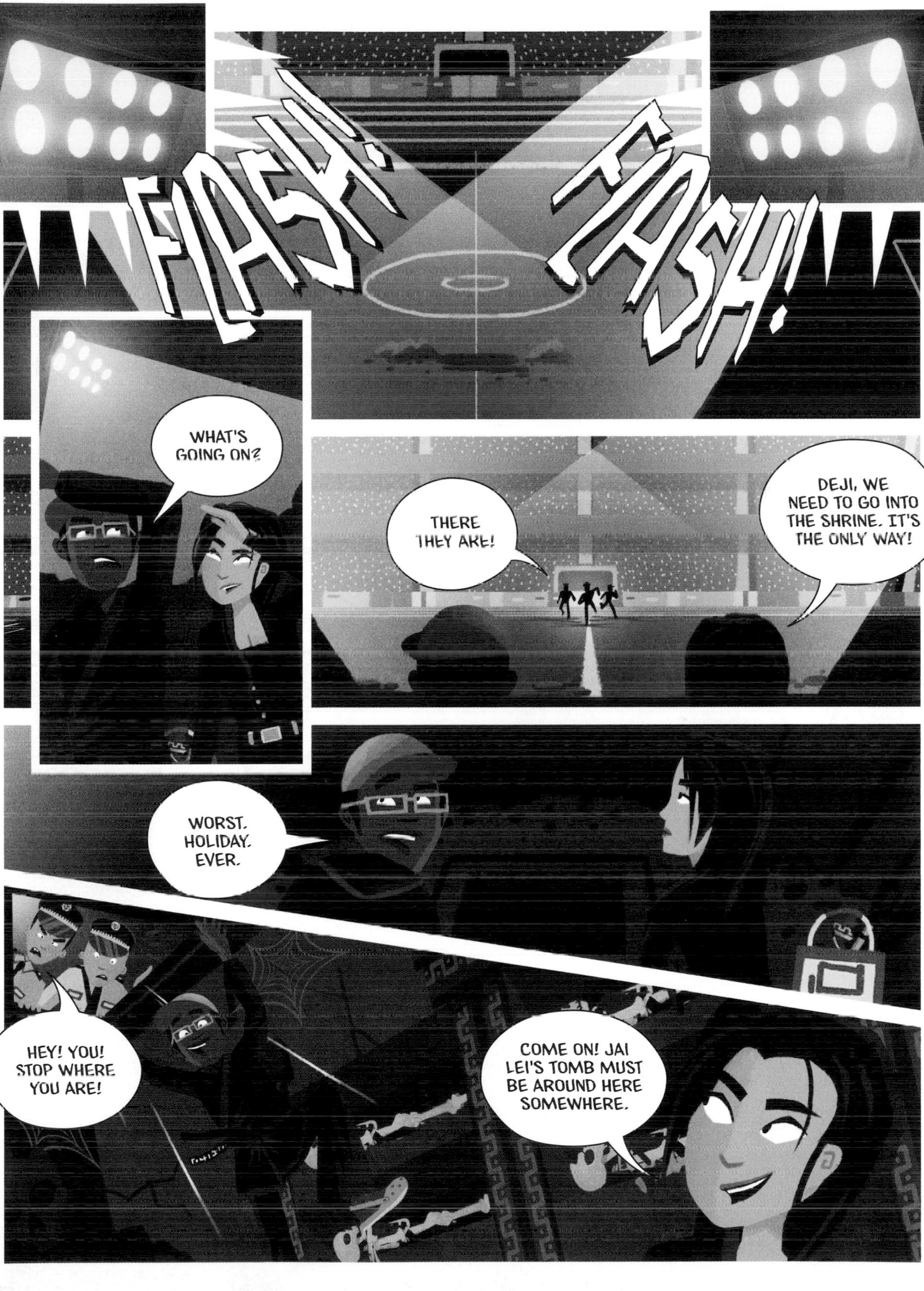
FLASH!
FLASH!
WHAT'S GOING ON?
THERE THEY ARE!
DEJI, WE NEED TO GO INTO THE SHRINE. IT'S THE ONLY WAY!
WORST. HOLIDAY. EVER.
HEY! YOU! STOP WHERE YOU ARE!
COME ON! JAI LEI'S TOMB MUST BE AROUND HERE SOMEWHERE.

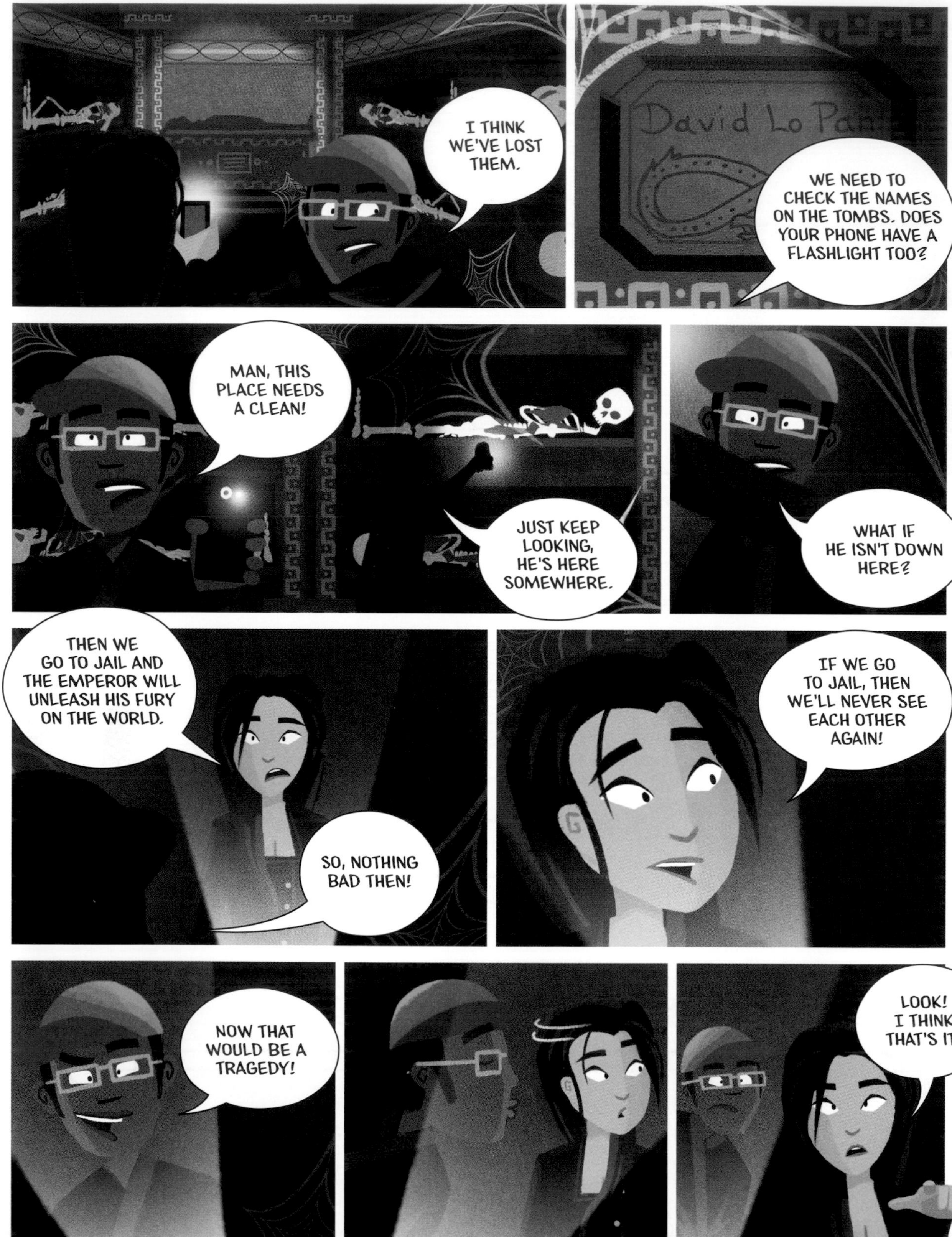
I THINK WE'VE LOST THEM.
David Lo Pan
WE NEED TO CHECK THE NAMES ON THE TOMBS. DOES YOUR PHONE HAVE A FLASHLIGHT TOO?
MAN, THIS PLACE NEEDS A CLEAN!
JUST KEEP LOOKING, HE'S HERE SOMEWHERE.
WHAT IF HE ISN'T DOWN HERE?
THEN WE GO TO JAIL AND THE EMPEROR WILL UNLEASH HIS FURY ON THE WORLD.
SO, NOTHING BAD THEN!
IF WE GO TO JAIL, THEN WE'LL NEVER SEE EACH OTHER AGAIN!
NOW THAT WOULD BE A TRAGEDY!
LOOK! I THINK THAT'S IT!

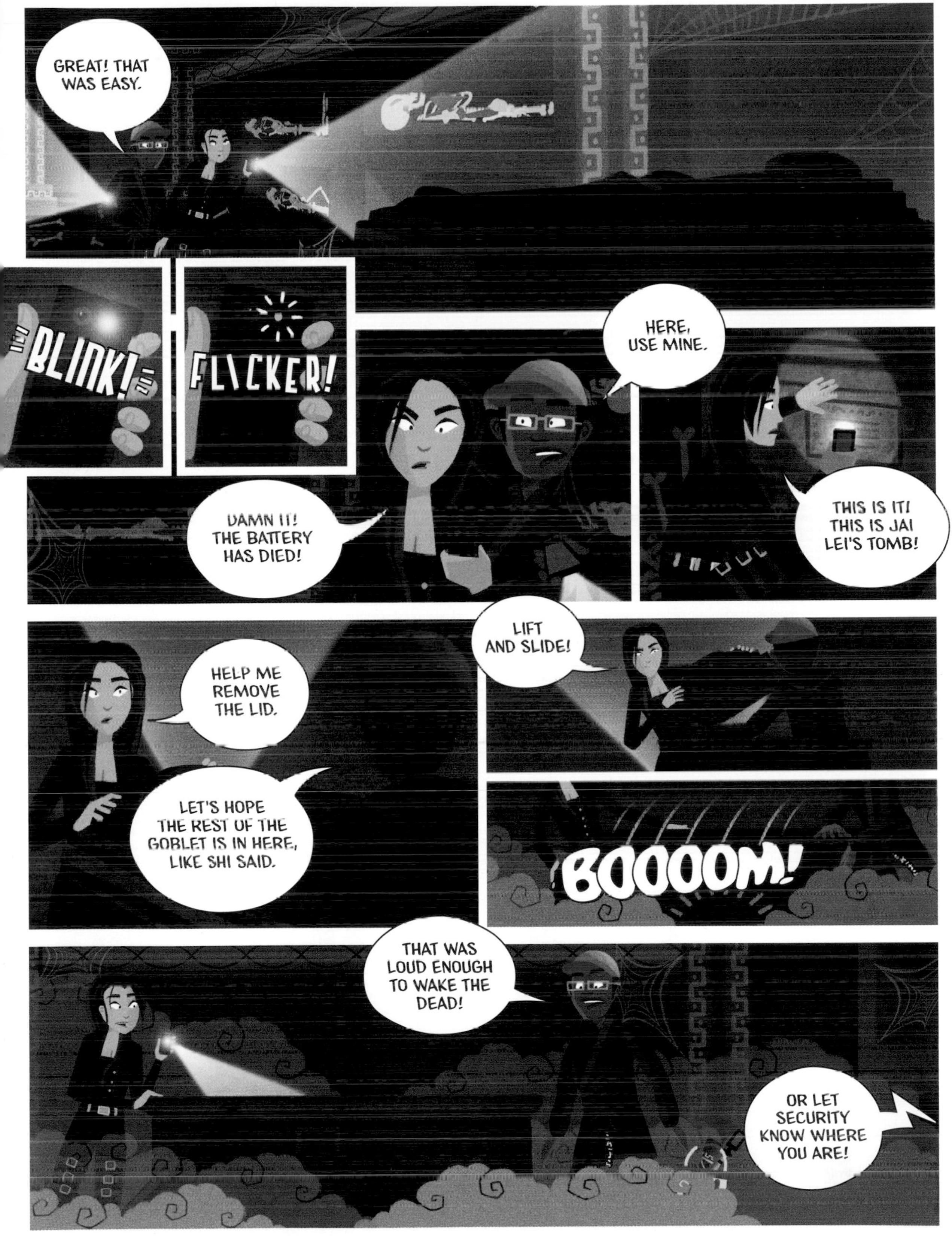
GREAT! THAT WAS EASY.
BLINK!
FLICKER!
DAMN IT! THE BATTERY HAS DIED!
HERE, USE MINE.
THIS IS IT! THIS IS JAI LEI'S TOMB!
HELP ME REMOVE THE LID.
LET'S HOPE THE REST OF THE GOBLET IS IN HERE, LIKE SHI SAID.
LIFT AND SLIDE!
BOOOOM!
THAT WAS LOUD ENOUGH TO WAKE THE DEAD!
OR LET SECURITY KNOW WHERE YOU ARE!

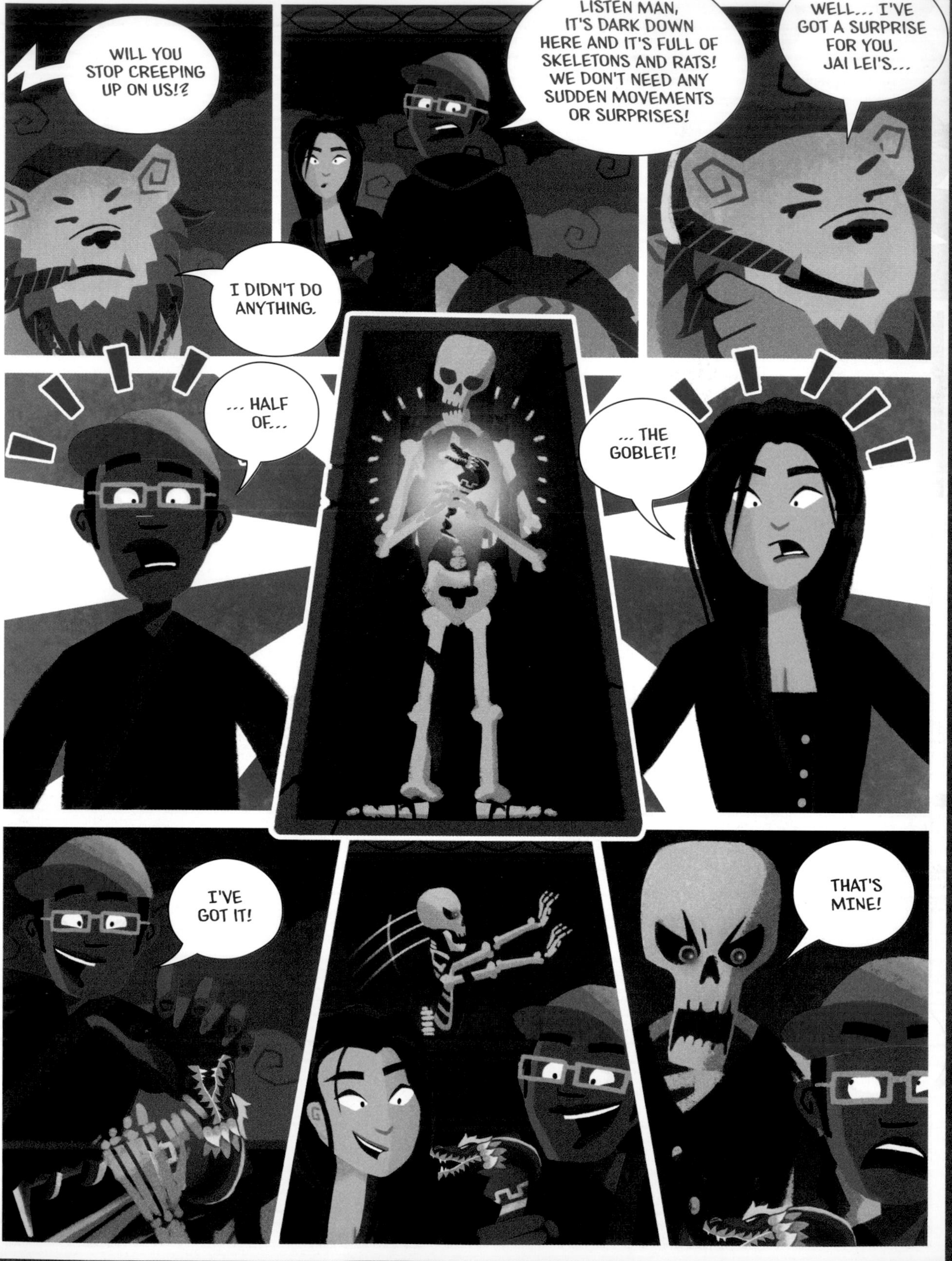
WILL YOU STOP CREEPING UP ON US!?
I DIDN'T DO ANYTHING.
LISTEN MAN, IT'S DARK DOWN HERE AND IT'S FULL OF SKELETONS AND RATS! WE DON'T NEED ANY SUDDEN MOVEMENTS OR SURPRISES!
WELL... I'VE GOT A SURPRISE FOR YOU. JAI LEI'S...
... HALF OF...
... THE GOBLET!
I'VE GOT IT!
THAT'S MINE!

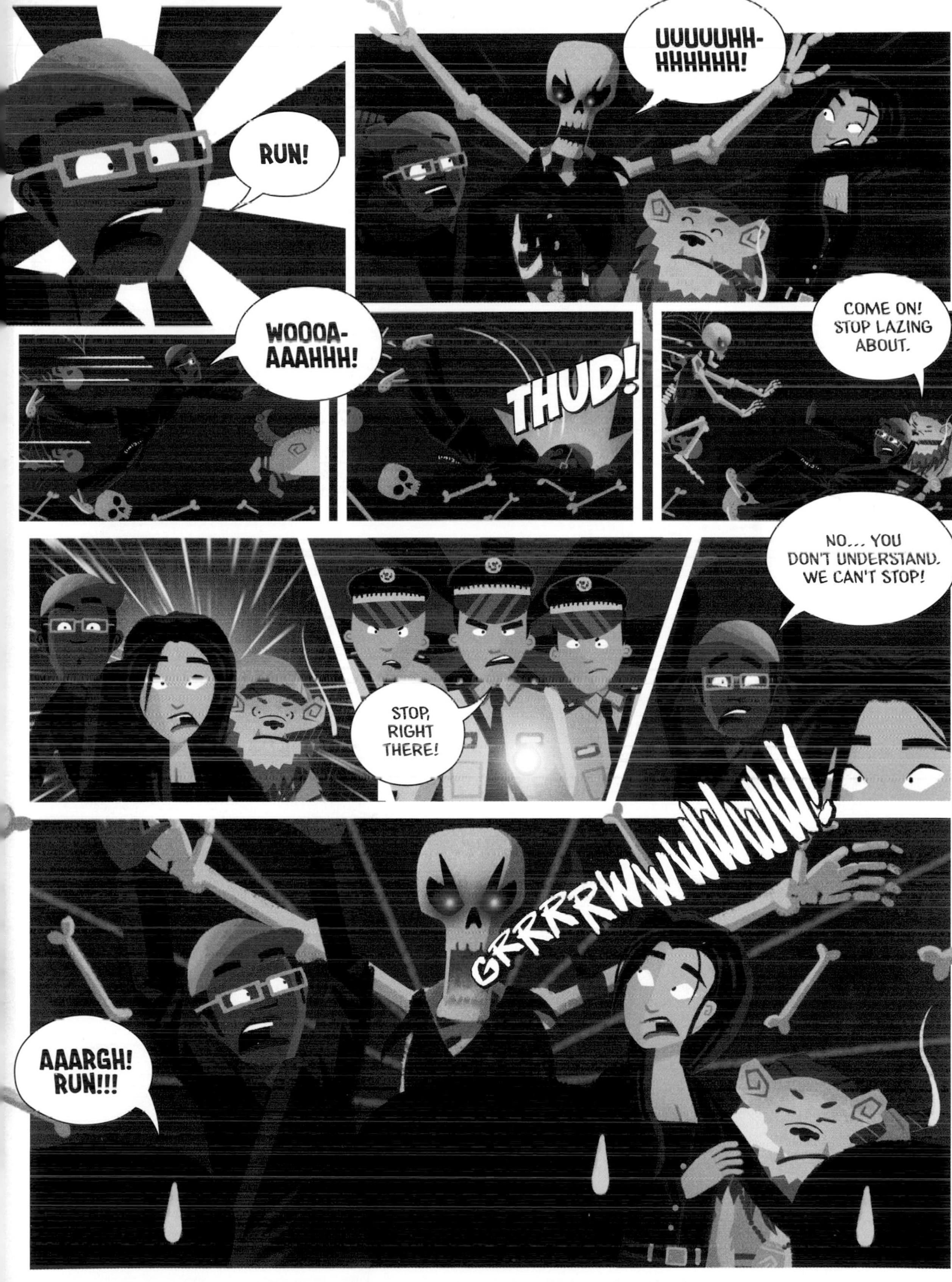
RUN!
UUUUUHH-HHHHHH!
WOOOA-AAAHHH!
THUD!
COME ON! STOP LAZING ABOUT.
NO... YOU DON'T UNDERSTAND. WE CAN'T STOP!
STOP, RIGHT THERE!
GRRRRWWWWWW!
AAARGH! RUN!!!

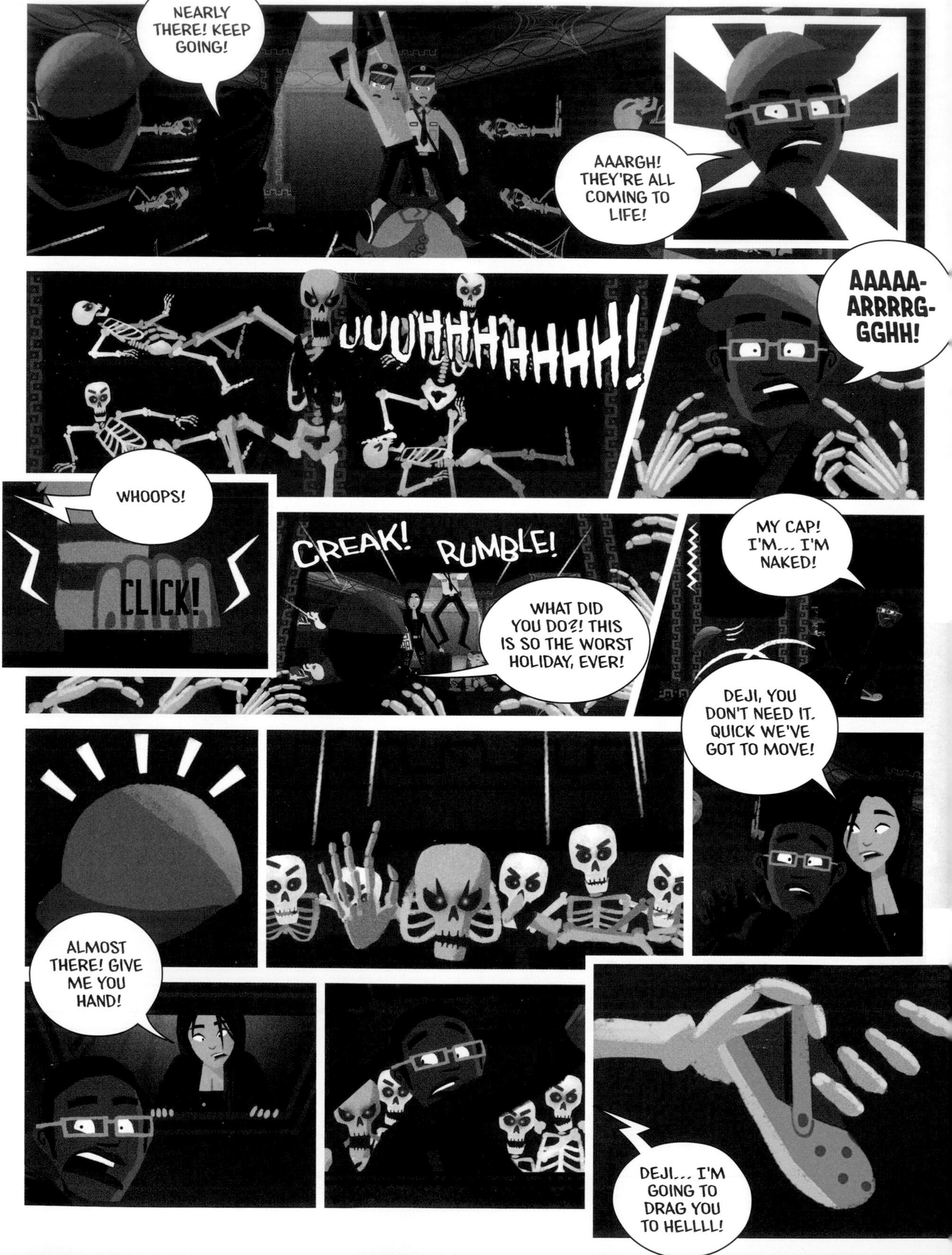
NEARLY THERE! KEEP GOING!
AAARGH! THEY'RE ALL COMING TO LIFE!
UUUHHHHHHH!
AAAAA-ARRRRG-GGHH!
WHOOPS!
CLICK!
CREAK! RUMBLE!
WHAT DID YOU DO?! THIS IS SO THE WORST HOLIDAY, EVER!
MY CAP! I'M... I'M NAKED!
DEJI, YOU DON'T NEED IT. QUICK WE'VE GOT TO MOVE!
ALMOST THERE! GIVE ME YOU HAND!
DEJI... I'M GOING TO DRAG YOU TO HELLLL!

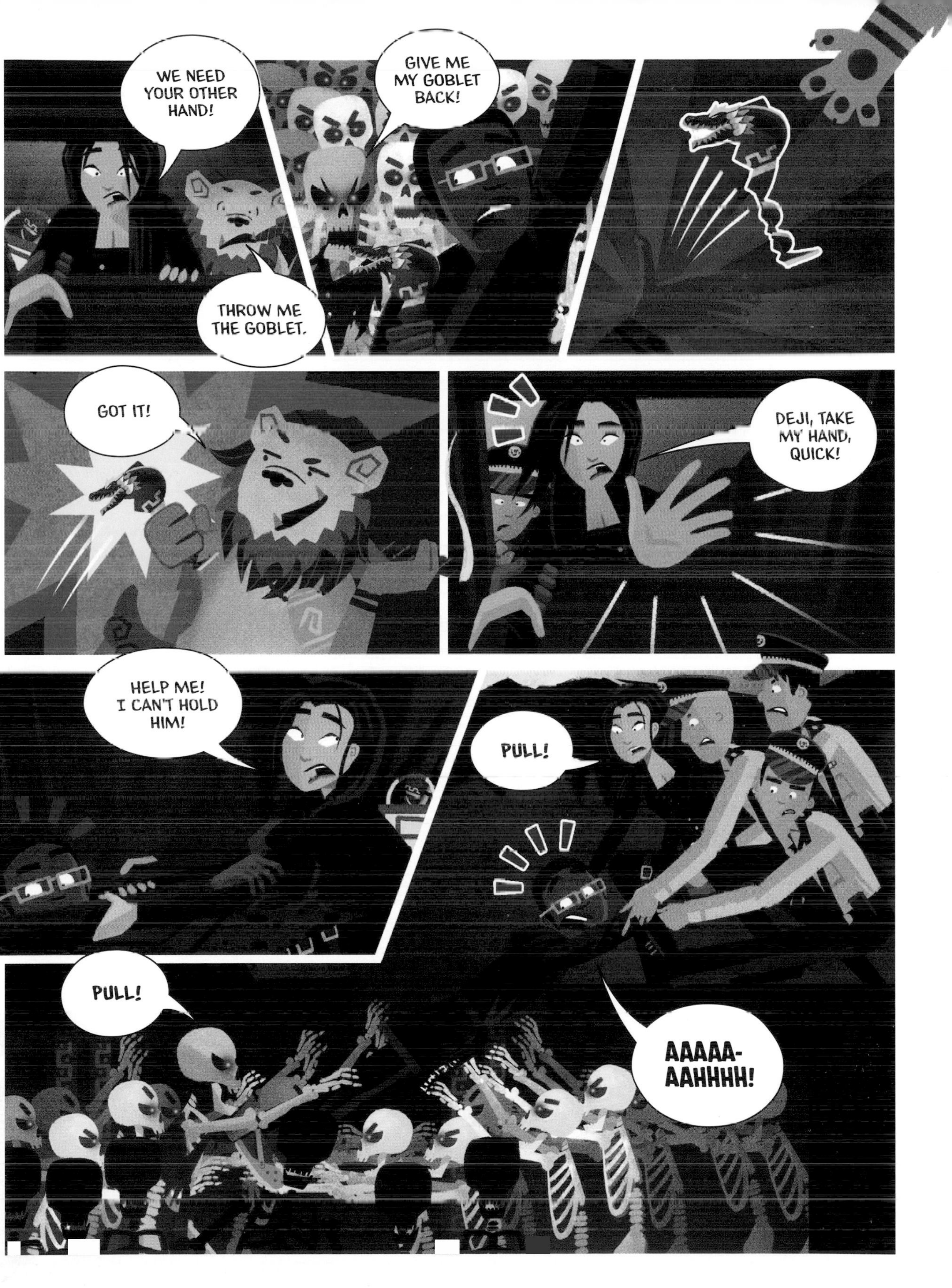
WE NEED YOUR OTHER HAND!
THROW ME THE GOBLET.
GIVE ME MY GOBLET BACK!
GOT IT!
DEJI, TAKE MY HAND, QUICK!
HELP ME! I CAN'T HOLD HIM!
PULL!
PULL!
AAAAA-AAHHHH!

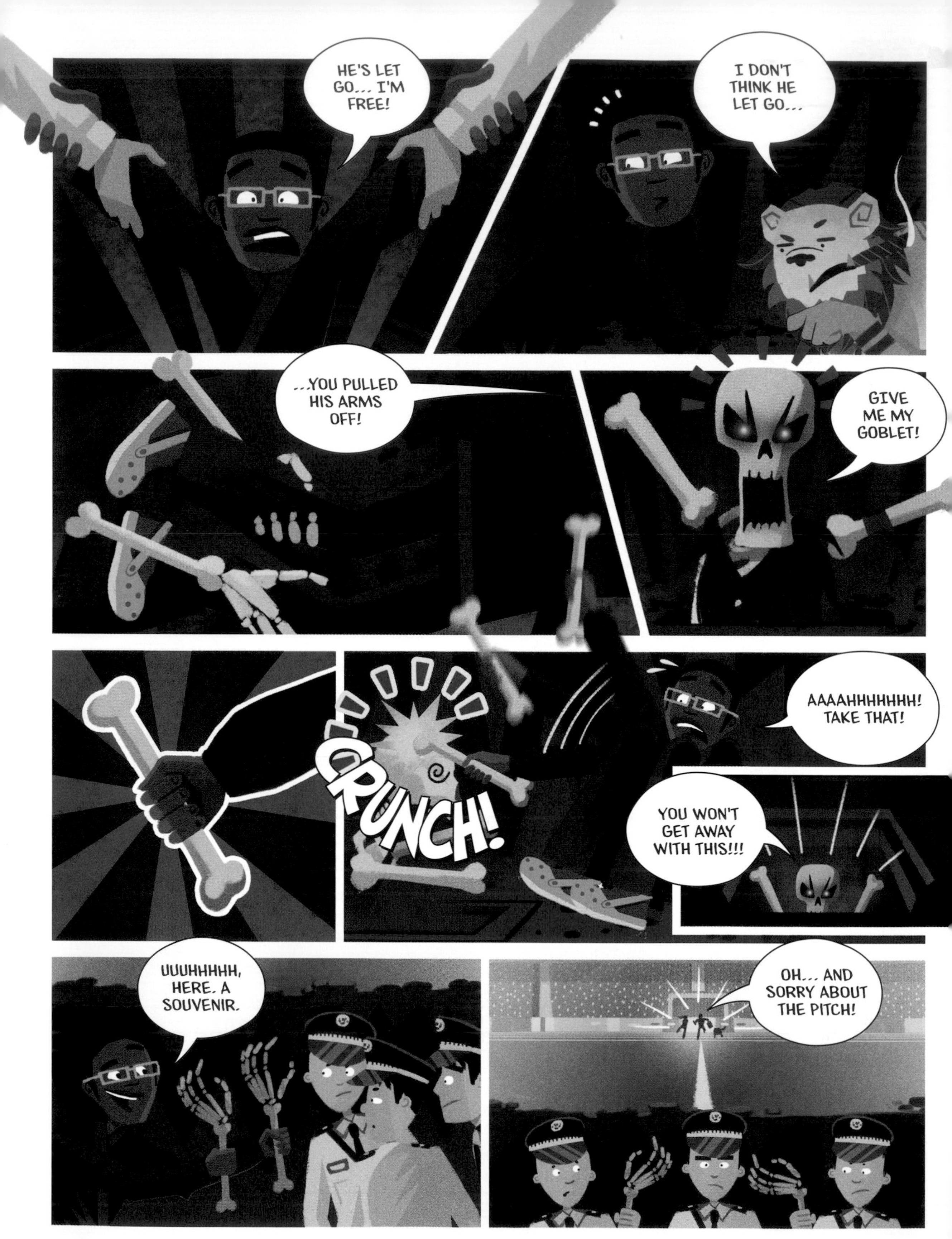
HE'S LET GO... I'M FREE!
I DON'T THINK HE LET GO...
...YOU PULLED HIS ARMS OFF!
GIVE ME MY GOBLET!
AAAAHHHHHHH! TAKE THAT!
CRUNCH!
YOU WON'T GET AWAY WITH THIS!!!
UUUHHHHH, HERE. A SOUVENIR.
OH... AND SORRY ABOUT THE PITCH!

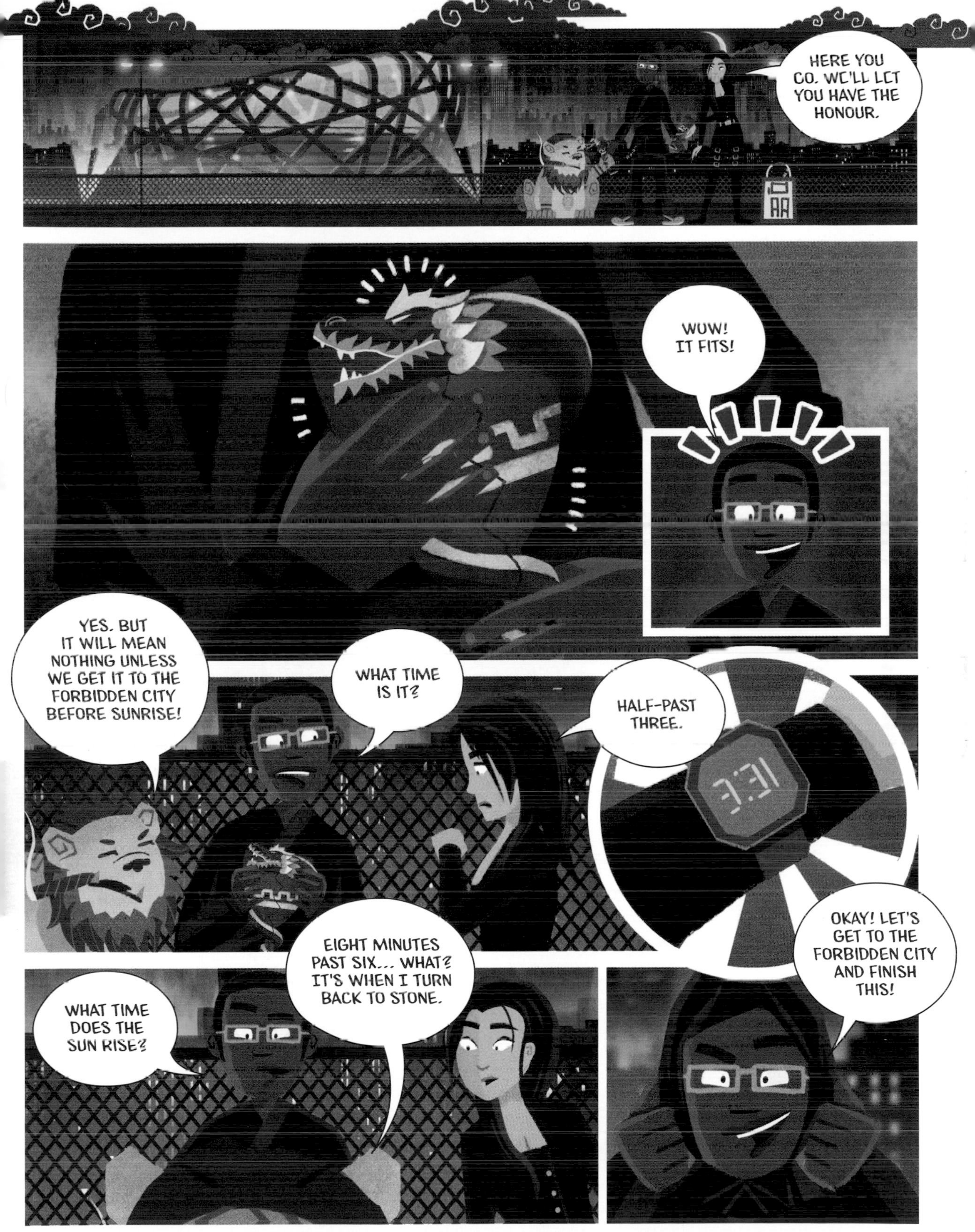
HERE YOU GO. WE'LL LET YOU HAVE THE HONOUR.
WOW! IT FITS!
YES. BUT IT WILL MEAN NOTHING UNLESS WE GET IT TO THE FORBIDDEN CITY BEFORE SUNRISE!
WHAT TIME IS IT?
HALF-PAST THREE.
WHAT TIME DOES THE SUN RISE?
EIGHT MINUTES PAST SIX... WHAT? IT'S WHEN I TURN BACK TO STONE.
OKAY! LET'S GET TO THE FORBIDDEN CITY AND FINISH THIS!

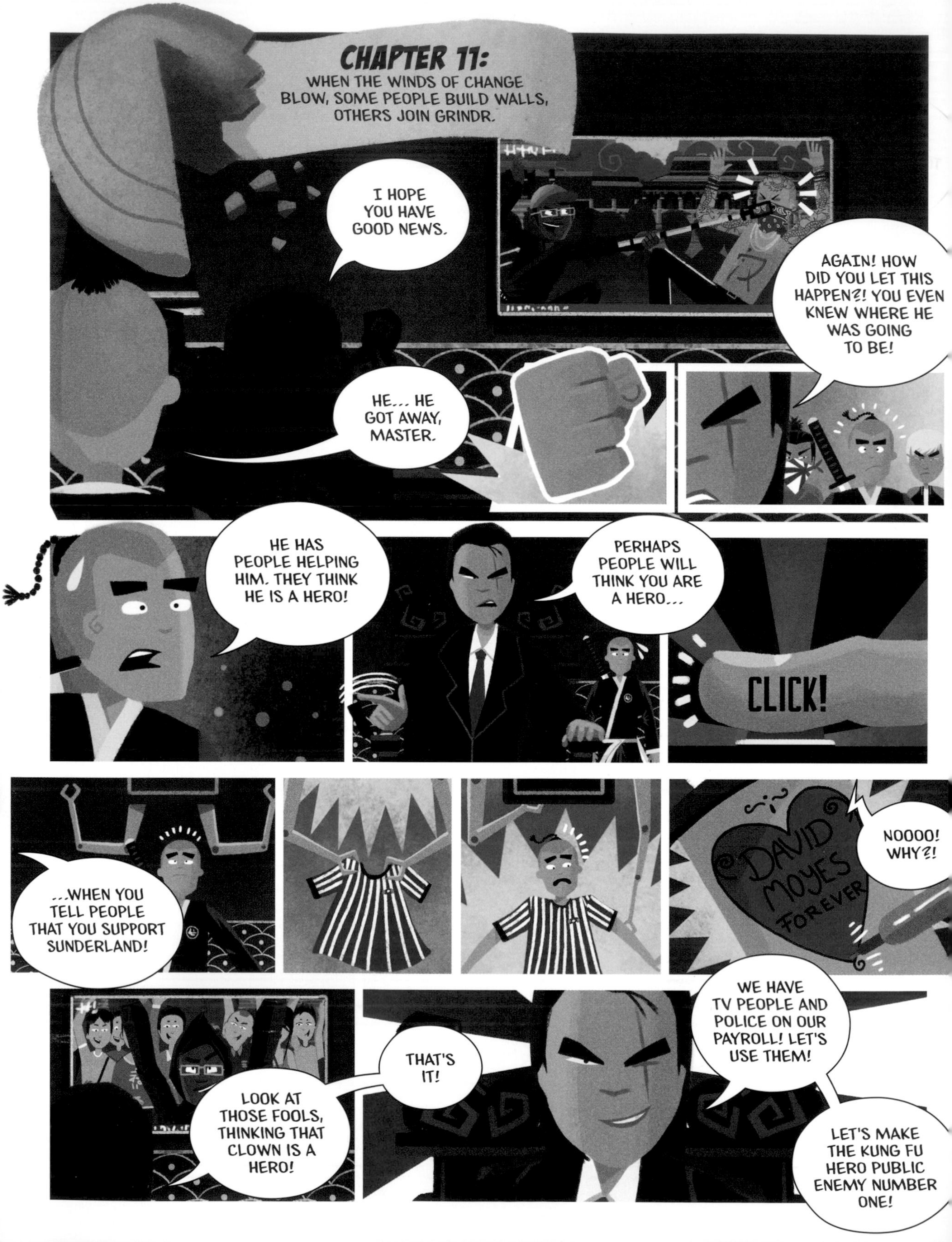
CHAPTER 11:
WHEN THE WINDS OF CHANGE BLOW, SOME PEOPLE BUILD WALLS, OTHERS JOIN GRINDR.
I HOPE YOU HAVE GOOD NEWS.
HE... HE GOT AWAY, MASTER.
AGAIN! HOW DID YOU LET THIS HAPPEN?! YOU EVEN KNEW WHERE HE WAS GOING TO BE!
HE HAS PEOPLE HELPING HIM. THEY THINK HE IS A HERO!
PERHAPS PEOPLE WILL THINK YOU ARE A HERO...
CLICK!
...WHEN YOU TELL PEOPLE THAT YOU SUPPORT SUNDERLAND!
DAVID MOYES FOREVER
NOOOO! WHY?!
LOOK AT THOSE FOOLS, THINKING THAT CLOWN IS A HERO!
THAT'S IT!
WE HAVE TV PEOPLE AND POLICE ON OUR PAYROLL! LET'S USE THEM!
LET'S MAKE THE KUNG FU HERO PUBLIC ENEMY NUMBER ONE!

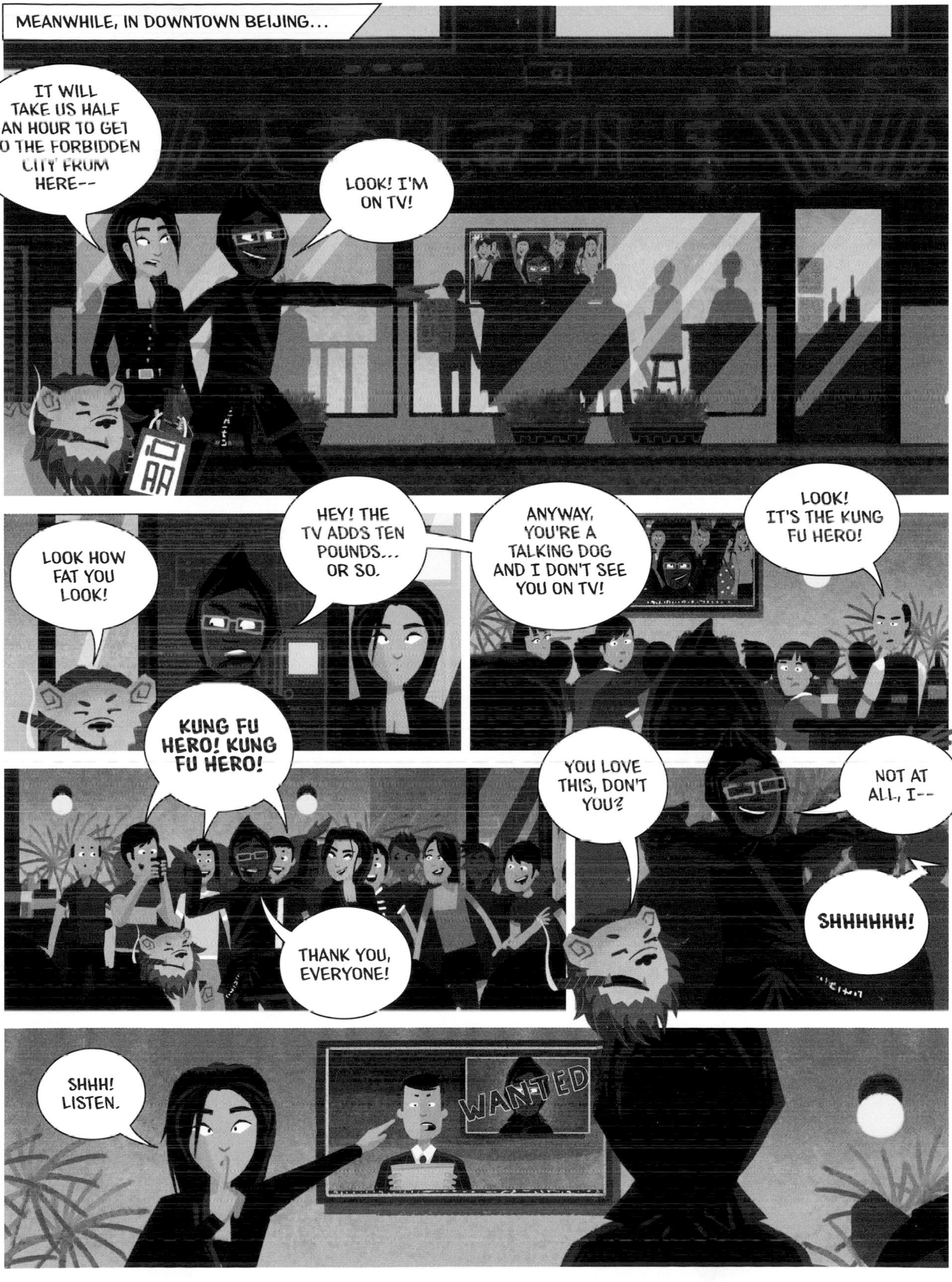
MEANWHILE, IN DOWNTOWN BEIJING...
IT WILL TAKE US HALF AN HOUR TO GET TO THE FORBIDDEN CITY FROM HERE--
LOOK! I'M ON TV!
LOOK HOW FAT YOU LOOK!
HEY! THE TV ADDS TEN POUNDS... OR SO.
ANYWAY, YOU'RE A TALKING DOG AND I DON'T SEE YOU ON TV!
LOOK! IT'S THE KUNG FU HERO!
KUNG FU HERO! KUNG FU HERO!
THANK YOU, EVERYONE!
YOU LOVE THIS, DON'T YOU?
NOT AT ALL, I--
SHHHHHH!
SHHH! LISTEN.
WANTED

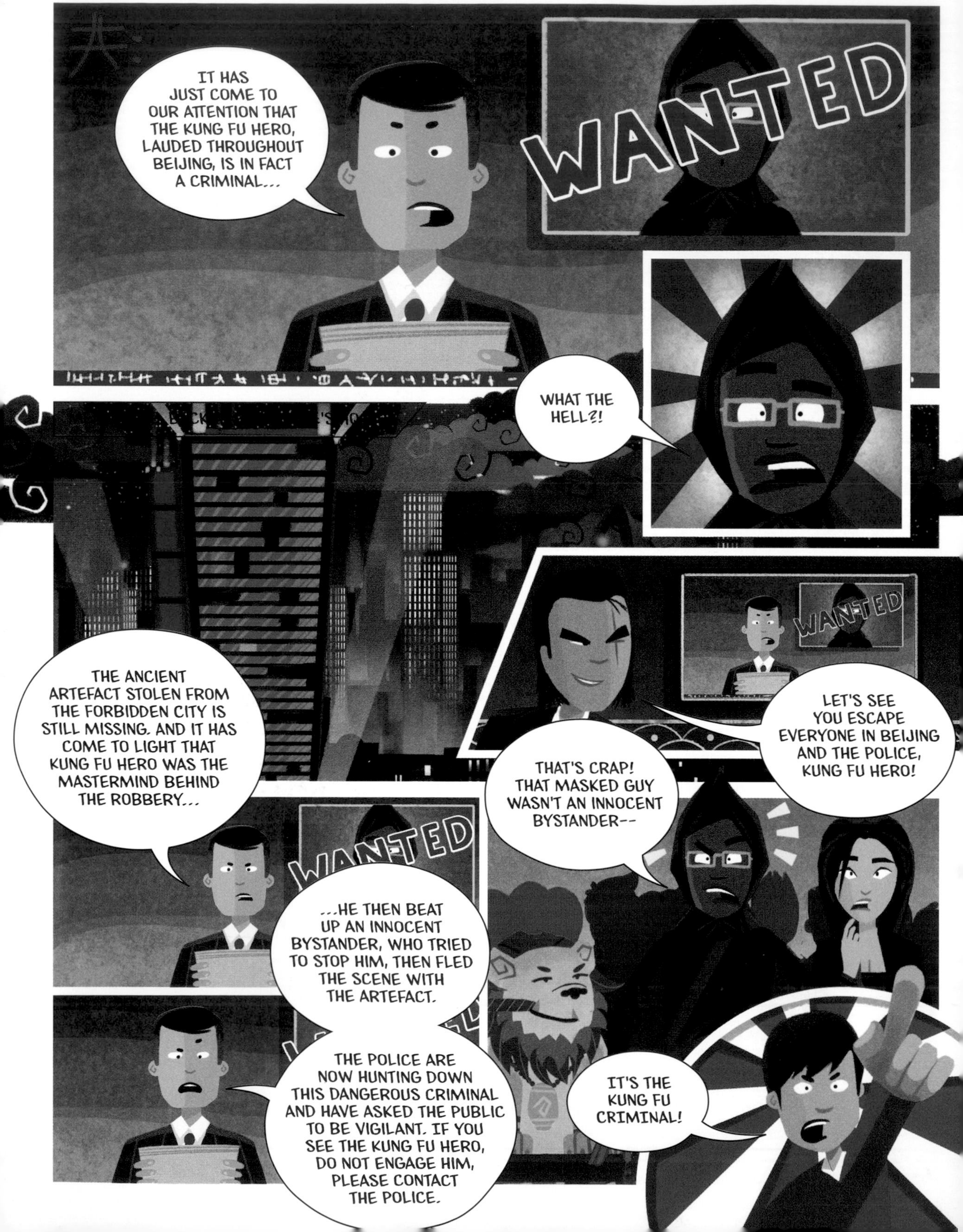
IT HAS JUST COME TO OUR ATTENTION THAT THE KUNG FU HERO, LAUDED THROUGHOUT BEIJING, IS IN FACT A CRIMINAL...
WANTED
WHAT THE HELL?!
WANTED
LET'S SEE YOU ESCAPE EVERYONE IN BEIJING AND THE POLICE, KUNG FU HERO!
THE ANCIENT ARTEFACT STOLEN FROM THE FORBIDDEN CITY IS STILL MISSING. AND IT HAS COME TO LIGHT THAT KUNG FU HERO WAS THE MASTERMIND BEHIND THE ROBBERY...
WANTED
...HE THEN BEAT UP AN INNOCENT BYSTANDER, WHO TRIED TO STOP HIM, THEN FLED THE SCENE WITH THE ARTEFACT.
THE POLICE ARE NOW HUNTING DOWN THIS DANGEROUS CRIMINAL AND HAVE ASKED THE PUBLIC TO BE VIGILANT. IF YOU SEE THE KUNG FU HERO, DO NOT ENGAGE HIM, PLEASE CONTACT THE POLICE.
THAT'S CRAP! THAT MASKED GUY WASN'T AN INNOCENT BYSTANDER--
IT'S THE KUNG FU CRIMINAL!

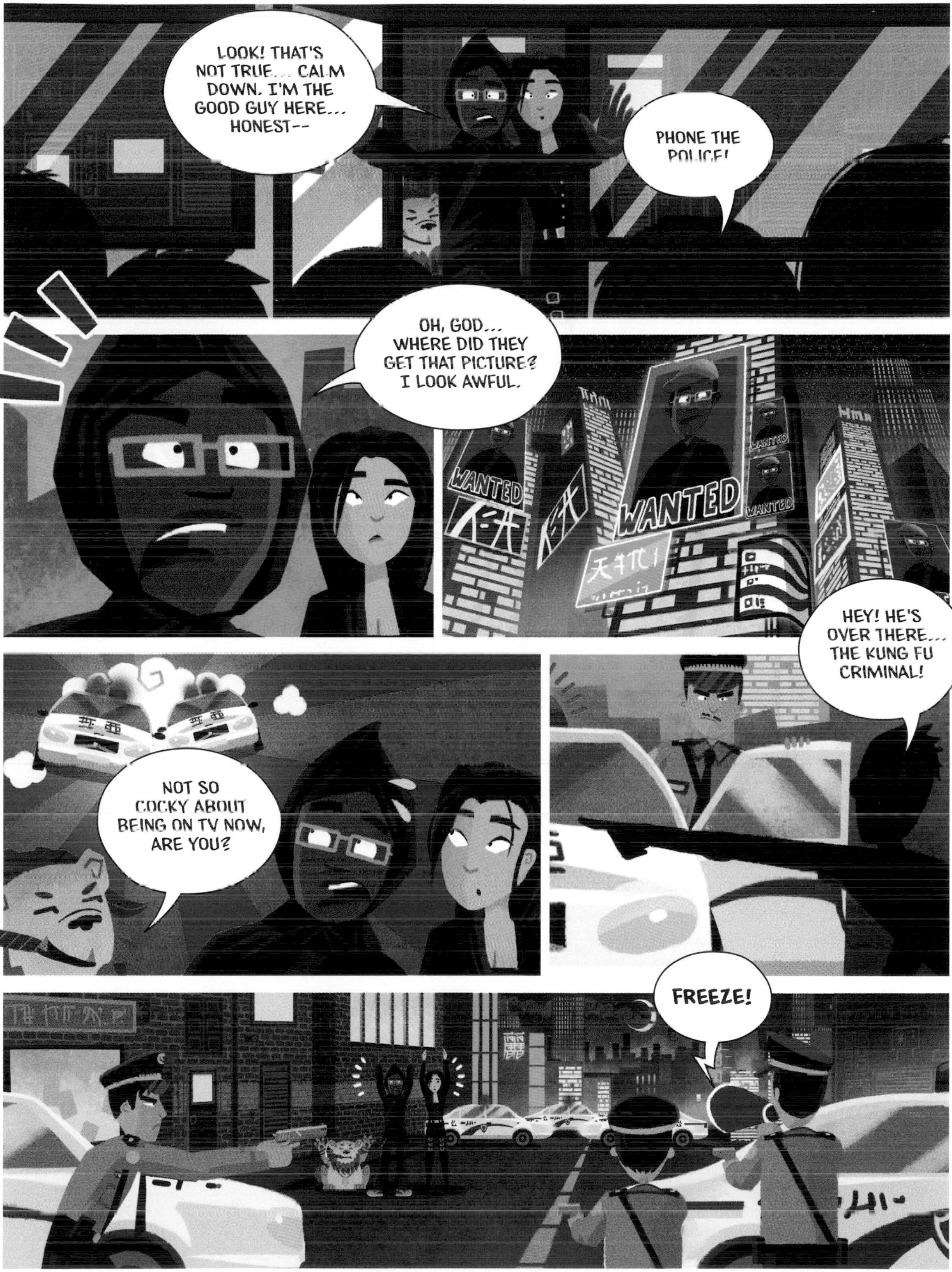
LOOK! THAT'S NOT TRUE... CALM DOWN. I'M THE GOOD GUY HERE... HONEST--
PHONE THE POLICE!
OH, GOD... WHERE DID THEY GET THAT PICTURE? I LOOK AWFUL.
WANTED
WANTED
WANTED
WANTED
HEY! HE'S OVER THERE... THE KUNG FU CRIMINAL!
NOT SO COCKY ABOUT BEING ON TV NOW, ARE YOU?
FREEZE!

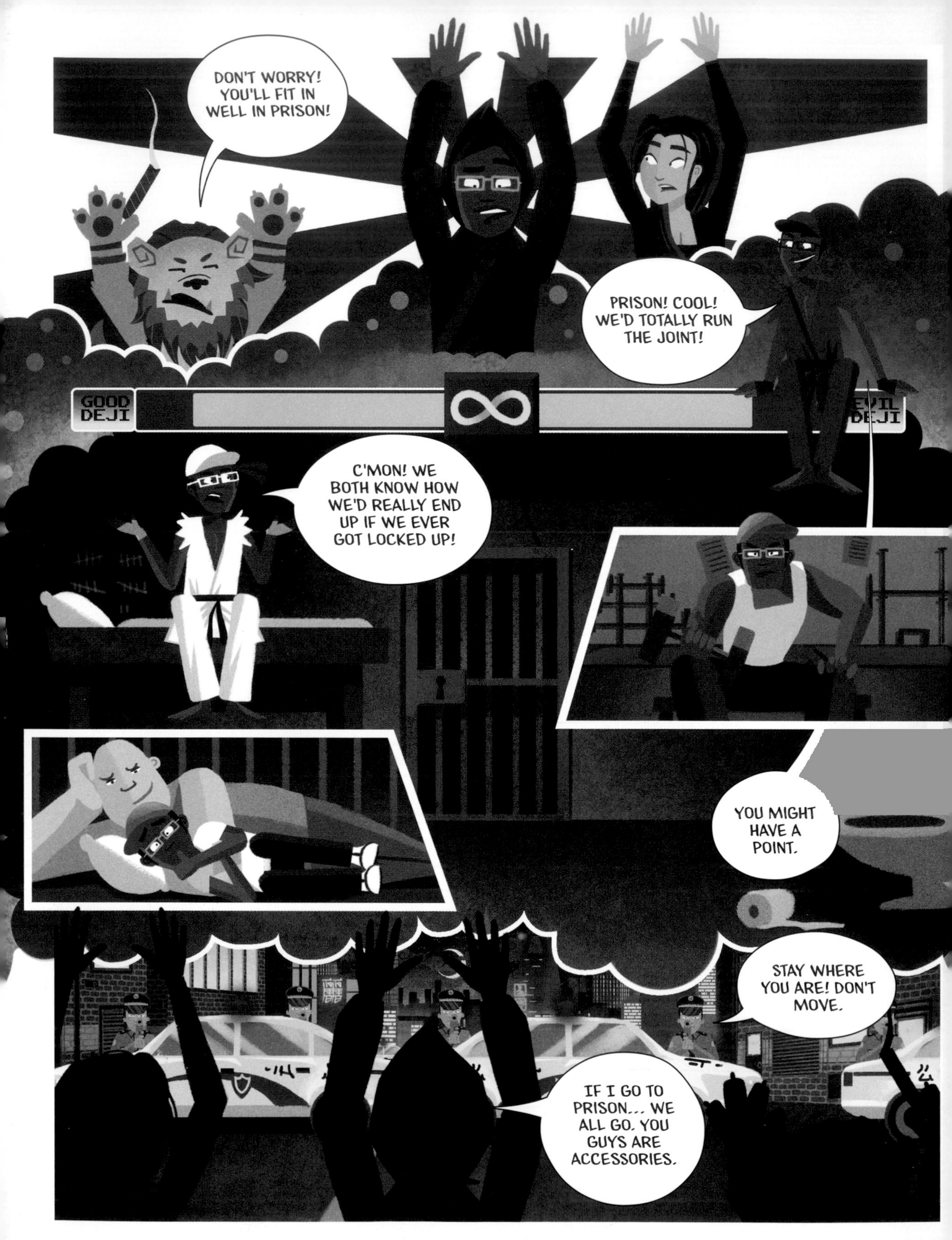
DON'T WORRY! YOU'LL FIT IN WELL IN PRISON!
PRISON! COOL! WE'D TOTALLY RUN THE JOINT!
GOOD DEJI
EVIL DEJI
C'MON! WE BOTH KNOW HOW WE'D REALLY END UP IF WE EVER GOT LOCKED UP!
YOU MIGHT HAVE A POINT.
STAY WHERE YOU ARE! DON'T MOVE.
IF I GO TO PRISON... WE ALL GO. YOU GUYS ARE ACCESSORIES.

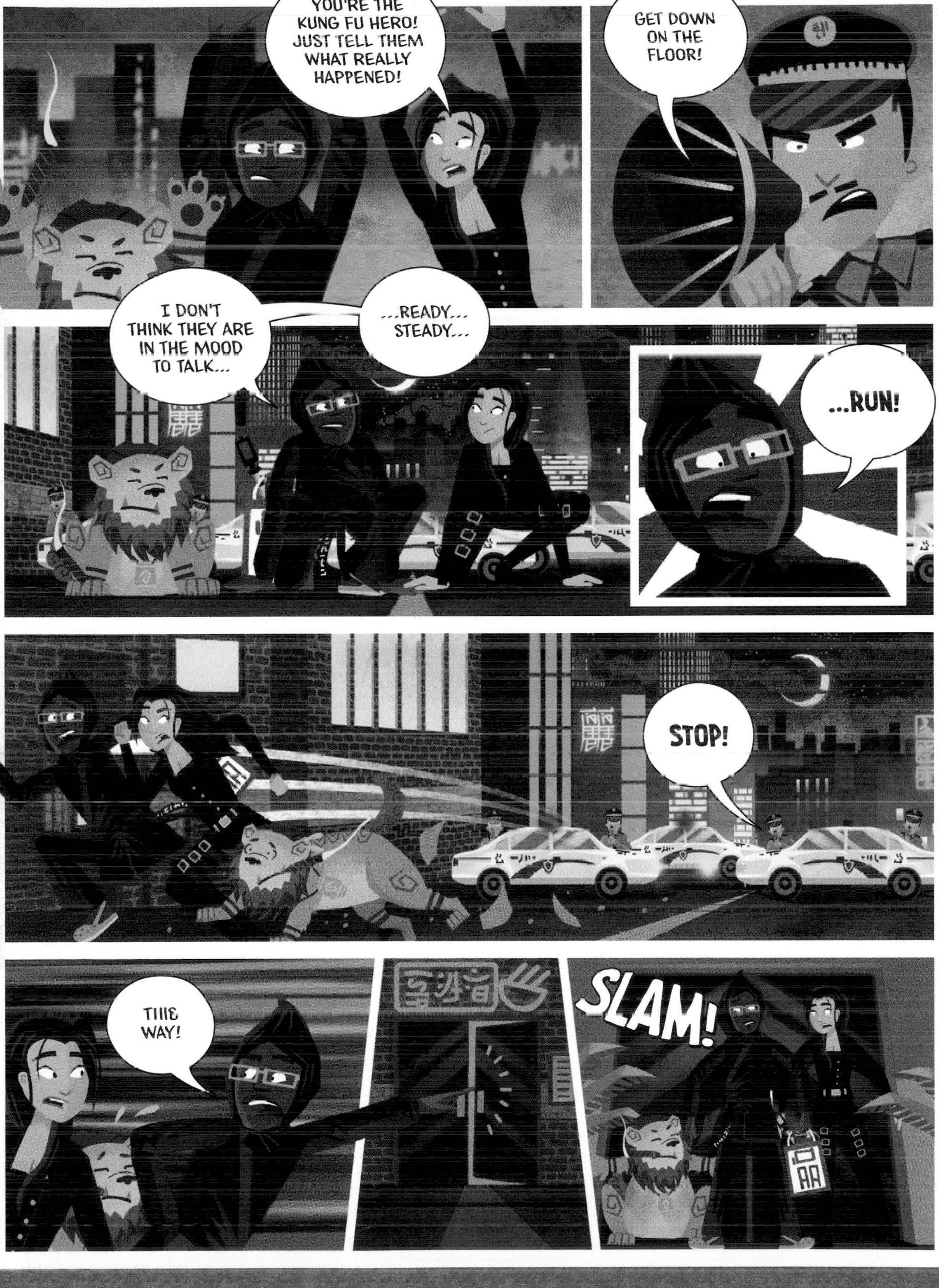
YOU'RE THE KUNG FU HERO! JUST TELL THEM WHAT REALLY HAPPENED!
GET DOWN ON THE FLOOR!
I DON'T THINK THEY ARE IN THE MOOD TO TALK...
...READY... STEADY...
...RUN!
STOP!
THIS WAY!
SLAM!

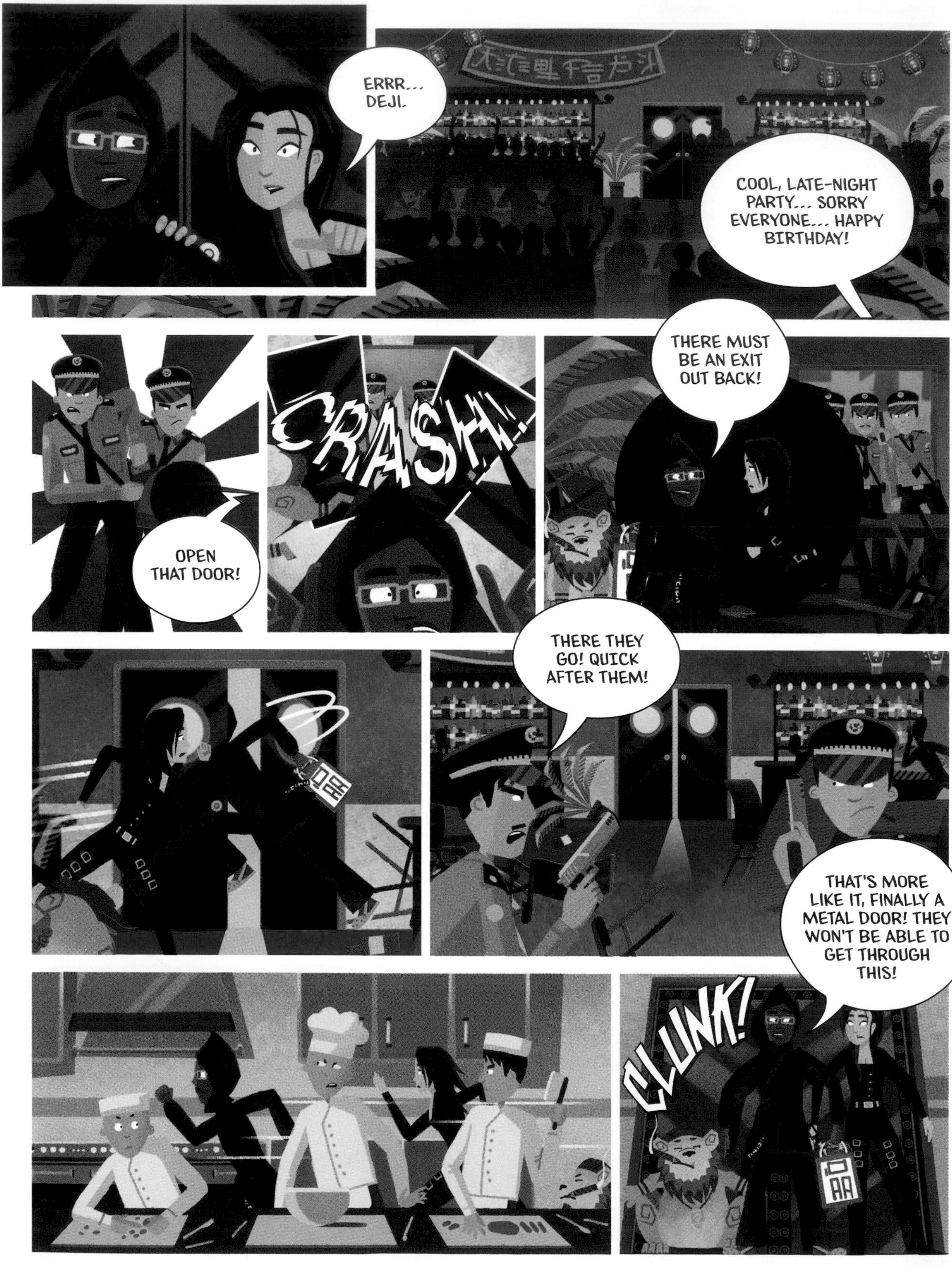

ERRR... DEJI.
COOL, LATE-NIGHT PARTY... SORRY EVERYONE... HAPPY BIRTHDAY!
OPEN THAT DOOR!
CRASH!
THERE MUST BE AN EXIT OUT BACK!
THERE THEY GO! QUICK AFTER THEM!
THAT'S MORE LIKE IT, FINALLY A METAL DOOR! THEY WON'T BE ABLE TO GET THROUGH THIS!
CLUNK!

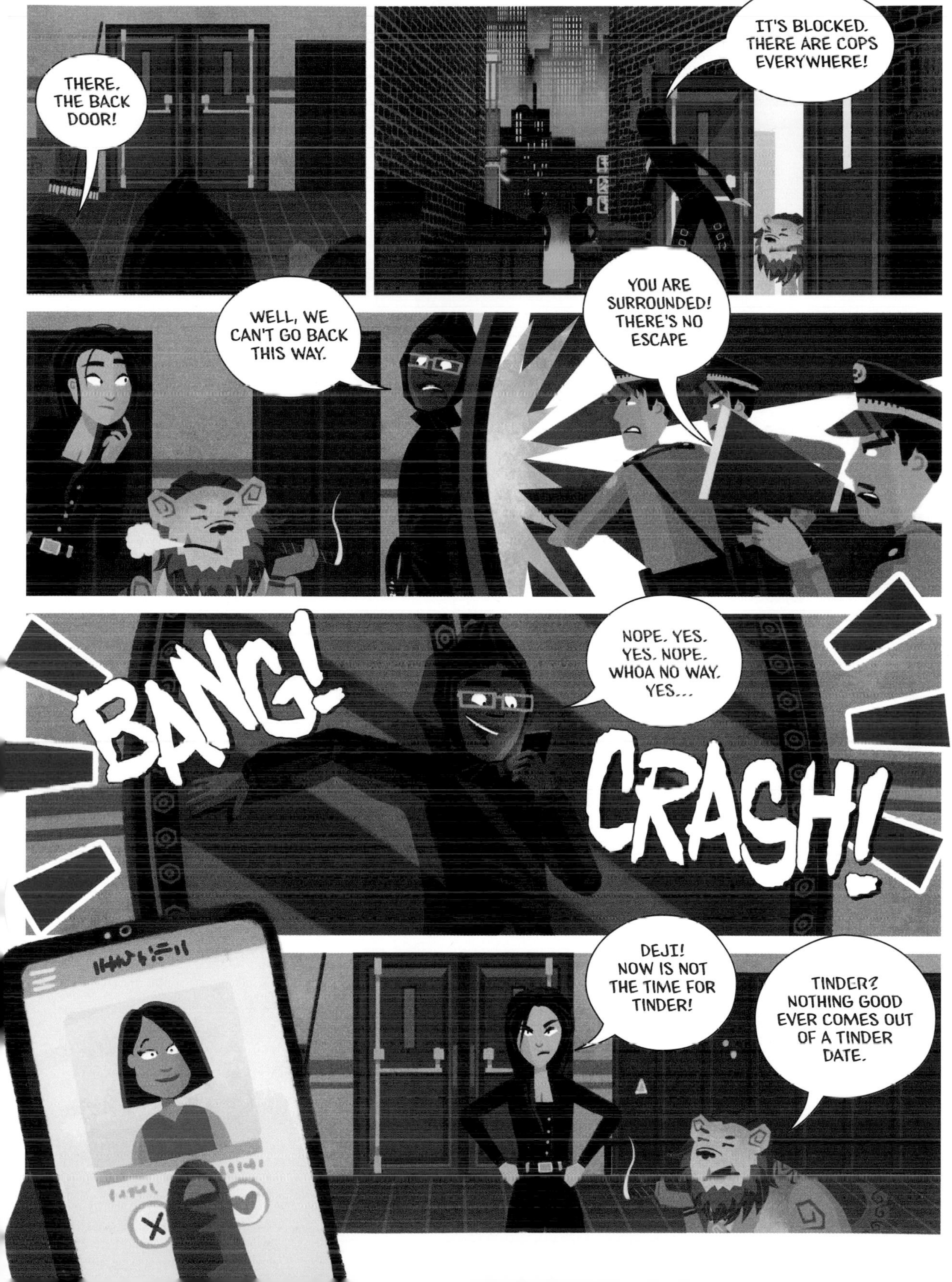
THERE. THE BACK DOOR!
IT'S BLOCKED. THERE ARE COPS EVERYWHERE!
WELL, WE CAN'T GO BACK THIS WAY.
YOU ARE SURROUNDED! THERE'S NO ESCAPE
BANG!
NOPE. YES. YES. NOPE. WHOA NO WAY. YES...
CRASH!
DEJI! NOW IS NOT THE TIME FOR TINDER!
TINDER? NOTHING GOOD EVER COMES OUT OF A TINDER DATE.

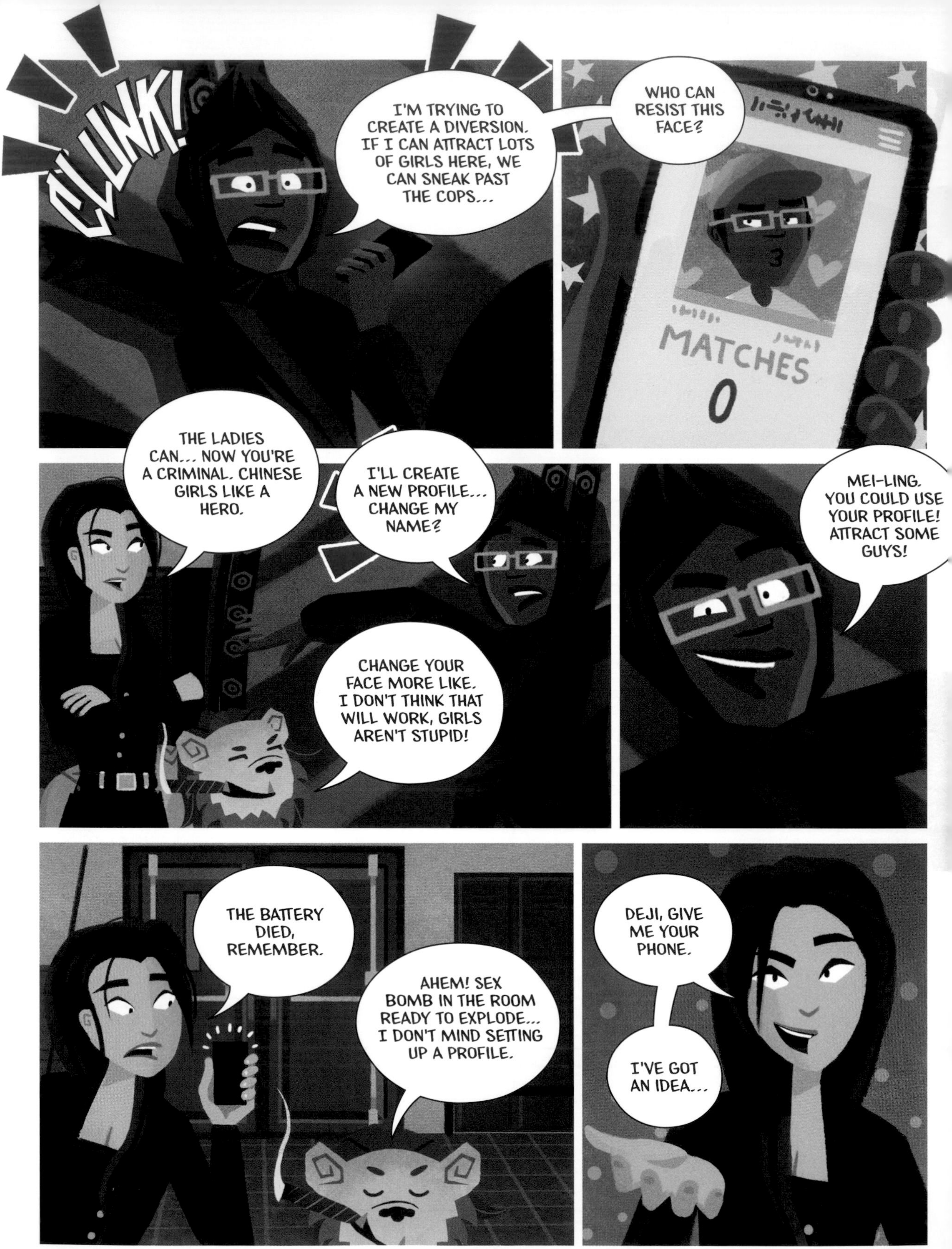
CLUNK!
I'M TRYING TO CREATE A DIVERSION. IF I CAN ATTRACT LOTS OF GIRLS HERE, WE CAN SNEAK PAST THE COPS...
WHO CAN RESIST THIS FACE?
MATCHES
0
THE LADIES CAN... NOW YOU'RE A CRIMINAL. CHINESE GIRLS LIKE A HERO.
I'LL CREATE A NEW PROFILE... CHANGE MY NAME?
CHANGE YOUR FACE MORE LIKE. I DON'T THINK THAT WILL WORK, GIRLS AREN'T STUPID!
MEI-LING. YOU COULD USE YOUR PROFILE! ATTRACT SOME GUYS!
THE BATTERY DIED, REMEMBER.
AHEM! SEX BOMB IN THE ROOM READY TO EXPLODE... I DON'T MIND SETTING UP A PROFILE.
DEJI, GIVE ME YOUR PHONE.
I'VE GOT AN IDEA...

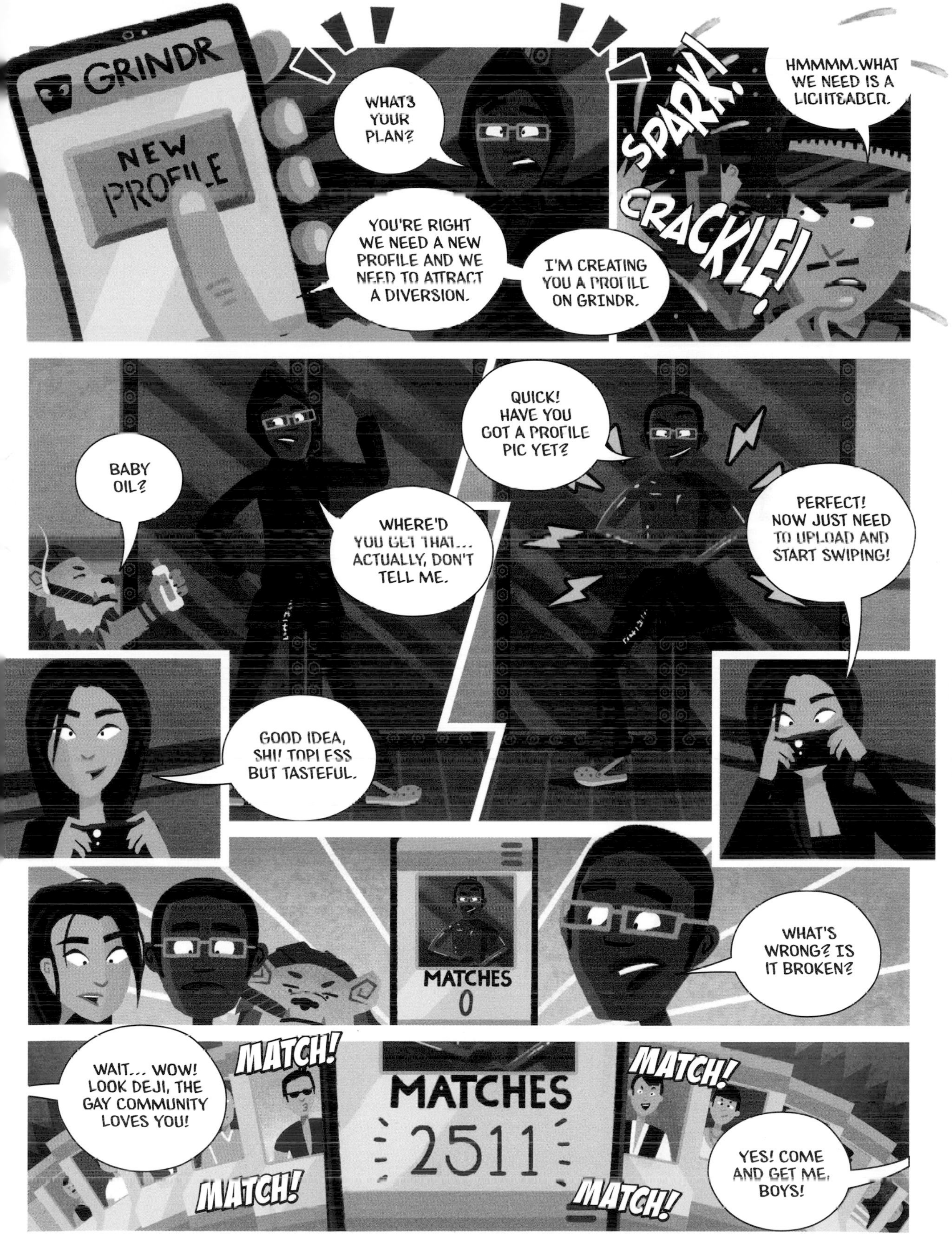
GRINDR
NEW PROFILE
WHAT'S YOUR PLAN?
YOU'RE RIGHT WE NEED A NEW PROFILE AND WE NEED TO ATTRACT A DIVERSION.
I'M CREATING YOU A PROFILE ON GRINDR.
SPARK!
CRACKLE!
HMMMM. WHAT WE NEED IS A LIGHTSABER.
BABY OIL?
WHERE'D YOU GET THAT... ACTUALLY, DON'T TELL ME.
QUICK! HAVE YOU GOT A PROFILE PIC YET?
PERFECT! NOW JUST NEED TO UPLOAD AND START SWIPING!
GOOD IDEA, SHI! TOPLESS BUT TASTEFUL.
MATCHES
0
WHAT'S WRONG? IS IT BROKEN?
WAIT... WOW! LOOK DEJI, THE GAY COMMUNITY LOVES YOU!
MATCH!
MATCHES
2511
MATCH!
MATCH!
MATCH!
YES! COME AND GET ME, BOYS!

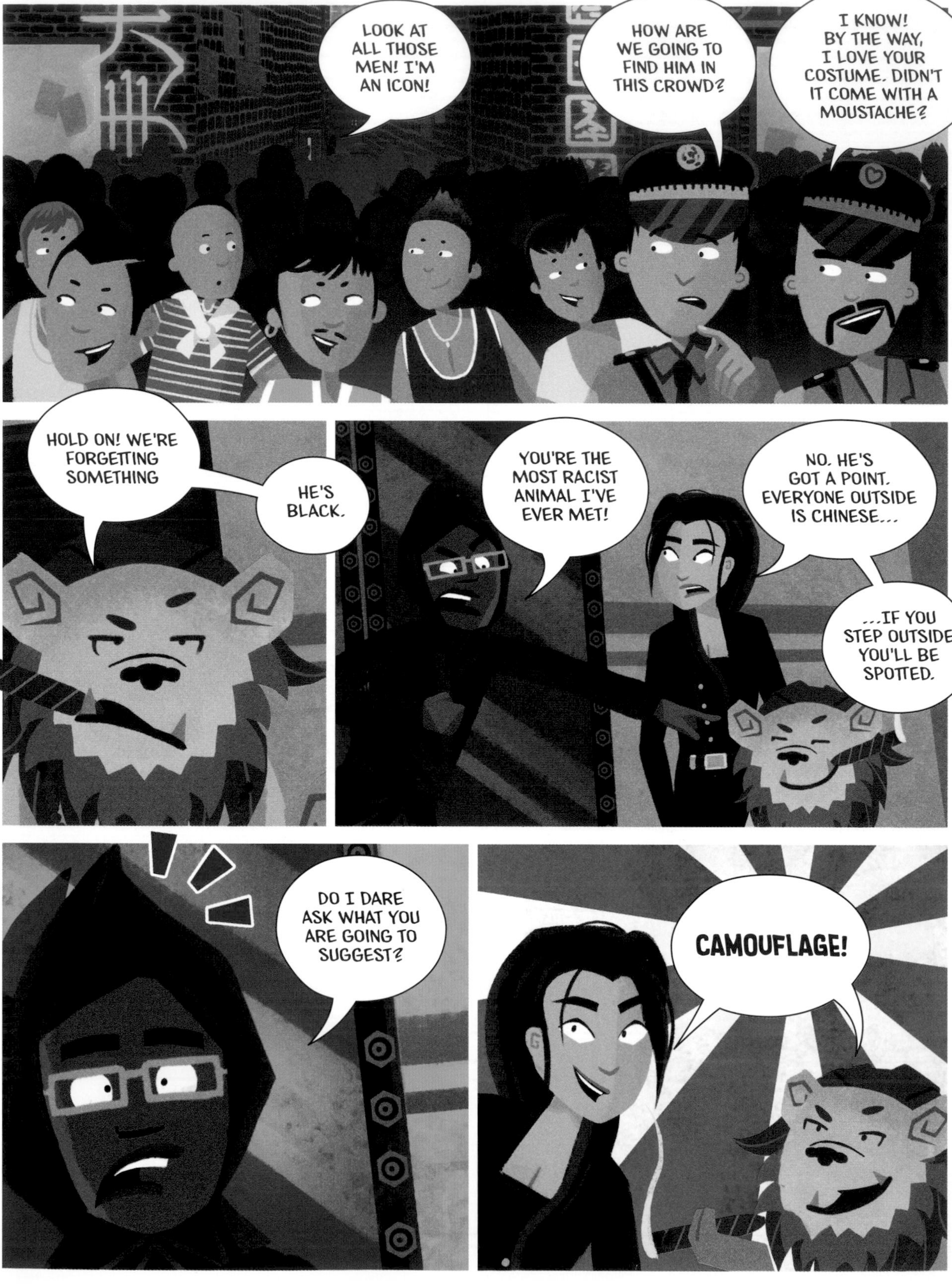

LOOK AT ALL THOSE MEN! I'M AN ICON!
HOW ARE WE GOING TO FIND HIM IN THIS CROWD?
I KNOW! BY THE WAY, I LOVE YOUR COSTUME. DIDN'T IT COME WITH A MOUSTACHE?
HOLD ON! WE'RE FORGETTING SOMETHING
HE'S BLACK.
YOU'RE THE MOST RACIST ANIMAL I'VE EVER MET!
NO. HE'S GOT A POINT. EVERYONE OUTSIDE IS CHINESE...
...IF YOU STEP OUTSIDE YOU'LL BE SPOTTED.
DO I DARE ASK WHAT YOU ARE GOING TO SUGGEST?
CAMOUFLAGE!

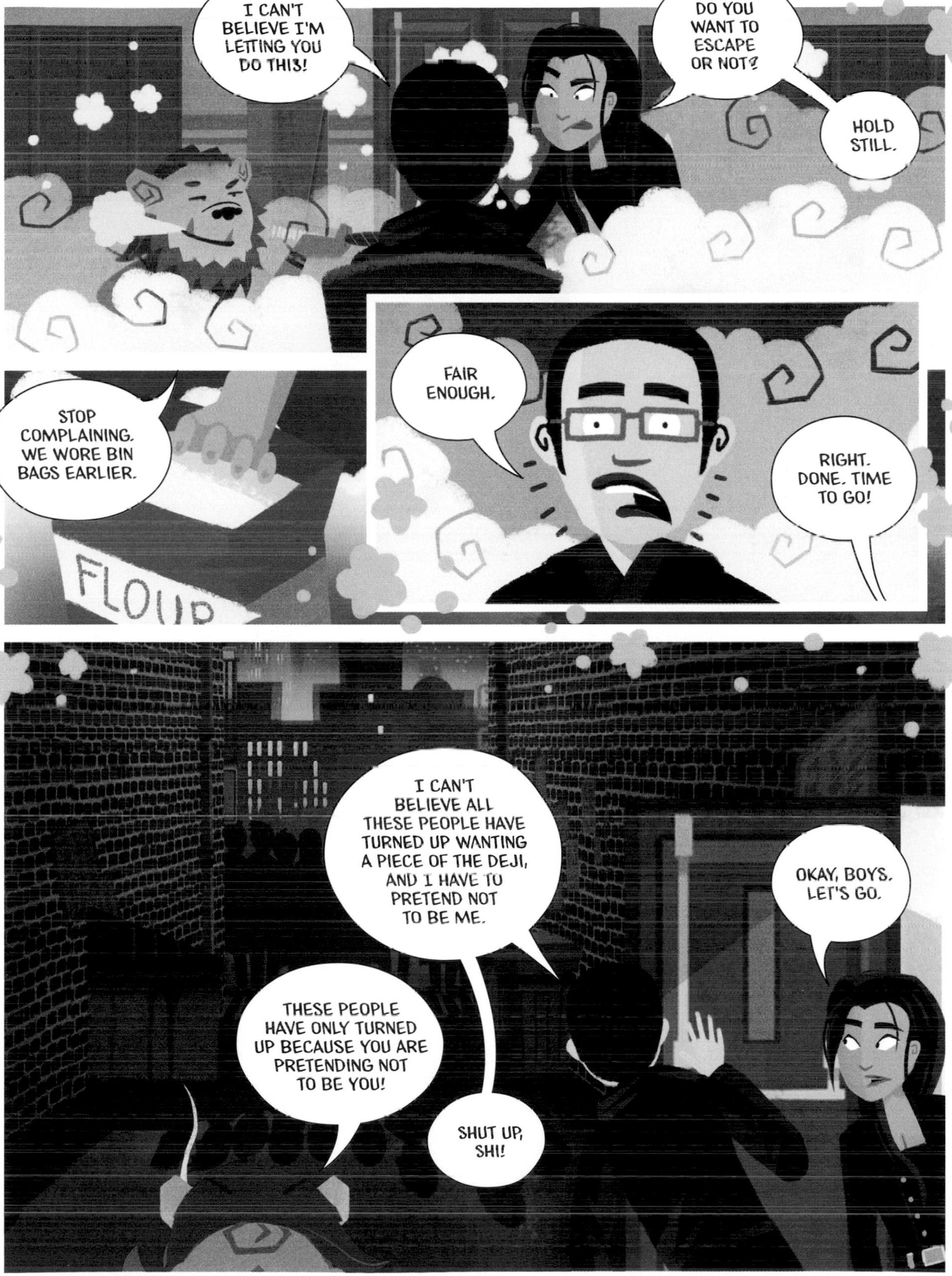
I CAN'T BELIEVE I'M LETTING YOU DO THIS!
DO YOU WANT TO ESCAPE OR NOT?
HOLD STILL.
STOP COMPLAINING. WE WORE BIN BAGS EARLIER.
FAIR ENOUGH.
RIGHT. DONE. TIME TO GO!
FLOUR
I CAN'T BELIEVE ALL THESE PEOPLE HAVE TURNED UP WANTING A PIECE OF THE DEJI, AND I HAVE TO PRETEND NOT TO BE ME.
OKAY, BOYS. LET'S GO.
THESE PEOPLE HAVE ONLY TURNED UP BECAUSE YOU ARE PRETENDING NOT TO BE YOU!
SHUT UP, SHI!

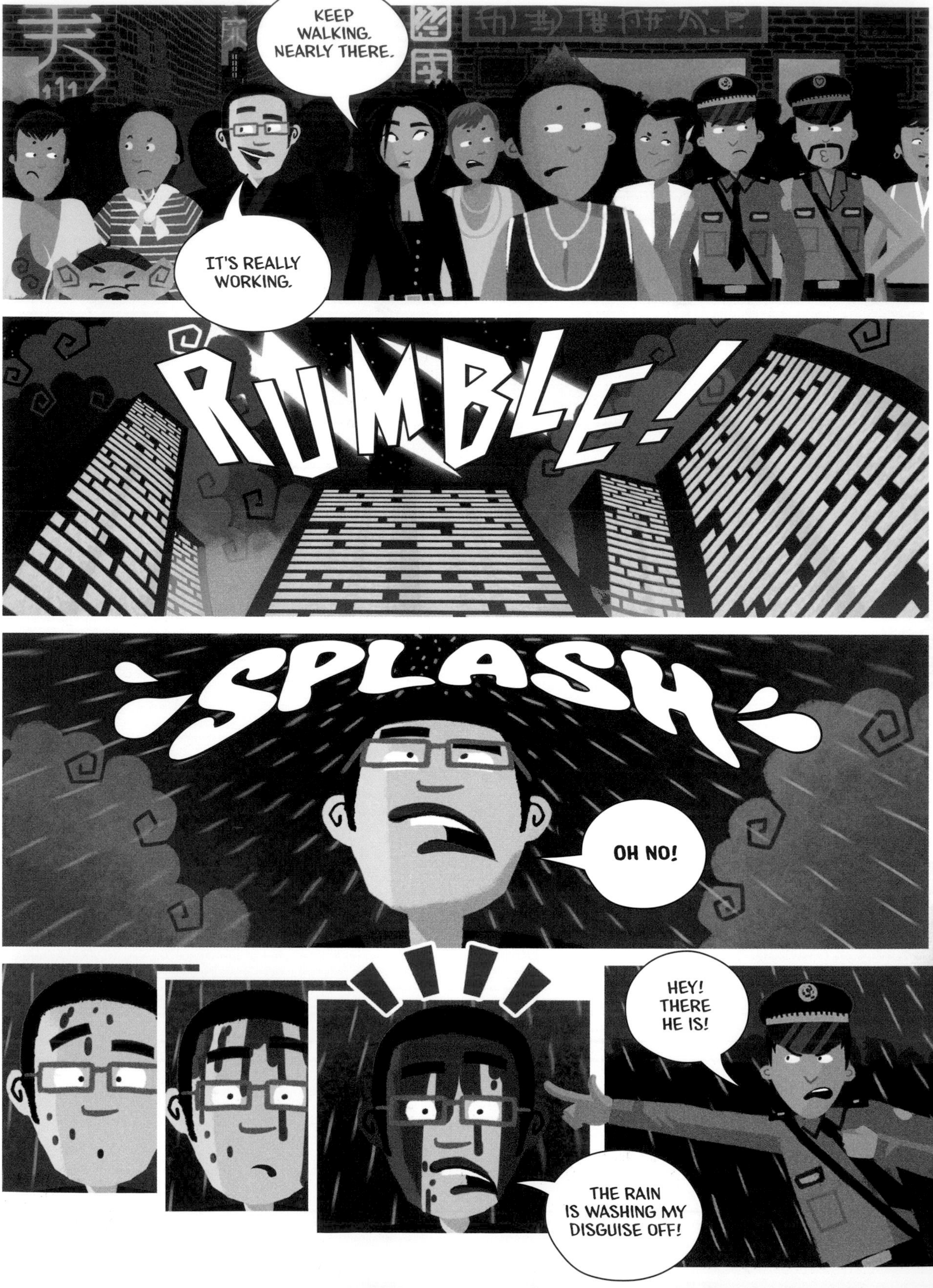
KEEP WALKING. NEARLY THERE.
IT'S REALLY WORKING.
RUMBLE!
SPLASH
OH NO!
THE RAIN IS WASHING MY DISGUISE OFF!
HEY! THERE HE IS!

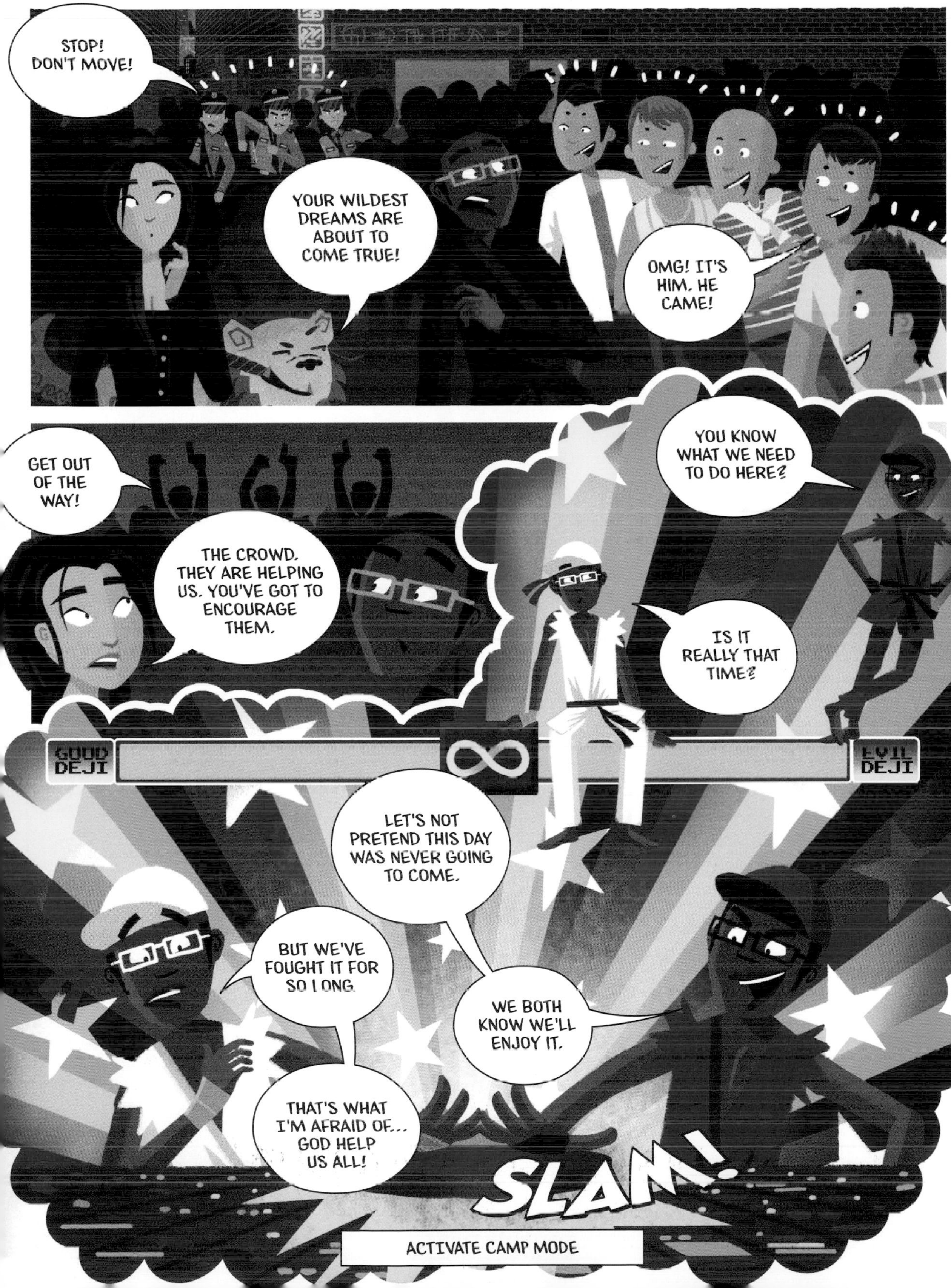
STOP! DON'T MOVE!
YOUR WILDEST DREAMS ARE ABOUT TO COME TRUE!
OMG! IT'S HIM. HE CAME!
GET OUT OF THE WAY!
THE CROWD. THEY ARE HELPING US. YOU'VE GOT TO ENCOURAGE THEM.
YOU KNOW WHAT WE NEED TO DO HERE?
IS IT REALLY THAT TIME?
GOOD DEJI
EVIL DEJI
LET'S NOT PRETEND THIS DAY WAS NEVER GOING TO COME.
BUT WE'VE FOUGHT IT FOR SO LONG.
WE BOTH KNOW WE'LL ENJOY IT.
THAT'S WHAT I'M AFRAID OF... GOD HELP US ALL!
SLAM!
ACTIVATE CAMP MODE

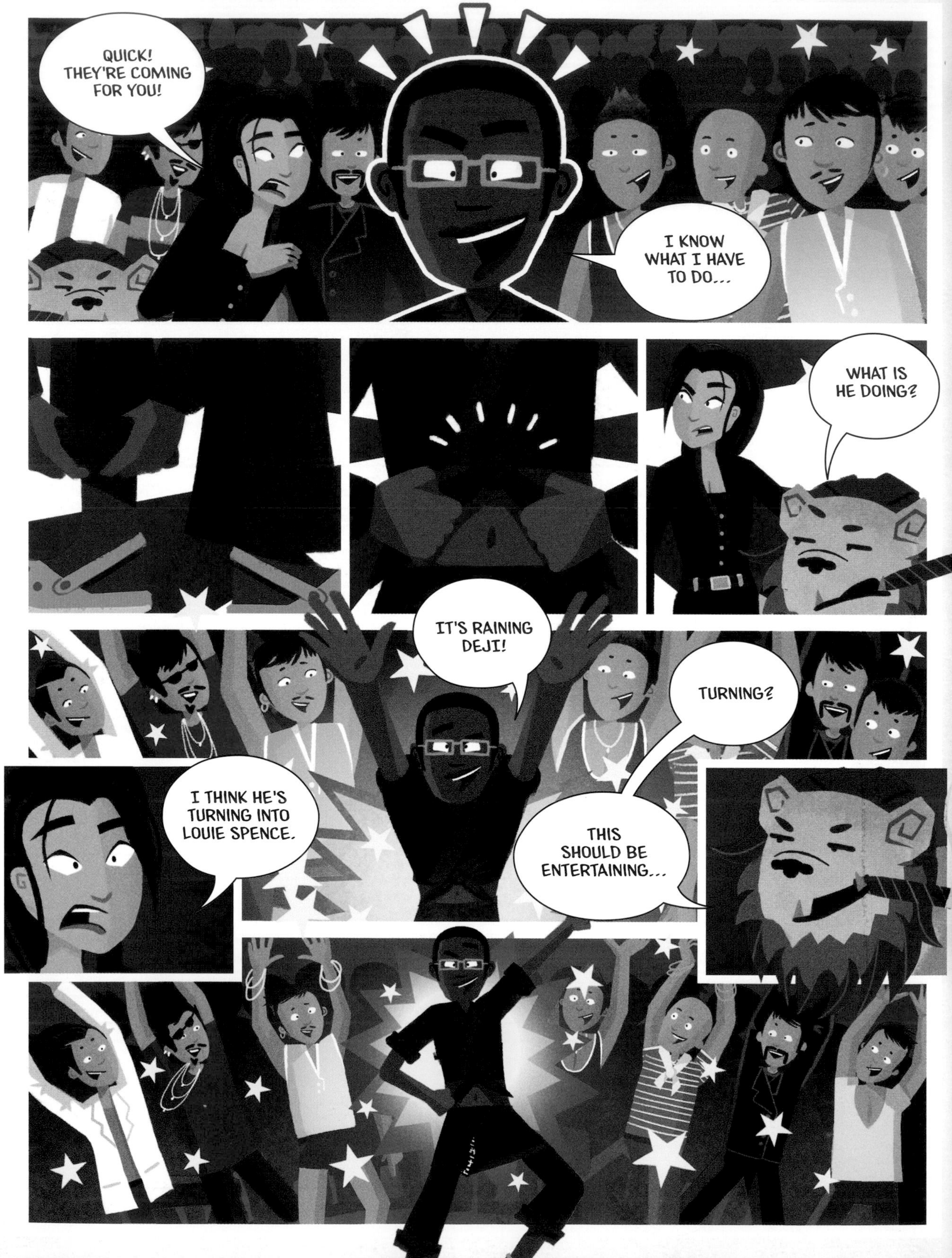
QUICK! THEY'RE COMING FOR YOU!
I KNOW WHAT I HAVE TO DO...
WHAT IS HE DOING?
IT'S RAINING DEJI!
TURNING?
I THINK HE'S TURNING INTO LOUIE SPENCE.
THIS SHOULD BE ENTERTAINING...

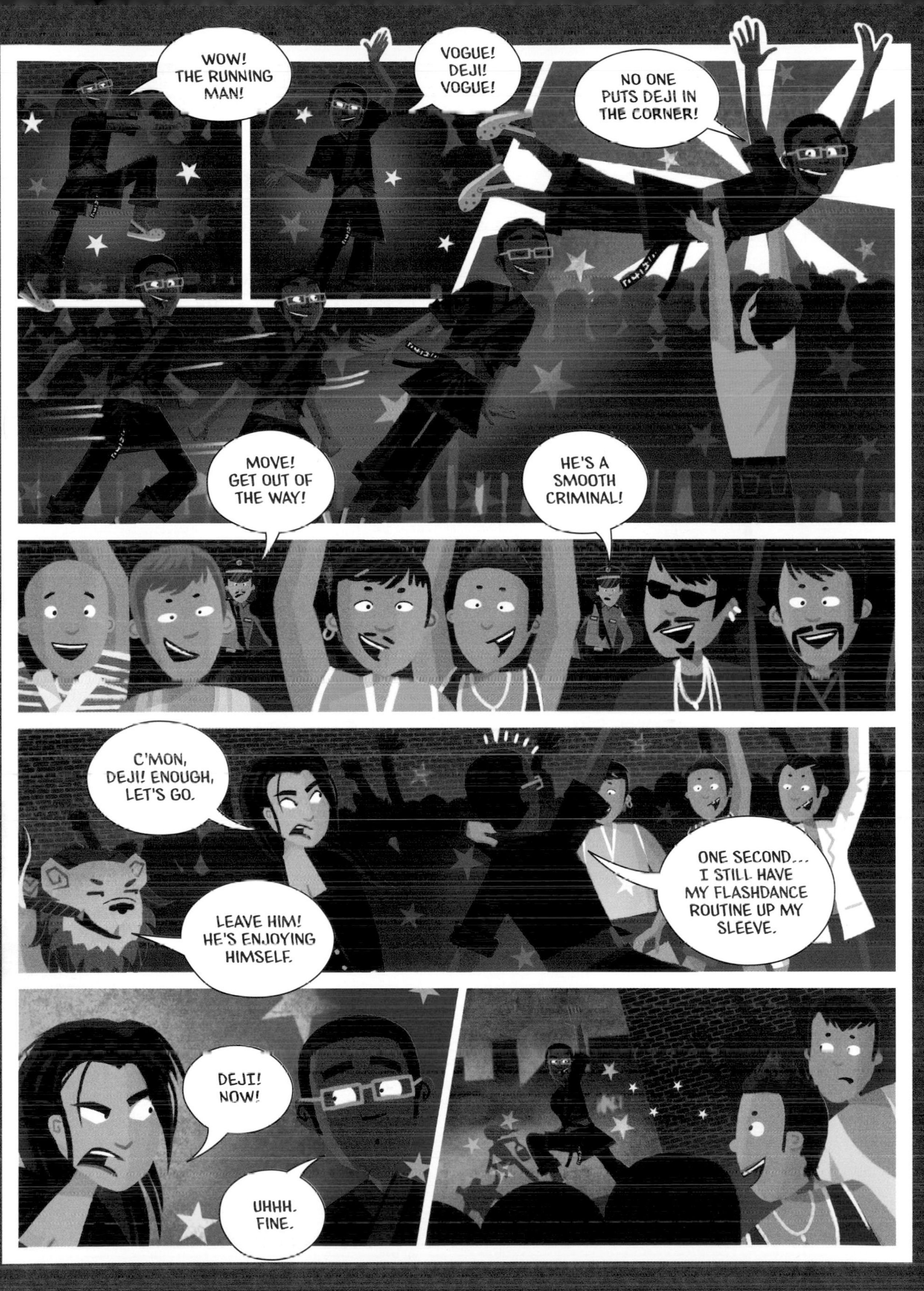
WOW! THE RUNNING MAN!
VOGUE! DEJI! VOGUE!
NO ONE PUTS DEJI IN THE CORNER!
MOVE! GET OUT OF THE WAY!
HE'S A SMOOTH CRIMINAL!
C'MON, DEJI! ENOUGH, LET'S GO.
LEAVE HIM! HE'S ENJOYING HIMSELF.
ONE SECOND... I STILL HAVE MY FLASHDANCE ROUTINE UP MY SLEEVE.
DEJI! NOW!
UHHH. FINE.

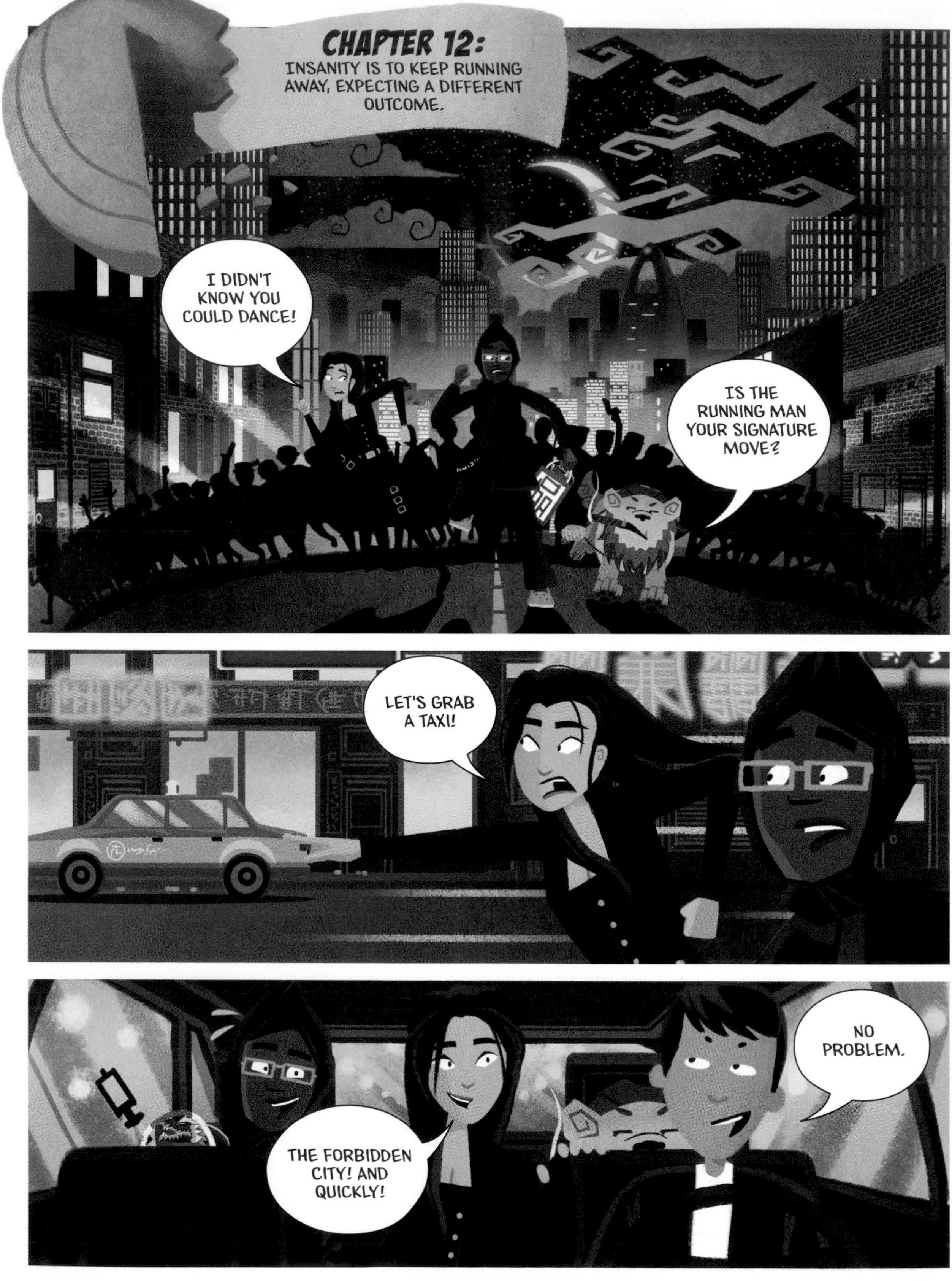
CHAPTER 12:
INSANITY IS TO KEEP RUNNING AWAY, EXPECTING A DIFFERENT OUTCOME.
I DIDN'T KNOW YOU COULD DANCE!
IS THE RUNNING MAN YOUR SIGNATURE MOVE?
LET'S GRAB A TAXI!
THE FORBIDDEN CITY! AND QUICKLY!
NO PROBLEM.

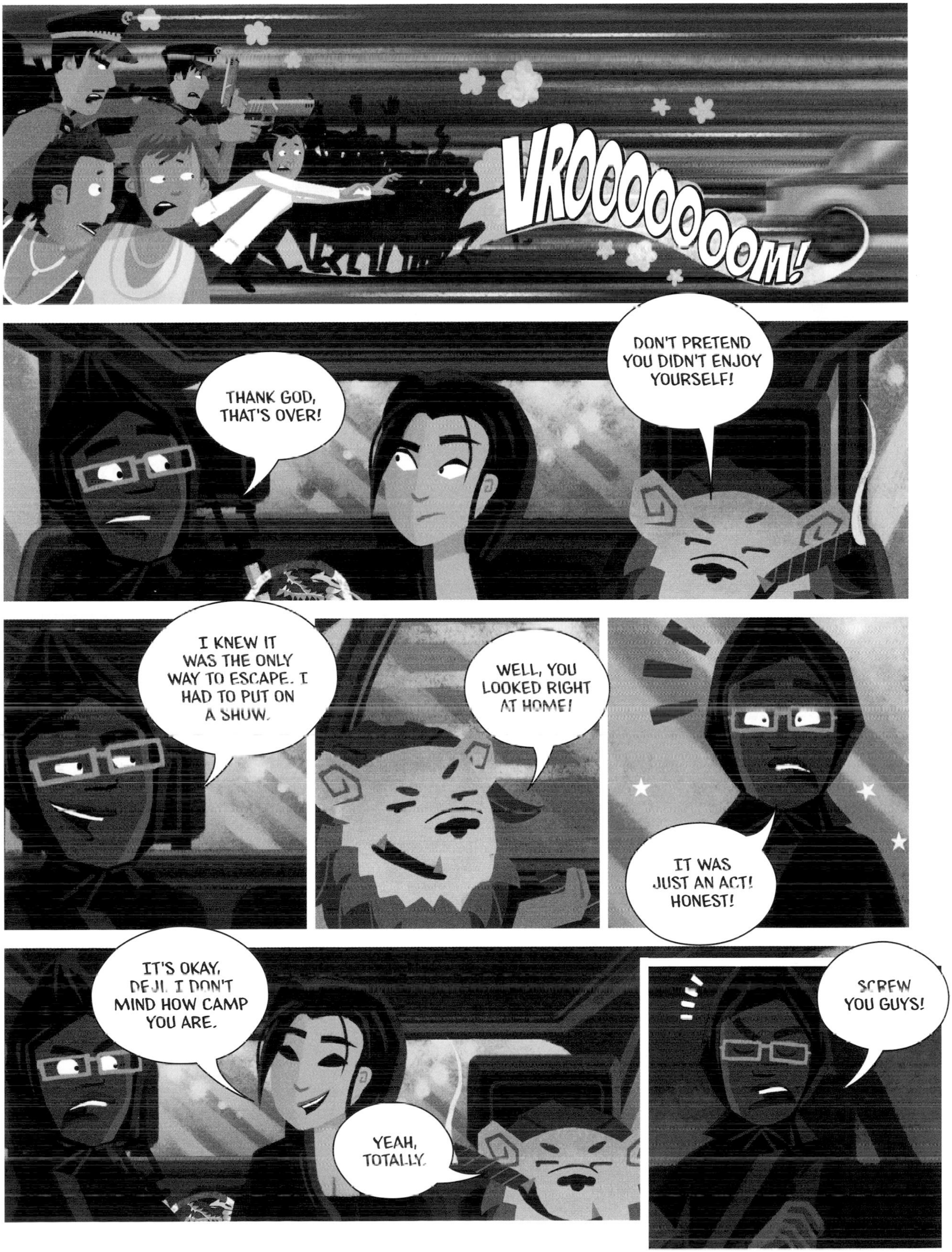
VROOOOOOOOM!
THANK GOD, THAT'S OVER!
DON'T PRETEND YOU DIDN'T ENJOY YOURSELF!
I KNEW IT WAS THE ONLY WAY TO ESCAPE. I HAD TO PUT ON A SHOW.
WELL, YOU LOOKED RIGHT AT HOME!
IT WAS JUST AN ACT! HONEST!
IT'S OKAY, DEJI. I DON'T MIND HOW CAMP YOU ARE.
YEAH, TOTALLY.
SCREW YOU GUYS!

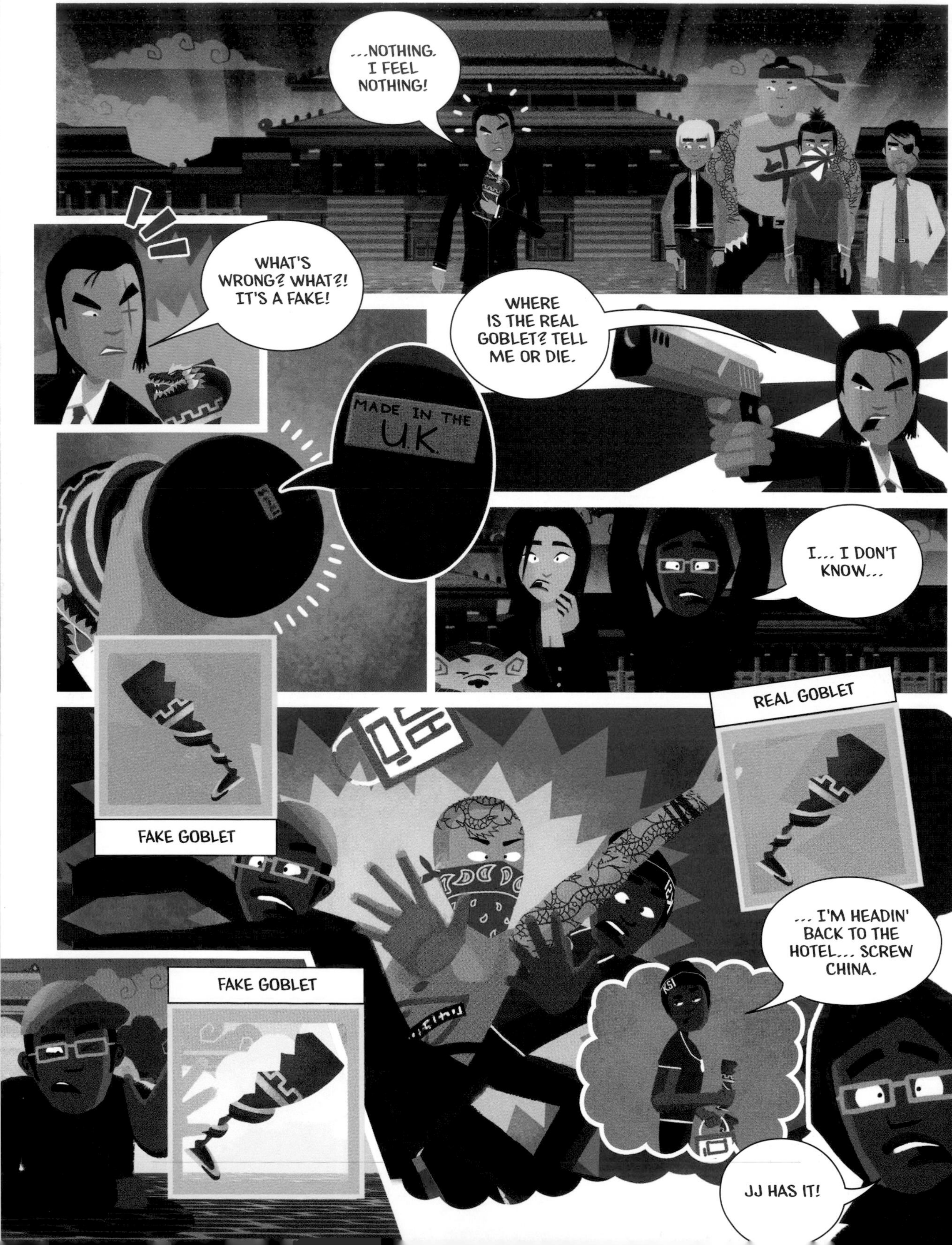
...NOTHING. I FEEL NOTHING!
WHAT'S WRONG? WHAT?! IT'S A FAKE!
WHERE IS THE REAL GOBLET? TELL ME OR DIE.
MADE IN THE U.K.
I... I DON'T KNOW...
FAKE GOBLET
REAL GOBLET
FAKE GOBLET
... I'M HEADIN' BACK TO THE HOTEL... SCREW CHINA.
JJ HAS IT!

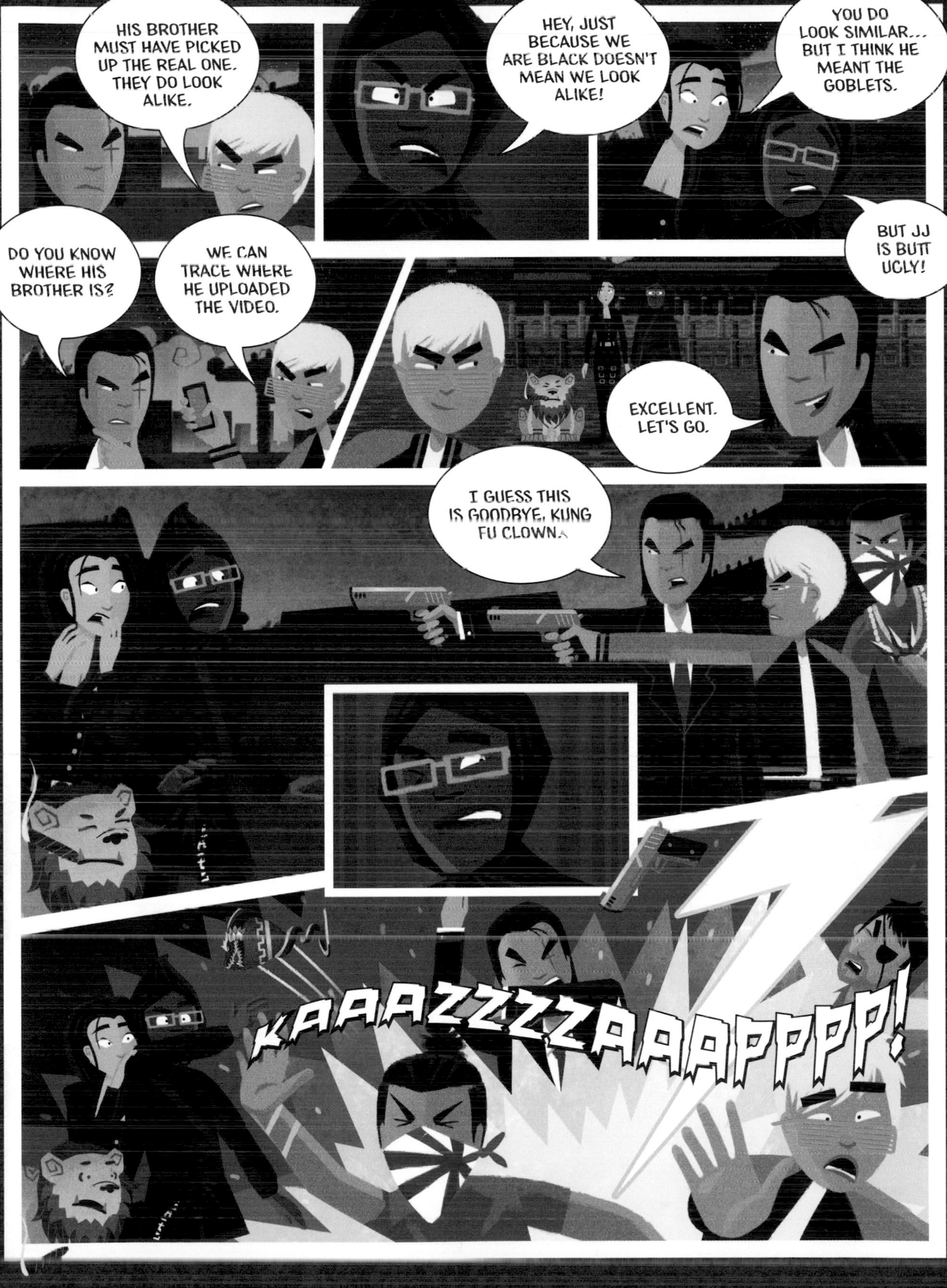
HIS BROTHER MUST HAVE PICKED UP THE REAL ONE. THEY DO LOOK ALIKE.
HEY, JUST BECAUSE WE ARE BLACK DOESN'T MEAN WE LOOK ALIKE!
YOU DO LOOK SIMILAR... BUT I THINK HE MEANT THE GOBLETS.
BUT JJ IS BUTT UGLY!
DO YOU KNOW WHERE HIS BROTHER IS?
WE CAN TRACE WHERE HE UPLOADED THE VIDEO.
EXCELLENT. LET'S GO.
I GUESS THIS IS GOODBYE, KUNG FU CLOWN.
KAAAZZZZZAAAAPPPPP!

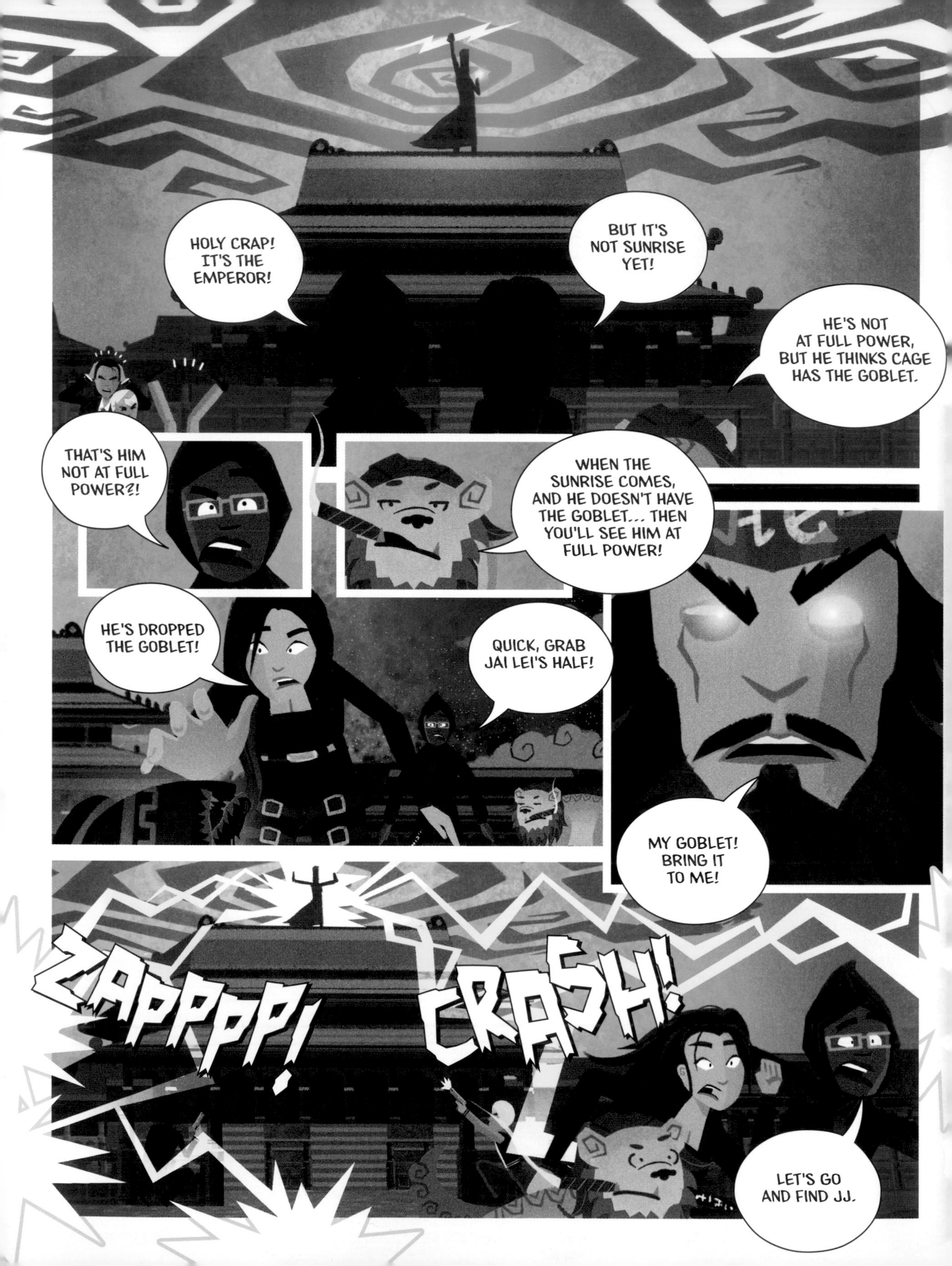
HOLY CRAP! IT'S THE EMPEROR!
BUT IT'S NOT SUNRISE YET!
HE'S NOT AT FULL POWER, BUT HE THINKS CAGE HAS THE GOBLET.
THAT'S HIM NOT AT FULL POWER?!
WHEN THE SUNRISE COMES, AND HE DOESN'T HAVE THE GOBLET... THEN YOU'LL SEE HIM AT FULL POWER!
HE'S DROPPED THE GOBLET!
QUICK, GRAB JAI LEI'S HALF!
MY GOBLET! BRING IT TO ME!
ZAPPPPP!
CRASH!
LET'S GO AND FIND JJ.

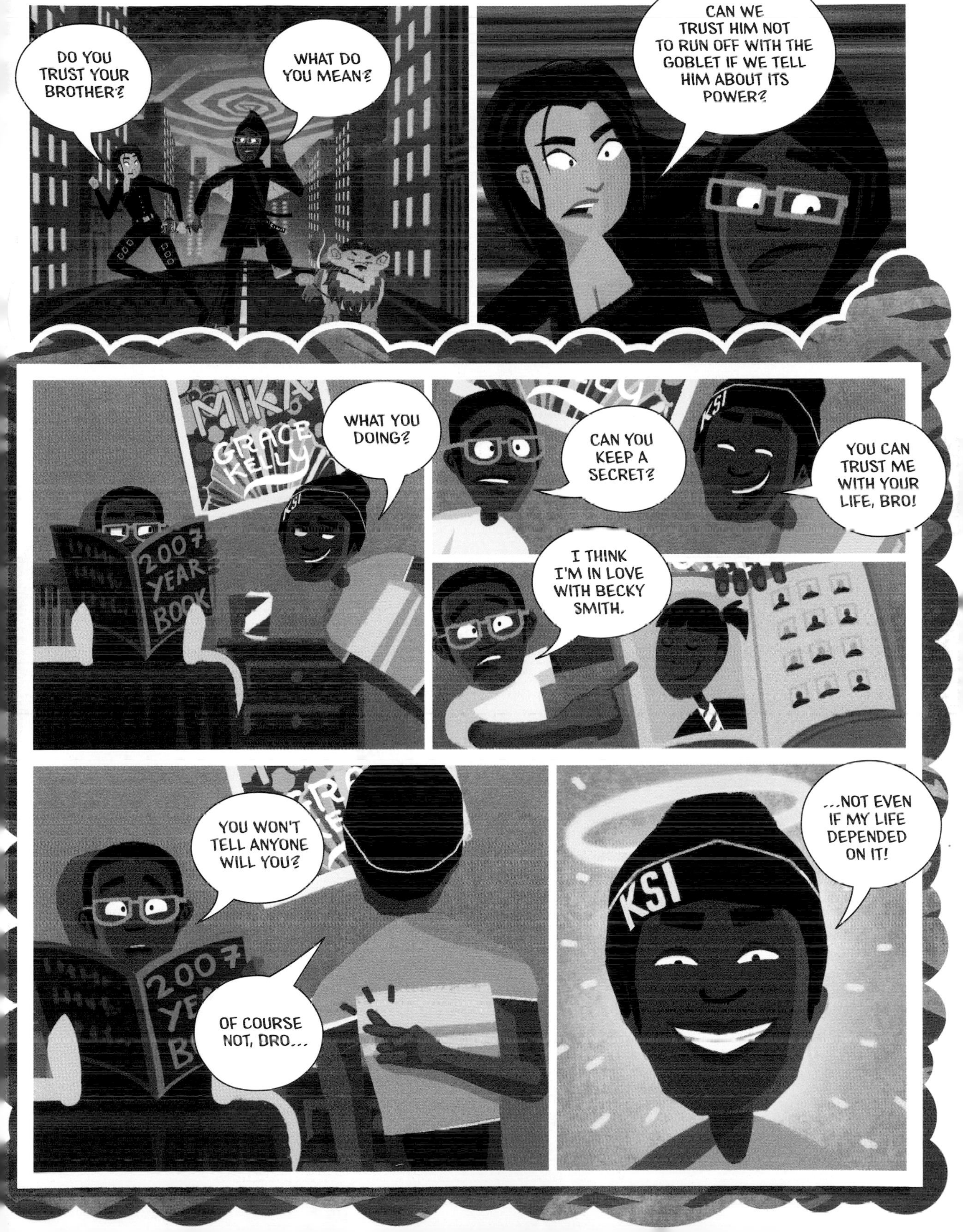
DO YOU TRUST YOUR BROTHER?
WHAT DO YOU MEAN?
CAN WE TRUST HIM NOT TO RUN OFF WITH THE GOBLET IF WE TELL HIM ABOUT ITS POWER?
MIKA
GRACE KELLY
2007 YEAR BOOK
WHAT YOU DOING?
KSI
CAN YOU KEEP A SECRET?
YOU CAN TRUST ME WITH YOUR LIFE, BRO!
I THINK I'M IN LOVE WITH BECKY SMITH.
YOU WON'T TELL ANYONE WILL YOU?
OF COURSE NOT, BRO...
...NOT EVEN IF MY LIFE DEPENDED ON IT!

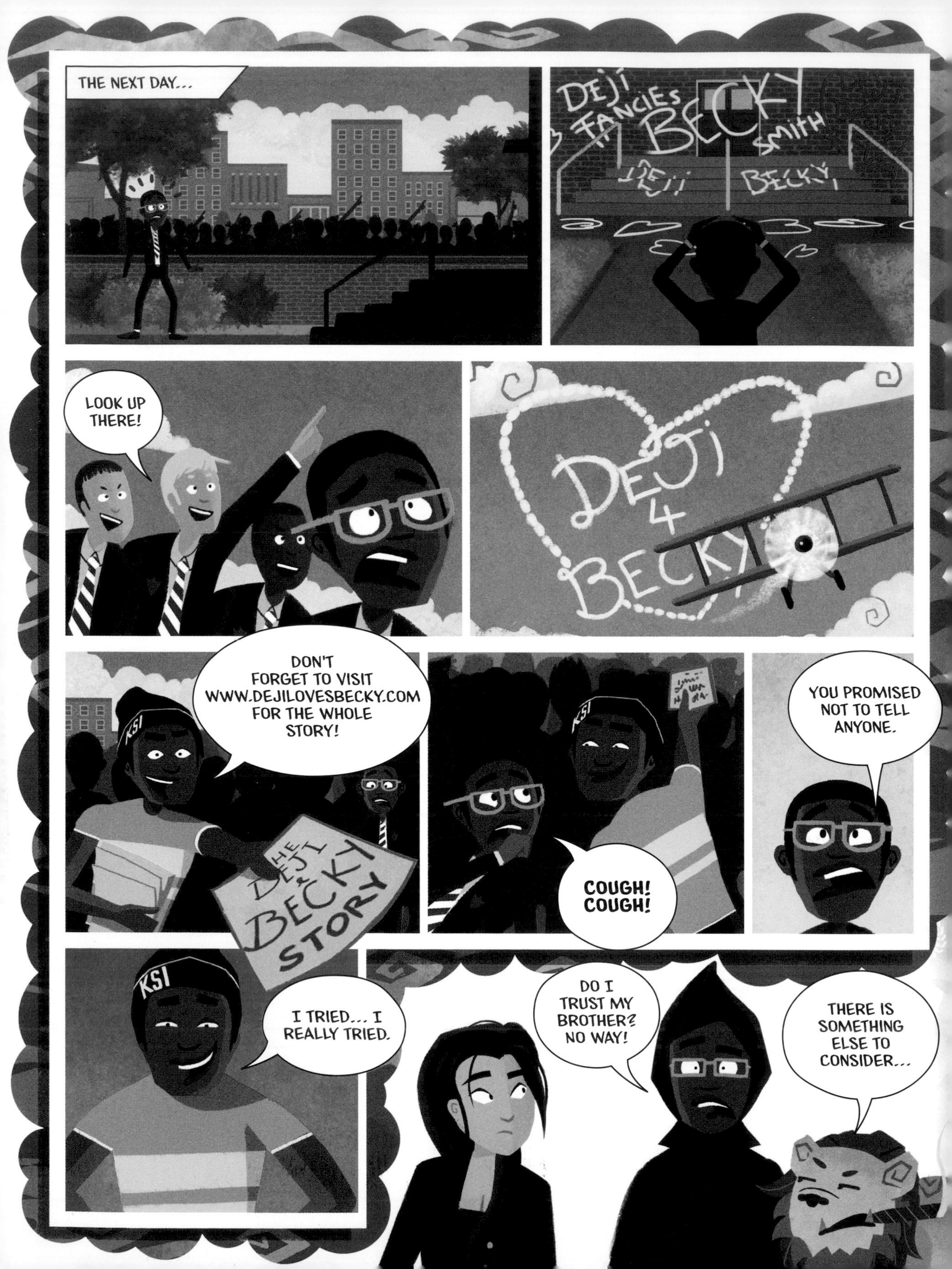
THE NEXT DAY...
DEJI FANCIES BECKY SMITH
DEJI BECKY
LOOK UP THERE!
DEJI 4 BECKY
DON'T FORGET TO VISIT WWW.DEJILOVESBECKY.COM FOR THE WHOLE STORY!
THE DEJI & BECKY STORY
COUGH! COUGH!
YOU PROMISED NOT TO TELL ANYONE.
KSI
I TRIED... I REALLY TRIED.
DO I TRUST MY BROTHER? NO WAY!
THERE IS SOMETHING ELSE TO CONSIDER...

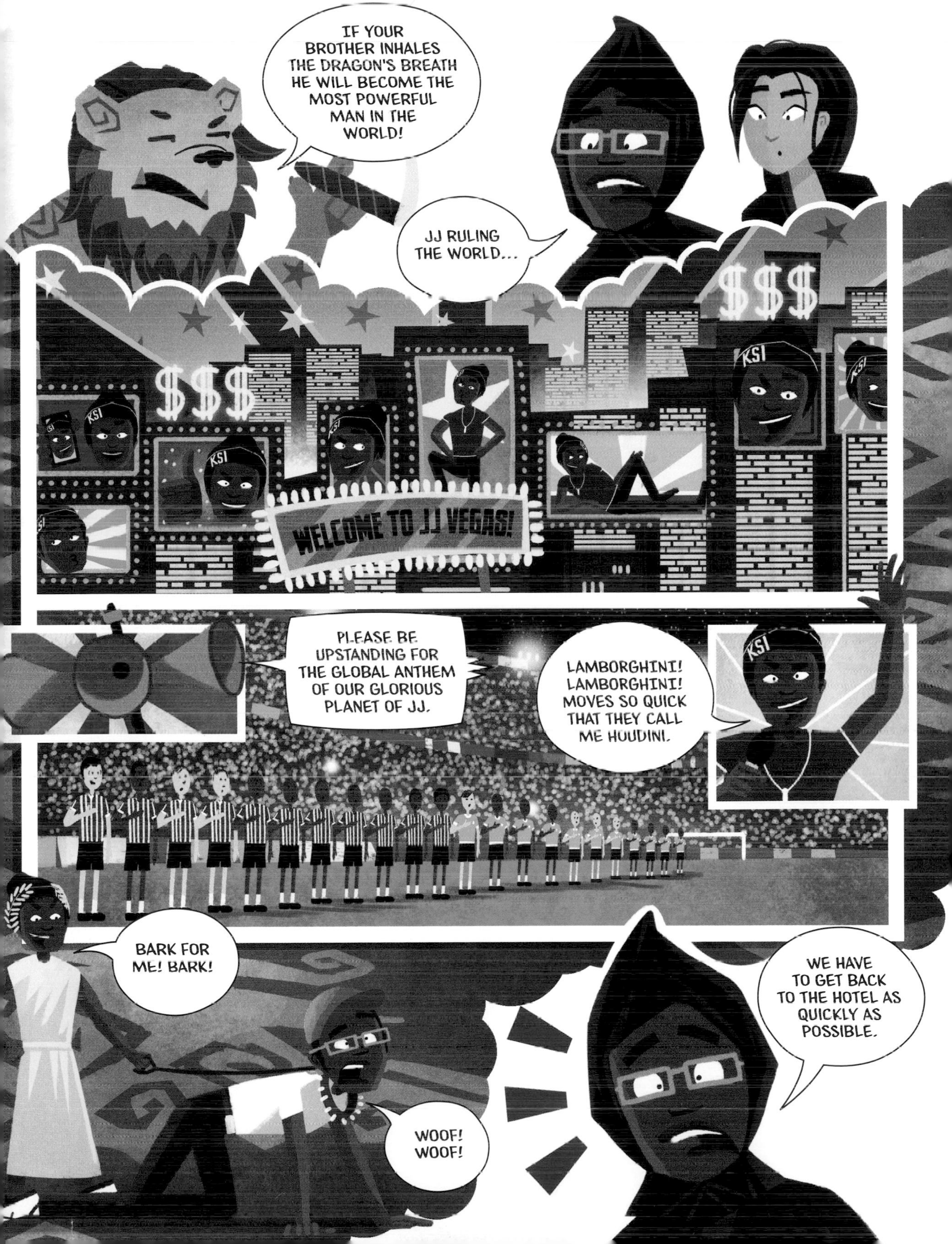
IF YOUR BROTHER INHALES THE DRAGON'S BREATH HE WILL BECOME THE MOST POWERFUL MAN IN THE WORLD!
JJ RULING THE WORLD...
WELCOME TO JJ VEGAS!
KSI
PLEASE BE UPSTANDING FOR THE GLOBAL ANTHEM OF OUR GLORIOUS PLANET OF JJ.
LAMBORGHINI! LAMBORGHINI! MOVES SO QUICK THAT THEY CALL ME HOUDINI.
BARK FOR ME! BARK!
WOOF! WOOF!
WE HAVE TO GET BACK TO THE HOTEL AS QUICKLY AS POSSIBLE.

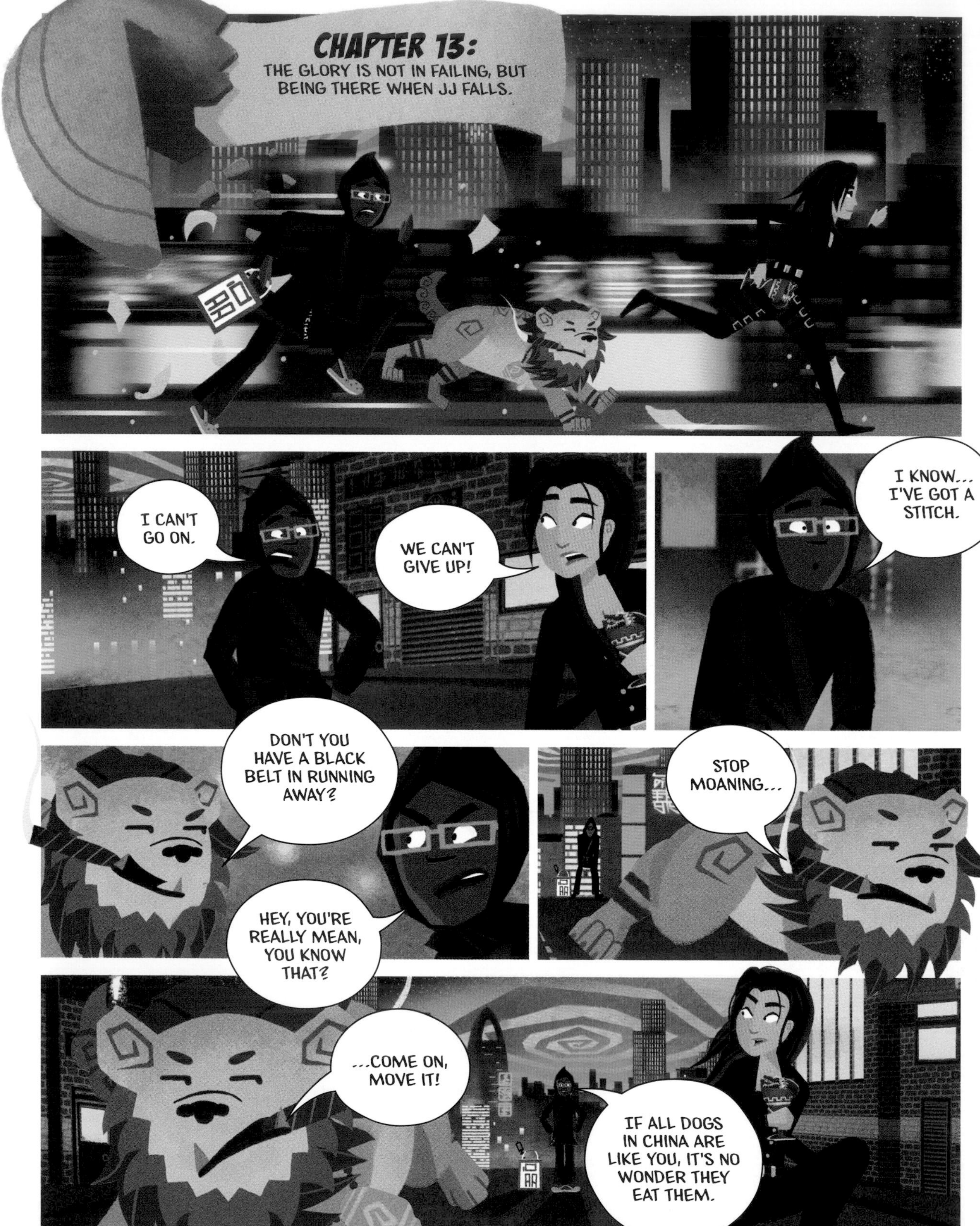

CHAPTER 13:
THE GLORY IS NOT IN FAILING, BUT BEING THERE WHEN JJ FALLS.
I CAN'T GO ON.
WE CAN'T GIVE UP!
I KNOW... I'VE GOT A STITCH.
DON'T YOU HAVE A BLACK BELT IN RUNNING AWAY?
HEY, YOU'RE REALLY MEAN, YOU KNOW THAT?
STOP MOANING...
...COME ON, MOVE IT!
IF ALL DOGS IN CHINA ARE LIKE YOU, IT'S NO WONDER THEY EAT THEM.

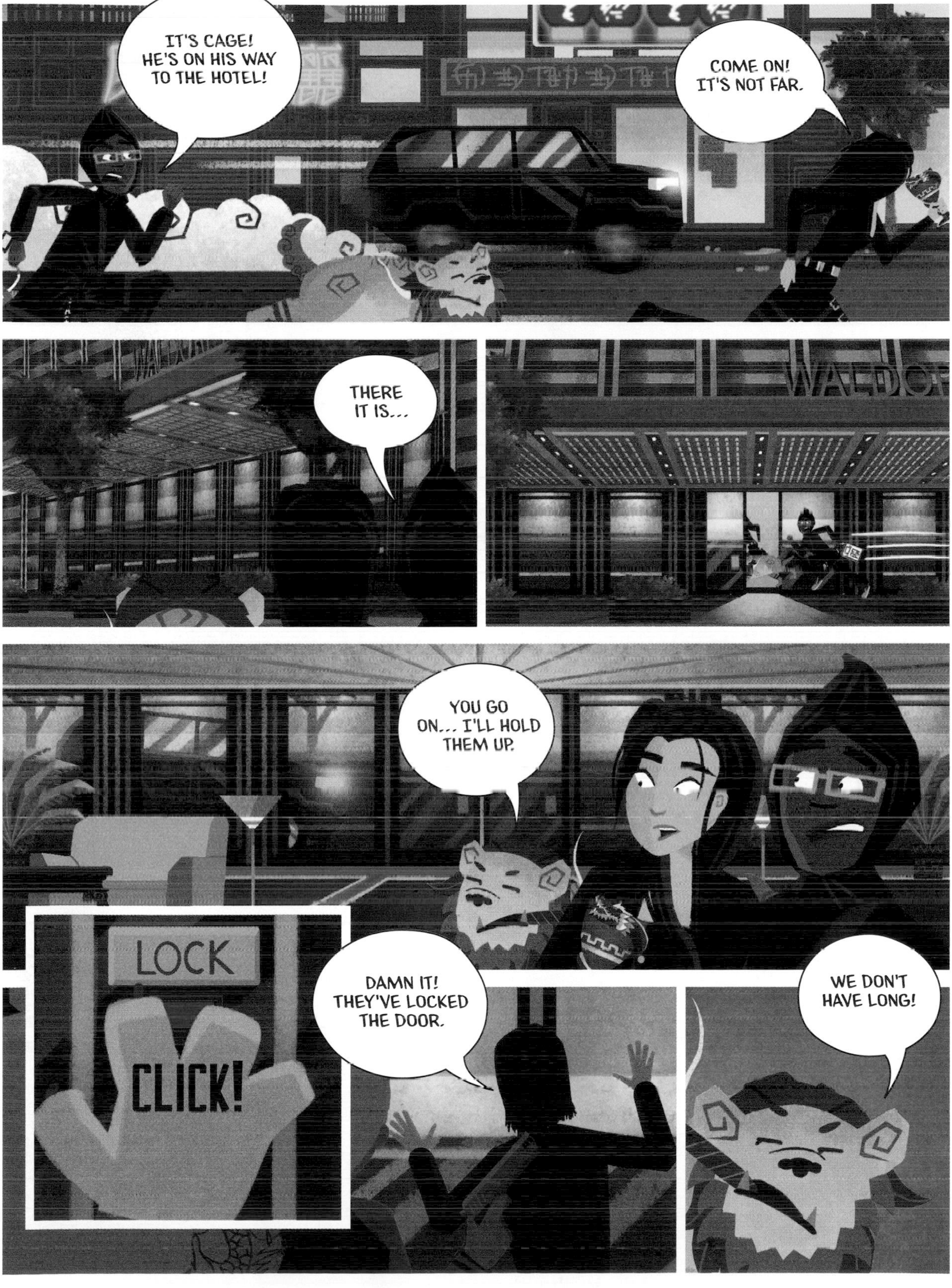
IT'S CAGE! HE'S ON HIS WAY TO THE HOTEL!
COME ON! IT'S NOT FAR.
THERE IT IS...
YOU GO ON... I'LL HOLD THEM UP.
LOCK
CLICK!
DAMN IT! THEY'VE LOCKED THE DOOR.
WE DON'T HAVE LONG!

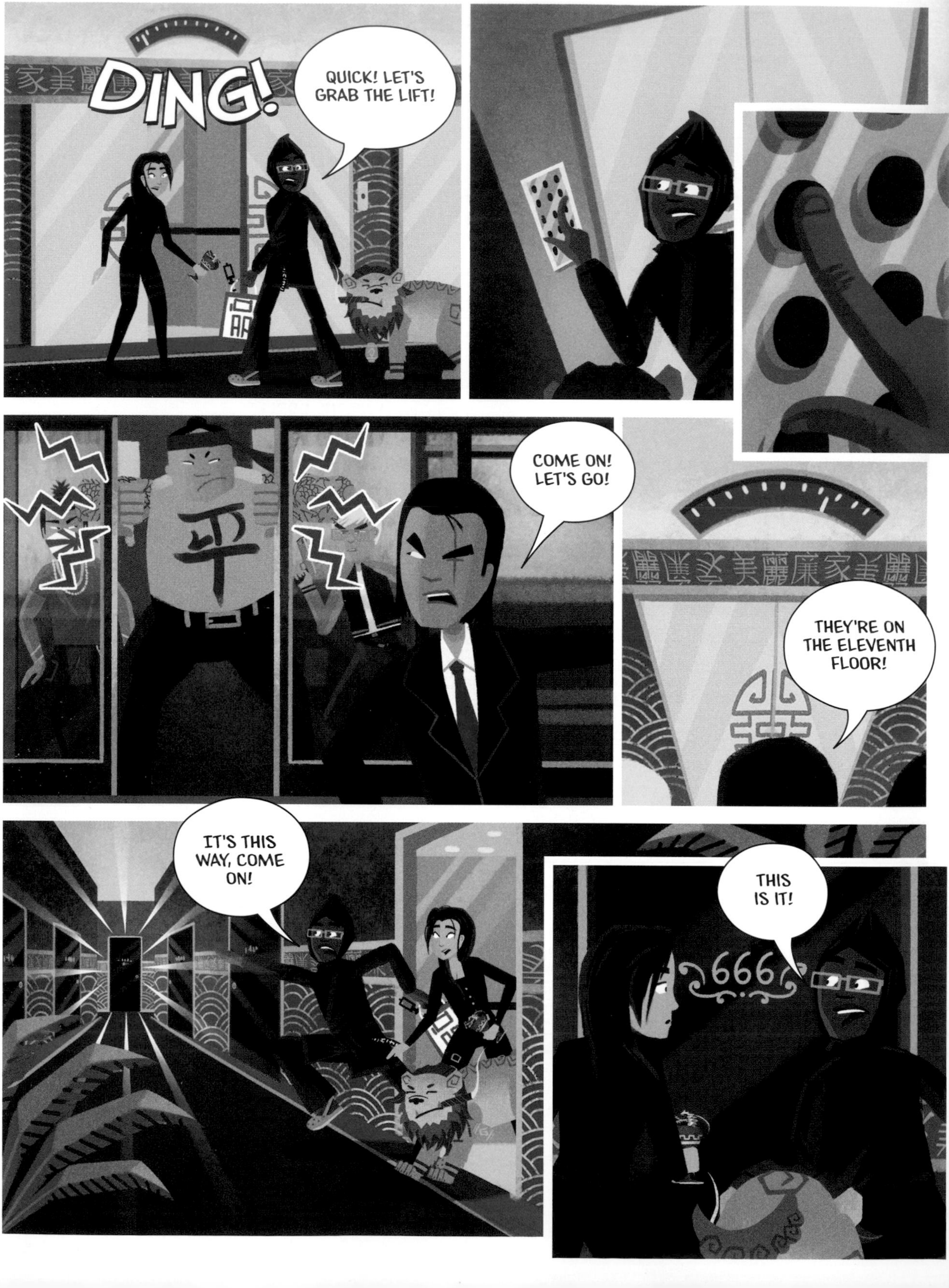
DING!
QUICK! LET'S GRAB THE LIFT!
COME ON! LET'S GO!
THEY'RE ON THE ELEVENTH FLOOR!
IT'S THIS WAY, COME ON!
THIS IS IT!
666

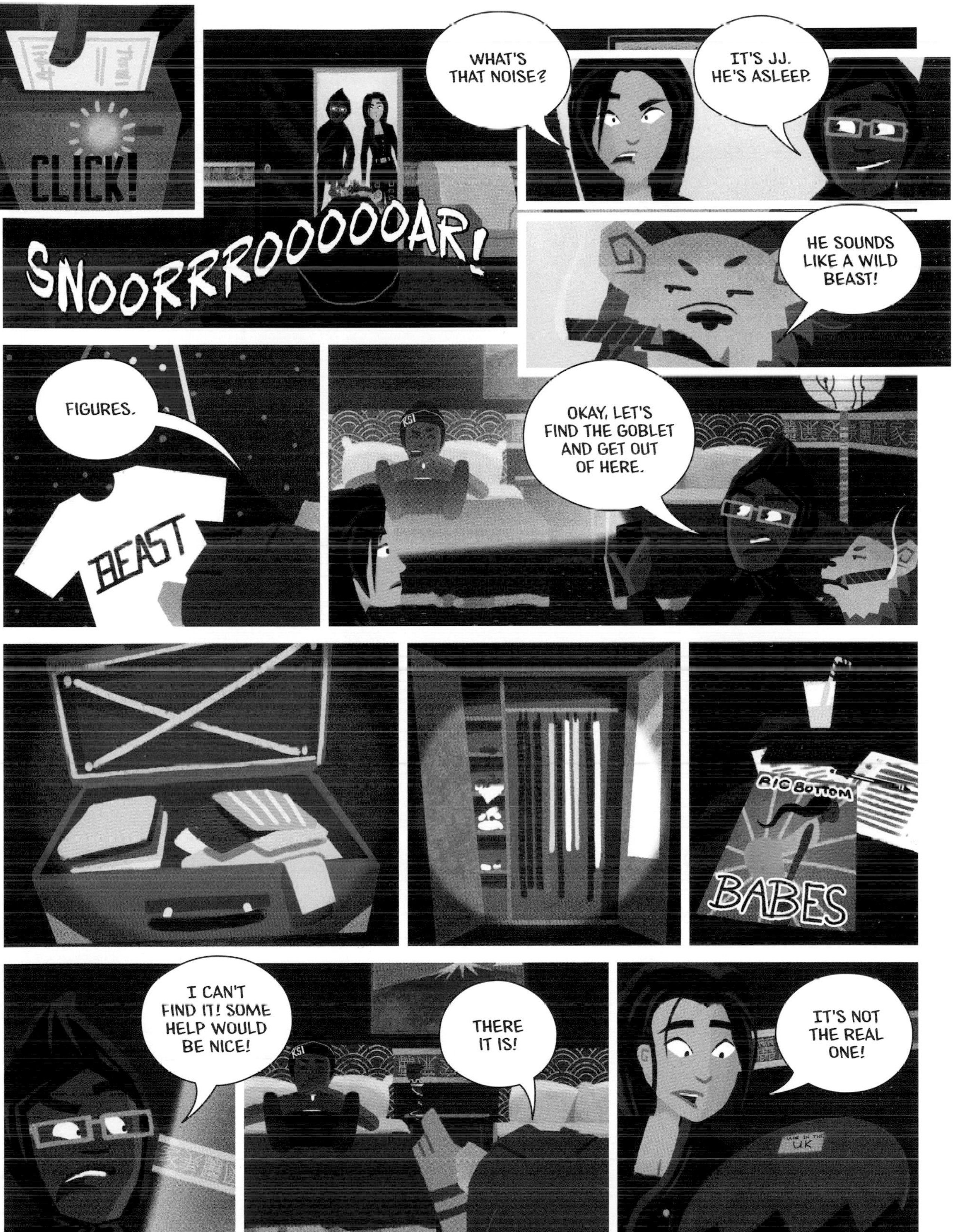
CLICK!
SNOORRROOOOOAR!
WHAT'S THAT NOISE?
IT'S JJ. HE'S ASLEEP.
HE SOUNDS LIKE A WILD BEAST!
FIGURES.
BEAST
OKAY, LET'S FIND THE GOBLET AND GET OUT OF HERE.
RSI
BIG BOTTOM
BABES
I CAN'T FIND IT! SOME HELP WOULD BE NICE!
RSI
THERE IT IS!
IT'S NOT THE REAL ONE!
MADE IN THE UK

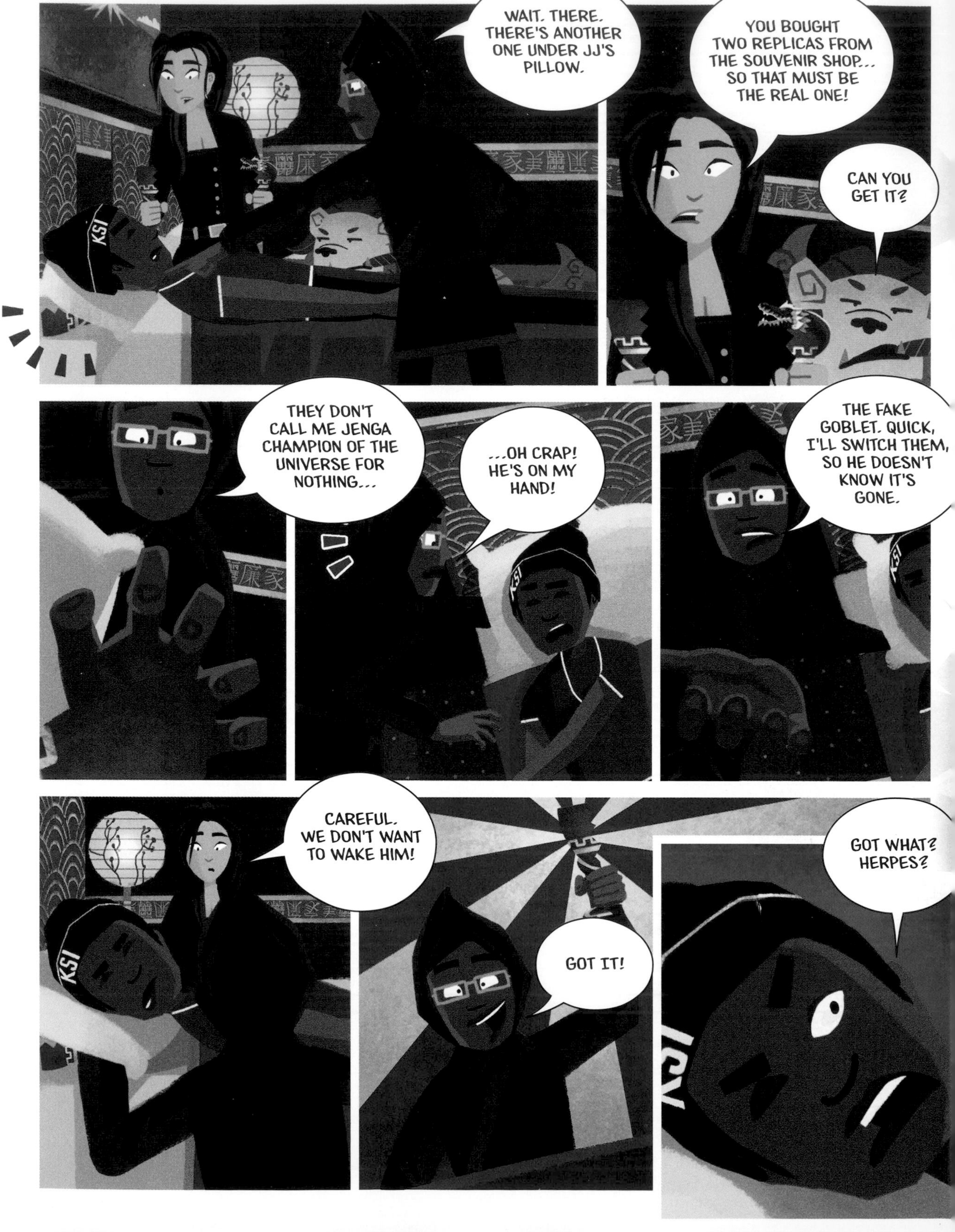
WAIT. THERE. THERE'S ANOTHER ONE UNDER JJ'S PILLOW.
YOU BOUGHT TWO REPLICAS FROM THE SOUVENIR SHOP... SO THAT MUST BE THE REAL ONE!
CAN YOU GET IT?
THEY DON'T CALL ME JENGA CHAMPION OF THE UNIVERSE FOR NOTHING...
...OH CRAP! HE'S ON MY HAND!
THE FAKE GOBLET. QUICK, I'LL SWITCH THEM, SO HE DOESN'T KNOW IT'S GONE.
CAREFUL. WE DON'T WANT TO WAKE HIM!
GOT IT!
GOT WHAT? HERPES?

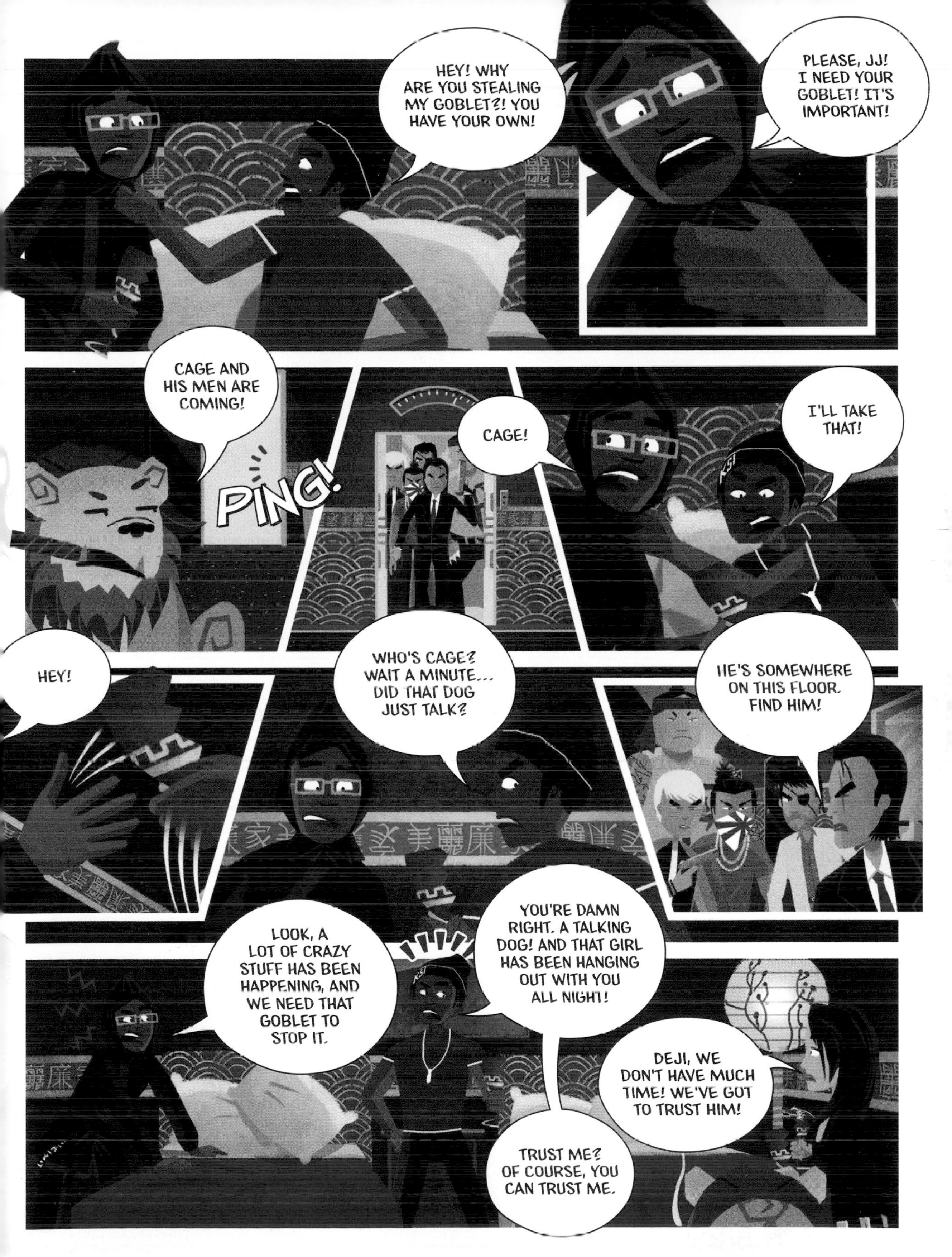

HEY! WHY ARE YOU STEALING MY GOBLET?! YOU HAVE YOUR OWN!
PLEASE, JJ! I NEED YOUR GOBLET! IT'S IMPORTANT!
CAGE AND HIS MEN ARE COMING!
PING!
CAGE!
I'LL TAKE THAT!
HEY!
WHO'S CAGE? WAIT A MINUTE... DID THAT DOG JUST TALK?
HE'S SOMEWHERE ON THIS FLOOR. FIND HIM!
LOOK, A LOT OF CRAZY STUFF HAS BEEN HAPPENING, AND WE NEED THAT GOBLET TO STOP IT.
YOU'RE DAMN RIGHT. A TALKING DOG! AND THAT GIRL HAS BEEN HANGING OUT WITH YOU ALL NIGHT!
DEJI, WE DON'T HAVE MUCH TIME! WE'VE GOT TO TRUST HIM!
TRUST ME? OF COURSE, YOU CAN TRUST ME.

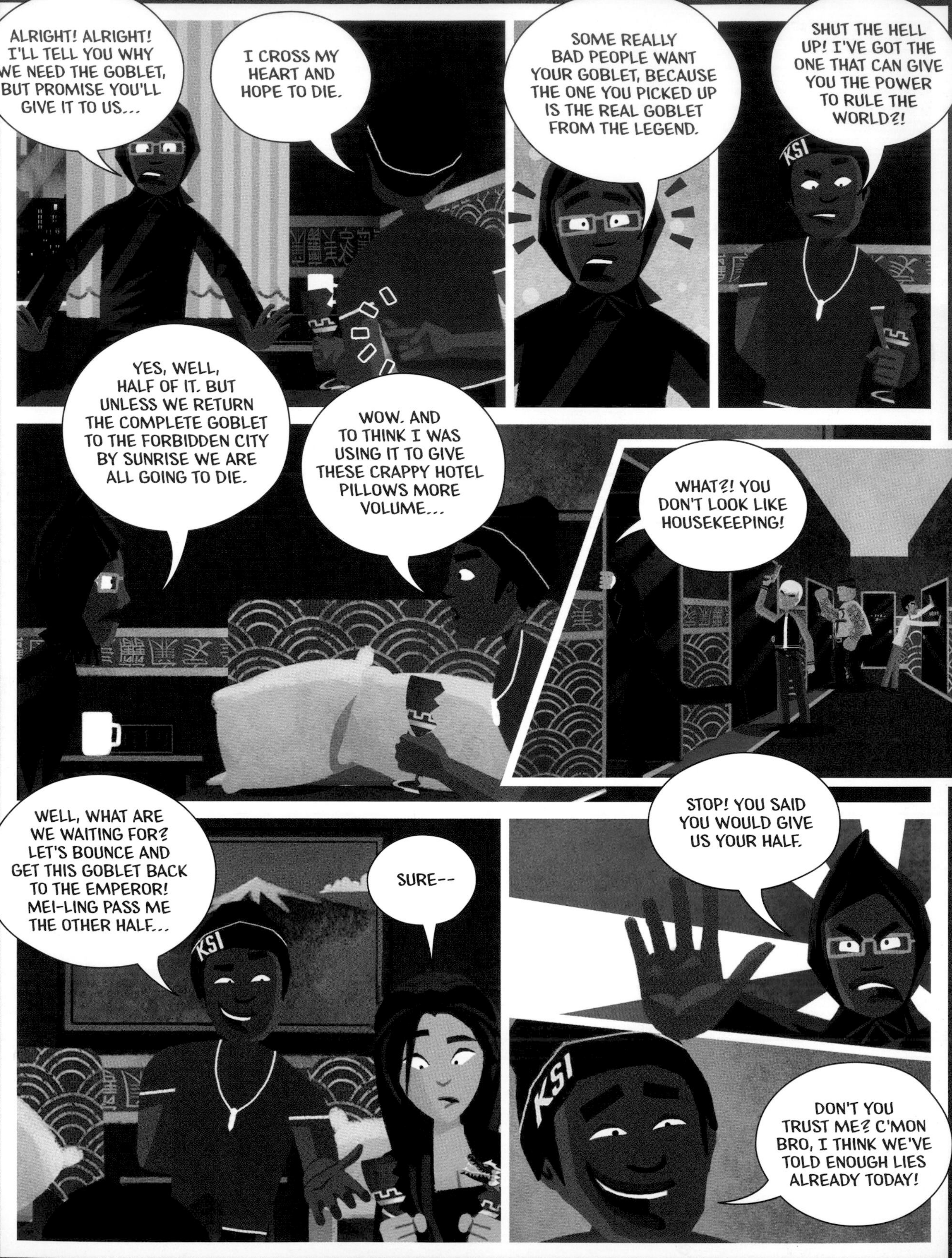
ALRIGHT! ALRIGHT! I'LL TELL YOU WHY WE NEED THE GOBLET, BUT PROMISE YOU'LL GIVE IT TO US...
I CROSS MY HEART AND HOPE TO DIE.
SOME REALLY BAD PEOPLE WANT YOUR GOBLET, BECAUSE THE ONE YOU PICKED UP IS THE REAL GOBLET FROM THE LEGEND.
SHUT THE HELL UP! I'VE GOT THE ONE THAT CAN GIVE YOU THE POWER TO RULE THE WORLD?!
YES, WELL, HALF OF IT. BUT UNLESS WE RETURN THE COMPLETE GOBLET TO THE FORBIDDEN CITY BY SUNRISE WE ARE ALL GOING TO DIE.
WOW. AND TO THINK I WAS USING IT TO GIVE THESE CRAPPY HOTEL PILLOWS MORE VOLUME...
WHAT?! YOU DON'T LOOK LIKE HOUSEKEEPING!
WELL, WHAT ARE WE WAITING FOR? LET'S BOUNCE AND GET THIS GOBLET BACK TO THE EMPEROR! MEI-LING PASS ME THE OTHER HALF...
SURE--
STOP! YOU SAID YOU WOULD GIVE US YOUR HALF.
DON'T YOU TRUST ME? C'MON BRO, I THINK WE'VE TOLD ENOUGH LIES ALREADY TODAY!

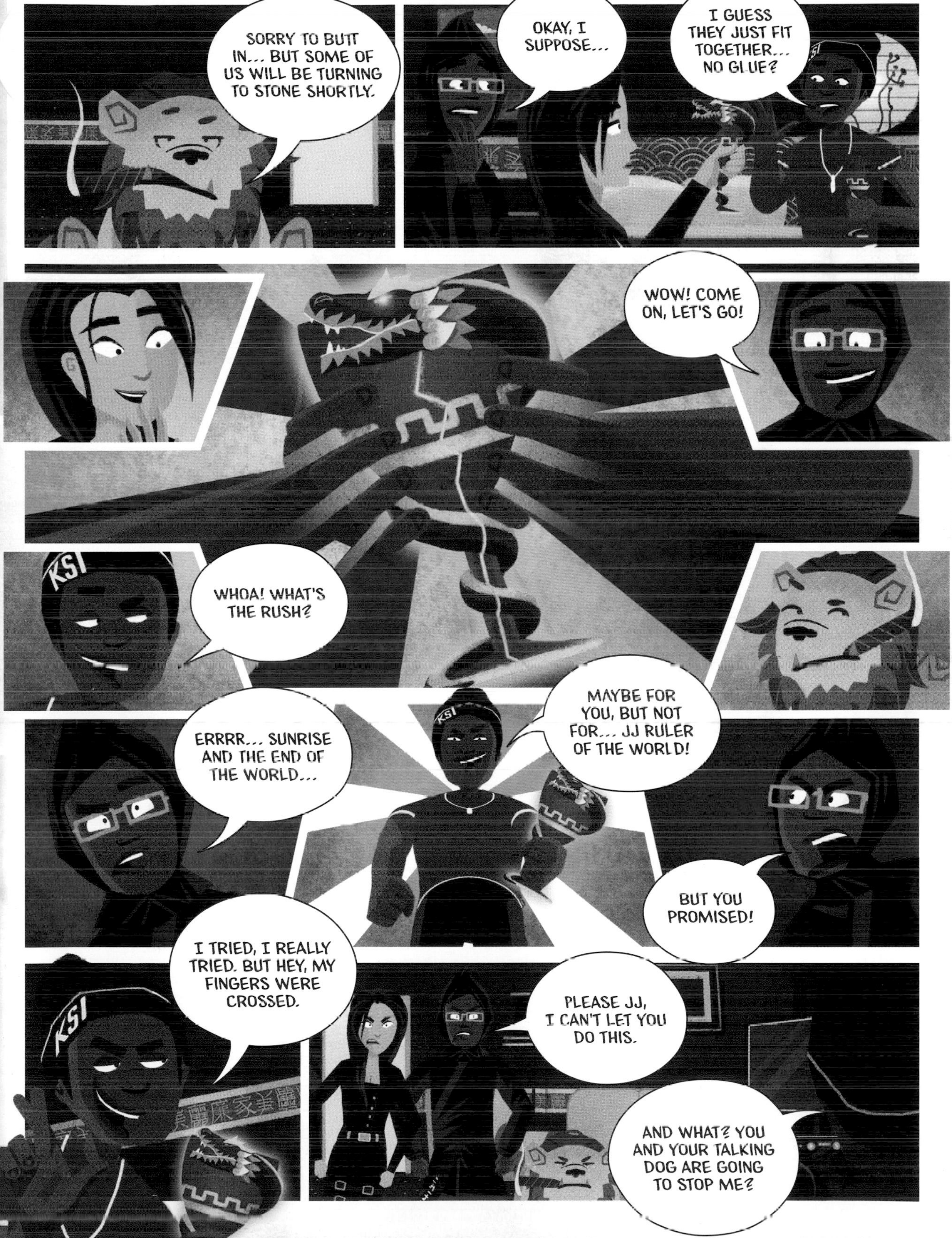
SORRY TO BUTT IN... BUT SOME OF US WILL BE TURNING TO STONE SHORTLY.
OKAY, I SUPPOSE...
I GUESS THEY JUST FIT TOGETHER... NO GLUE?
WOW! COME ON, LET'S GO!
WHOA! WHAT'S THE RUSH?
ERRRR... SUNRISE AND THE END OF THE WORLD...
MAYBE FOR YOU, BUT NOT FOR... JJ RULER OF THE WORLD!
BUT YOU PROMISED!
I TRIED, I REALLY TRIED. BUT HEY, MY FINGERS WERE CROSSED.
PLEASE JJ, I CAN'T LET YOU DO THIS.
AND WHAT? YOU AND YOUR TALKING DOG ARE GOING TO STOP ME?

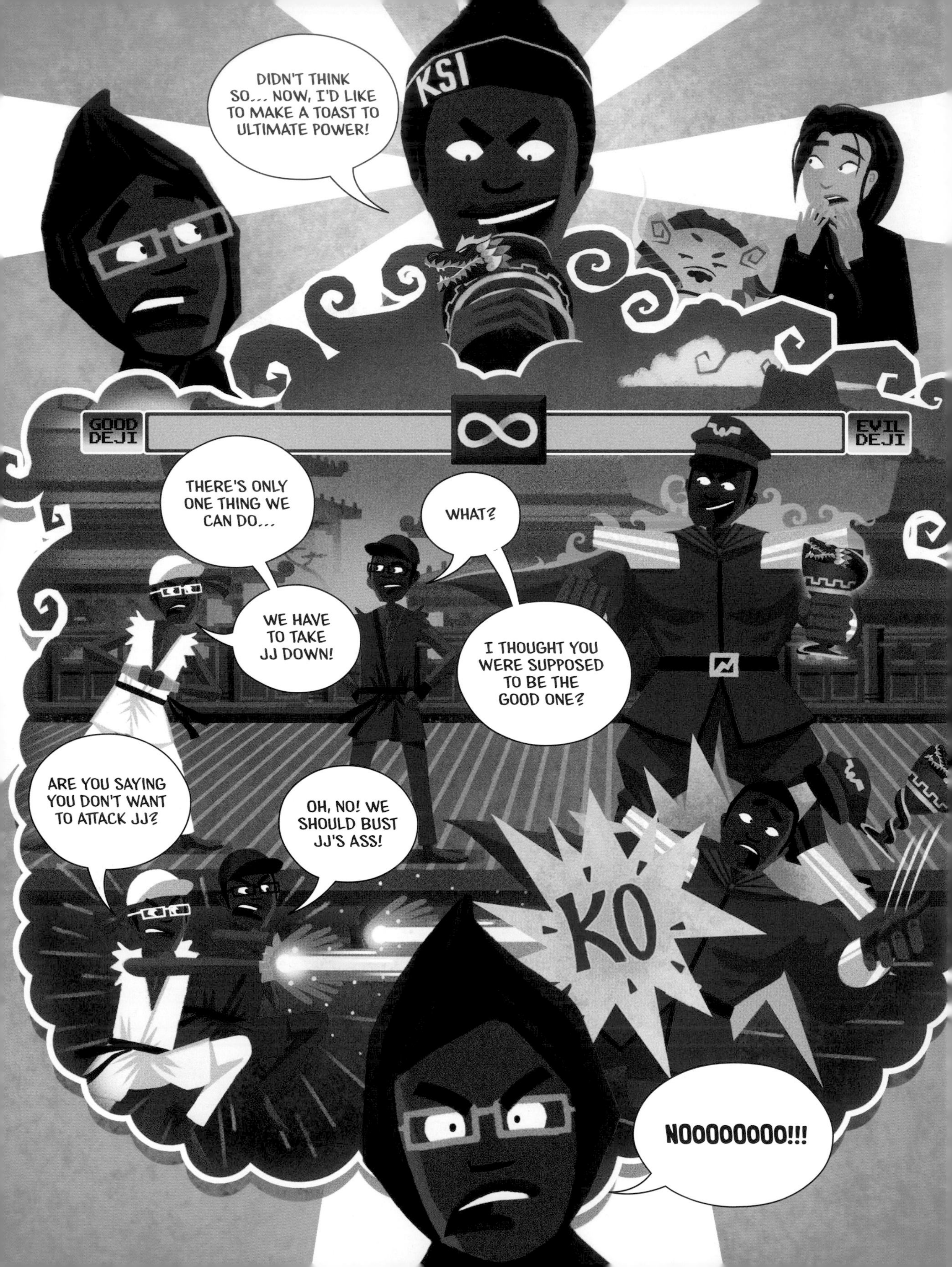
DIDN'T THINK SO... NOW, I'D LIKE TO MAKE A TOAST TO ULTIMATE POWER!
KSI
GOOD DEJI
EVIL DEJI
THERE'S ONLY ONE THING WE CAN DO...
WHAT?
WE HAVE TO TAKE JJ DOWN!
I THOUGHT YOU WERE SUPPOSED TO BE THE GOOD ONE?
ARE YOU SAYING YOU DON'T WANT TO ATTACK JJ?
OH, NO! WE SHOULD BUST JJ'S ASS!
KO
NOOOOOOOO!!!

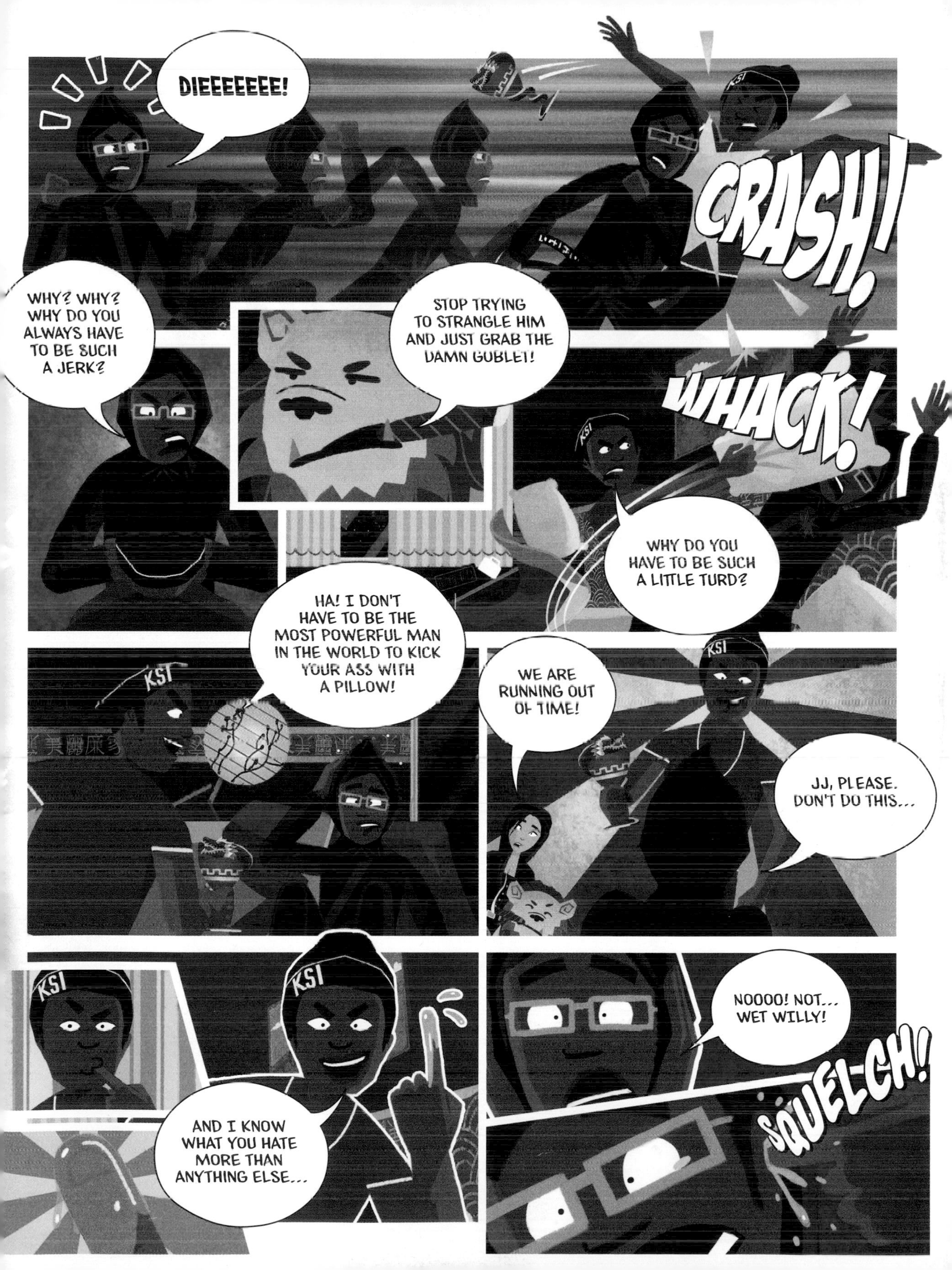
DIEEEEEEE!
CRASH!
WHY? WHY? WHY DO YOU ALWAYS HAVE TO BE SUCH A JERK?
STOP TRYING TO STRANGLE HIM AND JUST GRAB THE DAMN GOBLET!
WHACK!
WHY DO YOU HAVE TO BE SUCH A LITTLE TURD?
HA! I DON'T HAVE TO BE THE MOST POWERFUL MAN IN THE WORLD TO KICK YOUR ASS WITH A PILLOW!
WE ARE RUNNING OUT OF TIME!
JJ, PLEASE. DON'T DO THIS...
AND I KNOW WHAT YOU HATE MORE THAN ANYTHING ELSE...
NOOOO! NOT... WET WILLY!
SQUELCH!

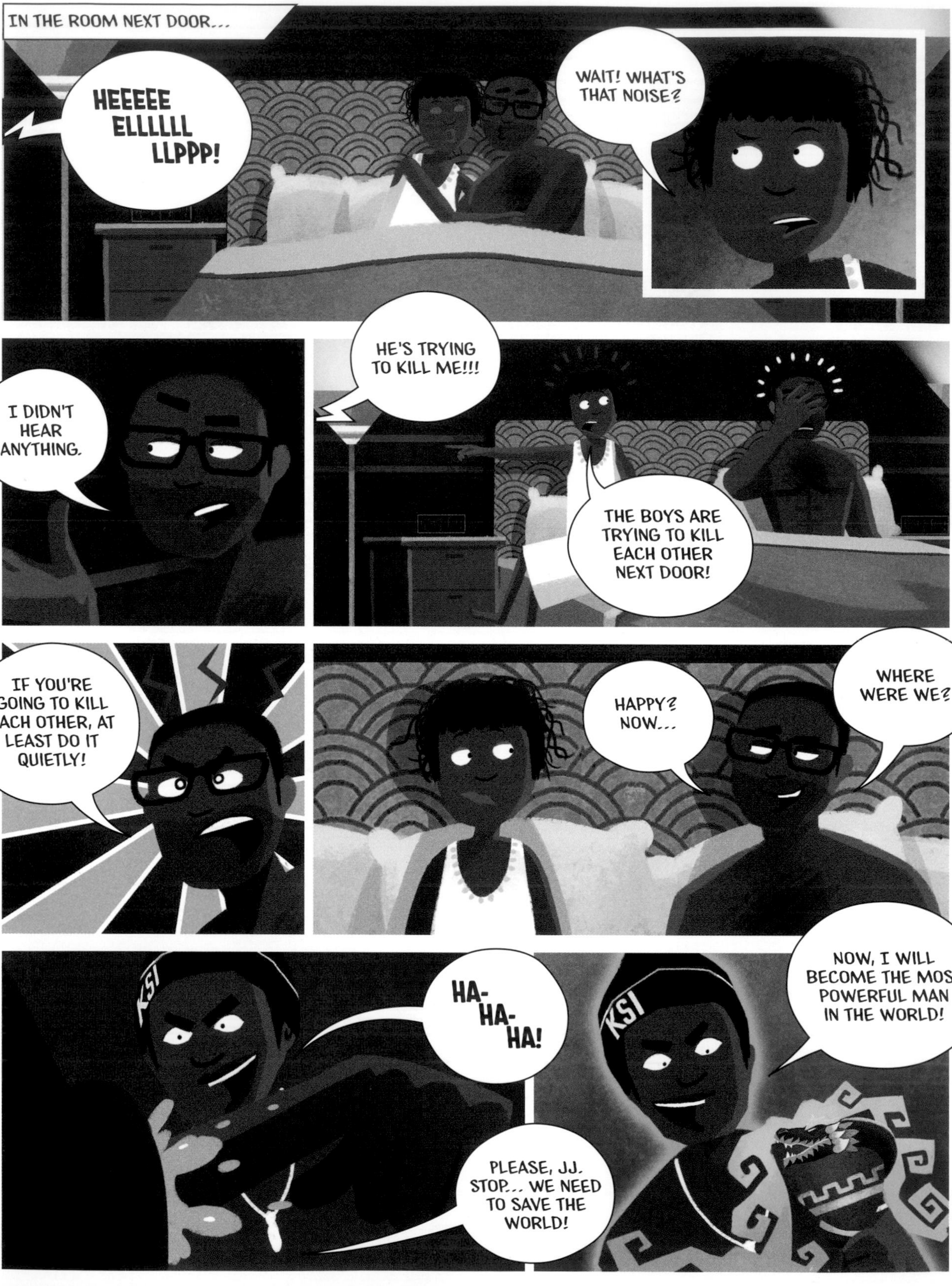
IN THE ROOM NEXT DOOR...
HEEEEE ELLLLLL LLPPP!
WAIT! WHAT'S THAT NOISE?
I DIDN'T HEAR ANYTHING.
HE'S TRYING TO KILL ME!!!
THE BOYS ARE TRYING TO KILL EACH OTHER NEXT DOOR!
IF YOU'RE GOING TO KILL EACH OTHER, AT LEAST DO IT QUIETLY!
HAPPY? NOW...
WHERE WERE WE?
KSI
HA-HA-HA!
PLEASE, JJ. STOP... WE NEED TO SAVE THE WORLD!
KSI
NOW, I WILL BECOME THE MOST POWERFUL MAN IN THE WORLD!

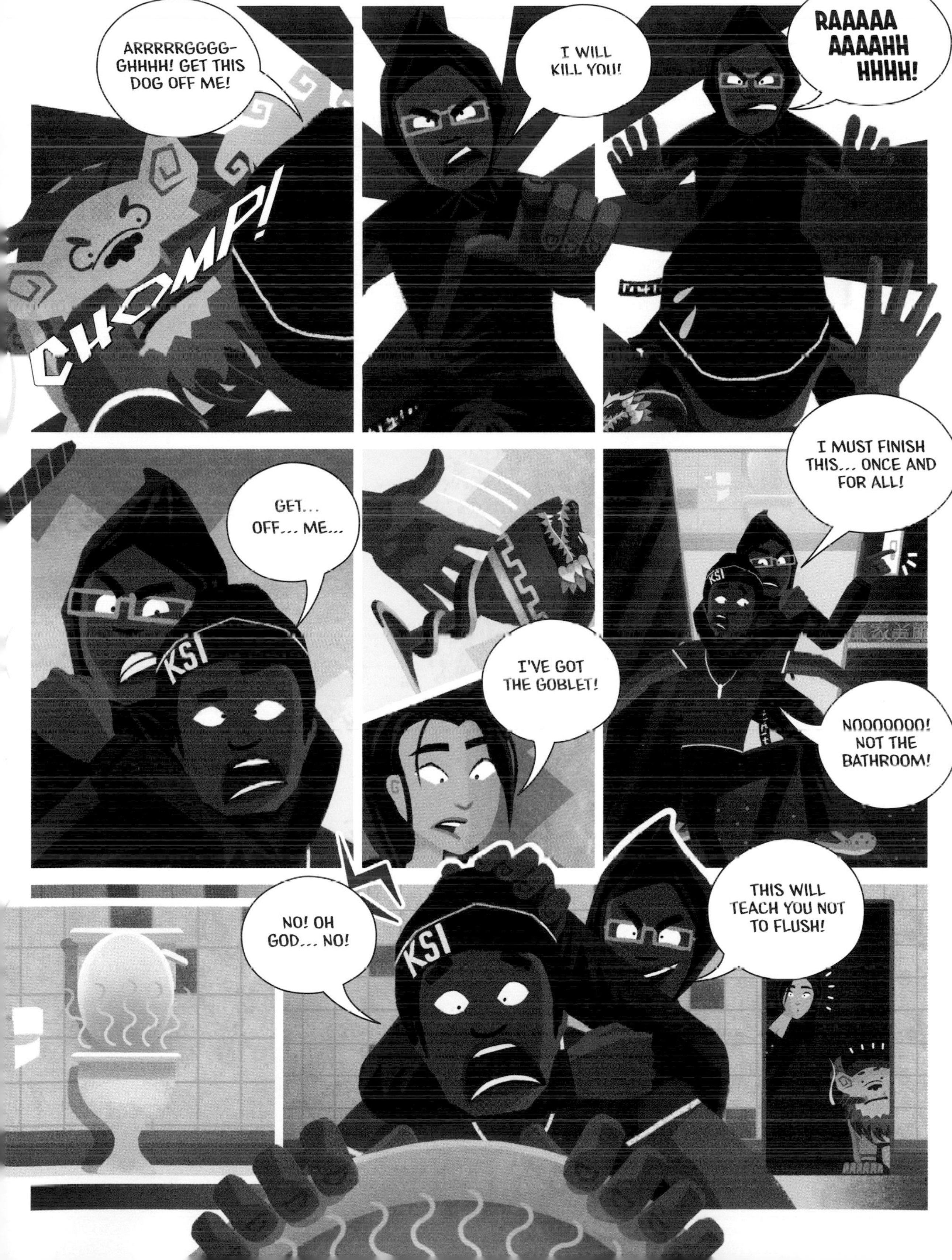
ARRRRRGGGG-GHHHH! GET THIS DOG OFF ME!
CHOMP!
I WILL KILL YOU!
RAAAAA AAAAHH HHHH!
GET... OFF... ME...
I'VE GOT THE GOBLET!
I MUST FINISH THIS... ONCE AND FOR ALL!
NOOOOOOO! NOT THE BATHROOM!
NO! OH GOD... NO!
THIS WILL TEACH YOU NOT TO FLUSH!
KSI

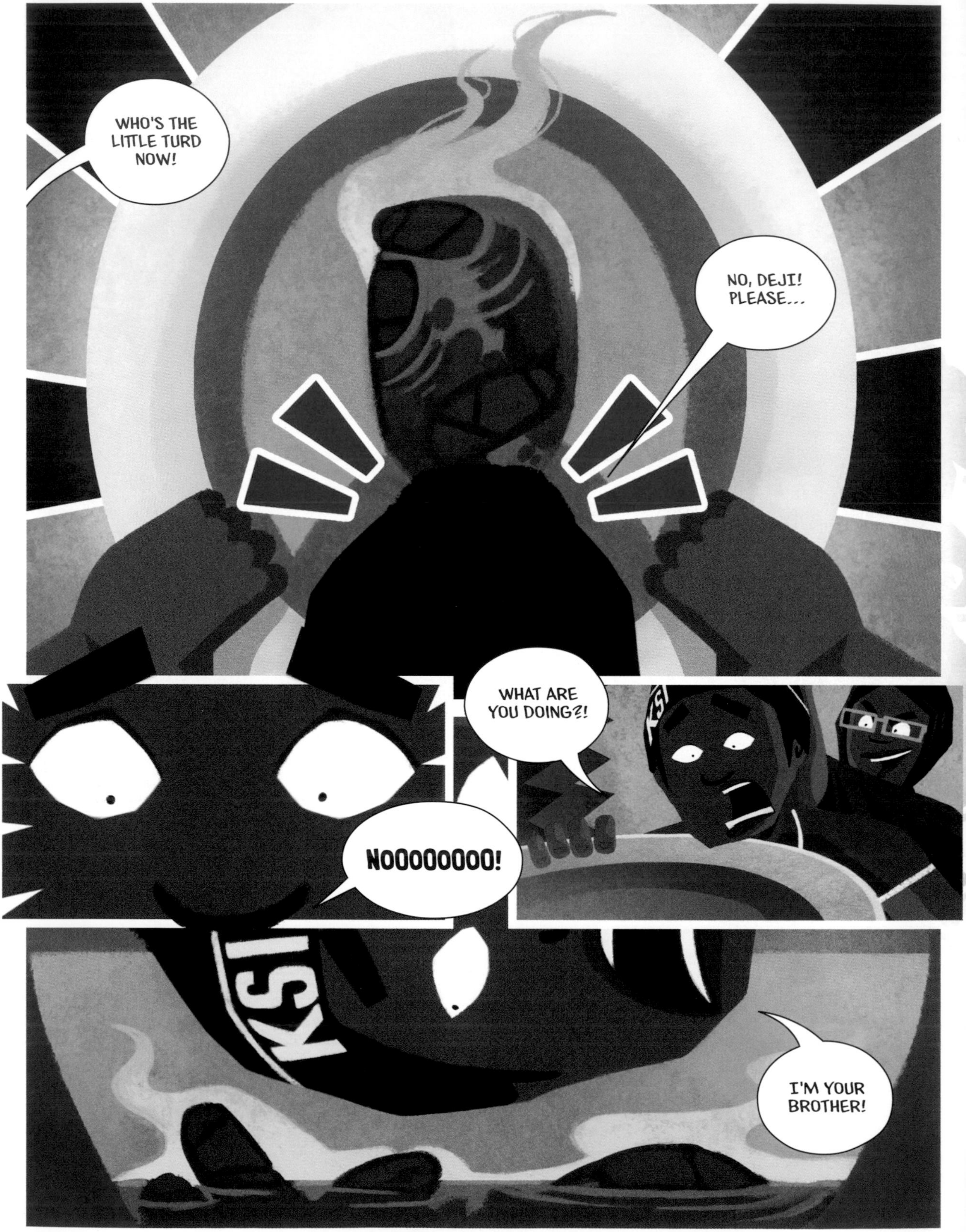
WHO'S THE LITTLE TURD NOW!
NO, DEJI! PLEASE...
WHAT ARE YOU DOING?!
NOOOOOOOO!
KSI
I'M YOUR BROTHER!

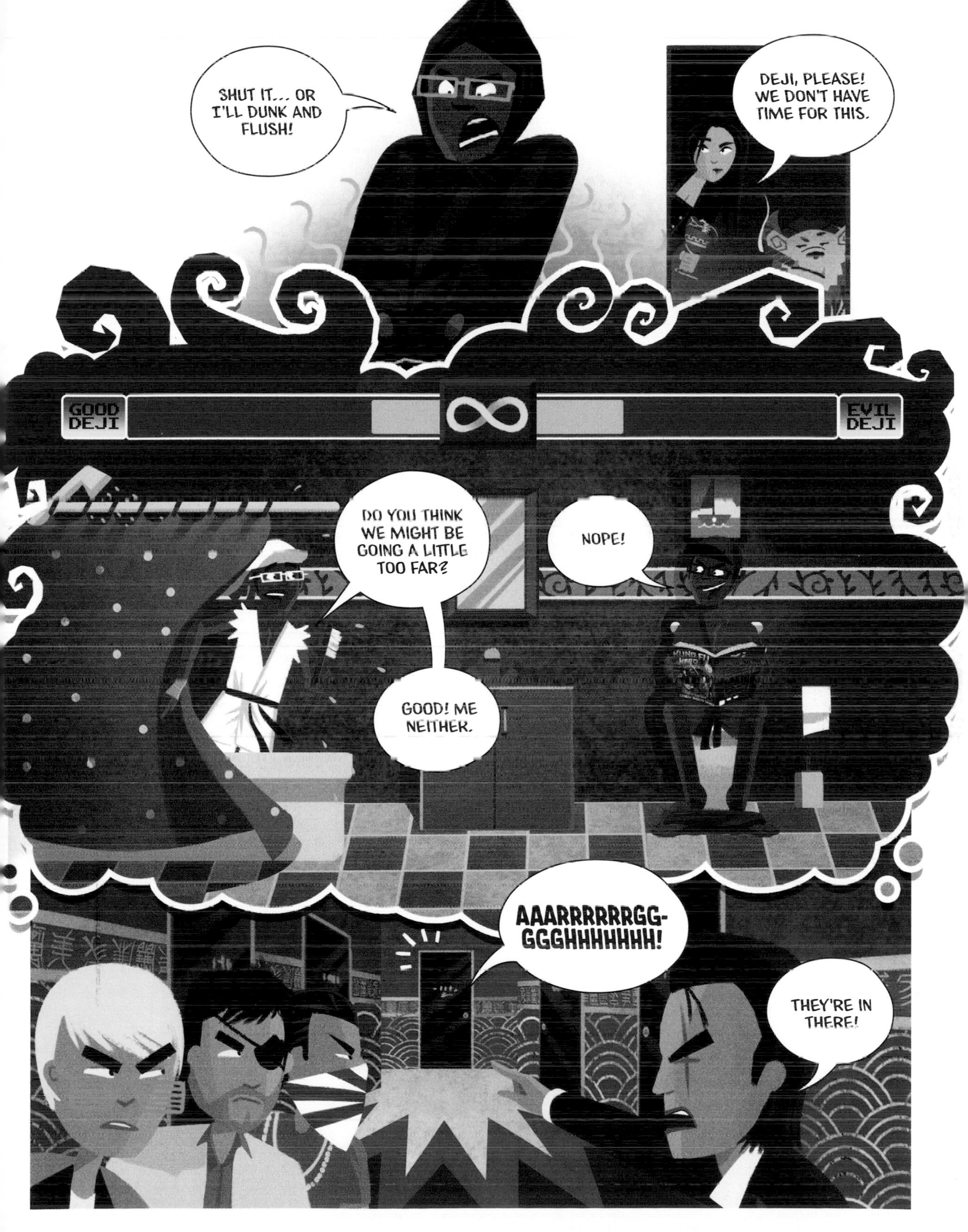
SHUT IT... OR I'LL DUNK AND FLUSH!
DEJI, PLEASE! WE DON'T HAVE TIME FOR THIS.
GOOD DEJI
EVIL DEJI
DO YOU THINK WE MIGHT BE GOING A LITTLE TOO FAR?
NOPE!
GOOD! ME NEITHER.
AAARRRRRRGG-GGGHHHHHHH!
THEY'RE IN THERE!

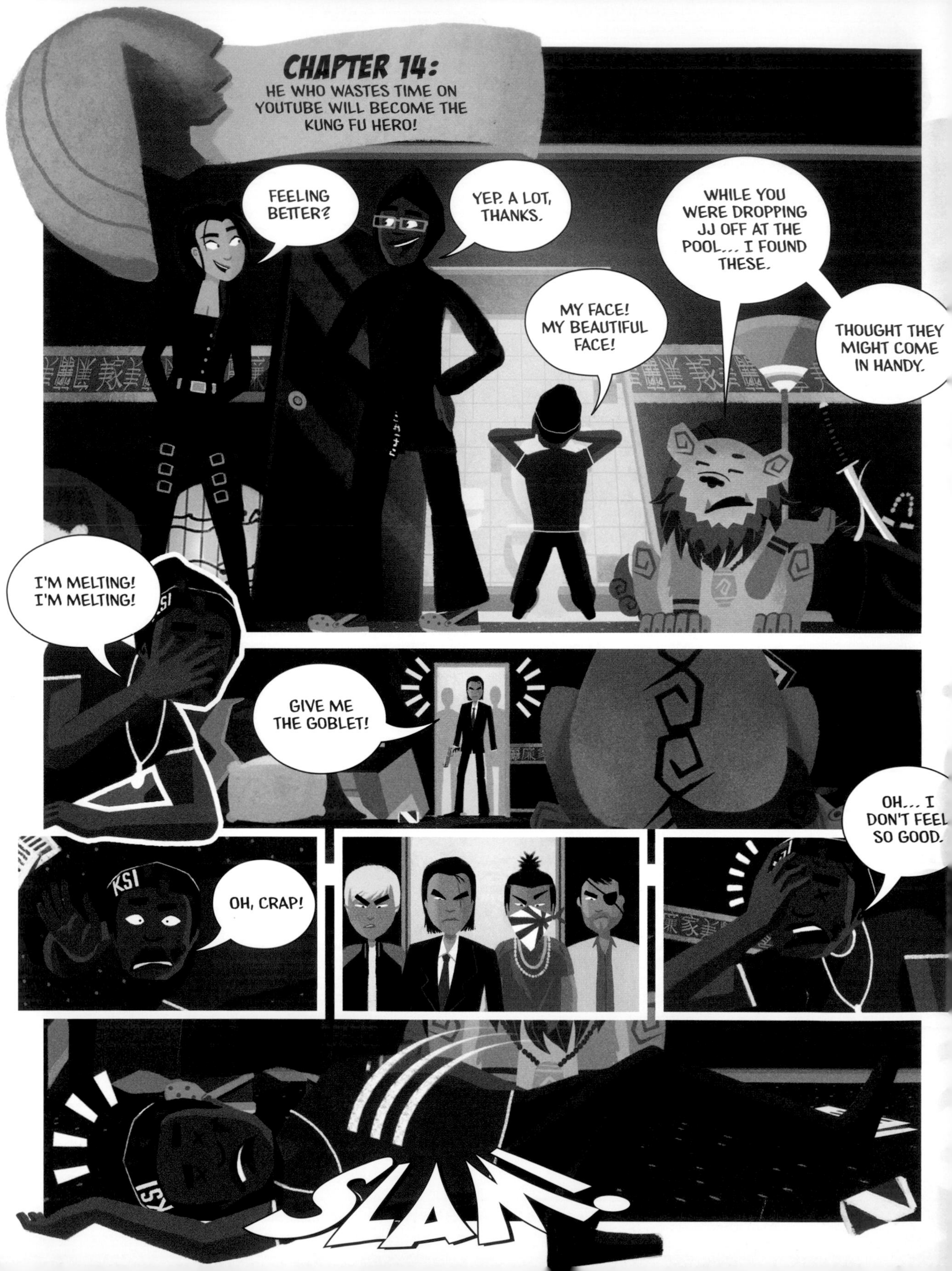
CHAPTER 14:
HE WHO WASTES TIME ON YOUTUBE WILL BECOME THE KUNG FU HERO!
FEELING BETTER?
YEP. A LOT, THANKS.
WHILE YOU WERE DROPPING JJ OFF AT THE POOL... I FOUND THESE.
THOUGHT THEY MIGHT COME IN HANDY.
MY FACE! MY BEAUTIFUL FACE!
I'M MELTING! I'M MELTING!
KSI
GIVE ME THE GOBLET!
KSI
OH, CRAP!
OH... I DON'T FEEL SO GOOD.
KSI
SLAM!

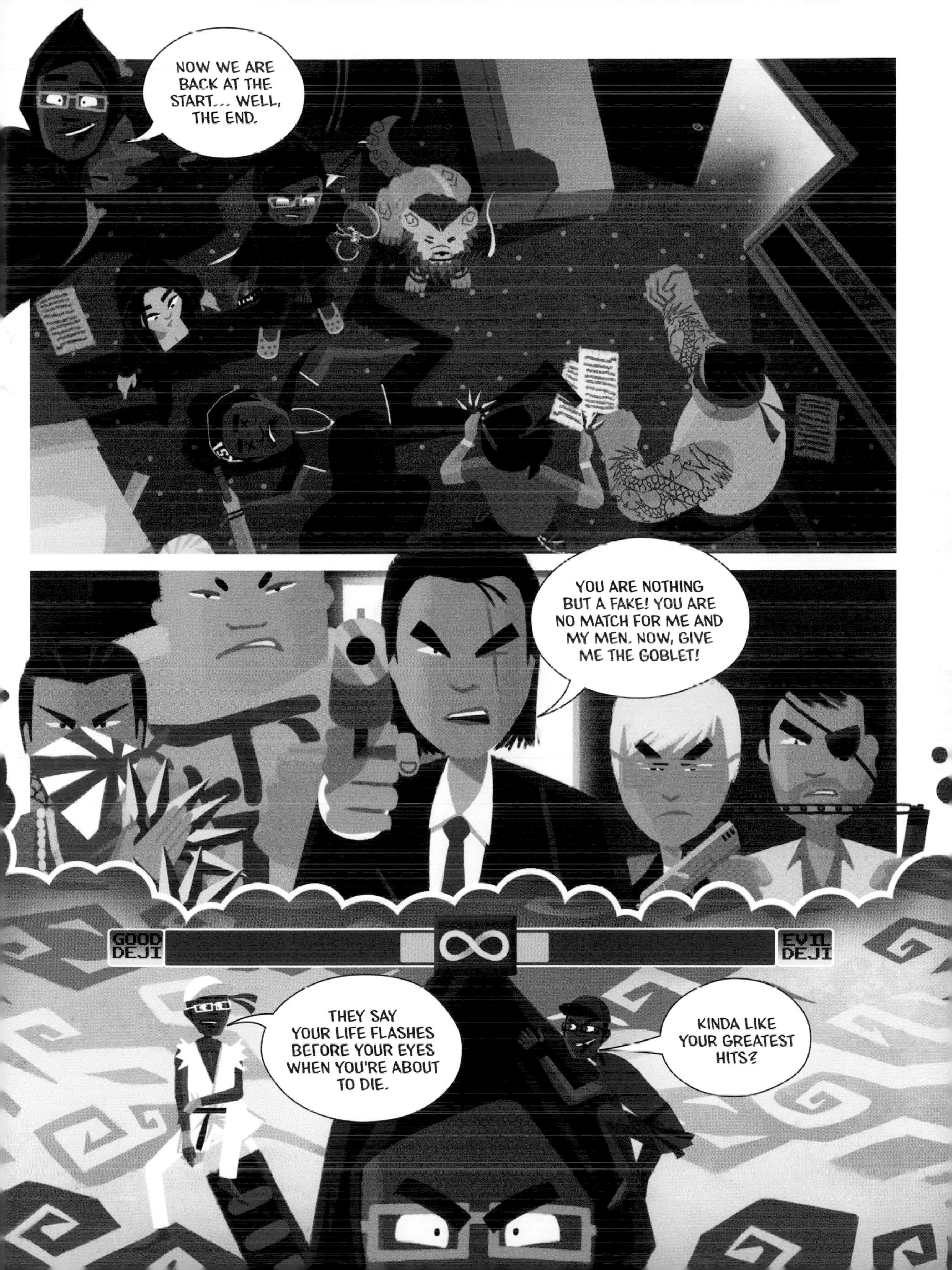
NOW WE ARE BACK AT THE START... WELL, THE END.
YOU ARE NOTHING BUT A FAKE! YOU ARE NO MATCH FOR ME AND MY MEN. NOW, GIVE ME THE GOBLET!
GOOD DEJI
EVIL DEJI
THEY SAY YOUR LIFE FLASHES BEFORE YOUR EYES WHEN YOU'RE ABOUT TO DIE.
KINDA LIKE YOUR GREATEST HITS?

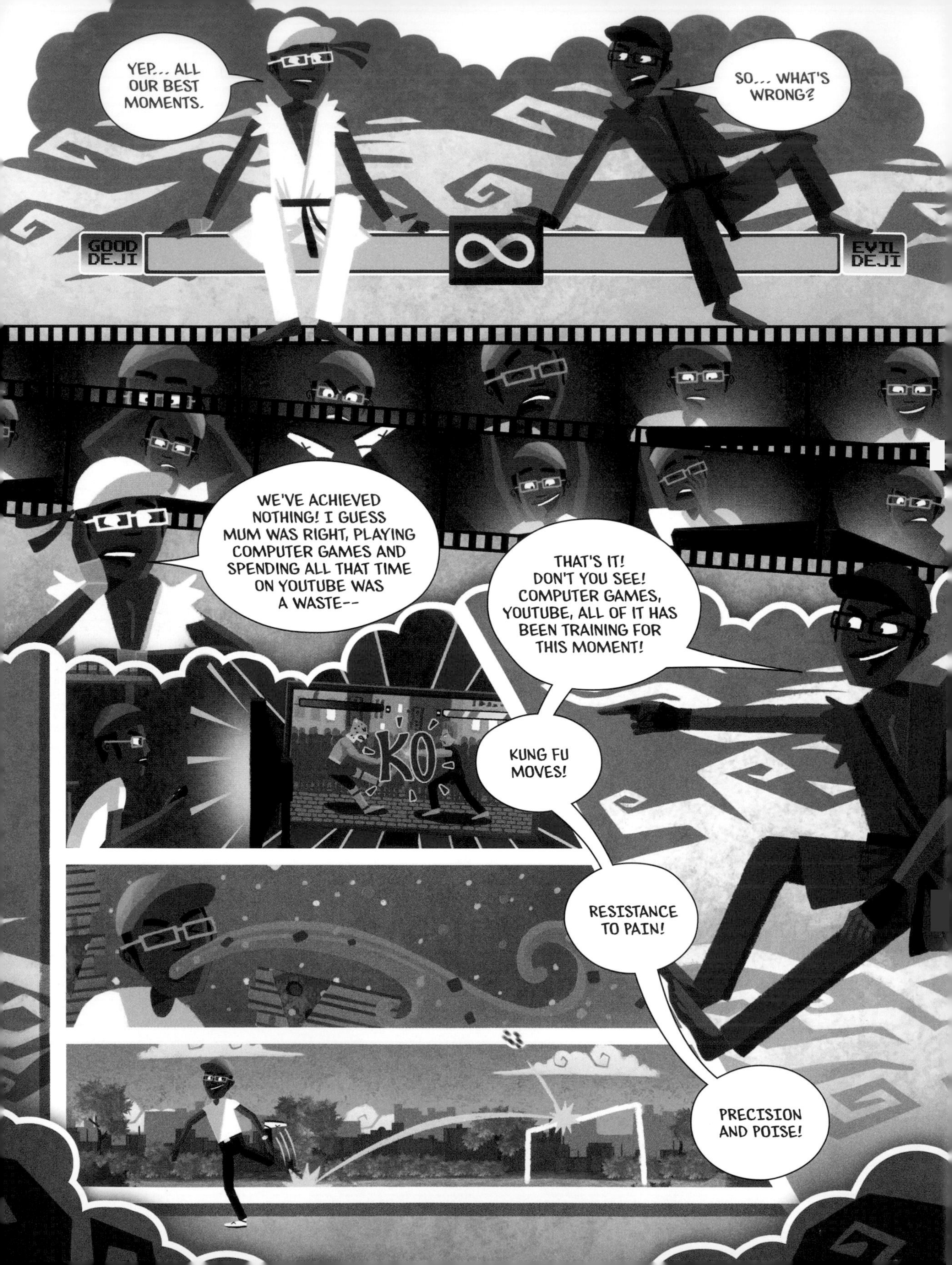
YEP... ALL OUR BEST MOMENTS.
SO... WHAT'S WRONG?
GOOD DEJI
EVIL DEJI
WE'VE ACHIEVED NOTHING! I GUESS MUM WAS RIGHT, PLAYING COMPUTER GAMES AND SPENDING ALL THAT TIME ON YOUTUBE WAS A WASTE--
THAT'S IT! DON'T YOU SEE! COMPUTER GAMES, YOUTUBE, ALL OF IT HAS BEEN TRAINING FOR THIS MOMENT!
KO
KUNG FU MOVES!
RESISTANCE TO PAIN!
PRECISION AND POISE!

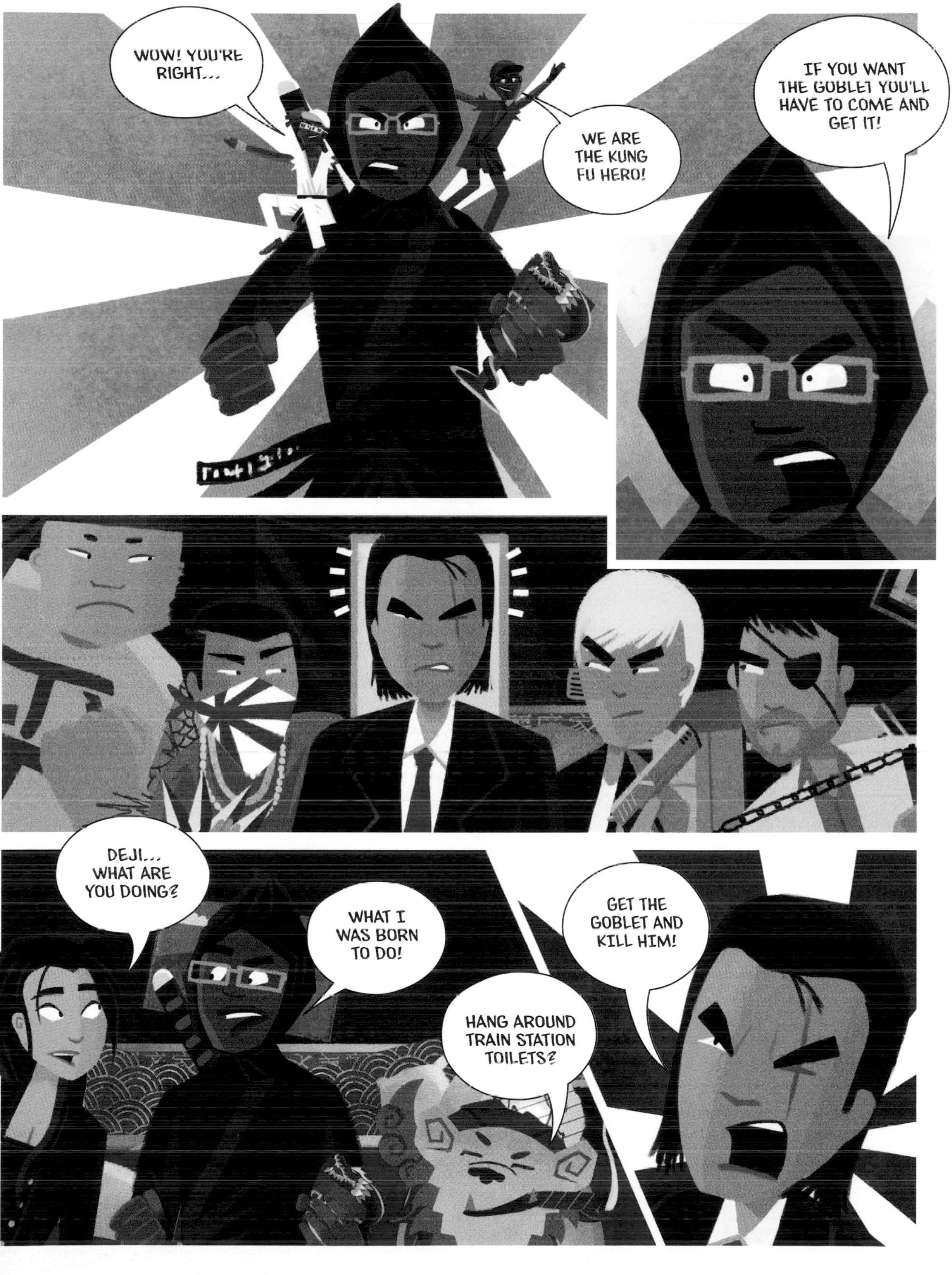
WOW! YOU'RE RIGHT...
WE ARE THE KUNG FU HERO!
IF YOU WANT THE GOBLET YOU'LL HAVE TO COME AND GET IT!
DEJI... WHAT ARE YOU DOING?
WHAT I WAS BORN TO DO!
HANG AROUND TRAIN STATION TOILETS?
GET THE GOBLET AND KILL HIM!

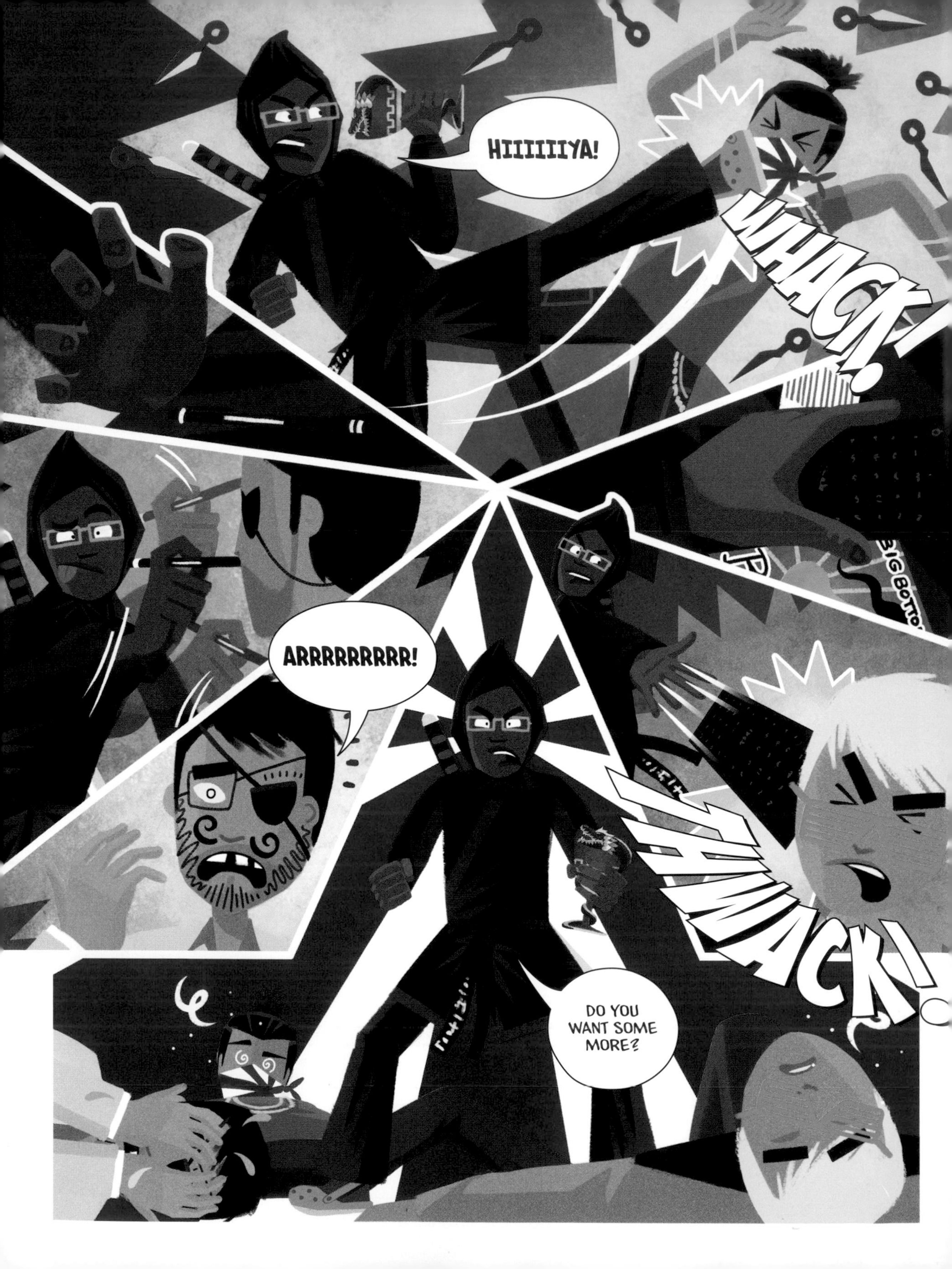
HIIIIIIYA!
WHACK!
ARRRRRRRRR!
THWACK!
DO YOU WANT SOME MORE?

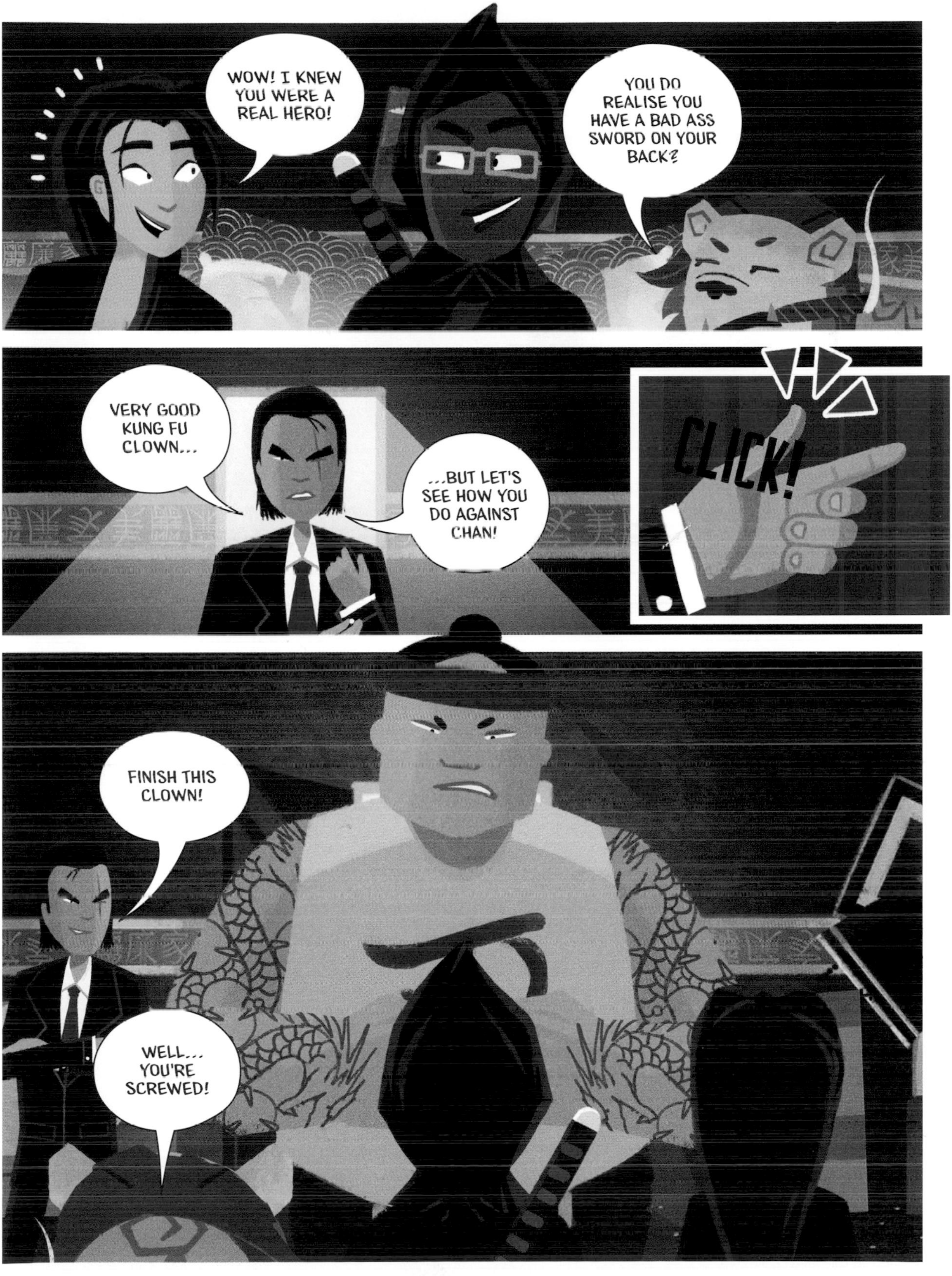
WOW! I KNEW YOU WERE A REAL HERO!
YOU DO REALISE YOU HAVE A BAD ASS SWORD ON YOUR BACK?
VERY GOOD KUNG FU CLOWN...
...BUT LET'S SEE HOW YOU DO AGAINST CHAN!
CLICK!
FINISH THIS CLOWN!
WELL... YOU'RE SCREWED!

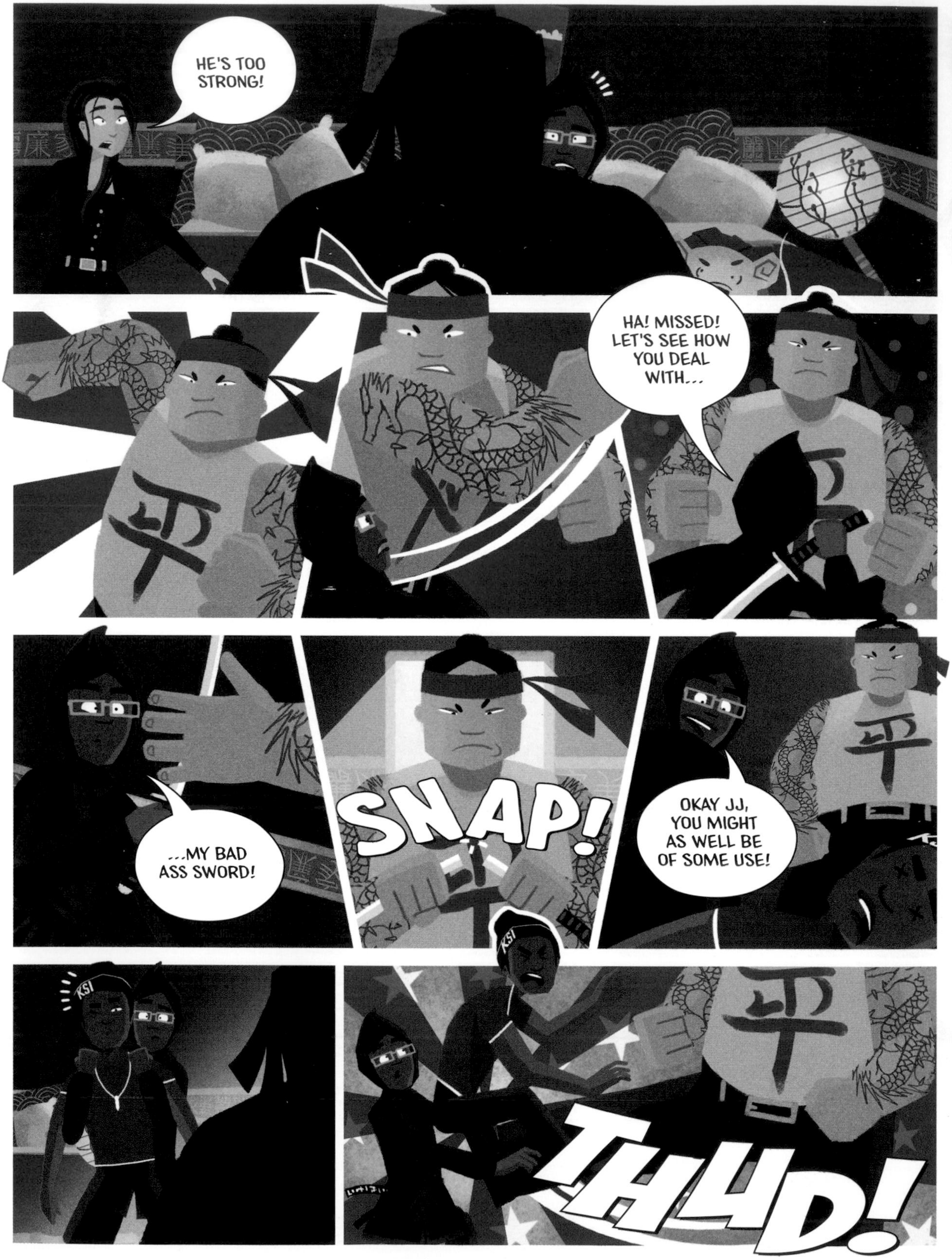
HE'S TOO STRONG!
HA! MISSED! LET'S SEE HOW YOU DEAL WITH...
...MY BAD ASS SWORD!
SNAP!
OKAY JJ, YOU MIGHT AS WELL BE OF SOME USE!
THUD!

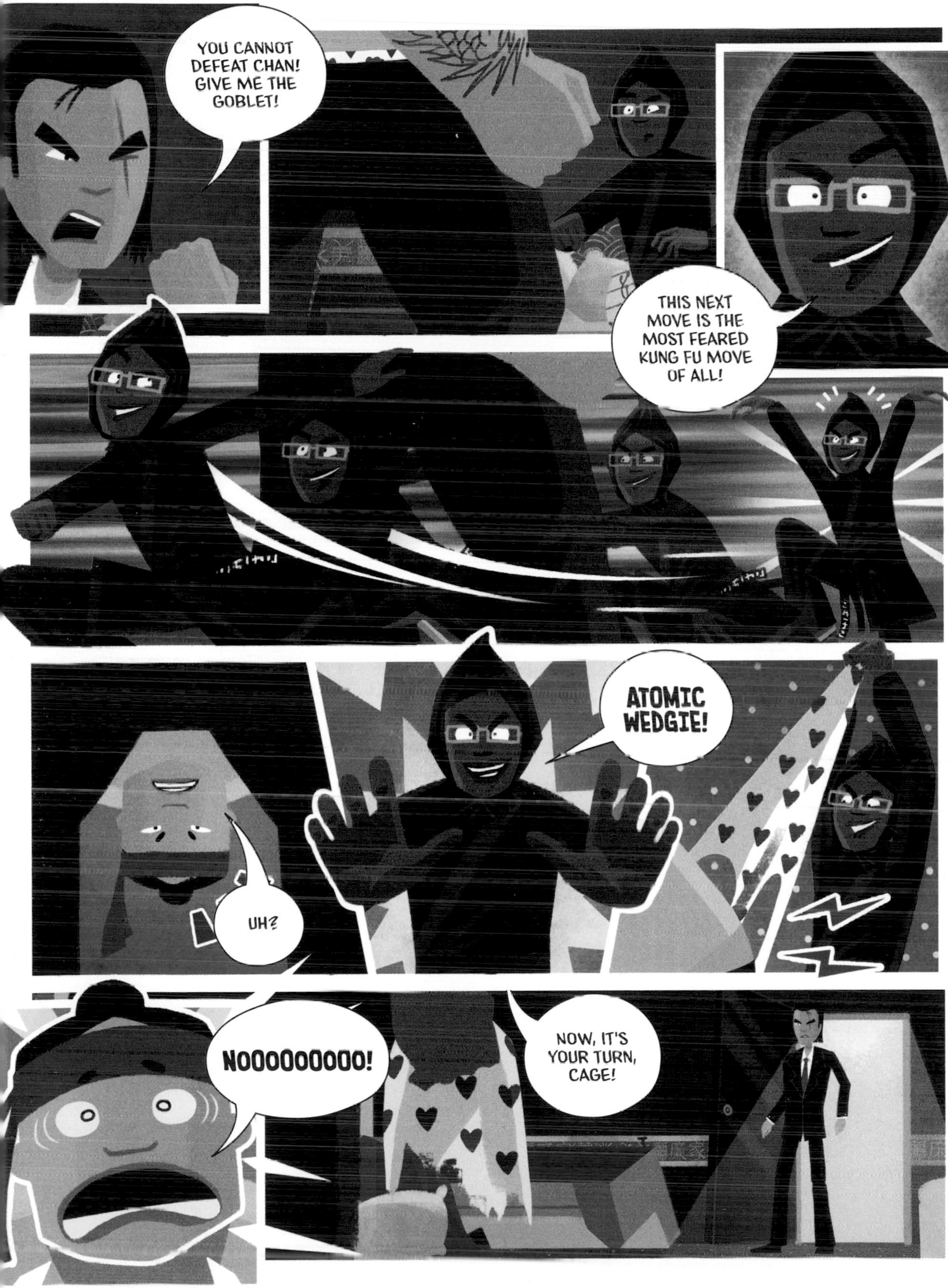
YOU CANNOT DEFEAT CHAN! GIVE ME THE GOBLET!
THIS NEXT MOVE IS THE MOST FEARED KUNG FU MOVE OF ALL!
ATOMIC WEDGIE!
UH?
NOOOOOOOOO!
NOW, IT'S YOUR TURN, CAGE!

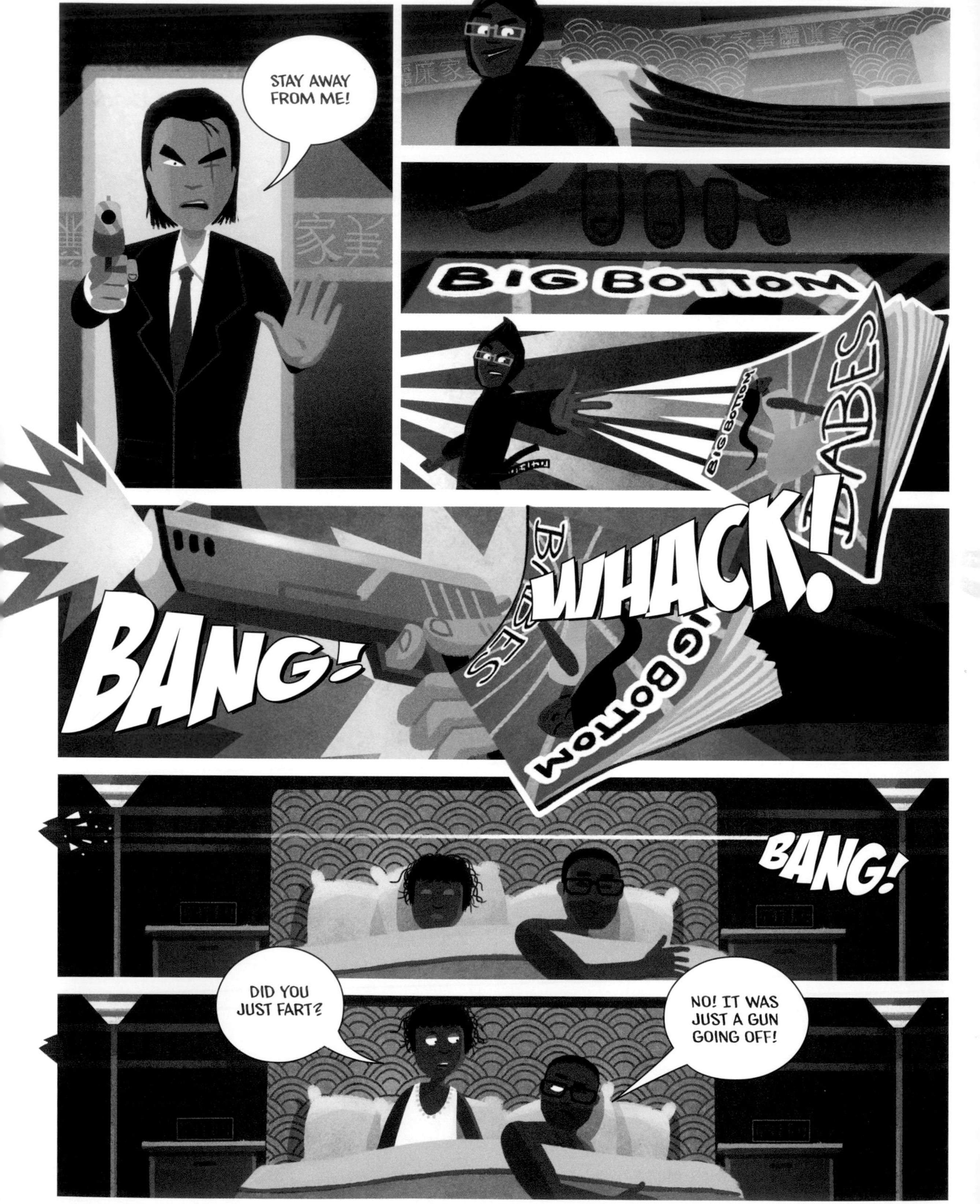
STAY AWAY FROM ME!
BIG BOTTOM
BIG BOTTOM BABES
BANG!
WHACK!
BIG BOTTOM BABES
BANG!
DID YOU JUST FART?
NO! IT WAS JUST A GUN GOING OFF!

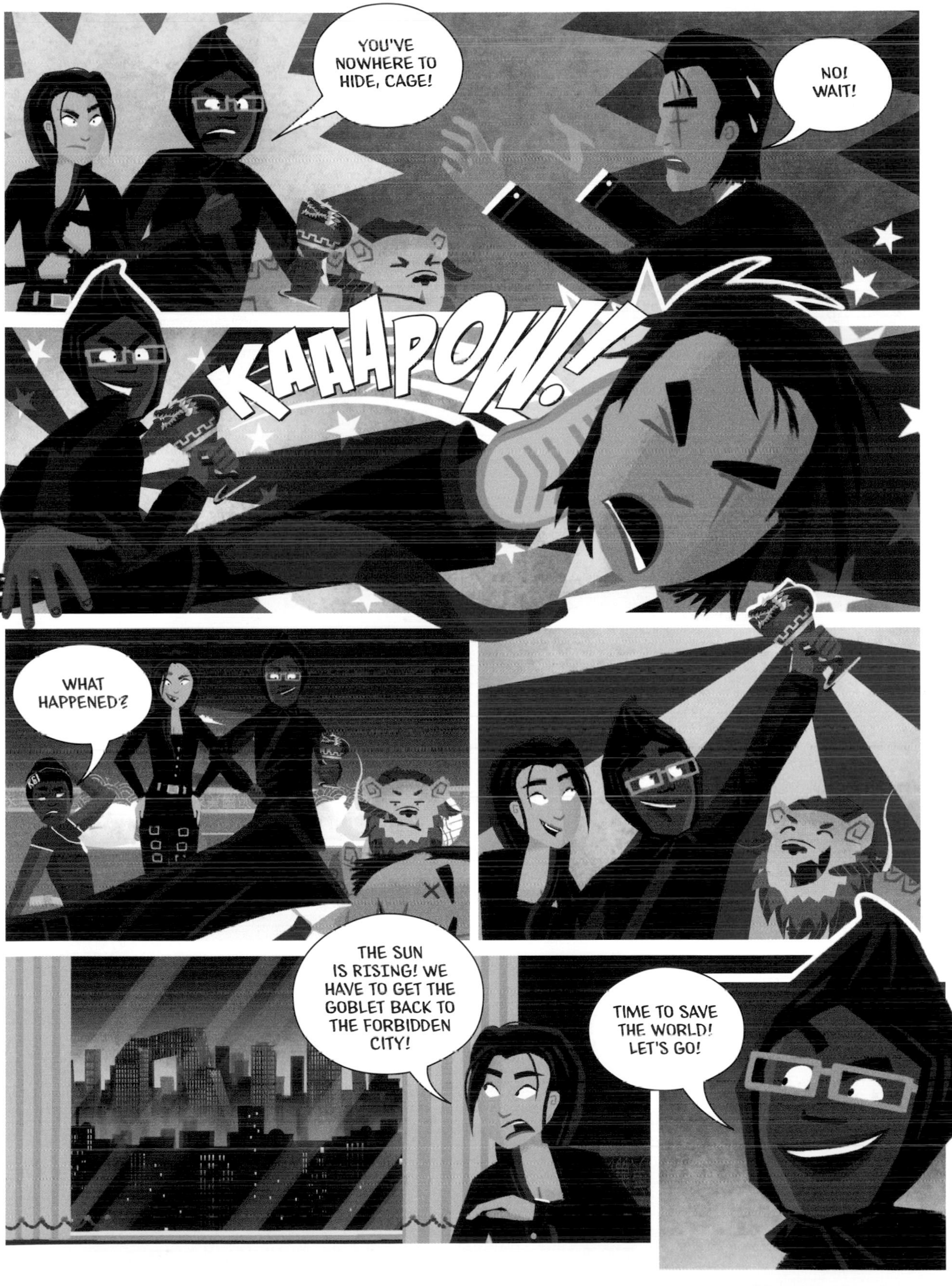
YOU'VE NOWHERE TO HIDE, CAGE!
NO! WAIT!
KAAAPOW!!
WHAT HAPPENED?
THE SUN IS RISING! WE HAVE TO GET THE GOBLET BACK TO THE FORBIDDEN CITY!
TIME TO SAVE THE WORLD! LET'S GO!

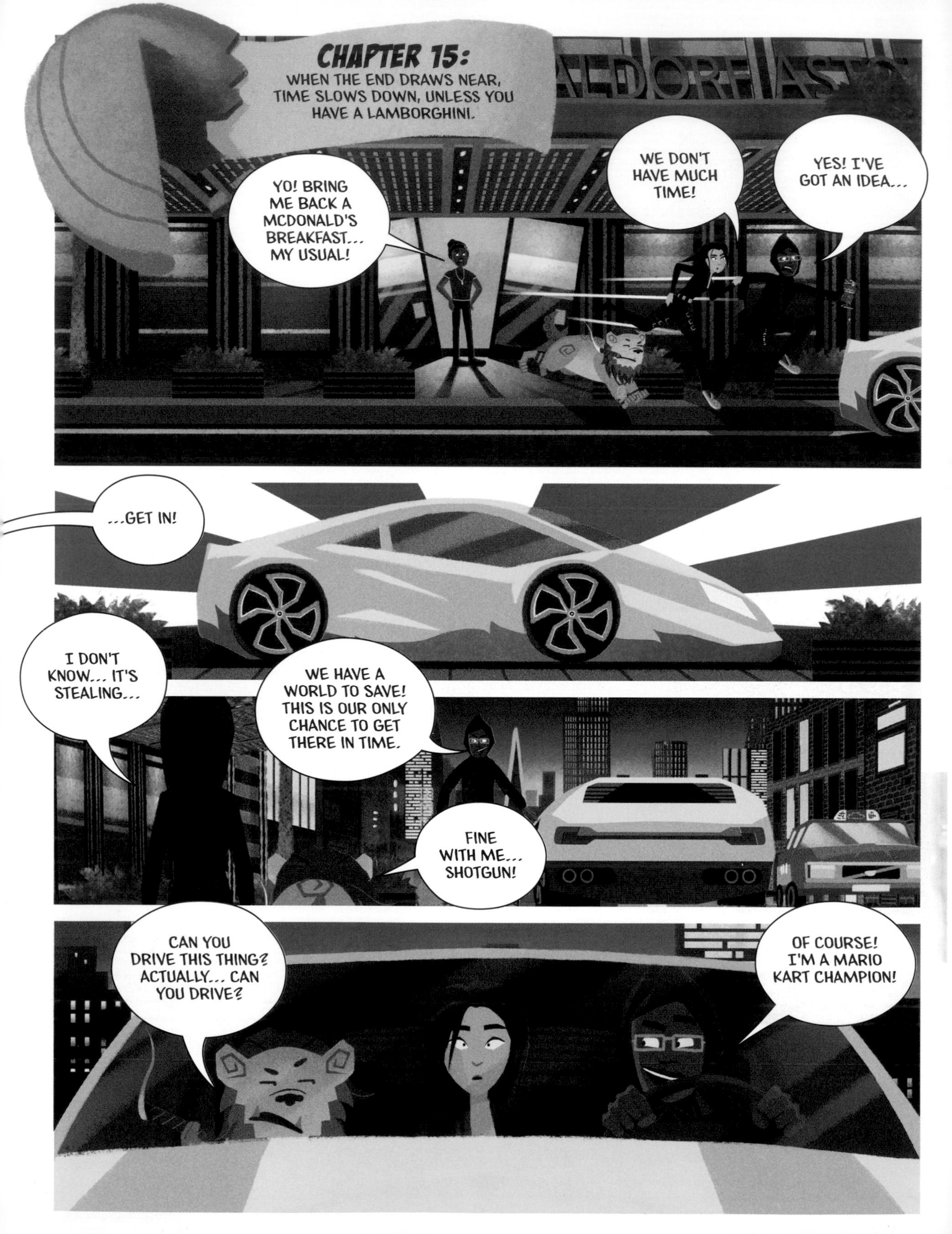
CHAPTER 15:
WHEN THE END DRAWS NEAR, TIME SLOWS DOWN, UNLESS YOU HAVE A LAMBORGHINI.
YO! BRING ME BACK A MCDONALD'S BREAKFAST... MY USUAL!
WE DON'T HAVE MUCH TIME!
YES! I'VE GOT AN IDEA...
...GET IN!
I DON'T KNOW... IT'S STEALING...
WE HAVE A WORLD TO SAVE! THIS IS OUR ONLY CHANCE TO GET THERE IN TIME.
FINE WITH ME... SHOTGUN!
CAN YOU DRIVE THIS THING? ACTUALLY... CAN YOU DRIVE?
OF COURSE! I'M A MARIO KART CHAMPION!

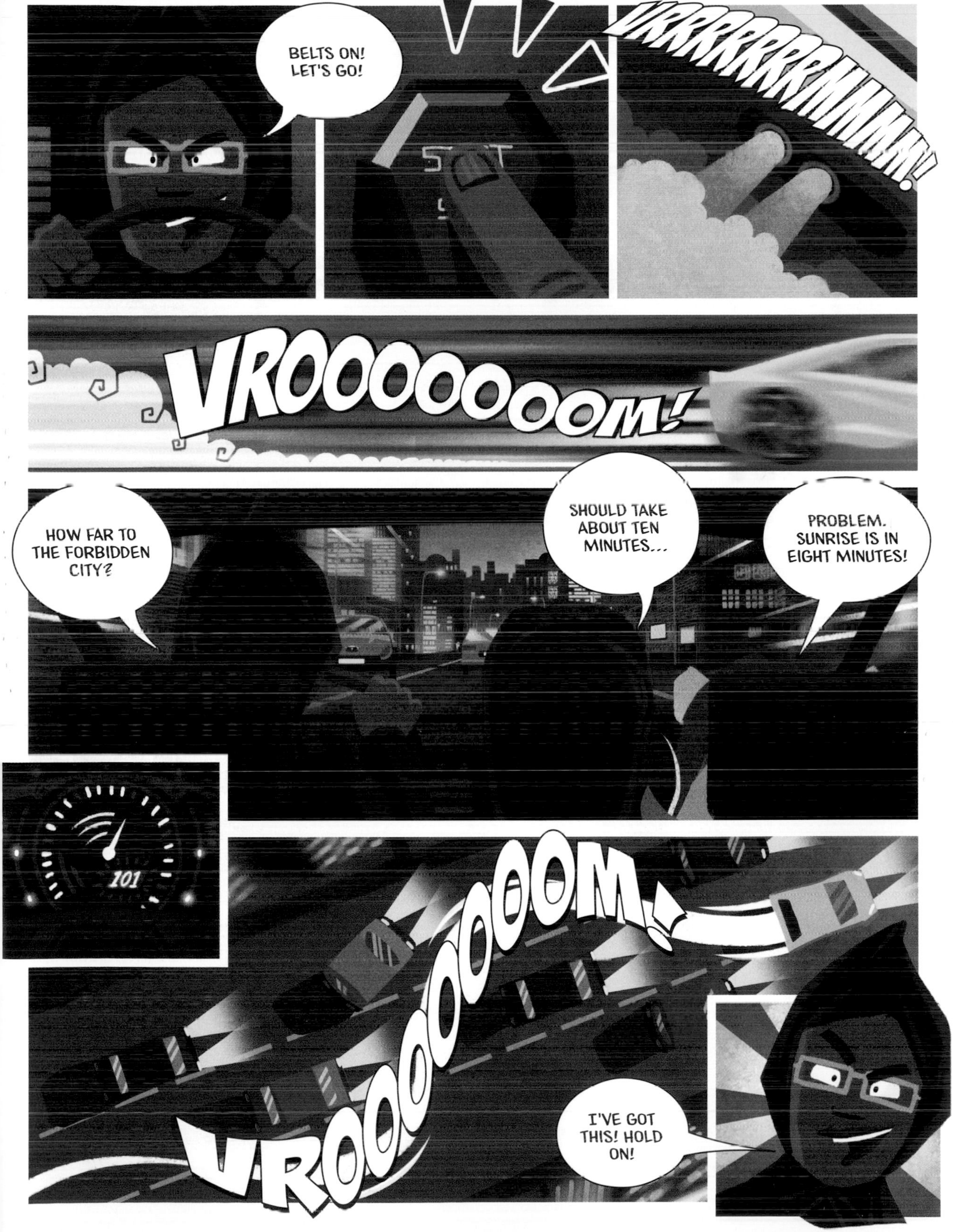
BELTS ON! LET'S GO!
START
VRRRRRRRMMMM!
VROOOOOOOM!
HOW FAR TO THE FORBIDDEN CITY?
SHOULD TAKE ABOUT TEN MINUTES...
PROBLEM. SUNRISE IS IN EIGHT MINUTES!
101
VROOOOOOOOOOM!
I'VE GOT THIS! HOLD ON!

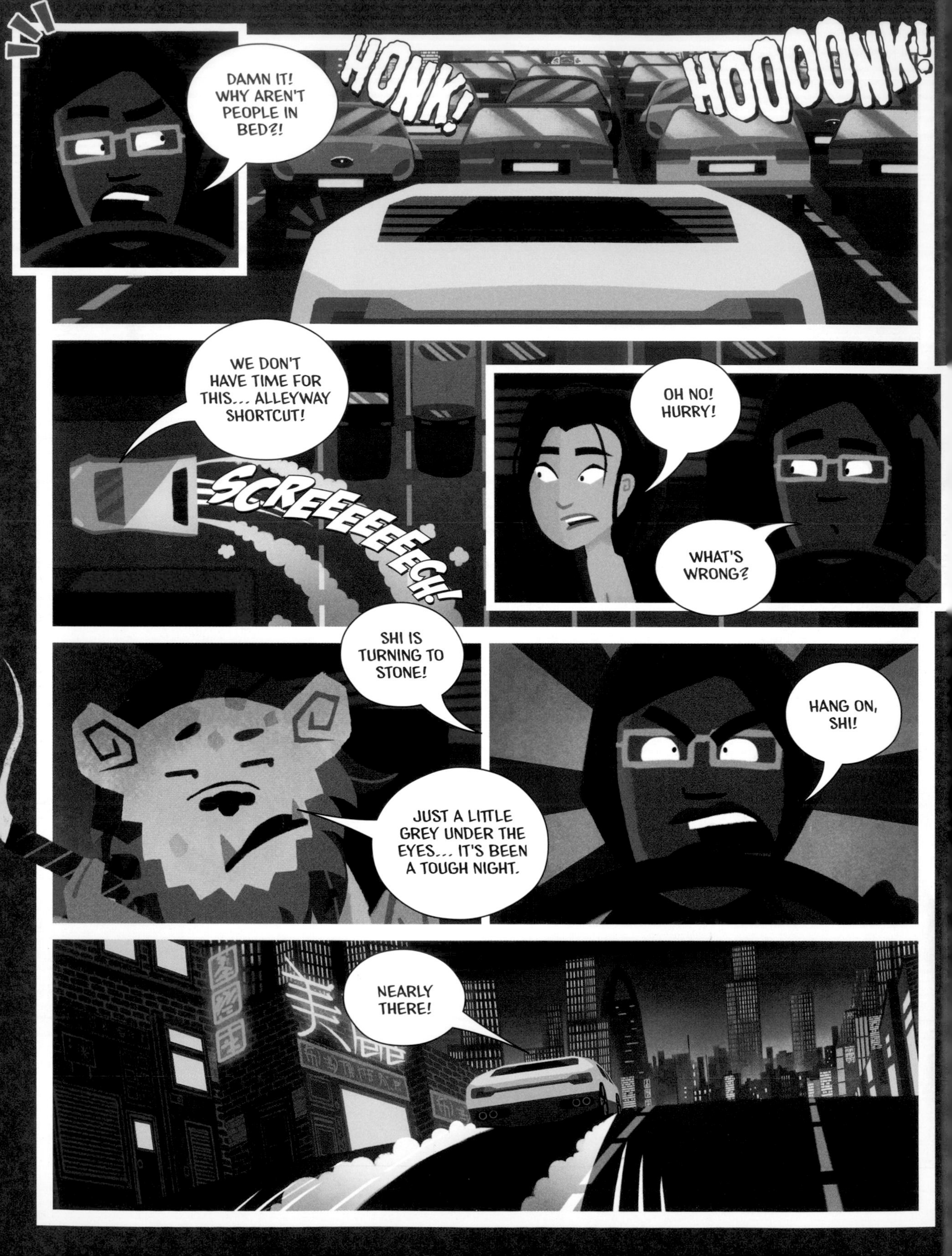
DAMN IT! WHY AREN'T PEOPLE IN BED?!
HONK!
HOOOONK!
WE DON'T HAVE TIME FOR THIS... ALLEYWAY SHORTCUT!
SCREEEEEEECH!
OH NO! HURRY!
WHAT'S WRONG?
SHI IS TURNING TO STONE!
HANG ON, SHI!
JUST A LITTLE GREY UNDER THE EYES... IT'S BEEN A TOUGH NIGHT.
NEARLY THERE!

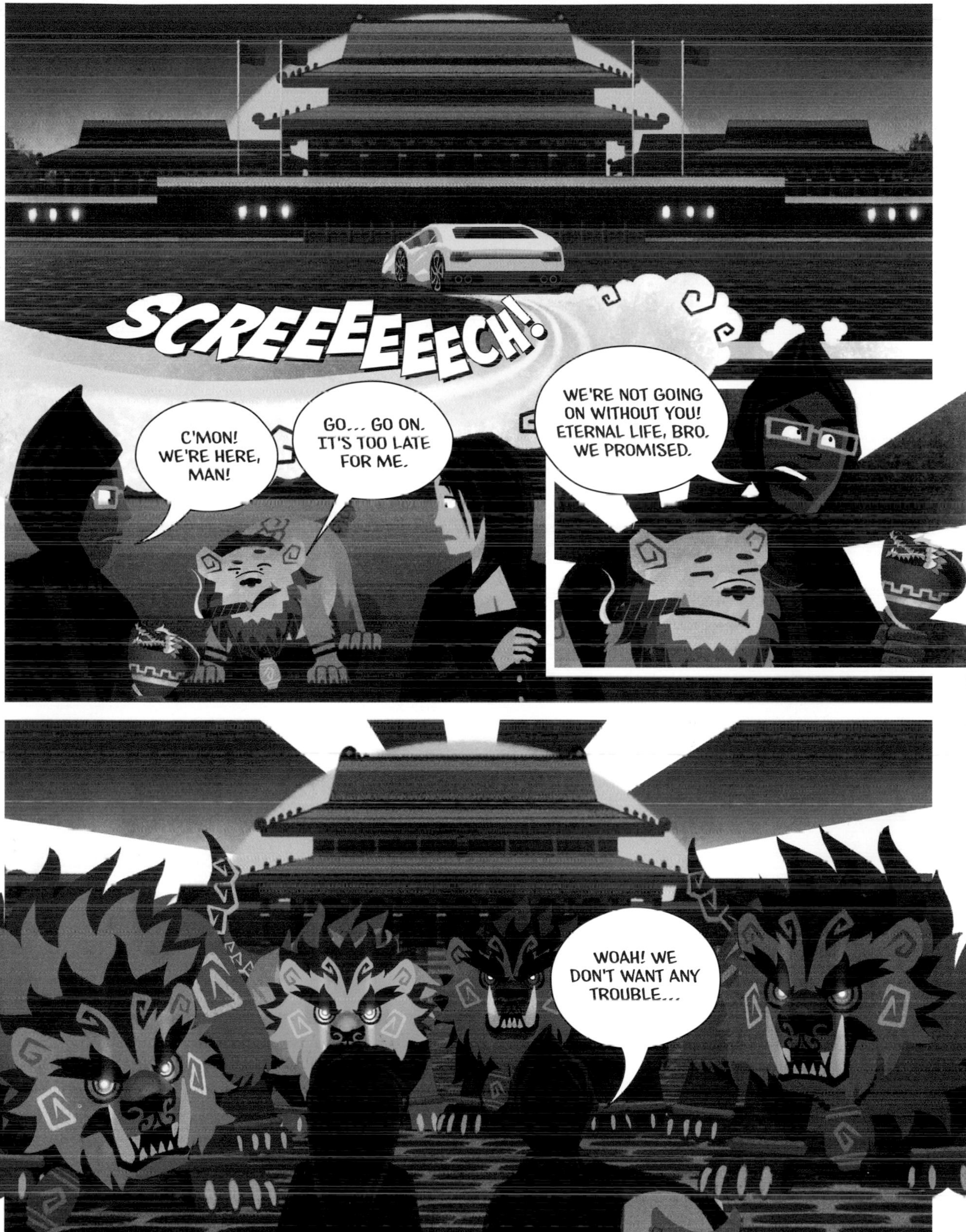
SCREEEEEEECH!
C'MON! WE'RE HERE, MAN!
GO... GO ON. IT'S TOO LATE FOR ME.
WE'RE NOT GOING ON WITHOUT YOU! ETERNAL LIFE, BRO. WE PROMISED.
WOAH! WE DON'T WANT ANY TROUBLE...

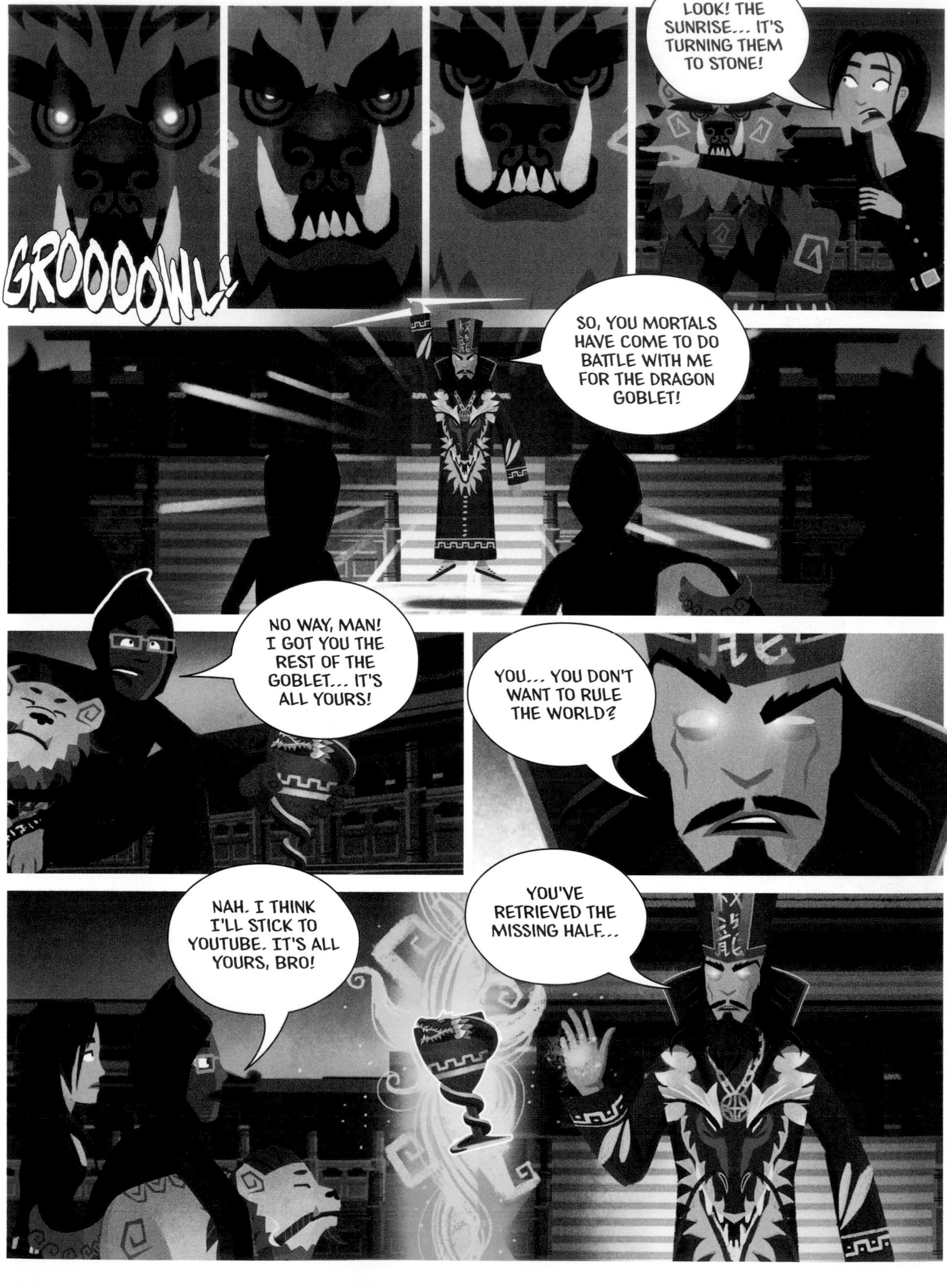
GROOOOWL!
LOOK! THE SUNRISE... IT'S TURNING THEM TO STONE!
SO, YOU MORTALS HAVE COME TO DO BATTLE WITH ME FOR THE DRAGON GOBLET!
NO WAY, MAN! I GOT YOU THE REST OF THE GOBLET... IT'S ALL YOURS!
YOU... YOU DON'T WANT TO RULE THE WORLD?
NAH. I THINK I'LL STICK TO YOUTUBE. IT'S ALL YOURS, BRO!
YOU'VE RETRIEVED THE MISSING HALF...

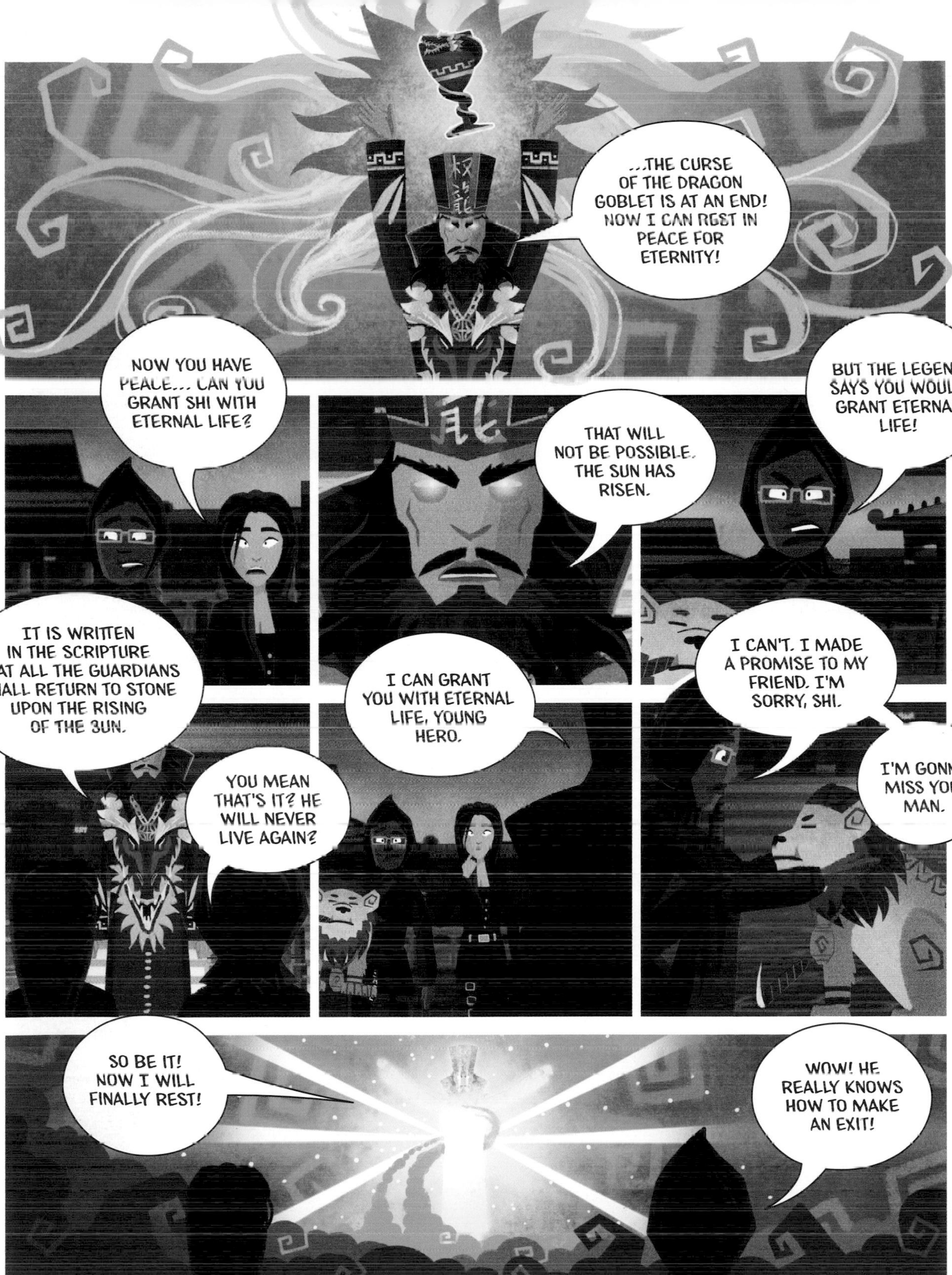
...THE CURSE OF THE DRAGON GOBLET IS AT AN END! NOW I CAN REST IN PEACE FOR ETERNITY!
NOW YOU HAVE PEACE... CAN YOU GRANT SHI WITH ETERNAL LIFE?
THAT WILL NOT BE POSSIBLE. THE SUN HAS RISEN.
BUT THE LEGEND SAYS YOU WOULD GRANT ETERNAL LIFE!
IT IS WRITTEN IN THE SCRIPTURE THAT ALL THE GUARDIANS SHALL RETURN TO STONE UPON THE RISING OF THE SUN.
YOU MEAN THAT'S IT? HE WILL NEVER LIVE AGAIN?
I CAN GRANT YOU WITH ETERNAL LIFE, YOUNG HERO.
I CAN'T. I MADE A PROMISE TO MY FRIEND. I'M SORRY, SHI.
I'M GONNA MISS YOU, MAN.
SO BE IT! NOW I WILL FINALLY REST!
WOW! HE REALLY KNOWS HOW TO MAKE AN EXIT!

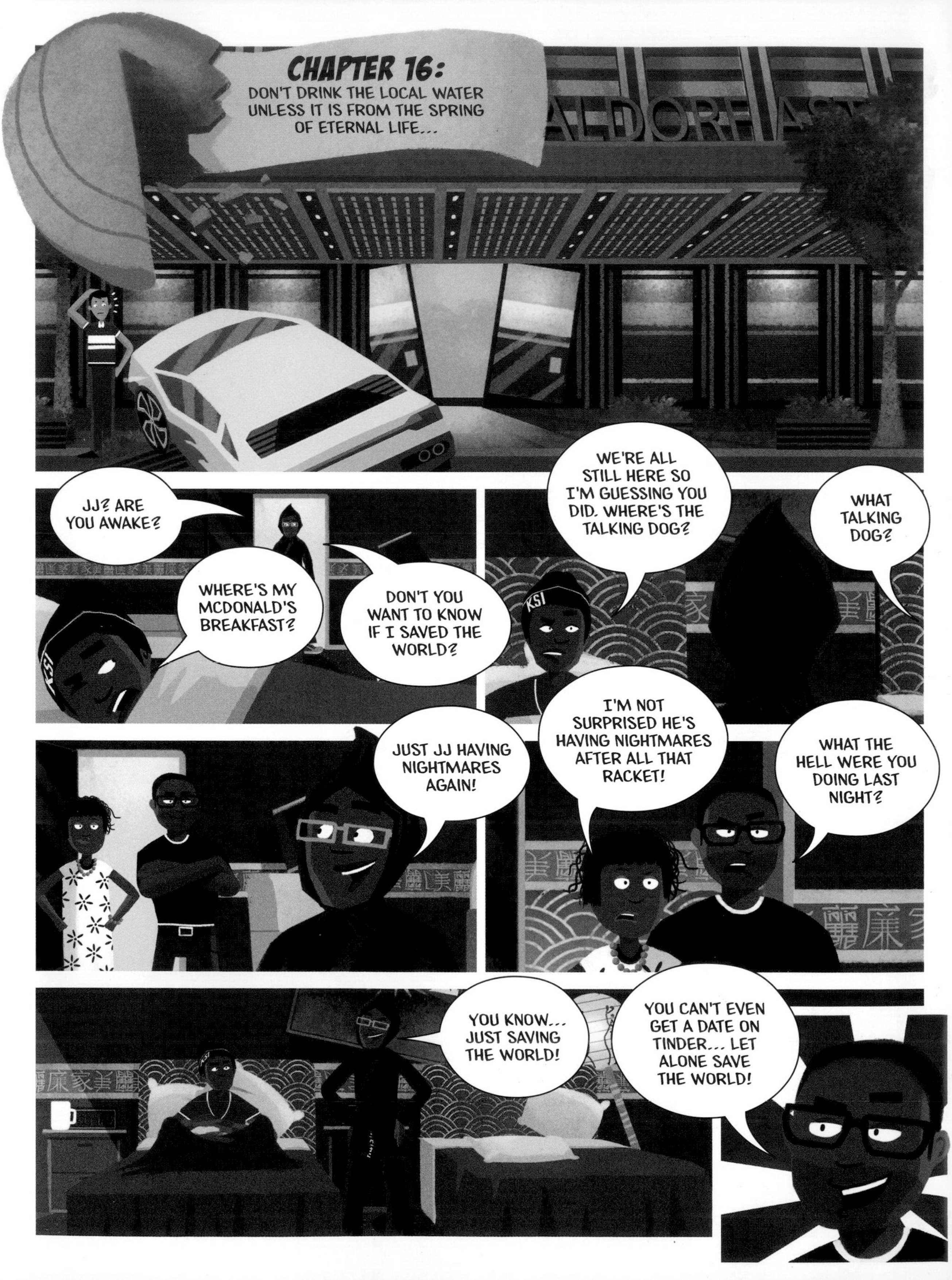
CHAPTER 16:
DON'T DRINK THE LOCAL WATER UNLESS IT IS FROM THE SPRING OF ETERNAL LIFE...
JJ? ARE YOU AWAKE?
WHERE'S MY MCDONALD'S BREAKFAST?
DON'T YOU WANT TO KNOW IF I SAVED THE WORLD?
WE'RE ALL STILL HERE SO I'M GUESSING YOU DID. WHERE'S THE TALKING DOG?
WHAT TALKING DOG?
JUST JJ HAVING NIGHTMARES AGAIN!
I'M NOT SURPRISED HE'S HAVING NIGHTMARES AFTER ALL THAT RACKET!
WHAT THE HELL WERE YOU DOING LAST NIGHT?
YOU KNOW... JUST SAVING THE WORLD!
YOU CAN'T EVEN GET A DATE ON TINDER... LET ALONE SAVE THE WORLD!

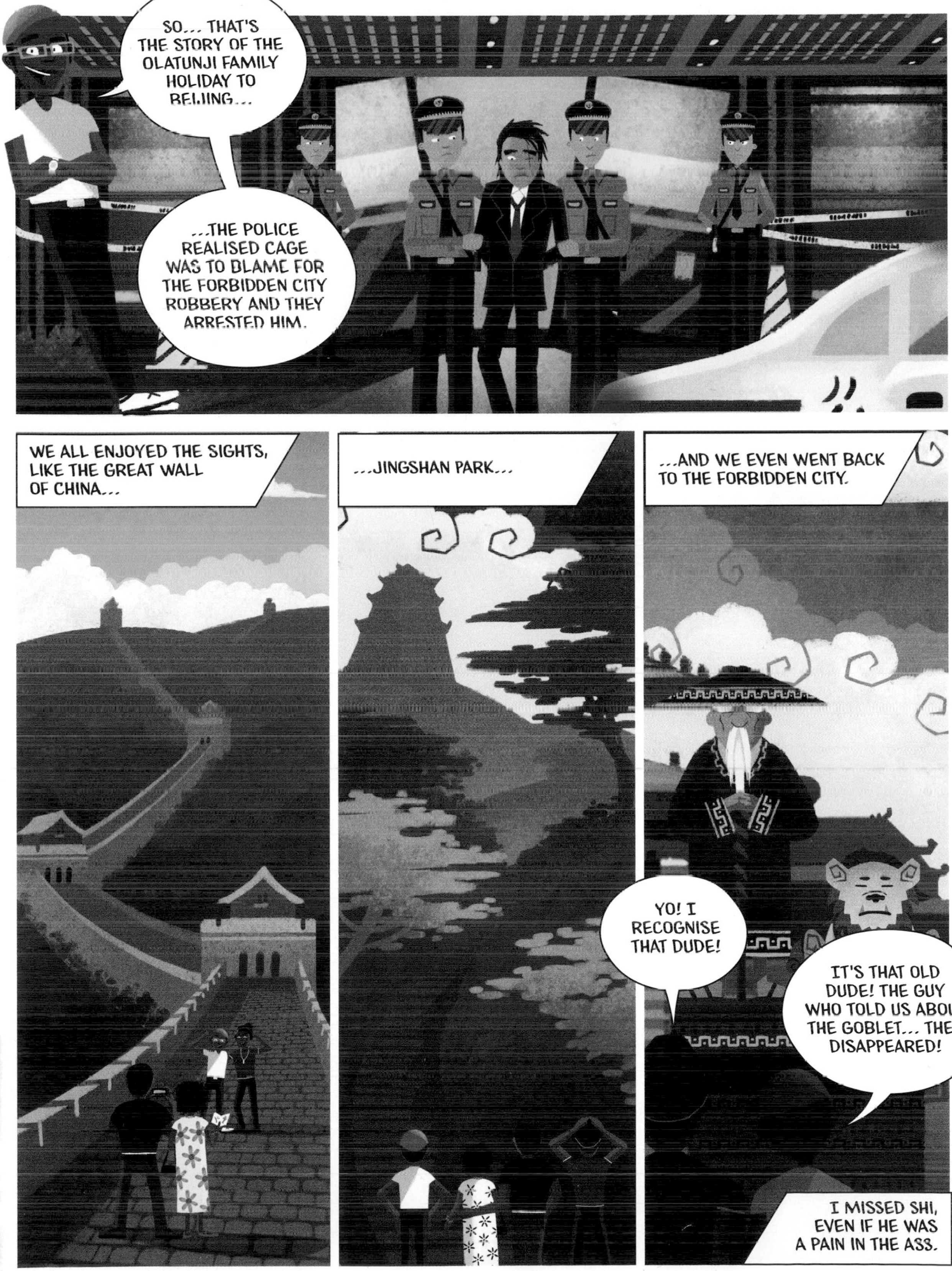
SO... THAT'S THE STORY OF THE OLATUNJI FAMILY HOLIDAY TO BEIJING...
...THE POLICE REALISED CAGE WAS TO BLAME FOR THE FORBIDDEN CITY ROBBERY AND THEY ARRESTED HIM.
WE ALL ENJOYED THE SIGHTS, LIKE THE GREAT WALL OF CHINA...
...JINGSHAN PARK...
...AND WE EVEN WENT BACK TO THE FORBIDDEN CITY.
YO! I RECOGNISE THAT DUDE!
IT'S THAT OLD DUDE! THE GUY WHO TOLD US ABOUT THE GOBLET... THEN DISAPPEARED!
I MISSED SHI, EVEN IF HE WAS A PAIN IN THE ASS.

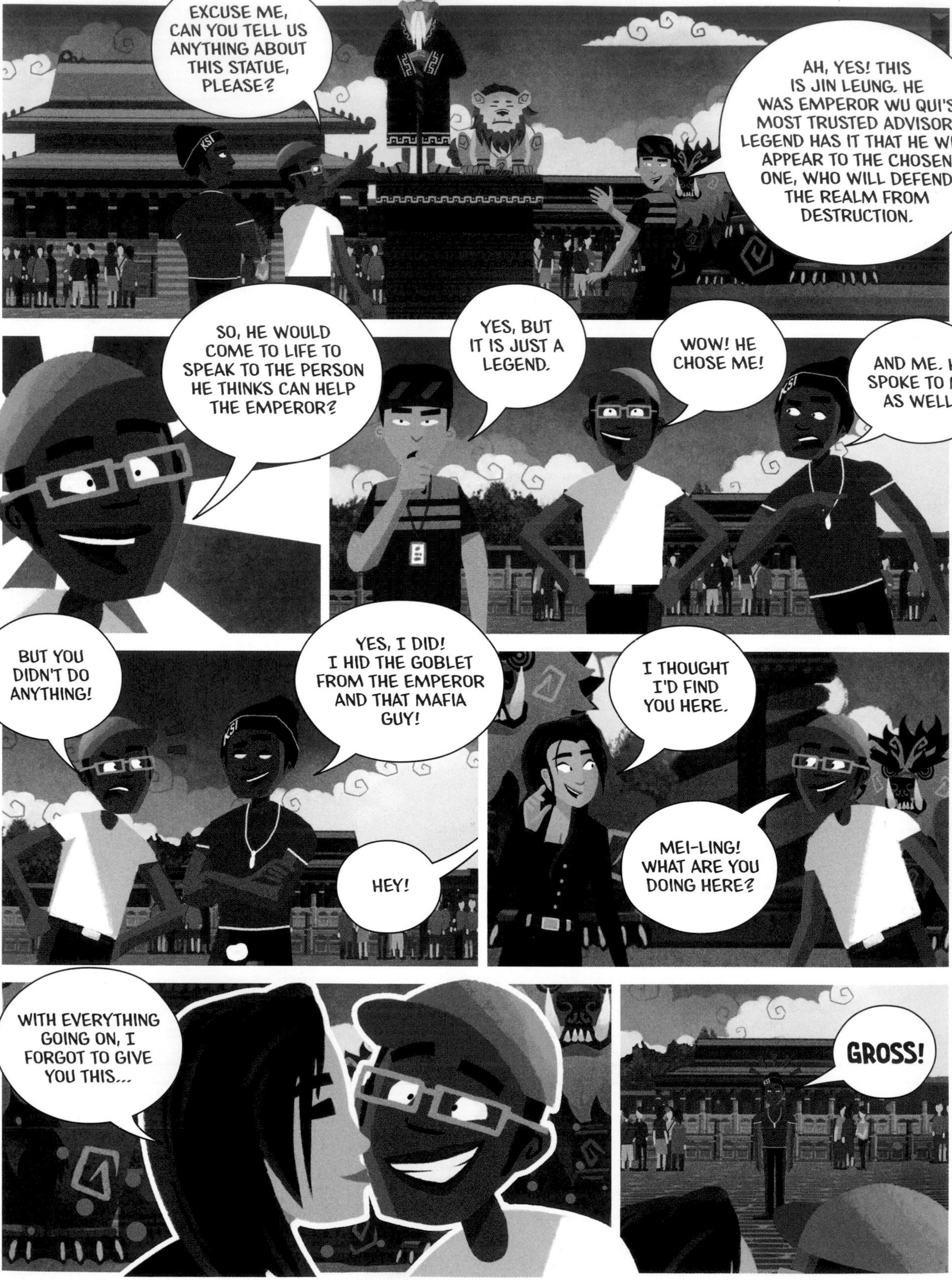
EXCUSE ME, CAN YOU TELL US ANYTHING ABOUT THIS STATUE, PLEASE?
AH, YES! THIS IS JIN LEUNG. HE WAS EMPEROR WU QUI'S MOST TRUSTED ADVISOR. LEGEND HAS IT THAT HE WILL APPEAR TO THE CHOSEN ONE, WHO WILL DEFEND THE REALM FROM DESTRUCTION.
SO, HE WOULD COME TO LIFE TO SPEAK TO THE PERSON HE THINKS CAN HELP THE EMPEROR?
YES, BUT IT IS JUST A LEGEND.
WOW! HE CHOSE ME!
AND ME. HE SPOKE TO ME AS WELL!
BUT YOU DIDN'T DO ANYTHING!
YES, I DID! I HID THE GOBLET FROM THE EMPEROR AND THAT MAFIA GUY!
HEY!
I THOUGHT I'D FIND YOU HERE.
MEI-LING! WHAT ARE YOU DOING HERE?
WITH EVERYTHING GOING ON, I FORGOT TO GIVE YOU THIS...
GROSS!

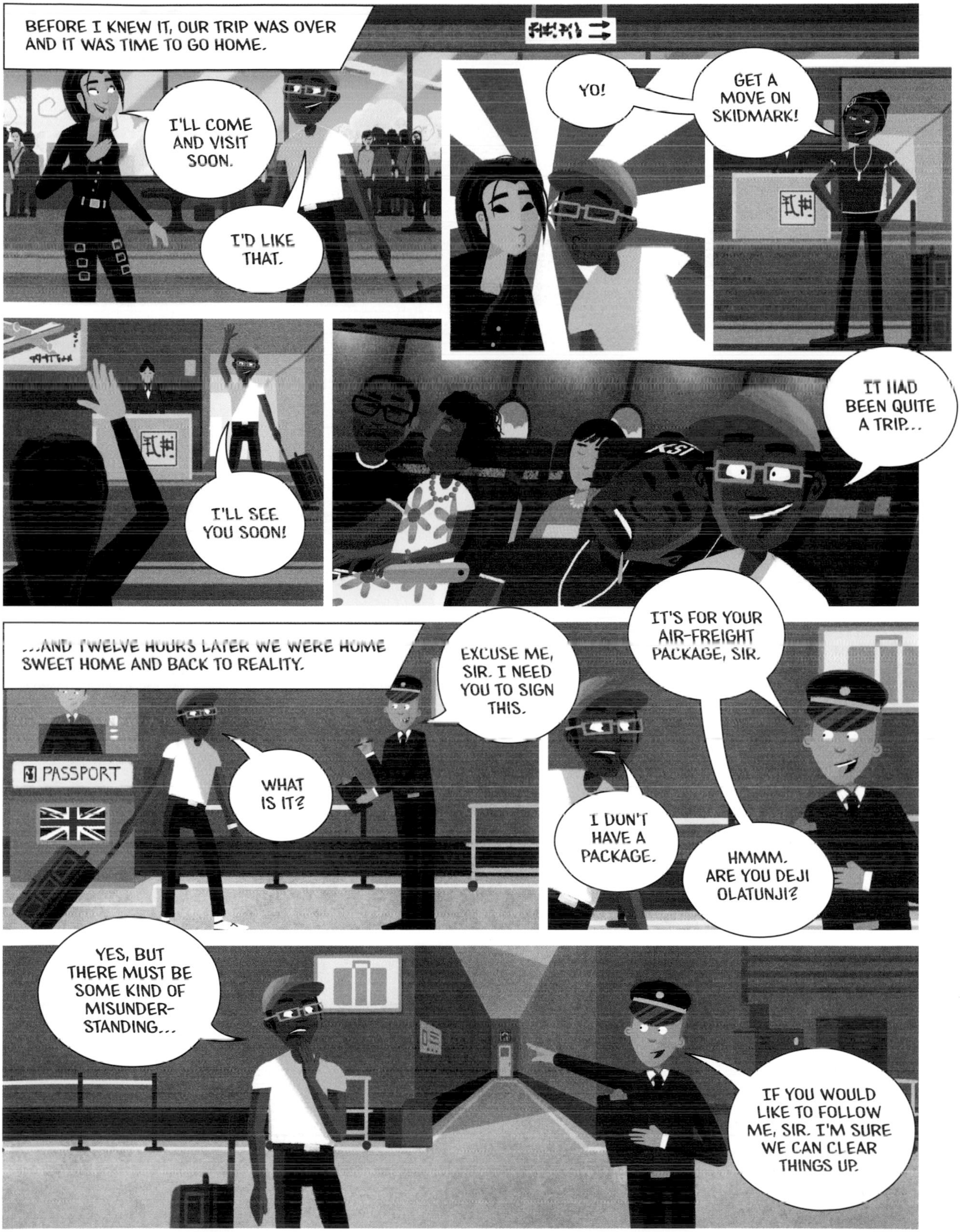
BEFORE I KNEW IT, OUR TRIP WAS OVER AND IT WAS TIME TO GO HOME.
I'LL COME AND VISIT SOON.
I'D LIKE THAT.
YO!
GET A MOVE ON SKIDMARK!
I'LL SEE YOU SOON!
IT HAD BEEN QUITE A TRIP...
...AND TWELVE HOURS LATER WE WERE HOME SWEET HOME AND BACK TO REALITY.
PASSPORT
EXCUSE ME, SIR. I NEED YOU TO SIGN THIS.
WHAT IS IT?
IT'S FOR YOUR AIR-FREIGHT PACKAGE, SIR.
I DON'T HAVE A PACKAGE.
HMMM. ARE YOU DEJI OLATUNJI?
YES, BUT THERE MUST BE SOME KIND OF MISUNDER-STANDING...
IF YOU WOULD LIKE TO FOLLOW ME, SIR. I'M SURE WE CAN CLEAR THINGS UP.

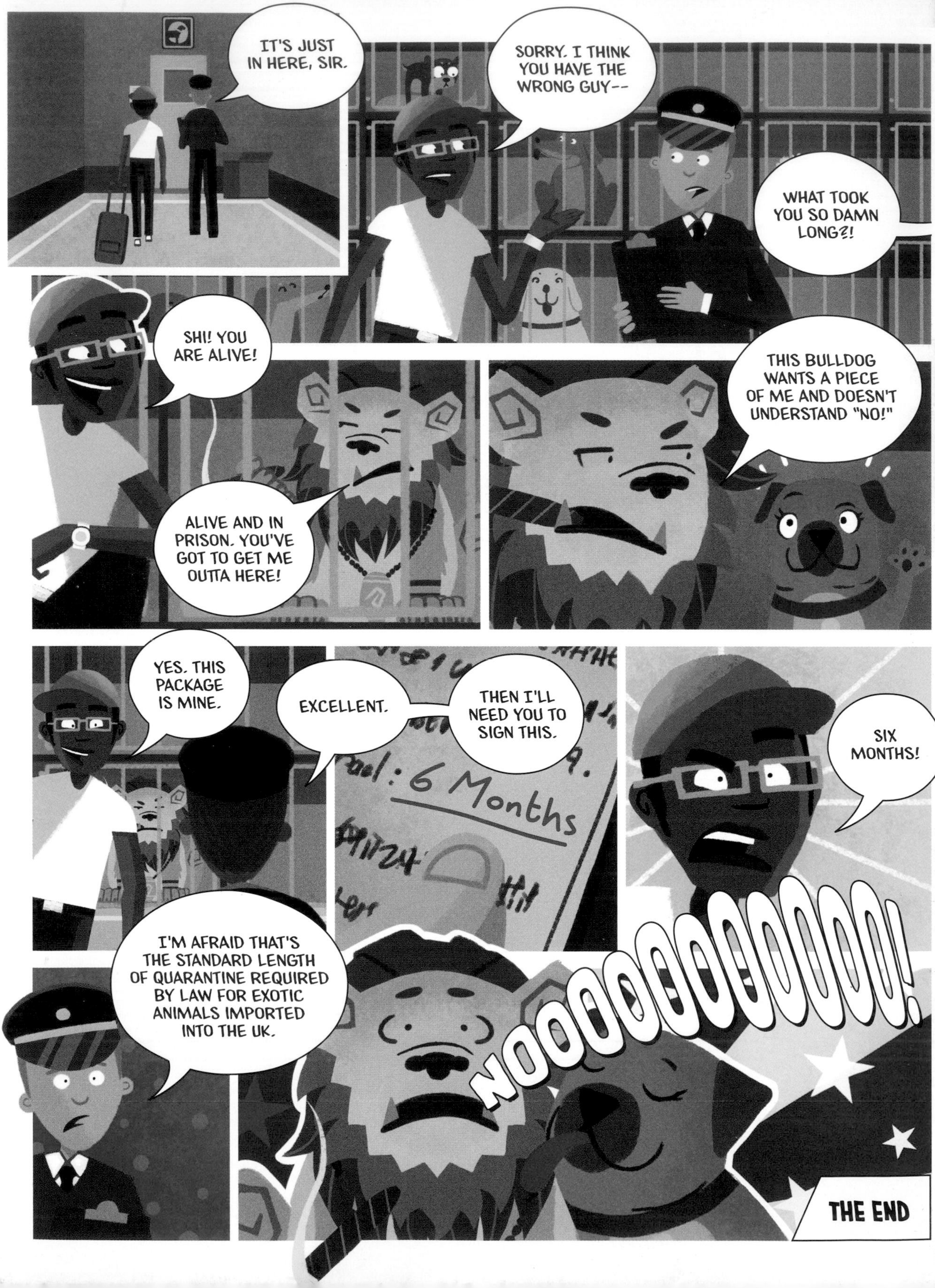
IT'S JUST IN HERE, SIR.
SORRY. I THINK YOU HAVE THE WRONG GUY--
WHAT TOOK YOU SO DAMN LONG?!
SHI! YOU ARE ALIVE!
ALIVE AND IN PRISON. YOU'VE GOT TO GET ME OUTTA HERE!
THIS BULLDOG WANTS A PIECE OF ME AND DOESN'T UNDERSTAND "NO!"
YES. THIS PACKAGE IS MINE.
EXCELLENT.
THEN I'LL NEED YOU TO SIGN THIS.
6 Months
SIX MONTHS!
I'M AFRAID THAT'S THE STANDARD LENGTH OF QUARANTINE REQUIRED BY LAW FOR EXOTIC ANIMALS IMPORTED INTO THE UK.
NOOOOOOOOOOOOO!
THE END

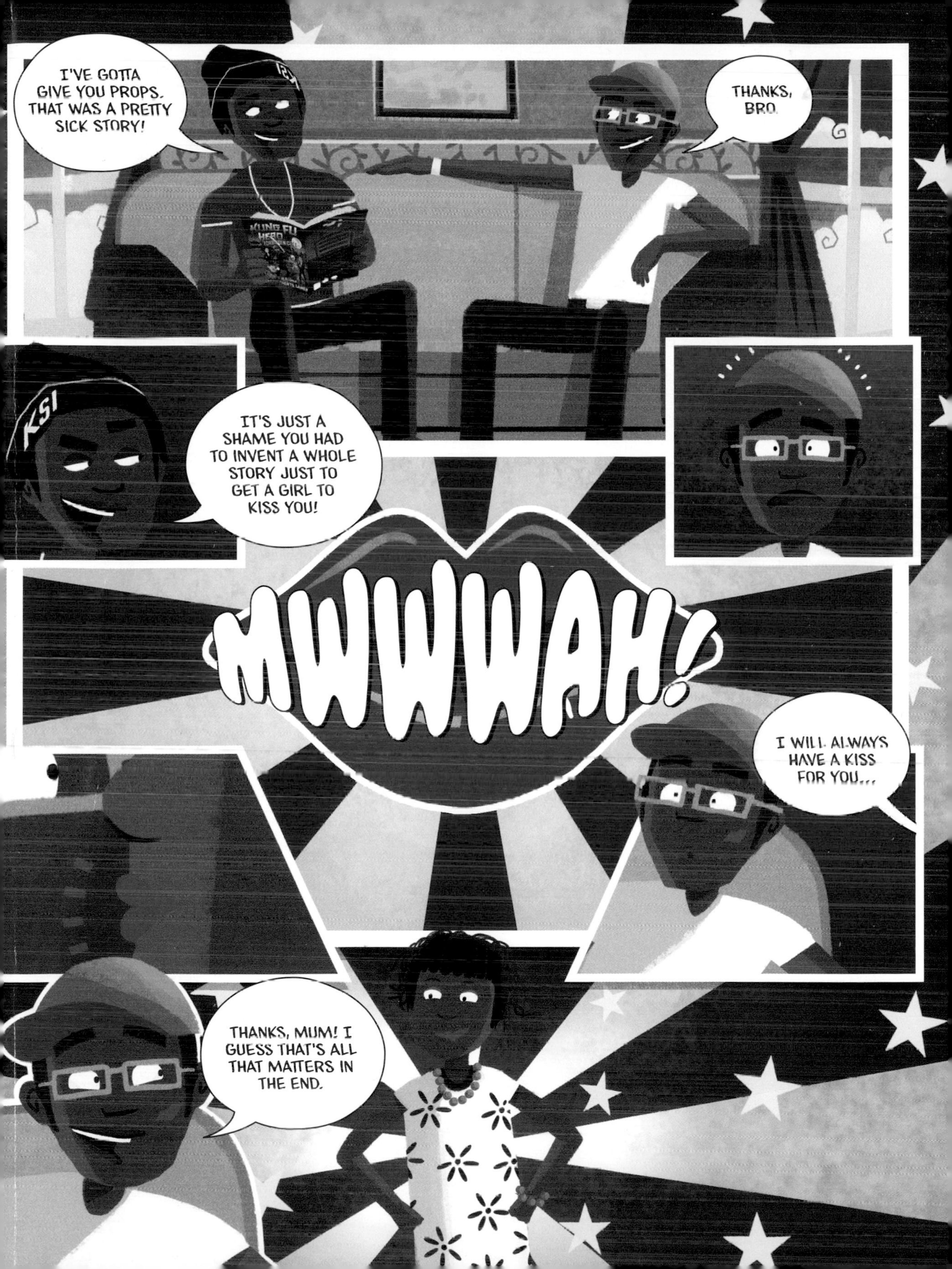
I'VE GOTTA GIVE YOU PROPS. THAT WAS A PRETTY SICK STORY!
THANKS, BRO.
IT'S JUST A SHAME YOU HAD TO INVENT A WHOLE STORY JUST TO GET A GIRL TO KISS YOU!
MWWWAH!
I WILL ALWAYS HAVE A KISS FOR YOU...
THANKS, MUM! I GUESS THAT'S ALL THAT MATTERS IN THE END.

TEAM DEJI

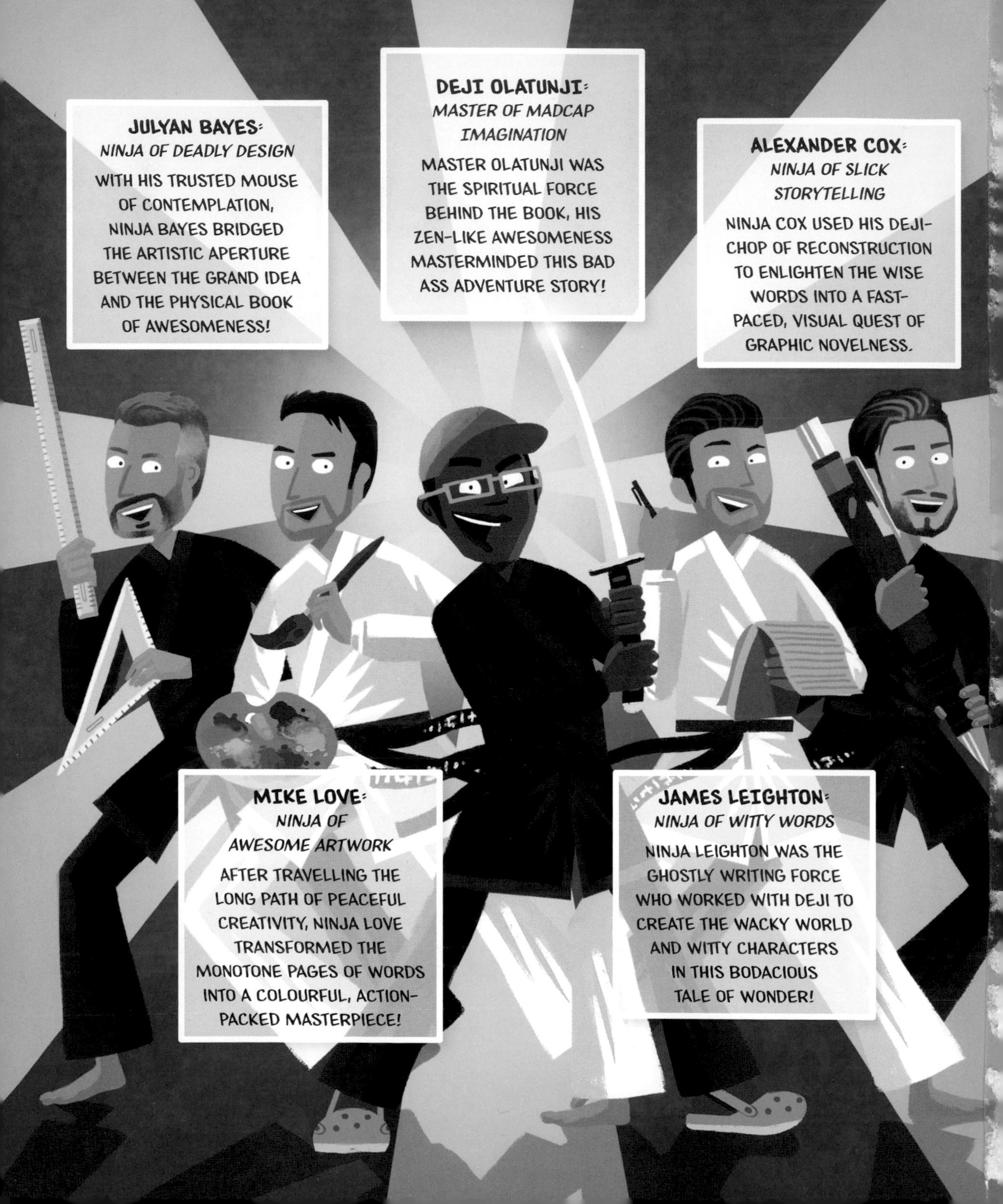
DEJI OLATUNJI: MASTER OF MADCAP IMAGINATION
MASTER OLATUNJI WAS THE SPIRITUAL FORCE BEHIND THE BOOK, HIS ZEN-LIKE AWESOMENESS MASTERMINDED THIS BAD ASS ADVENTURE STORY!
JULYAN BAYES: NINJA OF DEADLY DESIGN
WITH HIS TRUSTED MOUSE OF CONTEMPLATION, NINJA BAYES BRIDGED THE ARTISTIC APERTURE BETWEEN THE GRAND IDEA AND THE PHYSICAL BOOK OF AWESOMENESS!
ALEXANDER COX: NINJA OF SLICK STORYTELLING
NINJA COX USED HIS DEJI-CHOP OF RECONSTRUCTION TO ENLIGHTEN THE WISE WORDS INTO A FAST-PACED, VISUAL QUEST OF GRAPHIC NOVELNESS.
MIKE LOVE: NINJA OF AWESOME ARTWORK
AFTER TRAVELLING THE LONG PATH OF PEACEFUL CREATIVITY, NINJA LOVE TRANSFORMED THE MONOTONE PAGES OF WORDS INTO A COLOURFUL, ACTION-PACKED MASTERPIECE!
JAMES LEIGHTON: NINJA OF WITTY WORDS
NINJA LEIGHTON WAS THE GHOSTLY WRITING FORCE WHO WORKED WITH DEJI TO CREATE THE WACKY WORLD AND WITTY CHARACTERS IN THIS BODACIOUS TALE OF WONDER!